The Security+ Cram Sheet

1. Access control includes MAC, DAC, and RBAC (Rule-Based Access Control or Role-Based Access Control)

2. Authentication involves determining the identity of the account attempting access to resources. Here are some key points:

   - Kerberos authentication is a ticket-based, symmetric-key authentication system involving a KDC. Kerberos v5 supports mutual authentication.
   - CHAP involves the exchange of hashed values for authentication.
   - Certificates are used within a PKI to provide an asymmetric-key solution.
   - Username and password combinations are the most common form of authentication.
   - Token-based authentication is a strong form requiring possession of the token item.
   - Biometric authentication uses parts of the human body (hand, finger, iris, and so on) for authentication.

3. Nonessential services and protocols should be disabled, which requires an understanding of the following:

   - The role of each server, along with its current configuration
   - Required or critical services, protocols, and applications
   - Configuration changes that should be made to existing servers

ATTACKS

4. Denial of service (DoS) and distributed denial of service (DDoS) attacks involve the disruption of normal network services and include the following types:

   - *Smurf*—An attack based on the ICMP echo reply
   - *Fraggle*—Smurf-like attack based on UDP packets
   - *Ping flood*—Blocks service through repeated pings

   - *SYN flood*—Repeated SYN requests without ACK
   - *Land*—Exploits TCP/IP stacks using spoofed SYNs (where the same source address and port appears in both source and destination elements)
   - *Teardrop*—An attack using overlapping, fragmented UDP packets that can't be reassembled correctly
   - *Bonk*—An attack on port 53 using fragmented UDP packets with bogus reassembly information
   - *Boink*—Bonk-like attack on multiple ports

5. A back door allows access to a system without normal security checks.

6. Spoofing is the process of making data look as if it came from somewhere other than its origin.

7. Man-in-the-middle attacks involve the interception of traffic between two systems using a third system pretending to be the others.

8. Replay attacks involve the reposting of captured data.

9. TCP/IP hijacking involves taking control of a TCP/IP session.

10. Mathematical attacks involve cryptographic key cracking.

11. Password-guessing, brute-force, and dictionary attacks involve repeated guessing of logons and passwords.

12. Forms of malicious code include the following:

    - *Viruses*—Infect systems and spread copies of themselves
    - *Trojan horses*—Disguise malicious code within apparently useful applications
    - *Logic bombs*—Trigger on a particular condition
    - *Worms*—Self-replicating forms of other types of malicious code
    - *Java and ActiveX controls*—Automatically execute when sent via email

13. Social engineering involves manipulating human psychology to gain access to something of value.

- *Renewal*—If needed, a new key pair can be generated and the certificate renewed.
- *Recovery*—Recovery is possible if a certifying key is compromised but the holder is still valid and trusted.
- *Archiving*—The certificates and their uses are stored.

61. Key management may be either centralized or decentralized.

62. An escrow agent maintains a copy of the private key signed by the CA.

63. Multiple key pairs will require multiple certificates.

OPERATIONAL/ORGANIZATIONAL SECURITY

PHYSICAL SECURITY

64. Access control includes considerations of direct access, network access, facilities, and the environment supporting a system.

65. Social engineering involves extracting useful information from an authorized user, whereas reverse social engineering involves convincing an authorized user of the attacker's authorization or expertise so that the user will ask for assistance.

66. A disaster recovery plan (DRP) details considerations for backup and restoration, including secure recovery methods. Some of the items within the DRP are impact and risk assessments and service-level agreements (SLAs) with suppliers and vendors.

67. A business continuity plan details the procedures to follow in order to reestablish proper connectivity as well as the facilities needed to restore data in the event of a catastrophic loss. Items of consideration include network connectivity, facilities, clustering, and fault tolerance.

SECURITY POLICIES AND PROCEDURES

68. Security policies define guidelines and specifications for general types of security considerations. Procedures are step-by-step items defined within each policy that specify the responsible agents, actions to be taken, and methods for proper reporting. Procedures must be followed. Policies include risk assessment, security, acceptable use, and compliance. Focus details may include due care, privacy, separation of duties, need to know, password management, retention, disposal and destruction, incident response, and Human Resources policies.

69. Privilege management may be user based, group based, or role based, reflecting a MAC, DAC, or RBAC configuration.

70. Risk identification includes asset identification, risk assessment, threat identification and classification, and identification of vulnerabilities.

71. Education is required to ensure that users are aware of required and recommended security guidelines.

72. All aspects of security must be documented, including security policies, architecture documentation, as well as retention and disposal procedures for each form of documentation.

73. Computer forensic analysis includes the need to establish a clear chain of custody, properly collect the evidence, correctly perform the investigation, document all actions and findings, preserve all evidence and documentation, and prepare to provide expert testimony or consultation if required.

42. Tunneling is the process of transmitting data encapsulated within a second protocol to prevent direct eavesdropping using a packet sniffer.

INTRUSION DETECTION

43. An IDS monitors packet data using behavior-based or knowledge-based methods, operating in network-based or host-based configurations.

44. Honeypots and honeynets are used to study the actions of hackers and to distract them from more valuable data.

45. Incident handling may include detection, deflection, or countermeasures.

46. A security baseline is a measure of normal network activity against which behavior-based IDSs measure network traffic to detect anomalies.

47. Hardening is the process of securing a host, network, or application to resist attacks. Some key services that should be considered during hardening are Web, email, FTP, DNS, NNTP, DHCP, file, print, and data repository servers.

BASICS OF CRYPTOGRAPHY

ALGORITHMS

48. A hashing algorithm uses a mathematical formula to verify data integrity. Examples include the SHA and the Message Digest Series algorithms (MD2, MD4, and MD5).

49. Symmetric-key algorithms depend on a shared single key for encryption and decryption. Examples include DES, 3DES, AES, Blowfish, IDEA, and the Rivest ciphers (RC2, RC4, RC5, and RC6).

50. Asymmetric-key algorithms use a public key for encryption and a private key for decryption. Examples include the RSA, Diffie-Hellman, El Gamal, and Elliptic Curve Cryptography standards.

CONCEPTS OF USING CRYPTOGRAPHY

51. Cryptographic encryption improves confidentiality.

52. Error checking within encryption/decryption schemes ensures data integrity. Digital signatures are used to sign data so that the recipient can verify the data's origin.

53. Cryptographic routines can perform user authentication and provide for nonrepudiation of data origin.

54. Cryptographic methods may be used for access control.

PUBLIC KEY INFRASTRUCTURE (PKI)

55. PKI relies on asymmetric-key cryptography using certificates issued by an authentication Certificate Authority (CA) such as VeriSign.

56. Certificates are digitally signed blocks of data that may be used within a PKI setting. Some things to remember about certificates include the following:

   - Certificate policies specify the uses for a certificate as well as additional technical data.
   - A Certificate Practice Statement (CPS) is a legal document that details the purpose of conveying information using a certificate.
   - Certificates can be revoked before their expiration date.

57. Certificate Authorities may be grouped into several trust models, including the following:

   - *Single CA*—Uses a single CA
   - *Hierarchical CA*—Uses a root CA and subordinate CAs
   - *Bridge CA*—Uses a bridge CA and principal CAs

58. The IETF Working Group on X.509 standards for PKI is PKIX.

59. IPSec consists of AH, ESP, IPComp, and IKE.

KEY MANAGEMENT AND CERTIFICATE LIFECYCLE

60. Key management and the certificate lifecycle support PKI solutions through the process of creating, using, and then destroying public keys and the digital certificates they are associated with. The lifecycle includes the following parts:

   - *Key generation*—A public key pair is created and held by the CA.
   - *Identity submission*—The requesting entity submits its identity to the CA.
   - *Registration*—The CA registers the request and verifies the submission identity.
   - *Certification*—The CA creates a certificate signed by its own digital certificate.
   - *Distribution*—The CA publishes the generated certificate.
   - *Usage*—The receiving entity is authorized to use the certificate only for its intended use.
   - *Revocation and expiration*—The certificate will expire or may be revoked earlier if needed.

AUDITING

14. Auditing is the process of tracking user actions on the network.

15. System scanning involves probing service ports.

REMOTE ACCESS

16. Remote access includes these items:
    - 802.11x wireless networking (Wi-Fi)
    - Virtual Private Network (VPN) connections
    - Dial-up using RADIUS, TACACS, or TACACS+
    - SSL connections
    - Packet-level authentication via IPSec in the Network layer (layer 3) of the OSI model

17. VPN connections use PPTP or L2TP connectivity.

18. SSH functions as a secure Telnet.

SECURING CONNECTIVITY

19. Email can be secured using the S/MIME or PGP protocols.

20. Email and Instant Messaging suffer from undesired messages (spam) and hoaxes.

21. Web connectivity can be secured using HTTPS, SSL, and TLS.

ONLINE VULNERABILITIES

22. Web vulnerabilities include the following:
    - Java and JavaScript
    - ActiveX controls
    - Cookies
    - CGI vulnerabilities
    - SMTP relay vulnerabilities

23. Protocol vulnerabilities include the following:
    - TLS
    - LDAP
    - FTP vulnerabilities, including anonymous access and unencrypted authentication
    - Wireless vulnerabilities, including WEP key analysis

24. A site survey is necessary before deploying a WLAN.

BASIC NETWORK SECURITY DEVICES

25. Firewalls separate external and internal networks and include the following types:
    - Packet-filtering firewalls (Network layer, layer 3)
    - Proxy-service firewalls, including circuit-level (Session layer, layer 5) and application-level (Application layer, layer 7) gateways
    - Stateful-inspection firewalls (Application layer, layer 7)

26. Routers forward packets between subnets (Network layer, layer 3) using the following:
    - RIP
    - IGRP
    - EIGRP
    - OSPF
    - BGP
    - EGP
    - IS-IS

27. Switches segment broadcast networks (Data Link layer, layer 2).

28. Wireless devices provide broadcast-based connectivity.

29. Modems allow connection through audio telephony.

30. RAS allows remote dial-up (Telecom/PBX) or VPN connections.

31. Useful network diagnostic tools include the following:
    - Ping
    - Tracert/traceroute
    - Nslookup
    - Netstat
    - IPConfig/ifconfig
    - Telnet
    - SNMP

32. Workstations, servers, and mobile devices (such as PDAs) require configuration to improve security beyond the default.

MEDIA

33. The two main types of coaxial cable (coax) are 10Base2 (Thinnet) and 10Base5 (Thicknet).

34. Twisted pair cable is either unshielded (UTP) or shielded (STP). Both come in two speeds: Cat3 (10Mbps) or Cat5 (100Mbps).

35. Fiber-optic cable (fiber) speeds range from 100Mbps to 2Gbps (with higher speeds in the works).

36. Removable media includes tape, recordable compact discs (CD-R), hard drives, diskettes, flashcards, and smartcards.

37. Backups may be full, incremental, differential, or copy.

SECURITY TOPOLOGIES

38. Security zones support the management of a bastion host and screened host or screened subnet gateways.

39. Networks may be divided into intranets, extranets, DMZs, and the Internet.

40. A VLAN allows for computers on the same physical segment to be on different logical segments.

41. Network Address Translation (NAT) devices translate traffic between public and private address schemes.

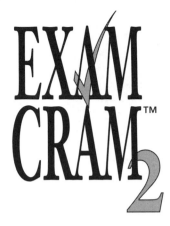

Security+

Kirk Hausman

Diane Barrett

Martin Weiss

CERTIFICATION

Security+ Exam Cram

International Standard Book Number: 0-7897-2910-5

Library of Congress Catalog Card Number: 2003100815

Printed in the United States of America

First Printing: April 2003

07   06   05   10   9   8   7   6

Trademarks

Warning and Disclaimer

Bulk Sales

Que Publishing offers excellent discounts on this book when ordered in quantity for bulk purchases or special sales. For more information, please contact

> **U.S. Corporate and Government Sales**
> **1-800-382-3419**
> corpsales@pearsontechgroup.com

For sales outside of the U.S., please contact

> **International Sales**
> international@pearsoned.com

Publisher
Paul Boger

Acquisitions Editor
Jeff Riley

Development Editor
Steve Rowe

Managing Editor
Charlotte Clapp

Project Editor
Tonya Simpson

Copy Editor
Bart Reed

Indexer
Chris Barrick

Proofreader
Suzanne Thomas

Technical Editors
Patrick Ramseier
Clement DuPuis

Team Coordinator
Pamalee Nelson

Multimedia Developer
Dan Scherf

Interior Designer
Gary Adair

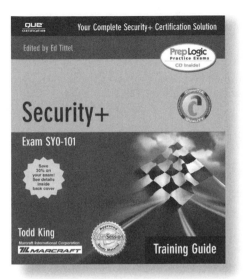

Que Certification • 800 East 96th Street • Indianapolis, Indiana 46240

A Note from Series Editor Ed Tittel

You know better than to trust your certification preparation to just anybody. That's why you, and more than two million others, have purchased an Exam Cram book. As Series Editor for the new and improved Exam Cram 2 series, I have worked with the staff at Que Certification to ensure you won't be disappointed. That's why we've taken the world's best-selling certification product—a finalist for "Best Study Guide" in a CertCities reader poll in 2002—and made it even better.

As a "Favorite Study Guide Author" finalist in a 2002 poll of CertCities readers, I know the value of good books. You'll be impressed with Que Certification's stringent review process, which ensures the books are high-quality, relevant, and technically accurate. Rest assured that at least a dozen industry experts—including the panel of certification experts at CramSession—have reviewed this material, helping us deliver an excellent solution to your exam preparation needs.

We've also added a preview edition of PrepLogic's powerful, full-featured test engine, which is trusted by certification students throughout the world.

As a 20-year-plus veteran of the computing industry and the original creator and editor of the Exam Cram series, I've brought my IT experience to bear on these books. During my tenure at Novell from 1989 to 1994, I worked with and around its excellent education and certification department. This experience helped push my writing and teaching activities heavily in the certification direction. Since then, I've worked on more than 70 certification-related books, and I write about certification topics for numerous Web sites and for *Certification* magazine.

In 1996, while studying for various MCP exams, I became frustrated with the huge, unwieldy study guides that were the only preparation tools available. As an experienced IT professional and former instructor, I wanted "nothing but the facts" necessary to prepare for the exams. From this impetus, Exam Cram emerged in 1997. It quickly became the best-selling computer book series since "...*For Dummies*," and the best-selling certification book series ever. By maintaining an intense focus on subject matter, tracking errata and updates quickly, and following the certification market closely, Exam Cram was able to establish the dominant position in cert prep books.

You will not be disappointed in your decision to purchase this book. If you are, please contact me at etittel@jump.net. All suggestions, ideas, input, or constructive criticism are welcome!

Ed Tittel

About the Authors

Kirk Hausman has been an IT professional for more than 20 years in the roles of consultant, trainer, programmer, database administrator, IT manager, and network administrator. He is currently working as a Computer Systems Manager and Lead Security Analyst for Texas A&M University, where he is active in many university-wide ERP planning committees and multidepartmental database-development efforts. He also is employed as the North American Online Manager for Fujitsu/ICL's online training division, KnowledgePool, Inc. Kirk has his Security+ certification, among others.

Diane Barrett is an instructor and technical reviewer. Currently, she instructs at Education America, where she has spent the last two years teaching in the Computer Networking program. She is also the president of NextGard Technology L.L.C., which specializes in security-awareness training and consulting. She is a member of InfraGard, the Sonoran Desert Users Security Group, HTCIA, and ISSA. Diane has done technical editing for the Coriolis Group and was a member of Transcender's technical evaluation program until it ceased in the spring of 2002. She had recently received her degree in Business Information Systems and is continually learning and advancing her education. She currently holds the following certifications: MSCE in Windows NT and 2000, CCNA, CompTIA A+, Net+, i-Net+, and Security+. You can reach Diane at dm_barrett@msn.com.

Martin Weiss is an Information Security Specialist with a large employee-benefits company. His other writings include *i-Net+ Exam Cram* and books on A+ certification and Windows 2000 Server. He currently holds the following certifications: CISSP, Security+, A+, i-Net+, Network+, MCSE, MCP+I, CCNA, and CNA. Martin lives in New England and enjoys snowboarding, candlelight dinners, and long walks on the beach. He currently attends graduate school at Rensselaer Polytechnic Institute. He can be reached via email at marty@castadream.com.

Acknowledgments

Kirk Hausman: Thanks go to Mary Burmeister for contacting me initially about this book. I also would like to extend thanks to Jeff Riley, the acquisitions editor at Que, for making this book possible, and to my agent, Jawahara Saidullah of Waterside Productions, for her indispensable assistance. Appreciation is also due to Steve Rowe, Tonya Simpson, and Bart Reed for their excellent editing, and to the technical reviewers, Clement DuPuis and Patrick Ramseier, for their technical comments and suggestions. Finally, thanks go to Diane Barrett and Martin Weiss for their assistance in bringing this book together.

Diane Barrett: Thank you to co-authors Kirk Hausman and Martin Weiss for their contributions. Thanks to Mary Burmeister for always having a sense of humor, and to her and Ed Tittel for their kindness and understanding when my brothers died. Special thanks to my husband, Bill, whose love, understanding, and patience never cease to amaze me.

Martin Weiss: Many thanks to the entire team who helped bring this book together, especially Ed Tittel and Mary Burmeister. To my son Kobe: I love you! Thank you to all the other fine folks in my life who rock, including Elizabeth Ballou and Taxi, as well as the many fine professionals I work with on a daily basis, especially Michael "Security Guru" Dalton. Finally, thanks to the great folks at Castadream.com. Lots of love to the rest of my family and peeps.

Contents at a Glance

Table of Contents

We Want to Hear from You!

As the reader of this book, *you* are our most important critic and commentator. We value your opinion and want to know what we're doing right, what we could do better, what areas you'd like to see us publish in, and any other words of wisdom you're willing to pass our way.

As an executive editor for Que, I welcome your comments. You can email or write me directly to let me know what you did or didn't like about this book—as well as what we can do to make our books better.

Please note that I cannot help you with technical problems related to the *topic* of this book. We do have a User Services group, however, where I will forward specific technical questions related to the book.

When you write, please be sure to include this book's title and author as well as your name, email address, and phone number. I will carefully review your comments and share them with the author and editors who worked on the book.

Email: feedback@quepublishing.com

Mail: Jeff Riley
          Que Certification
          800 East 96th Street
          Indianapolis, IN 46240 USA

For more information about this book or another Que title, visit our Web site at www.quepublishing.com. Type the ISBN (excluding hyphens) or the title of a book in the Search field to find the page you're looking for.

Introduction

Welcome to *Security+ Exam Cram 2*. This book is intended to prepare you to take and pass the CompTIA Security+ exam, number SY0-101, as administered by both the Prometric and VUE testing organizations. This introduction explains CompTIA's Security+ certification program in general and talks about how the *Exam Cram 2* series can help you prepare for that certification exam. You can learn more about Prometric by visiting its Web site at www.prometric.com, and you can learn more about VUE by visiting its Web site at www.vue.com.

Exam Cram 2 books help you understand and appreciate the subjects and materials you need to pass certification exams. *Exam Cram 2* books are aimed strictly at test preparation and review. They do not teach you everything you need to know about a topic. Instead, the series presents and dissects the questions and problems that you're likely to encounter on a test. In preparing this book, we've worked from preparation guides and tests and from a battery of third-party test-preparation tools. The aim of the *Exam Cram 2* series is to bring together as much information as possible about the certification exams that are its primary focus.

Nevertheless, to completely prepare yourself for any test, we recommend that you begin by taking the Self-Assessment immediately following this introduction. This tool will help you evaluate your knowledge base against the requirements for the CompTIA Security+ exam under both ideal and real circumstances.

Based on what you learn from that exercise, you might decide to begin your studies with some classroom training, or to pick up and read one of the many study guides available from third-party vendors, including Que Certification's *Training Guide* series. We also strongly recommend that you spend some time installing, configuring, and working with both Windows and Unix or Linux operating systems to patch and maintain them for the best and most current security possible, because the Security+ exam is focused on such activities—and the knowledge and skills they can provide for you—in large part.

Whom Is This Book For?

This book is for you if

➤ You are an IT professional who's already familiar with basic system and network administration concepts and who has a basic working knowledge of information security terms, concepts, tools, and technologies.

➤ Your job or work involves working in and around the Internet, particularly if it is related to managing or securing such access.

➤ Your job or work carries some explicit security considerations with it, be it managing access or permissions for a single system or for one or more networks and related servers.

➤ You are interested in moving into the information security specialization within IT and are seeking a good place to start your training and learning experiences.

This book is *not* for you if

➤ You are just getting started in computing and have little experience with systems or networks, or with information security terms, concepts, tools, and technologies.

➤ You are working in IT but have no systems or network administration experience, or explicitly security-related job duties or responsibilities.

➤ You seek a learning tool to teach you all the background, terms, and concepts necessary to understand information security as represented in the Security+ exam.

➤ You are curious about this suddenly popular IT specialization called "information security" and want to find out what the fuss is about.

If you fall into the category that indicates this book is not for you, you should start your Security+ certification path somewhere else. You might consider our other book, *Security+ Training Guide* (Que Certification, 2002, ISBN 0-7897-2836-2). It is full of explanations, background information, lots of examples and illustrations, and plenty of case studies and scenarios. (You will not find much of that type of information in this book, because it assumes you already know such things.)

CompTIA's Security+ and Other Certifications

The Computing Technology Industry Association (www.comptia.org) offers numerous IT certifications, primarily aimed at entry- and intermediate-level IT professionals. Here is a list of some other relevant CompTIA certifications, briefly annotated to document their possible relevance to Security+:

➤ *A+* —An exam that tests basic PC hardware and software installation, including installing, configuring, and managing systems, components, peripherals, operating systems, key applications, and basic networking. This exam is an excellent prequalifier for those interested in Security+ who may have little or no PC or computing skills or knowledge. For more information on this exam, see www.comptia.org/certification/a/default.asp.

➤ *Network+* —An exam that tests basic and intermediate networking skills and knowledge, including hardware, drivers, protocols, and troubleshooting topics. This exam is an excellent prequalifier for those interested in Security+ who have little or no networking skills or knowledge. For more information on this exam, go to www.comptia.org/certification/network/default.asp.

➤ *i-Net+* —An exam that tests basic Internet access, applications, connectivity management, and troubleshooting skills. CompTIA's information about this exam recommends taking A+ and Network+ to prepare, but itself provides an essential steppingstone to Security+, because so much of the activity involved in establishing and maintaining secure systems and networks revolves around controlling and managing Internet access (both coming and going). For more information about this exam, visit www.comptia.org/certification/i-net/default.asp.

The CompTIA exams are all vendor- and platform-neutral, which means they primarily test general skills and knowledge rather than focusing on vendor or product specifics. As such, they offer certification candidates a chance to demonstrate necessary general abilities that will be relevant in most workplaces. This explains why employers generally look at CompTIA certifications favorably as well.

Signing Up to Take the Exam

After you have studied this book, have taken the sample test, and feel ready to tackle the real thing, you can sign up to take the exam either at Prometric or at VUE. The Security+ exam costs $225 for individuals whose employers do not belong to CompTIA, and $175 for individuals who can claim active membership.

Signing Up with Prometric

You can contact Prometric to locate a nearby testing center that administers the test and to make an appointment. The last time we visited the Prometric Web site, a searching system to find the testing center nearest you was located at www.2ittrain.com. The sign-up Web page address for the exam itself is www.2test.com. You can also use this Web page (click the Contact Us button you'll find there) to obtain a telephone number for the company if you can't or don't want to sign up for the exam on the Web page.

Signing Up with VUE

You can contact Virtual University Enterprises (VUE) to locate a nearby testing center that administers the test and to make an appointment. The sign-up Web page address for the exam itself is www.vue.com/comptia/. You can also use this Web page (click the Contact button, click the View Telephone Directory by Sponsor link, and then click CompTIA) to obtain a telephone number for the company, if you can't or don't want to sign up for the exam on the Web page.

Scheduling the Security+ Exam

To schedule an exam, call at least one day in advance, but do not count on getting an early appointment. In some areas of the United States, tests are booked up for weeks in advance. To cancel or reschedule an exam, you must call at least 12 hours before the scheduled test time (or you may be charged). When calling Prometric, be sure have the following information ready for the telesales staffer who handles your call:

➤ Your name, organization, and mailing address.

➤ A unique test ID. For most U.S. citizens, this will be your Social Security number. Citizens of other nations can use their taxpayer IDs or make other arrangements with the order taker.

➤ The name and number of the exam you wish to take. For this book, the exam number is SY0-101, and the exam name is Security+.

➤ If you will be paying by credit card, be sure have your card handy as well. If you wish to pay by check or other means, you'll have to obtain the necessary information from the Prometric or VUE representative with whom you speak.

Taking the Test

When you show up for your appointment, be sure you bring two forms of identification that have your signature on them, including one with a photograph. You won't be allowed to take any printed material into the testing environment, but you can study the Cram Sheet from the front of this book while you are waiting. Try to arrive at least 15 minutes before the scheduled timeslot.

All exams are completely closed book. In fact, you will not be permitted to take anything with you into the testing area, but you will be furnished with a blank sheet of paper and a pen. We suggest that you immediately write down on that sheet of paper any of the information from the Cram Sheet you've had a hard time remembering.

You will have some time to compose yourself, to record memorized information, and even to take a sample orientation exam before you begin the real thing. We suggest you take the orientation test before taking your first exam, but because they're all more or less identical in layout, behavior, and controls, you probably won't need to do this more than once.

About This Book

Each topical *Exam Cram* chapter follows a regular structure, along with graphical clues about important or useful information. Here's the structure of a typical chapter:

➤ *Opening hotlists*—Each chapter begins with a list of the terms, tools, and techniques you must learn and understand before you can be fully conversant with that chapter's subject matter. We follow the hotlists with one or two introductory paragraphs to set the stage for the rest of the chapter.

➤ *Topical coverage*—After the opening hotlists, each chapter covers a series of at least four topics related to the chapter's subject title. Throughout this section, we highlight topics or concepts likely to appear on a test using a special Exam Alert layout, like this:

 This is what an Exam Alert looks like. Normally, an Exam Alert stresses concepts, terms, software, or activities that are likely to relate to one or more certification test questions. For that reason, any information found offset in an Exam Alert format is worthy of unusual attentiveness on your part.

Pay close attention to material flagged as an Exam Alert; although all the information in this book pertains to what you need to know to pass the exam, we flag certain items that are really important. You'll find what appears in the meat of each chapter to be worth knowing, too, when preparing for the test.

Because this book's material is very condensed, we recommend that you use this book along with other resources to achieve the maximum benefit.

► *Practice questions*—Although we talk about test questions and topics throughout each chapter, this section presents a series of mock test questions and explanations of both correct and incorrect answers. We also try to point out especially tricky questions by using a special icon, like this:

 Ordinarily, this icon flags the presence of a particularly devious inquiry, if not an outright trick question. Trick questions are calculated to be answered incorrectly if not read more than once—and carefully at that. Although they are not ubiquitous, such questions make occasional appearances on CompTIA exams. That is why we say exam questions are as much about reading comprehension as they are about knowing your material inside-out and backwards.

► *Details and resources*—Every chapter ends with a section titled "Need to Know More?" that provides direct pointers to security resources that offer more details on the chapter's subject. If you find a resource you like in this collection, use it, but don't feel compelled to use all the resources. On the other hand, we recommend only those resources we ourselves use regularly, so none of our recommendations will waste your time or money.

The bulk of the book follows this chapter structure slavishly, but there are a few other elements we'd like to point out. Chapters 12 and 14 each contain an entire sample test that provides a good review of the material presented throughout the book to ensure you're ready for the exam. Chapters 13 and 15 contain the corresponding answer keys to the sample test chapters that precede them. Additionally, you'll find appendixes at the back of the book that include the following information:

> ➤ A list of study, practice test, and other resources relevant to the Security+ exam (Appendix A)

> ➤ A list of security-related products, vendors, and technologies mentioned throughout the book (Appendix B)

> ➤ A glossary that explains terms

> ➤ An index you can use to track down terms as they appear in the text

Finally, the tear-out Cram Sheet attached next to the inside front cover of this *Exam Cram 2* book represents a condensed and compiled collection of facts, tricks, and tips we think you should memorize before taking the test. Because you can dump this information out of your head onto a piece of paper before answering any exam questions, you can master this information by brute force—you need to remember it only long enough to write it down when you walk into the test room. You might even want to look at it in the car or in the lobby of the testing center just before you walk in to take the test.

Typographic Conventions

In this book, configuration settings and script fragments are typeset in a monospaced font, as in the following example:

```
deny all
allow port 25 80 445
allow domain microsoft.com
allow protocols HTTP, SMTP, LDAP
```

This notation means that all access is denied, by default, and that only ports 25, 80, and 445 are allowed, as are the associated protocols SMTP (email), HTTP (Web), and LDAP (directory services). Likewise, only the domain microsoft.com is accessible under these filter definitions, which are abstract and do not correspond to exact syntax and structure for real-world routers or firewalls like those from Cisco, CheckPoint, Microsoft, or other vendors.

How to Use This Book

The order of chapters is what we consider to be a logical progression for someone who wants to review all the topics on the exam. If you feel that you are already up to speed on certain topics, you may elect to skip the chapter or chapters in which those topics are covered. In any case, you should try all the questions in the chapters and the sample tests in Chapters 12 and 14.

If you find errors, sections that could be worded more clearly, or questions that seem deceptive, feel free to let us know by email at `feedback` `@quepublishing.com`.

Self-Assessment

Based on recent statistics from CompTIA, as many as half a million individuals are at some stage of the certification process but have not yet received one of their various certification credentials. Recent polls in *Certification* magazine indicate that two to three times that number might be considering whether to obtain a CompTIA certification of some kind. That is a huge potential audience!

What we can't know yet—because the Security+ certification is relatively new as this book goes to press—are precise numbers for the Security+ certification itself. Based on recent salary and job interest surveys, we know security is a hot topic for IT professionals and a leading target for upcoming certification studies. But there are more than 50 security certifications of various types and parentage available in today's marketplace, so we can't know yet how well Security+ will fare in this densely populated and highly fragmented certification landscape. On the one hand, CompTIA certifications on popular topics tend to do fairly well, numbers-wise. On the other hand, with so many other options to choose from, only time will tell whether what's true for more certification topics in general is also true for security certifications in particular!

The reason we included a self-assessment in this *Exam Cram 2* book is to help you evaluate your readiness to tackle the CompTIA Security+ certification. It should also help you understand what you need to know to master the topic of this book—namely, Exam SY0-101, "Security+." But before you tackle this self-assessment, let's talk about concerns you might face when pursuing the Security+ certification, as well as what an ideal Security+ candidate might look like.

Security Professionals in the Real World

In the next section, we describe an ideal Security+ candidate, knowing full well that only a few real candidates will meet this ideal. In fact, our description of that ideal candidate might seem downright scary. But take heart: Although the requirements to obtain the Security+ credential might seem formidable, they are by no means impossible to meet. However, be keenly aware that getting through this process takes time, involves some expense, and requires real effort.

More than 100,000 IT professionals already hold information security certifications with more stringent requirements than Security+ demands, so it is an eminently attainable goal. You can get all the real-world motivation you need from knowing that many others have gone down similar paths before you, so you should be able to follow in their footsteps. If you're willing to tackle the process seriously and do what it takes to obtain the necessary experience and knowledge, you can take—and pass—the Security+ certification exam. In fact, we have designed our *Exam Cram 2* books to make it as easy on you as possible to prepare for these exams. But prepare you must!

The Ideal Security+ Candidate

Just to give you some idea of what an ideal Security+ candidate is like, here are some relevant statistics about the background and experience such an individual might have. Don't worry if you don't meet these qualifications, or don't come that close—this is a far from ideal world, and where you fall short is simply where you will have more work to do.

➤ Academic or professional training in information security theory, concepts, and operations. This includes everything from "general security concepts, communications security, infrastructure security," and "basics of cryptography" to "operational/organizational security," to quote straight from the CompTIA Web page on general Security+ exam information.

➤ Academic or professional training in networking, with a particular emphasis on TCP/IP. This includes everything from networking media and transmission techniques through network operating systems, services, and applications, to the details involved in installing, configuring, and using common TCP/IP-based networking services such as FTP, Web (HTTP), and news (NNTP), among others. The official CompTIA verbiage for this requirement reads "two years of networking experience and... a thorough knowledge of TCP/IP."

➤ Two or more years of professional networking experience, including experience with various networking media. This must include installation, configuration, upgrade, and troubleshooting experience. CompTIA recommends "that the Security+ test candidate have the knowledge and skills equivalent to those tested for in the CompTIA A+ and Network+ certification exams," to quote from the general exam information Web page yet again.

➤ General security concepts include access control, authentication tools and techniques, and services-management principles and practices. They also include understanding a broad variety of attacks, the various well-known types of malicious code or malware, and the insidious practices that lurk behind the innocuous-seeming term *social engineering*. Under this heading, candidates must also understand principles and practices related to system auditing, logging, and scanning techniques.

➤ Communications security covers a broad range of topics, including tools, protocols, and technologies relevant to managing security for remote access, email, Web services, directory services, file-transfer services, and wireless networking.

➤ Infrastructure security means learning the roles that key devices—routers, switches, firewalls, and so forth—play in creating safe and secure networking infrastructures. It also means understanding networking media and security topologies, such as security zones, VLANs, NAT, and so forth. Other relevant concepts under this heading include intrusion-detection systems and establishing and maintaining security baselines for networks, servers, and applications.

➤ Basics of cryptography cover key algorithms, related benefits and services, public key infrastructures, security standards and protocols, and what's involved in managing keys and digital certificates.

➤ Operational/organizational security covers the key concepts and best practices related to physical security, disaster recovery, business continuity, and what's involved in formulating and maintaining security policies and procedures. It also embraces principles and practices that govern managing user and group privileges, gathering and managing evidence of security attacks or breaches (under the heading of forensics), risk identification and assessment, plus user education and important security documentation concerns.

Fundamentally, this all boils down to a bachelor's degree in computer science with a strong focus on security topics, plus two years' experience working in a position involving network design, installation, configuration, maintenance, and security matters. We believe that under half of all certification candidates meet these requirements and that, in fact, most meet less than half of these requirements—at least, when they begin the certification process. But because so many other IT professionals who already have been certified in security topics have survived this ordeal, you can survive it, too, especially if you heed what our Self-Assessment can tell you about what you already know and what you need to learn.

Put Yourself to the Test

The following series of questions and observations is designed to help you figure out how much work you must do to pursue Security+ certification and what kinds of resources you might consult on your quest. Be absolutely honest in your answers, or you will end up wasting money on an exam you are not yet ready to take (and because the Security+ exam will cost you somewhere between $175 and $225, this isn't chump change). There are no right or wrong answers, only steps along the path to certification. Only you can decide where you really belong in the broad spectrum of aspiring candidates.

Two things should be clear from the outset, however:

➤ Even a modest background in computer science is helpful.

➤ Hands-on experience with networking and security products and technologies is a key ingredient to certification success.

Educational Background

1. Have you ever taken any computer-related classes? [Yes or No]

   If Yes, proceed to question 2; if No, proceed to question 4.

2. Have you taken any classes on computer operating systems? [Yes or No]

   If Yes, you will probably be able to handle various architecture and system component discussions that come up throughout the Security+ materials. If you are rusty, brush up on basic operating system concepts, especially virtual memory, buffer overflows, access controls, and general computer security topics.

   If No, consider some basic reading in this area. We strongly recommend a good general operating systems book, such as *Operating System Concepts, 6th Edition*, by Abraham Silberschatz, Peter Baer Galvin, and Greg Gagne (John Wiley & Sons, 2001, ISBN 0-471-41743-2). If this title doesn't appeal to you, check out reviews for other, similar titles at your favorite online bookstore.

3. Have you taken any networking concepts or technologies classes? [Yes or No]

If Yes, you will probably be able to handle the numerous mentions of networking terminology, concepts, and technologies that appear on the Security+ exam. If you are rusty, brush up on basic networking concepts and terminology, especially networking media, transmission types, the OSI Reference Model, basic networking technologies, and TCP/IP.

If No, you might want to read one or two books in this topic area. The two best general books that we know of are *Computer Networks, 4th Edition*, by Andrew S. Tanenbaum (Prentice-Hall, 2002, ISBN 0-13-066102-3) and *Computer Networks and Internets, 2nd Edition*, by Douglas E. Comer and Ralph E. Droms (Prentice-Hall, 2001, ISBN 0-130-91449-5). When it comes to TCP/IP, consider also Richard Steven's magnificent book *TCP/IP Illustrated, Volume 1: The Protocols* (Addison-Wesley, 1994, ISBN 0-201-63346-9) or *Guide to TCP/IP* by Laura Chappell and series editor Ed Tittel (Course Technology, 2002, ISBN 0-619-03530-7).

Skip to question 5.

4. Have you done any reading on operating systems or networks? [Yes or No]

If Yes, review the requirements stated in the first paragraphs after questions 2 and 3. If you meet those requirements, move on to question 5. If No, consult the recommended reading for both topics. A strong networking background will help you prepare for the Security+ exam in too many important ways to recount them all.

5. Have you taken any security concepts or information security classes? [Yes or No]

If Yes, you will probably be able to handle the primary focus on information security terminology, concepts, and technologies that drive the Security+ exam. If you are rusty, brush up on basic security concepts and terminology, especially the topics mentioned explicitly in the Security+ exam objectives (read them online at www.comptia.org/certification/Security/objectives.asp). If you are not sure you are completely up on these topics, pick and read one of the general information security references mentioned in the following paragraph.

If No, you might want to read one or two books in this topic area. The two best general information security books that we know of are *Network Security: Private Communication in a Public World, 2nd Edition*, by Charlie Kaufmann, Radia Perlman, and Mike Speciner (Prentice Hall PTR, 2002, ISBN 0-130-46019-2) and *Computer Security*, by Dieter Gollmann (John Wiley & Sons, 1999, ISBN 0-471-97844-2). In fact, this is such a huge area for background reading that series editor Ed Tittel has compiled a comprehensive, two-part bibliography called "The Computer Security Bookshelf" for InformIT.com that provides lots of additional pointers. To access these articles, visit www.informit.com and search on "Tittel Security Bookshelf" (do not include the quotation marks in your search string). This should provide direct pointers to both items.

6. Have you done any reading on general security concepts or information security? [Yes or No]

   If Yes, review the requirements stated in the first paragraphs after question 5. If you meet those requirements, move on to the next section.

   If No, consult the recommended reading for those topics. A strong information security background is essential when preparing for the Security+ exam.

Hands-on Experience

An important key to success on the Security+ exam lies in obtaining hands-on experience, especially with Windows 2000 Server and Professional, and/or with some relatively recent version of Linux or Unix in both server and workstation configurations. There is simply no substitute for time spent installing, configuring, and using the various Microsoft and/or Linux or Unix services, protocols, and configuration settings about which you will be asked repeatedly on the Security+ exam. That said, such coverage stresses concepts and principles much more than exact installation or configuration details; it is a vendor-neutral exam, after all.

7. Have you installed, configured, and worked with:

   ➤ Windows 2000 Server? [Yes or No]

   If Yes, make sure you understand basic concepts as covered in Microsoft MCP Exam 70-215. You should also study the TCP/IP interfaces, utilities, and services for Microsoft MCP Exam 70-216, plus implement the security features for Microsoft Exam 70-220. Microsoft MCP Exam 70-214 can also shed light on the Microsoft slant on information security, which will help you prepare for the Security+ exam as well.

You can download objectives, practice exams, and other data about Microsoft exams from the Training and Certification page at **www.microsoft.com/train_cert/**. Use the "Find an Exam" link to obtain specific exam info. We provided a pointer to the Security+ exam objectives earlier in this chapter.

If you haven't worked with Windows 2000 Server, TCP/IP, and the Internet Security and Accelerator (ISA) Server, you should obtain one or two machines and a copy of Windows 2000 Server. Then, learn the operating system. Do the same for TCP/IP and any other software components on which you will also be tested.

➤ Some version of Linux or Unix configured as a server? [Yes or No]

If Yes, be sure you understand basic concepts behind Linux or Unix installation, configuration, operation, and maintenance. You also should study the TCP/IP interfaces, utilities, and related services as well as specific security utilities and related configuration tools to make sure you can put Security+ concepts and terms into an operational context.

In fact, we recommend that you obtain two computers, each with a network interface, and set up a two-node network on which to practice. With decent Windows 2000- and Unix/Linux-capable computers selling for under $500 these days, this shouldn't be too great a financial hardship. You may have to scrounge to come up with the necessary software, but if you scour the Microsoft Web site, you can usually find low-cost options to obtain evaluation copies of most of the software you will need. Linux is open source, which means you can get it for free (if you don't mind building your own installations without software assistance) or for under $100 (if you'd prefer to get a self-installing version of the software).

➤ Windows 2000 Professional? [Yes or No]

If Yes, make sure you understand the concepts covered in Microsoft MCP Exam 70-210.

If No, you will want to obtain a copy of Windows 2000 Professional and learn how to install, configure, and maintain it. You should also review the objectives for Microsoft MCP Exam 70-210 and pay attention to topics and coverage that overlap with the Security+ exam objectives.

 For any and all Microsoft topics, the company's Resource Kits for the topics involved are a great information resource. You can purchase soft cover Resource Kits from Microsoft Press (search at **mspress.microsoft.com/**), but they also appear on TechNet (**www.microsoft.com/technet**).

If No, you will want to obtain a copy of Windows 2000 Professional and learn how to install, configure, and maintain it. You can use *MCSE Windows 2000 Professional Exam Cram* to guide your activities and studies, or work straight from Microsoft's test objectives if you prefer.

➤ Some version of Linux or Unix configured as a workstation or desktop machine? [Yes or No]

If Yes, make sure you understand the concepts involved in installing, configuring, and managing Linux or Unix desktop machines. Here again, you will need to pay special attention to installing, configuring, and maintaining a Linux or Unix desktop as well as to client-side security settings, tools, and utilities.

Testing Your Exam-Readiness

Whether you attend a formal class on a specific topic to get ready for an exam or use written materials to study on your own, some preparation for the Security+ certification exam is essential. At $175 to $225 a try (the lower price applies if you or your employer belong to CompTIA; otherwise, you'll pay the higher price), pass or fail, you want to do everything you can to pass on your first try. That is where studying comes in.

We have included two practice exams in this book, so if you don't score that well on the first test, you can study more and then tackle the second test. If you still don't hit a score of at least 90% after these tests, you will want to investigate the practice test resources we mention here (feel free to use your favorite search engine to look for more; this list is by no means exhaustive):

➤ *MeasureUp*—www.measureup.com

➤ *Transcender*—www.transcender.com

➤ *PrepLogic*—www.preplogic.com

➤ *Self Test Software*—www.selftestsoftware.com

For any given subject, consider taking a class if you have tackled self-study materials, taken the test, and failed anyway. The opportunity to interact with an instructor and fellow students can make all the difference in the world, if you can afford that privilege. For information about Security+ classes, use your favorite search engine with a string such as "Security+ class" or "Security+ training." Even if you can't afford to spend much at all, you should still invest in some low-cost practice exams from commercial vendors.

CompTIA also maintains a list of pointers to Security+ training venues on its Web site. Visit **www.comptia.org/certification/Security/get_training.asp** for more details.

8. Have you taken a Security+ practice exam? [Yes or No]

If Yes, and you scored 90% or better, you are probably ready to tackle the real thing. If your score isn't above that threshold, keep at it until you break that barrier.

If No, obtain all the free and low-budget practice tests you can find (check pointers at www.examcram.com and www.cramsession.com, or scope out offerings from the for-a-fee practice test vendors listed earlier in this chapter) and get to work. Keep at it until you can break the passing threshold comfortably.

When it comes to assessing your test readiness, there is no better way than to take a good-quality practice exam and pass with a score of 85% or better. When we are preparing ourselves, we shoot for better than 90%, just to leave room for the "weirdness factor" that sometimes depresses exam scores when taking the real thing. (The passing score on Security+ is 85% or higher; that is why we recommend shooting for 90%, to leave some margin for the impact of stress when taking the real thing.)

Assessing Readiness for the Security+ Exam

In addition to the general exam-readiness information in the previous section, there are several things you can do to prepare for the Security+ exam. As you're getting ready for the Security+, visit the Web sites at www.examcram.com and www.cramsession.com. You can sign up for "Question of the Day" services for this exam, join ongoing discussion groups on the exam, and look for pointers to exam resources, study materials, and related tips.

Onward, Through the Fog!

Once you have assessed your readiness, undertaken the right background studies, obtained the hands-on experience that will help you understand the products and technologies at work, and reviewed the many sources of information to help you prepare for the test, you will be ready to take a round of practice tests. When your scores come back positive enough to get you through the exam, you are ready to go after the real thing. If you follow our assessment regime, you will not only know what you need to study, but when you are ready to make a test date at Prometric or VUE. Good luck!

CompTIA
Certification Exams

. . . .

Terms you'll need to understand:

✓ Radio button
✓ Check box
✓ Careful reading
✓ Exhibits
✓ Multiple-choice question formats
✓ Process of elimination

Techniques you'll need to master:

✓ Preparing to take a certification exam
✓ Practicing to take a certification exam
✓ Making the best use of the testing software
✓ Budgeting your time
✓ Saving the hardest questions until last
✓ Guessing (as a last resort)

No matter how well prepared you might be, exam taking is not something that most people look forward to. In most cases, familiarity helps relieve test anxiety. You probably won't be as nervous when you take your fourth or fifth CompTIA certification exam as you'll be when you take your first one.

Whether it's your first exam or your tenth, understanding the finer points of exam taking (how much time to spend on questions, the setting you will be in, and so on) and the exam software will help you concentrate on the questions at hand rather than on the surroundings. Likewise, mastering some basic exam-taking skills should help you recognize—and perhaps even outsmart—some of the tricks and traps you are bound to find in several of the exam questions.

Besides explaining the CompTIA Security+ certification program, exam environment, and software, this chapter describes some proven exam-taking strategies you should be able to use to your advantage.

CompTIA Certification Programs Launch Your Career

Many companies prefer to hire people with certifications. CompTIA certification programs are vendor-neutral. They are known throughout the technology community as one of the best ways to break into the Information Technology field and build a solid career. If you are already certified, acquiring additional CompTIA certifications will add to your current credentials and increase the chances of leading to more lucrative and challenging positions. Top technology companies such as Cisco, Hewlett-Packard, IBM, Intel, Microsoft, and Novell use CompTIA certifications as electives or equivalents to their own certification tracks.

Development of the CompTIA Security+ Certification

Leading industry experts from all sectors of the IT industry developed the CompTIA Security+ certification exam. They include government, training and academic organizations, consulting firms, and other affiliated associations. The test questions were written by an experienced group of IT security professionals. All questions are subject to a multilevel review process, making sure they are accurate and pertinent to the subject matter.

The Exam Situation

When you arrive at the testing center where you scheduled your exam, you will need to sign in with an exam proctor. He or she will ask you to show two forms of identification, one of which must be a photo ID. After you have signed in, you will be asked to deposit any books, bags, or other items you brought with you. Then you'll be escorted into the closed room that houses the exam seats.

All exams are completely closed book. In fact, you won't be permitted to take anything with you into the testing area. You will be furnished with a pen or pencil and a blank sheet of paper—or, in some cases, an erasable plastic sheet and an erasable felt-tip pen. You are allowed to write down any information you want on both sides of this sheet. It would be a good idea to memorize as much of the material that appears on the Cram Sheet (inside the front cover of this book) as you can, so you can write that information on the blank sheet as soon as you are seated in front of the computer. At the beginning of each test is a tutorial you can go through if you are unfamiliar with the testing environment. This tutorial time can also be used to write additional information on your sheet. You can refer to the note sheet anytime you like during the test, but you will have to turn in the sheet when you leave the room.

Typically, the room will be furnished with anywhere from one to half a dozen computers, and each workstation will be separated from the others by dividers designed to keep you from seeing what is happening on someone else's computer.

Most test rooms feature a wall with a large picture window. This permits the exam proctor to monitor the room, to prevent exam takers from talking to one another, and to observe anything out of the ordinary that might go on. The exam proctor will have preloaded the appropriate CompTIA certification exam—for this book, that's the Security+ Certification Exam—and you'll be permitted to start as soon as you are seated in front of the computer.

All CompTIA certification exams allow a predetermined maximum amount of time in which to complete your work (this time is indicated on the exam by an onscreen counter/clock in the upper-right corner of the screen, so you can check the time remaining whenever you like). All exams are computer generated and use a multiple-choice format. The Security+ exam consists of 100 randomly selected questions from a pool of several hundred questions. You may take up to 90 minutes to complete the exam.

Although this might sound quite simple, the questions are formulated to thoroughly check your mastery of the material. Often, you will be asked to give more than one answer to a question. Likewise, you might be asked to select the best or most effective solution to a problem from a range of choices, all of which technically are correct. Taking the exam is quite an adventure, and it involves real thinking as well as skill and managing your time. This book shows you what to expect and how to deal with the potential problems, puzzles, and predicaments you are likely to encounter.

When you complete a CompTIA certification exam, the software will tell you whether you have passed or failed. Results are broken into several topic or domain areas. Even if you fail, you should ask for, and keep, the detailed report the test proctor prints for you. You can use this report to help you prepare for another go-round, if needed. If you need to retake an exam, you will have to schedule a new test with Prometric or VUE and pay for another exam. (The amount of the retake exam is determined by what you paid for the original exam.) Keep in mind that because the questions come from a pool, you will receive different questions the second time around. CompTIA also has a retake policy, which can be found on its Web site.

In the following section, you will learn more about how CompTIA test questions look and how they must be answered.

Exam Layout and Design

Some exam questions require you to select a single answer, whereas others ask you to select multiple correct answers. The following multiple-choice question requires you to select a single correct answer. Following the question is a brief summary of each answer selection and why it is either correct or incorrect.

Question 1

As the network administrator, you are implementing a policy for passwords. What is the best option for creating user passwords?

○ A. Uppercase and lowercase letters combined with numbers and symbols

○ B. A randomly generated password

○ C. A word that is familiar to the user with a number attached to the end

○ D. The user's last name spelled backwards

Answer A is correct. A combination of both uppercase and lowercase letters, along with numbers and symbols will make guessing the password difficult. It will also take longer to crack using brute force. Answer B is incorrect because randomly generated passwords are difficult if not impossible for users to remember. This causes them to be written down, thereby increasing the risk of other people finding them. Answers C and D are incorrect because both can easily be guessed or cracked.

This sample question format corresponds closely to the CompTIA Security+ Certification Exam format—the only difference on the exam is that questions are not followed by answer keys. To select an answer, position the cursor over the radio button next to the answer and then click the mouse button to select the answer. See the practice exam CD that comes with this book for a general idea of what the questions will look like.

Next, we examine a question that requires choosing multiple answers. This type of question provides check boxes rather than radio buttons for marking all appropriate selections. These types of questions can either specify how many answers to choose or instruct you to choose all the appropriate answers.

Question 2

Digital signatures are used to authenticate the sender. Which of the following are true of digital signatures? [Choose the two best answers.]

- ❑ A. They use the skipjack algorithm.
- ❑ B. They can be automatically time-stamped.
- ❑ C. They allow the sender to repudiate that the message was sent.
- ❑ D. They can't be imitated by someone else.

Answers B and D are correct. A digital signature is applied to a message, which keeps it from being modified or imitated. Digital signatures can also be automatically time-stamped. Answer A is incorrect because digital signatures are based on an asymmetric scheme. Skipjack is a symmetric key algorithm designed by the U.S. National Security Agency (NSA). Answer C is incorrect because digital signatures allow for nonrepudiation. This means the sender cannot deny that the message was sent.

For this type of question, more than one answer is required. Such questions are scored as wrong unless all the required selections are chosen. In other words, a partially correct answer does not result in partial credit when the test is scored. If you are required to provide multiple answers and you do not provide the number of answers the question asks for, the testing software will mark the question for you and indicate at the end of the test that you did not complete that question. For Question 2, you have to check the boxes next to answers B and D to obtain credit for this question. Realize that choosing the correct answers also means knowing why the other answers are incorrect!

Although these two basic types of questions can appear in many forms, they are the premise on which all the Security+ Certification Exam questions are based. More complex questions may include exhibits, which are usually screenshots. For some of these questions, you will be asked to make a selection by clicking the portion of the exhibit that answers the question.

Other questions involving exhibits use charts or diagrams to help document a workplace or network scenario that you'll be asked to troubleshoot or configure. Careful attention to such exhibits is the key to success. In these instances, you may have to toggle between the exhibit and the question to absorb all the information being shown and to properly answer the question.

Using CompTIA's Exam Software Effectively

A well-known principle when taking exams is to first read over the entire exam from start to finish while answering only those questions you feel absolutely sure of. The next time around, you can delve into the more complex questions. Knowing how many such questions you have left helps you spend your exam time wisely.

Fortunately, the CompTIA exam software makes this approach easy to implement. At the top of each question, in the left corner, is a check box that permits you to mark the question for later review.

NOTE Marking questions makes review easier, but you can return to any question if you are willing to click the Forward or Back button located across the bottom of the screen.

As you read each question, if you answer only those you are sure of, and mark those you are unsure of for review, you can continue working through a dwindling list of questions as you answer the less complex ones first.

There is at least one potential benefit to reading the exam before answering the trickier questions: Sometimes, information stated in later questions will actually answer earlier questions. Other times, information you read in later questions might spark your memory about facts or behaviors that also will help with earlier questions. No matter how you look at it, you will come out ahead if you hold off answering those questions you are not absolutely sure of.

Work through the marked questions until you are certain of all your answers or until you know you will run out of time. If questions remain unanswered, you will want to go through them quickly and guess. Leaving a question unanswered means you won't receive credit for it, and a guess has at least a chance of being correct.

 At the very end of your exam period, you are better off guessing than leaving questions unanswered.

Exam-Taking Techniques

The most important advice about taking any exam is this: Read each question carefully. Some questions are deliberately ambiguous, some use double negatives, and others use terminology in incredibly precise ways. The authors have taken numerous exams—both practice and live—and in nearly every one have missed at least one question because they didn't read it closely or carefully enough.

Here are some suggestions on how to deal with the tendency to jump to an answer too quickly:

➤ Be sure you read every word in the question. If you find yourself impatiently skipping ahead, go back and start over.

➤ As you read, try to reformulate the question in your own words. If you can do this, you should be able to pick the correct answer(s) much more easily.

➤ When returning to a question after your initial read-through, read every word again carefully; otherwise, your mind can fall into a rut. Sometimes, rereading a question after turning your attention elsewhere lets you see something you missed, but the tendency is to see what you have seen before. Try not to let that happen.

➤ If you return to a question more than twice, ask yourself what you don't understand about the question, why the answers don't appear to make sense, or what appears to be missing? If you think about the subject for a while, your subconscious might provide the details that are lacking or you might notice a "trick" that will point to the correct answer.

Above all, try to deal with each question by thinking through what you know about security—the characteristics, behaviors, and facts involved. By reviewing what you know (and what you have written down on your information sheet), you will often recall or understand enough to be able to deduce the answer to the question.

Question-Handling Strategies

Based on exams the authors have taken, some interesting trends have become apparent. For those questions that take only a single answer, usually two or three of the answers will be obviously incorrect, and two of the answers will be possible—of course, only one can be correct. Unless the answer leaps out at you, begin the process of answering by eliminating those answers that are most obviously wrong. A word of caution: If the answer seems too obvious, reread the question to look for a trick. Often those are the ones you are most likely to get wrong.

Things to look for in obviously wrong answers include nonexistent methods of access control, incorrect vulnerability names, inconsistent matches between server types and protocols, and terminology you have never seen. If you have done your homework for an exam, no valid information should be completely new to you. In that case, unfamiliar or bizarre terminology most likely indicates a bogus answer.

As you work your way through the exam, budget your time by making sure you have completed one-quarter of the questions one-quarter of the way through the exam period and three-quarters of them three-quarters of the way through the exam. This ensures that you will have time to go through them all.

As mentioned earlier, you might consider marking the more wordy questions and the ones you are unsure of, answering only the questions you know the first time around. You can always come back to the more complex questions later. This allows you to go through all the questions. You can then review the ones you have marked.

Be cautious about changing your answers and second-guessing yourself. Many times the first selection is right and changing your answer may cause you to miss questions that were originally answered correctly.

If you are not finished when 95% of the time has elapsed, use the last few minutes to guess your way through the remaining questions. Remember that guessing is potentially more valuable than not answering, because blank answers are always wrong, but a guess may turn out to be right. If you don't have a clue about any of the remaining questions, pick answers at random, or choose all A's, B's, and so on. The important thing is to submit an exam for scoring that has an answer for every question.

Mastering the Inner Game

Knowledge breeds confidence, and confidence breeds success. If you study the information in this book carefully and review all the practice questions at the end of each chapter, you should become aware of those areas where you need additional learning and studying.

Follow up by reading some or all of the materials recommended in the "Need to Know More?" section at the end of each chapter. Don't hesitate to look for more resources online. Remember that the idea is to become familiar enough with the concepts and situations you find in the sample questions that you can reason your way through similar scenarios on a real exam. If you know the material, you have every right to be confident that you can pass the exam.

After you have worked your way through the book, take the sample tests in Chapters 12 and 14. This will provide a reality check and help you identify areas you need to study further. Answer keys to these exams can be found in Chapters 13 and 15.

Be sure you follow up and review materials related to the questions you miss on the sample test before scheduling a real exam. The key is to know the why and how. If you memorize the answers, you do yourself a great injustice and may not pass the exam. Only when you have covered all the ground and feel comfortable with the whole scope of the sample test should you take a real one.

If you take the sample test and don't score at least 90% correct, you will want to practice further. When you practice, remember that it is important to know why the answer is correct or incorrect. If you memorize the answers instead, it will trip you up when taking the exam.

With the information in this book and the determination to supplement your knowledge, you should be able to pass the certification exam. However, you need to work at it. Otherwise, you will have to pay for the exam more than once before you finally pass. As long as you get a good night's sleep and prepare thoroughly, you should do just fine. Good luck!

Weighted Averages of the Skill Sets

The Security+ exam encompasses five skill sets, and each is weighted according to the percentages shown in Table 1.1.

Table 1.1	Weighted Objectives	
Domain	Skill Set	Weight
1.0	General Security Concepts	30%
2.0	Communication Security	20%
3.0	Infrastructure Security	20%
4.0	Basics of Cryptography	15%
5.0	Operational/Organizational Security	15%

Here is a quick breakdown of the various domains:

➤ *Domain 1.0 (General Security Concepts)*—You need to be proficient in several aspects of access control, authentication, attacks, malicious code, social engineering, and auditing.

➤ *Domain 2.0 (Communication Security)*—Tests your knowledge of remote access, email, Web, directory, file-transfer, and wireless technologies as well as the vulnerabilities associated with each.

➤ *Domain 3.0 (Infrastructure Security)*—Requires that you be familiar with network devices and media, security topologies, intrusion detection, and security baselines.

➤ *Domain 4.0 (Basics of Cryptography)*—Tests your understanding of algorithms as well as the concepts of using and deploying cryptography and PKI.

➤ *Domain 5.0 (Operational/Organizational Security)*—Assesses your ability to plan physical security, disaster recovery, business continuity, and policy and procedures.

Study Guide Checklist

As you read through this book, use the following checklist to ensure you understand all the skill sets the Security+ exam will cover. The criteria parallel those found on the CompTIA Web site and follow the domain structure for the test.

Domain 1.0: General Security Concepts

1.1. Access Control
➤ 1.1.1. MAC/DAC/RBAC

1.2. Authentication
➤ 1.2.1. Kerberos

➤ 1.2.2. CHAP

➤ 1.2.3. Certificates

➤ 1.2.4. Username/Password

➤ 1.2.5. Tokens

➤ 1.2.6. Multifactor

➤ 1.2.7. Mutual Authentication

➤ 1.2.8. Biometrics

These objectives are covered in Chapter 2, "General Security Practices."

1.3. Nonessential Services and Protocols

1.4. Attacks
➤ 1.4.1. DOS/DDOS

➤ 1.4.2. Back Door

➤ 1.4.3. Spoofing

➤ 1.4.4. Man in the Middle

➤ 1.4.5. Replay

➤ 1.4.6. TCP/IP Hijacking

➤ 1.4.7. Weak Keys

➤ 1.4.8. Mathematical

➤ 1.4.9. Social Engineering

➤ 1.4.10. Birthday

➤ 1.4.11. Password Guessing

    ➤ 1.4.11.1. Brute Force

    ➤ 1.4.11.2. Dictionary

➤ 1.4.12. Software Exploitation

1.5. Malicious Code

➤ 1.5.1. Viruses

➤ 1.5.2. Trojan Horses

➤ 1.5.3. Logic Bombs

➤ 1.5.4. Worms

1.6. Social Engineering

1.7. Auditing

These objectives are covered in Chapter 3, "Nonessential Services and Attacks."

Domain 2.0: Communication Security

2.1. Remote Access

➤ 2.1.1. 802.1x

➤ 2.1.2. VPN

➤ 2.1.3. RADIUS

➤ 2.1.4. TACACS/+

➤ 2.1.5. L2TP/PPTP

➤ 2.1.6. SSH

➤ 2.1.7. IPSec

➤ 2.1.8. Vulnerabilities

2.2. Email

➤ 2.2.1. S/MIME

➤ 2.2.2. PGP

➤ 2.2.3. Vulnerabilities

    ➤ 2.2.3.1. Spam

    ➤ 2.2.3.2. Hoaxes

2.3. Web

➤ 2.3.1. SSL/TLS

➤ 2.3.2. HTTP/S

➤ 2.3.3. Instant Messaging

    ➤ 2.3.3.1. Vulnerabilities

    ➤ 2.3.3.2. 8.3 Naming Conventions

    ➤ 2.3.3.3. Packet Sniffing

    ➤ 2.3.3.4. Privacy

These objectives are covered in Chapter 4, "Communication Security."

➤ 2.3.4. Vulnerabilities

    ➤ 2.3.4.1. Java Script

    ➤ 2.3.4.2. ActiveX

    ➤ 2.3.4.3. Buffer Overflows

    ➤ 2.3.4.4. Cookies

    ➤ 2.3.4.5. Signed Applets

    ➤ 2.3.4.6. CGI

    ➤ 2.3.4.7. SMTP Relay

2.4. Directory

➤ 2.4.1. SSL/TLS

➤ 2.4.2. LDAP

2.5. File Transfer

➤ 2.5.1. S/FTP

➤ 2.5.2. Blind FTP/Anonymous

➤ 2.5.3. File Sharing

➤ 2.5.4. Vulnerabilities

    ➤ 2.5.4.1. Packet Sniffing

2.6. Wireless

➤ 2.6.1. WTLS

➤ 2.6.2. 802.11x

➤ 2.6.3. WEP/WAP

➤ 2.6.4. Vulnerabilities

    ➤ 2.6.4.1. Site Surveys

These objectives are covered in Chapter 5, "Online Vulnerabilities."

Domain 3.0: Infrastructure Security

3.1. Devices

➤ 3.1.1. Firewalls

➤ 3.1.2. Routers

➤ 3.1.3. Switches

➤ 3.1.4. Wireless

➤ 3.1.5. Modems

➤ 3.1.6. RAS

➤ 3.1.7. Telecom/PBX

➤ 3.1.8. VPN

➤ 3.1.9. IDS

➤ 3.1.10. Network Monitoring/Diagnostic

➤ 3.1.11. Workstations

➤ 3.1.12. Servers

➤ 3.1.13. Mobile Devices

3.2. Media

➤ 3.2.1. Coax

➤ 3.2.2. UTP/STP

➤ 3.2.3. Fiber

➤ 3.2.4. Removable Media

   ➤ 3.2.4.1. Tape

   ➤ 3.2.4.2. CDR

   ➤ 3.2.4.3. Hard drives

   ➤ 3.2.4.4. Diskettes

   ➤ 3.2.4.5. Flashcards

   ➤ 3.2.4.6. Smartcards

3.3. Security Topologies

➤ 3.3.1. Security Zones

   ➤ 3.3.1.1. DMZ

   ➤ 3.3.1.2. Intranet

   ➤ 3.3.1.3. Extranet

➤ 3.3.2. VLANs

➤ 3.3.3. NAT

➤ 3.3.4. Tunneling

These objectives are covered in Chapter 6, "Infrastructure Security."

3.4. Intrusion Detection

➤ 3.4.1. Network Based

  ➤ 3.4.1.1. Active Detection

  ➤ 3.4.1.2. Passive Detection

➤ 3.4.2. Host Based

  ➤ 3.4.2.1. Active Detection

  ➤ 3.4.2.2. Passive Detection

➤ 3.4.3. Honey Pots

➤ 3.4.4. Incident Response

3.5. Security Baselines

➤ 3.5.1. OS/NOS Hardening

  ➤ 3.5.1.1. File System

  ➤ 3.5.1.2. Updates (Hotfixes, Service Packs, Patches)

➤ 3.5.2. Network Hardening

  ➤ 3.5.2.1. Updates (Firmware)

  ➤ 3.5.2.2. Configuration

    ➤ 3.5.2.2.1. Enabling and Disabling Services and Protocols

    ➤ 3.5.2.2.2. Access Control Lists

➤ 3.5.3. Application Hardening

  ➤ 3.5.3.1. Updates (Hotfixes, Service Packs, Patches)

  ➤ 3.5.3.2. Web Servers

  ➤ 3.5.3.3. Email Servers

  ➤ 3.5.3.4. FTP Servers

  ➤ 3.5.3.5. DNS Servers

  ➤ 3.5.3.6. NNTP Servers

  ➤ 3.5.3.7. File/Print Servers

  ➤ 3.5.3.8. DHCP Servers

➤ 3.5.3.9. Data Repositories

   ➤ 3.5.3.9.1. Directory Services

   ➤ 3.5.3.9.2. Databases

These objectives are covered in Chapter 7, "Intrusion Detection and Security Baselines."

Domain 4.0: Basics of Cryptography

4.1. Algorithms
➤ 4.1.1. Hashing

➤ 4.1.2. Symmetric

➤ 4.1.3. Asymmetric

4.2. Concepts of Using Cryptography
➤ 4.2.1. Confidentiality

➤ 4.2.2. Integrity

   ➤ 4.2.2.1. Digital Signatures

➤ 4.2.3. Authentication

➤ 4.2.4. Nonrepudiation

   ➤ 4.2.4.1. Digital Signatures

➤ 4.2.5. Access Control

4.3. PKI
➤ 4.3.1. Certificates

   ➤ 4.3.1.1. Certificate Policies

   ➤ 4.3.1.2. Certificate Practice Statements

➤ 4.3.2. Revocation

➤ 4.3.3. Trust Models

These objectives are covered in Chapter 8, "Basics of Cryptography."

4.4. Standards and Protocols

4.5. Key Management/Certificate Lifecycle

➤ 4.5.1. Centralized vs. Decentralized

➤ 4.5.2. Storage

    ➤ 4.5.2.1. Hardware vs. Software

    ➤ 4.5.2.2. Private Key Protection

➤ 4.5.3. Escrow

➤ 4.5.4. Expiration

➤ 4.5.5. Revocation

    ➤ 4.5.5.1. Status Checking

➤ 4.5.6. Suspension

    ➤ 4.5.6.1. Status Checking

➤ 4.5.7. Recovery

    ➤ 4.5.7.1. M of N Control

➤ 4.5.8. Renewal

➤ 4.5.9. Destruction

➤ 4.5.10. Key Usage

    ➤ 4.5.10.1. Multiple Key Pairs (Single, Dual)

These objectives are covered in Chapter 9, "Deploying Cryptography."

Domain 5.0: Operational/Organizational Security

5.1. Physical Security

➤ 5.1.1. Access Control

    ➤ 5.1.1.1. Physical Barriers

    ➤ 5.1.1.2. Biometrics

➤ 5.1.2. Social Engineering

➤ 5.1.3. Environment

  ➤ 5.1.3.1. Wireless Cells

  ➤ 5.1.3.2. Location

  ➤ 5.1.3.3. Shielding

  ➤ 5.1.3.4. Fire Suppression

5.2. Disaster Recovery

➤ 5.2.1. Backups

  ➤ 5.2.1.1. Offsite Storage

➤ 5.2.2. Secure Recovery

  ➤ 5.2.2.1. Alternate Sites

➤ 5.2.3. Disaster Recovery Plan

5.3. Business Continuity

➤ 5.3.1. Utilities

➤ 5.3.2. High Availability / Fault Tolerance

➤ 5.3.3. Backups

5.4. Policy and Procedures

➤ 5.4.1. Security Policy

  ➤ 5.4.1.1. Acceptable Use

  ➤ 5.4.1.2. Due Care

  ➤ 5.4.1.3. Privacy

  ➤ 5.4.1.4. Separation of Duties

  ➤ 5.4.1.5. Need to Know

  ➤ 5.4.1.6. Password Management

  ➤ 5.4.1.7. SLA

  ➤ 5.4.1.8. Disposal/Destruction

➤ 5.4.1.9. HR Policy

➤ 5.4.1.9.1 Termination

➤ 5.4.1.9.2 Hiring

➤ 5.4.1.9.3 Code of Ethics

➤ 5.4.2. Incident Response Policy

These objectives are covered in Chapter 10, "Organizational Security."

5.5. Privilege Management

➤ 5.5.1. User/Group/Role Management

➤ 5.5.2. Single Sign-On

➤ 5.5.3. Centralized vs. Decentralized

➤ 5.5.4. Auditing (Privilege, Usage, Escalation)

➤ 5.5.5. MAC/DAC/RBAC

5.6. Forensics

➤ 5.6.1. Chain of Custody

➤ 5.6.2. Preservation of Evidence

➤ 5.6.3. Collection of Evidence

5.7. Risk Identification

➤ 5.7.1. Asset Identification

➤ 5.7.2. Risk Assessment

➤ 5.7.3. Threat Identification

➤ 5.7.4. Vulnerabilities

5.8. Education

➤ 5.8.1. Communication

➤ 5.8.2. User Awareness

➤ 5.8.3. Education

➤ 5.8.4. Online Resources

5.9. Documentation

➤ 5.9.1. Standards and Guidelines

➤ 5.9.2. Systems Architecture

➤ 5.9.3. Change Documentation

➤ 5.9.4. Logs and Inventories

➤ 5.9.5. Classification

    ➤ 5.9.5.1. Notification

➤ 5.9.6. Retention/Storage

➤ 5.9.7. Destruction

These objectives are covered in Chapter 11, "Privilege Management, Forensics, Risk Identification, Education, and Documentation."

Additional Resources

A good source of information about CompTIA certification exams comes from CompTIA itself. The best place to go for exam-related information is online. The CompTIA Security+ home page resides at `http://www.comptia.com/certification/security/default.asp`.

Coping with Change on the Web

Sooner or later, all the information we have shared about Web-based resources mentioned throughout this book may go stale or be replaced by newer information. There is always a way to find what you want on the Web if you are willing to invest some time and energy. CompTIA's site has a site map to help you find your way around. Most large or complex Web sites offer search engines. Finally, feel free to use general search tools to search for related information.

General Security Practices

Terms you'll need to understand:

✓ Mandatory Access Control (MAC)
✓ Discretionary Access Control (DAC)
✓ Rule-Based Access Control (RBAC)
✓ Role-Based Access Control (RBAC)
✓ Kerberos authentication
✓ Challenge Handshake Authentication Protocol (CHAP)
✓ Certificates
✓ Tokens
✓ Biometrics

Techniques you'll need to master:

✓ Recognizing the forms of access control (MAC/DAC/RBAC)
✓ Understanding the process of authentication and the various forms of authentication available
✓ Recognizing asymmetric and symmetric encryption methods
✓ Understanding biometrics and the part they play in security

The concept of security within the network environment includes aspects drawn from all operating systems, application software packages, hardware solutions, and networking configurations present within the network to be secured, as well as within any network sharing connectivity directly or indirectly with the network to be secured. Clients studying for the Security+ exam need to develop the broadest set of skills possible, gaining experience from the most specific to the most general of security concepts.

You need to be aware of general security concepts, and this chapter and Chapter 3, "Nonessential Services and Attacks," provide an overview of the general concepts you should familiarize yourself with in particular. As a prospective security professional, you should also take every opportunity you can find to expand your skill base beyond these. The practice of a security professional is never an end unto itself but rather a never-ending path threaded through constant change and ever-evolving possibility.

Access Control

Before discussing identity verification of security principles, we review the methods of access authorization that may be utilized once authentication has occurred. Planning for access control may affect the methods utilized in the authentication process—for example, if there will only be a need for anonymous access to a public read-only HTML document, there is no need for a complex authentication process.

 Whenever you're confronted by a solution involving the determination of proper levels of access, remember the phrase "Less is more." This is a convenient reminder of the security practice known as *least privilege*, where an account is granted no more access rights than the bare minimum needed to perform assigned tasks. Remember you are dealing with human beings when you give users access. It is always better received when rights or privileges are added than when taken away.

Access control generally refers to the process of making resources available to accounts that should have access, while limiting that access to only what is required. The forms of access control you need to know include the following:

➤ Mandatory Access Control (MAC)

➤ Discretionary Access Control (DAC)

➤ Rule-Based Access Control (RBAC)

➤ Role-Based Access Control (RBAC)

We discuss these types of access control in the following sections.

 The Trusted Computer System Evaluation Criteria (TCSEC) specification used by many government networks explicitly specifies only the MAC and DAC forms of access control.

Mandatory Access Control

Mandatory Access Control (MAC) is often found in government systems, although it is not restricted to them. It is a strict, hierarchical model. What is important to understand with MAC is that the operating system controls the access and that a data owner cannot override this control. All objects are given security labels, also referred to as *sensitivity labels*. Users are assigned security clearances, such as top secret or confidential, and data is also classified accordingly. This classification is stored in the resource security label.

Besides the classification, the security label contains categories. Categories can be used to define such things as levels of management, departments, or projects. When a user requests access to an object, the system checks the user's security clearance and the classification of the object to determine accessibility. In other words, the system determines access by comparing the labels of the user and the object. Because labels have classifications and categories, if you have top-secret clearance but are not in a certain department, you will not have access to that department's information, even though you have top-secret clearance.

Discretionary Access Control

Discretionary Access Control (DAC) is a model where the data owners decide who has access to data. This is most commonly found in the PC environment. Access is restricted based on permissions granted to the users. The creator/owner of a file can determine who has access to the file. The basis of DAC is the use of *access control lists (ACLs)*. These lists are enforced by the operating system but are determined by the owners and set by the network administrator. For example, suppose you want to give Mary access to your hard drive but not John. All you do is set the share and/or security permissions to mirror this. Mary then has access to the hard drive; John does not. Note that in MAC, the operating system determines the access, and in DAC, the data owner determines the access. Therefore, in this situation, if you were using MAC and the security labels did not allow Mary access to your hard drive, she would not be able to access it no matter what you did.

Rule-Based Access Control

Two access control methods share the same acronym, RBAC. The first of these is *Rule-Based Access Control*, and the second is *Role-Based Access Control*. Rule-Based Access Control is also based on ACLs. The basis of this type of access is to determine what can happen to an object based on a set of rules. The most common use of this is on routers and firewalls. Access is determined by looking at a request to see whether it matches a predefined set of conditions. An example would be if you configured your router to deny any IP addresses from the 10.10.0.0 subnet and allow addresses from the 192.168.10.0 network. When a machine with an address of 192.168.10.15 requests access, the router looks at the rules and accepts the request. In Rule-Based Access Control, the administrator sets the rules. This is considered a type of mandatory control because the users cannot change these rules. In other words, if the administrator sets the aforementioned router conditions, you, as a user, cannot have the router accept requests from a 10.10.0.25 address.

 Rule-Based Access Control is based on a predefined set of rules that determines the object's access.

In a Rule-Based Access Control solution, accounts may be granted varying levels of access, such as Read, Write, or Edit. These rights may vary by account, by group membership, by time of day, or by many other forms of conditional testing. An example of this would be setting the filtering of IP packets on a proxy server or firewall. Say you want to keep the production staff from downloading BMP files, but you want to allow the development staff to do so. Before you allow any file to be downloaded, you check conditions such as the file type and the group membership. Remember that the most common form of Rule-Based Access Control involves testing against an ACL that details systems and accounts with access rights and the limits of their access for the resources. ACLs are used within operating systems such as Novell NetWare, Microsoft Windows, DEC OpenVMS, and most Unix and Linux packages.

Role-Based Access Control

The second type of access control that utilizes the RBAC acronym is the *Role-Based Access Control* method. This method of access is based on an organization's structure and the roles the users play in the organization. In this type of access control, it is determined what job functions each employee performs and then access is assigned based on those functions. Role-Based Access Control is also known as *Nondiscretionary Access Control.*

Because users are assigned roles and then permissions are assigned to these roles, this may sound similar to a group membership. However, this is not necessarily so. Roles and groups both provide ways of controlling user access, but in a group environment, users can belong to other groups. In a role-based model, users can only be assigned one role. Another difference is that sometimes in a group environment, users are assigned separate or individual permissions. A role-based model does not support this. Therefore, if you are assigned to the role of "developer," you have access to the resources that are allowed for that role—nothing more, and nothing less.

Many times, this type of access control model will be used in companies that use a lot of independent contractors or have a high turnover. This saves on administrative overhead because the administrator can more easily remove and add users to a role. For example, let's look at the difference between a user in a group scenario and a user in a role scenario.

Your company had a developer who belonged to the following groups: development, testing, and production. He also had administrative permissions on two of the servers in the development office. He has left the company, and a new developer has been hired to replace him. Because you don't want the new developer to have the excessive permissions the original developer had, you cannot just rename the old account. This creates a lot of work for you as the administrator, and if turnover is high in your company, before you know it, you will have very little control or will be spending all your time setting permissions.

If the preceding situation is designed as a role-based scenario, the permissions are much cleaner because the developer can only be assigned one role. Therefore, when a new developer is hired, he either has the same role as the previous developer or is assigned a different one, but he can only have one role, making administration much easier.

The Role-Based Access Control model can use task-based access, lattice-based access, and role-based access. Task-based access is similar to role-based access, except tasks instead of roles are defined. Lattice-based access defines the upper and lower bounds of a user's permissions. This is found in MAC situations. Let's say the developer role has a security clearance of top-secret. The upper bound would be top-secret, and the lower bound would be anything the public would have access to. So you see, role-based access can be used in MAC. It can also be used in DAC. In DAC, the data owners decide on the permissions; therefore, administrators can make roles and the data owners can then decide to which roles to give access.

Authentication

Before authorization may occur, for anything other than anonymous access to wholly public resources, the identity of the account attempting to access a resource must first be determined. This process is known as *authentication*. The most well known form of authentication is the use of a logon account identifier and password combination to access controlled resources. Access is not possible without both required account authentication parts, thus a level of protection is provided.

 The shortcoming of any authentication system is that keys used may be easily falsi-fied. This can lead to access rights being granted to an unauthorized access attempt. Null or easily guessed passwords are among the most widespread examples of the potential for this weakness.

The relative strength of an authentication system involves the difficulty associated with falsifying or circumventing its process. Anonymous or open access represents the weakest possible form of authentication, whereas the requirement for both a logon identifier and password combination may be considered the most basic of actual account verification. Beyond this, authentication may involve restricting access only when occurring from specific network addresses, or if an identified digital key or security token, such as an access smartcard, is present.

In theory, the strongest security would be offered by identifying biometric keys that are unique to a particular user's person or physical body, such as fingerprints and retinal or iris patterns, combined with other authentication methods, such as access passwords or token-based security that requires the possession of a physical smartcard key.

Obviously, the needs for authentication are going to be relative to the value assigned to a particular resource's security. Adding more layers of authentication increases both the administrative overhead required for management and the difficulty users will have gaining access to needed resources. As an example, consider the differences in authentication requirements for access to a high-security solution such as the Federal Reserve's banking network, as opposed to those needed to access an unprivileged local account in a public kiosk.

Obviously, in the first scenario, to establish authentication for rightful access, the use of a combination of biometric, token-based, and password-form access methods may be mandatory. You may also use these access methods with even more complex forms of authentication, such as the use of dedicated lines of communication, time-of day restrictions, synchronized shifting-key hardware encryption devices, and redundant-path comparisons. You would use these to ensure that each account attempting to make a transaction is properly identified. In the second scenario, authentication might be as simple as an automatic anonymous guest logon shared by all visitors.

In the following section, we discuss the various methods of authentication. These include Kerberos, which uses tickets; Challenge Handshake Authentication Protocol (CHAP), which uses a challenge/response mechanism; certificates, which use encryption; tokens, which are hardware devices; and biometrics, which combines each individual's unique traits with technology.

Kerberos Authentication

The most basic aspects of authentication, within a completely isolated network, would only include the need to determine the identity of an account. If a network is itself physically or logically accessible to external parties that might seek to sniff (that is, capture and examine) data being transmitted between systems, the problem arises as to how to keep the authentication keys themselves safe.

Here is an example. A basic File Transfer Protocol (FTP) access session involves the client sending a logon identifier and a password to the FTP server, which accepts or rejects this access. The logon identifier and password, by default, are sent in plaintext form, readable by any agent with access to the data as it is transmitted from the client to the server. This information could then be used later to allow an unauthorized party to access the server, pretending to be the authorized user.

To avoid the process of sending the actual logon information across an unsecured network, a solution created by the Athena project at MIT can be used—the symmetric-key authentication protocol known as *Kerberos*. The term *symmetric key* means that both the client and server must agree to use a single key in both the encryption and decryption processes (see Figure 2.1).

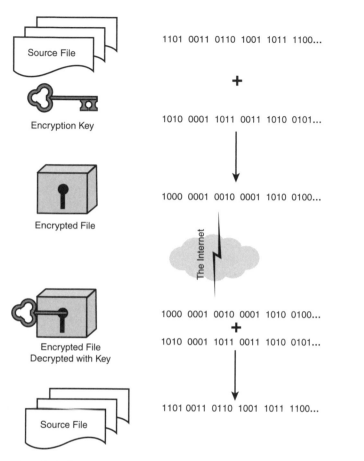

Figure 2.1 Example of a symmetric-key encrypted data transfer.

In Kerberos authentication, a client sends its authentication details not to the target server but rather to a Key Distribution Center (KDC) through the following process:

1. The Authentication Service (AS) receives the client request and verifies the user ID and request in a database.

2. Once the request has been verified, a timestamped session key is created with a limited duration (by default, eight hours) using the client's key, as well as a randomly generated key that includes the identification of the target service.

3. This information is sent back to the client in the form of a ticket-granting ticket (TGT).

4. The client then submits the TGT to a ticket-granting server (TGS).

5. This server then generates a timestamped key encrypted with the service's key and returns both to the client.

6. The client then uses its key to decrypt its ticket, contacts the server, and offers the encrypted ticket to the service.

7. The service uses its key to decrypt the ticket and verify that the timestamps match and the ticket remains valid.

8. The service contacts the KDC and receives a timestamped session-keyed ticket, which it returns to the client.

9. The client then decrypts the keyed ticket using its key. After both agree that the other is the proper account and that the keys are within their valid lifetime, communication occurs.

The short lifespan of a ticket ensures that if someone attempts to intercept the encrypted data to try to break its key, the key will have changed before that person can break the key using cryptographic algorithms. The handshaking between the client and the KDC, and the service and the KDC, provides verification that the current session is valid without requiring the transmission of logon or password information between client and service.

The strengths of Kerberos authentication come from its time-synchronized connections and the use of registered client and service keys within the KDC. These circumstances also create some drawbacks, such as the need to use a standard time base for all systems involved as well as the difficulties that can result if the KDC is unavailable or the cached client and service credentials were accessed directly from the granting servers.

Mutual Authentication

Kerberos v.5 includes support for a process known as *mutual authentication*, in which both client and server verify that the computer with which they are communicating is the proper system. This process helps to prevent man-in-the-middle attacks, where an unauthorized party intercepts communications between two systems and pretends to be each to the other, passing some data intact, modifying other data, or inserting entirely new sets of values to accomplish the desired tasks. (See Chapter 3 for more on man-in-the-middle attacks.)

In mutual authentication, one system creates a challenge code based on a random number and then sends this code to the other system. The receiving system generates a response code using the original challenge code and also creates a challenge code of its own, sending both back to the originating system. The originating system verifies the response code as a value and returns its own response code to the second system, generated from the challenge code returned with the first response code. Once the second system has verified its returned response code, it notifies the originating system, and both systems consider themselves mutually authenticated.

Challenge Handshake Authentication Protocol (CHAP)

The Challenge Handshake Authentication Protocol (CHAP) can be used to provide on-demand authentication within an ongoing data transmission. CHAP uses a one-way hashing function that first involves a service requesting a CHAP response from the client. The client creates a hashed value that is derived using the Message Digest (MD5) hashing algorithm and sends this value to the service, which also calculates the expected value itself. The server, referred to as the *authenticator*, compares these two values. If they match, the transmission continues. This process is repeated at random intervals during a session of data transaction.

Several items are worth reviewing from the previous paragraph. The CHAP process is repeated at random intervals during the session. This helps eliminate the possibility of a replay attack. The process of authenticating is called a *three-way process*. Actually, four steps are involved because the first step is establishing the connection, but the authentication process itself is a three-way process.

Remember that CHAP functions over Point-to-Point Protocol (PPP) connections. Also, you should be able to recognize the two forms of CHAP that are Microsoft specific: MS-CHAP and MS-CHAPv2.

Certificates

One of the most rigorous forms of authentication involves the use of *digital certificates* within a Public Key Infrastructure (PKI). These certificates are used to establish encrypted communication streams through unsecured networks. Public key systems utilize an asymmetric cryptographic process in which the encryption and decryption keys are not the same, as opposed to a symmetric cryptographic process like that used in Kerberos authentication.

PKI is the basis for many commonly encountered data encryption solutions, including the use of the X.509-compliant keys used in establishing Secure Sockets Layer (SSL) connections most often seen in secured Web site forms (HTTPS on port 443). PKI is discussed in detail in Chapter 8, "Basics of Cryptography."

In public key encryption, a public key and private key are generated by a Certificate Authority (CA), and these keys are returned to the client in the form of digital certificates. The public key is given to those who need to encrypt data and send it to the client. The client then decrypts the data using its private key, which only the client has. The public key is used to encrypt a message, and the public key is used to decrypt the results. So, if you send Diane a message, you can find out her public key from a central authority and encrypt a message to her using that public key. When she receives it, she decrypts it with her private key. Besides encrypting messages, she can also authenticate herself to you by using her private key to encrypt a digital certificate. When you receive it, you then use her public key to decrypt it. The purpose of encrypting messages is to ensure privacy. The purpose of encrypting signatures is to validate the identity of the person who sent the message.

 To send an encrypted message, the receiver's public key (the security key open to anybody who can be found from a central authority) is used. To decrypt a message, the receiver's private key (the security key only known by the recipient) is used. If you want to send a message using an encrypted signature, the sender uses his private key. To decrypt an encrypted signature, the sender's public key is used.

A Registration Authority (RA) provides authentication to the Certificate Authority of the validity of a client's certificate request. One of the most commonly used Certificate and Registration Authorities is VeriSign, a vendor specializing in the issuance of X.509 certificates for secure Web site connections.

Username and Password

The most common form of authentication is the combination of a username and a password or passphrase. If both match values stored within a locally stored table, the user is authenticated for a connection. Password strength is a measure of the difficulty involved in guessing or breaking the password through cryptographic techniques or library-based automated testing of alternate values.

A weak password might be very short or only use alphanumeric characters, making decryption simple. A weak password can also be one that is easily guessed by someone profiling the user, such as a birthday, nickname, address, name of a pet or relative, or a common word such as *God, love, money,* or *password.*

Stronger passwords can be derived from events or things the user knows. For example, let's say the password requirements are that the length be nine characters and a combination of letters, numbers, and special characters must be used. So, let's say a user is going to the Bahamas on June 6, 2003, with his spouse, Judy. The phrase "Going to the Bahamas on June 6, 2003 with Judy" can become gtB6603@J. The user now has a complex password that is easy to remember!

Tokens

One of the best methods of authentication involves the use of a *token*, which may either be a physical device or a one-time password issued to the user. Tokens include solutions such as the chip-integrated smartcard or a digital token such as RSA Security's SecurID token. Without the proper token, access is denied. Because the token is unique and only granted to the user, it is harder to pretend to be (spoof) the properly authorized user. Digital tokens are typically only used one time; therefore, they cannot be captured and reused later by an unauthorized party.

Biometrics

Obviously, the most unique quality of a user is his body and its unique physical characteristics, such a fingerprints, retinal patterns, iris patterns, facial blood-vessel patterns, bone structure, and other forms of specific, unique biophysical qualities. Other values may be used, such as voice patterns or high-resolution cardiac patterns, but because of the manner in which these may change due to illness or exertion, they can be somewhat less dependable.

New systems are becoming available to allow authentication of a user by her body's measurements (biometrics), which are compared to values stored within a local table to provide authentication only if the biometric values match. Another alternative includes storing biometric data on smartcard tokens, so a user must have both to be authenticated within a widely distributed scheme, where transactions against a central server storing large and complex biometric values might be difficult.

Multifactor

The best possible authentication solution involves a combination of other methods. A multifactor solution like this might include the use of a smartcard token storing biometric values that are compared to those of the user, who might also be asked to enter a valid password. In other words, multifactor authentication combines something you have with something you know. The difficulty involved in gaining unauthorized access increases as more types of authentication are used, although the difficulty for users wishing to authenticate themselves is also increased similarly. The administrative overhead and cost of support also increase with the complexity of the authentication scheme, so a solution should be reasonable based on the sensitivity of data being secured.

Nonessential Services and Protocols

Systems installed in default configurations often include many unnecessary services that are configured automatically. These provide many potential avenues for unauthorized access to a system or network. Many services have known vulnerabilities that require specific actions to make them more secure or that might be used to simply impair system function by causing additional processing overhead.

NOTE

The denial of service (DoS) attack against an unneeded Web service is one example of a possible way in which a nonessential service could cause problems for an otherwise functional system.

Common default-configuration exploits include services, such as anonymous-access FTP servers, as well as network protocols, such as the Simple Network Management Protocol (SNMP).

ALERT

If you are presented with a question that asks you to choose "all that apply," you might be tempted to simply pick all the above to make sure that all requirements are covered. Be wary of this option, because it will generally also cause the installation of unnecessary services or protocols. Therefore, read the question carefully to determine exactly what is required.

Practice Questions

Question 1

> You are the network administrator responsible for selecting the access control method that will be used for a new kiosk system to be used in a local museum. The museum's donors want to have full access to information on all items, but visitors should only have access to those items in current displays. Which forms of access control would be most appropriate to this requirement? [Choose the two best answers.]
>
> ❑ A. Discretionary Access Control (DAC)
> ❑ B. Mandatory Access Control (MAC)
> ❑ C. Role-Based Access Control (RBAC)
> ❑ D. Rule-Based Access Control (RBAC)

Answers B and C are correct. A MAC solution involving labels such as DONOR and DISPLAY would suffice for the user access assignment. A Role-Based Access Control solution involving the roles of User and Donor would also be appropriate. Answer A is incorrect because the complexity of assigning by-user access rights over each item's files would involve a large amount of administrative overhead. Answer D is incorrect because the complexity of the requirement is not great enough to involve detailed conditional testing.

Question 2

> The relative strength of a password is a measure of how difficult it is to guess or cryptographically break. Of the following, which is the strongest password?
>
> ○ A. Username: Jane Fields, Password: t1ns3lt0wn
> ○ B. Username: Robert Shaw, Password: bobshaw
> ○ C. Username: John Doe, Password: PaSsWoRd
> ○ D. Username: Tina Weeks, Password: 7days

Answer A is correct. It is the strongest password because it contains the best variety of numbers and letters. Answer B is incorrect and the weakest password because it contains no numbers and no mix of uppercase and lowercase letters. Answer C is the second weakest password and is incorrect because it only contains letters. Answer D is the third-weakest password and is incorrect because it only contains one number and all lowercase letters.

Question 3

A Public Key Infrastructure relies on what type of authentication?

○ A. The exchange of tickets by the client and service

○ B. Public and private keys

○ C. Something you have along with something you know

○ D. A device that stores information on a user

Answer B is correct. A Public Key Infrastructure uses public and private keys. Answer A is incorrect because shared tickets are utilized by the Kerberos authentication process. Answer C is incorrect because something you have along with something you know is an example of multifactor authentication. Answer D is incorrect because it describes a token.

Question 4

When reviewing user access to a service or resource, what is the order of operation?

○ A. Access must be granted first and then authentication occurs.

○ B. Authentication occurs first and then access is determined.

○ C. Authentication and access control occur separately at the same time.

○ D. A user's access rights are determined by the method of authentication used.

Answer B is correct. Before access rights can be determined, a user must first be authenticated. Answers A and C are incorrect because authentication must precede access rights determination to avoid granting an unauthorized account access rights. Answer D is incorrect because the processes of authentication and access rights determination are not explicitly dependent on one another.

Question 5

Which type of authentication involves comparison of two values calculated using the Message Digest (MD5) hashing algorithm?

- ○ A. Biometric authentication
- ○ B. Challenge Handshake Authentication Protocol (CHAP)
- ○ C. Kerberos authentication
- ○ D. Mutual authentication
- ○ E. Public Key Infrastructure (PKI)

Answer B is correct. The Challenge Handshake Authentication Protocol uses two compared values created using the MD5 hashing algorithm. Answer A is incorrect because biometric authentication relies on biological patterns rather than calculated values. Answers C and D are incorrect because Kerberos and mutual authentication schemes involve timestamped ticket-based key exchange or time-based random code exchange rather than an MD5 calculated value. Answer E is incorrect because a PKI solution involves the use of digital certificates rather than a calculated hashed value.

Question 6

Many different keys may be used to perform user authentication. Which of the following are biometric authentication types? [Choose all correct answers.]

- ❑ A. One-use passcode
- ❑ B. Voice recognition
- ❑ C. Fingerprint
- ❑ D. Smartcard
- ❑ E. Facial recognition
- ❑ F. Iris identification

Answers B, C, E, and F are correct. These are all biometric authentication types. Answers A and D are incorrect because they are token authentication types.

Question 7

Which of the following is an example of the use of an asymmetric encryption method?

- O A. Biometric authentication
- O B. Challenge Handshake Authentication Protocol (CHAP)
- O C. Kerberos authentication
- O D. Username and password
- O E. Public Key Infrastructure (PKI)

Answer E is correct. A PKI solution involves an asymmetric encryption scheme in which a public key is used to encrypt data and a separate private key is used to decrypt the data. Answer A is incorrect because biometric identification relies on biological patterns and not encrypted values. Answers B and C are incorrect because both CHAP and Kerberos authentication involve the use of symmetric encryption schemes, where the same key values are used to calculate or encrypt and decrypt data by both client and service. Answer D is incorrect because the username and password are simply available values and don't involve encryption.

Question 8

You are the network administrator responsible for selecting the access control method that will be used for a new parking garage. Members of the Board of Directors must always be granted access, whereas other staff members should only be granted access to the parking garage when spaces are available. Visitors should be allowed access only during normal business hours. What form of access control would be best for this scenario?

- O A. Discretionary Access Control (DAC)
- O B. Mandatory Access Control (MAC)
- O C. Role-Based Access Control (RBAC)
- O D. Rule-Based Access Control (RBAC)

Answer D is correct. A Rule-Based Access Control solution would allow detailed conditional testing of the user's account type as well as the time of day and day of the week in order to allow or deny access. Answers A and B are incorrect because both solutions do not allow for conditional testing. Answer C is also incorrect because Role-Based Access Control involves testing against role-assigned access rights rather than by other qualities, such as a test for normal working hours.

Question 9

Which of the following might be used in multifactor authentication? [Choose all correct answers.]

- ❏ A. Biometric authentication
- ❏ B. Challenge Handshake Authentication Protocol (CHAP)
- ❏ C. Kerberos authentication
- ❏ D. Username and password
- ❏ E. Public Key Infrastructure (PKI)

Answers A, B, C, D, and E are correct. Any combination of authentication methods may be used in a multifactor solution.

Question 10

You are presented with an authentication scheme in which Computer A calculates a code it sends to Computer B, Computer B returns a calculated code based on the one from Computer A as well as one of its own, and then Computer A returns a calculated code to Computer B based on its transmitted code. What type of authentication is this?

- ○ A. Biometric authentication
- ○ B. Challenge Handshake Authentication Protocol (CHAP)
- ○ C. Kerberos authentication
- ○ D. Mutual authentication
- ○ E. Public Key Infrastructure (PKI)

Answer D is correct. In mutual authentication, both computers exchange calculated values and verify a returned code based on these. Answer A is incorrect because biometric authentication involves comparisons against stored biological values. Answer B is incorrect because CHAP is service-demanded and does not provide verification back to the client that the service is also authentic. Answer C is incorrect because Kerberos provides end-to-end security using symmetric key cryptography. Answer E is incorrect because PKI authentication involves the exchange and comparison of keys or certificates issued by a third agent (the Certificate Authority) rather than by direct negotiation between the two systems.

Need to Know More?

 Allen, Julia H. *The CERT Guide to System and Network Security Practices*. Addison-Wesley. Upper Saddle River, NJ, 2001. ISBN 020173723X.

 Krause, Micki, and Harold F. Tipton. *Information Security Management Handbook, Fourth Edition*. Auerbach Publications. New York, NY, 1999. ISBN 0849398290.

 The SANS "The Twenty Most Critical Internet Security Vulnerabilities" list: www.sans.org/top20/.

Nonessential Services and Attacks

Terms you'll need to understand:

✓ Nonessential services
✓ DoS/DDoS
✓ Back door
✓ Spoofing
✓ Man-in-the-middle attack
✓ Replay
✓ Transmission Control Protocol/Internet Protocol (TCP/IP) hijacking
✓ Password guessing (brute force/dictionary)
✓ Software exploitation
✓ Viruses
✓ Trojan horses
✓ Logic bombs
✓ Worms
✓ Social engineering
✓ Auditing

Techniques you'll need to master:

✓ Understanding and identifying common services that may be disabled or locked down to thwart unauthorized access
✓ Recognizing when an attack is happening and taking proper steps to end it

✓ Learning to identify which types of attacks you might be subject to and how to implement proper security to protect your environment

✓ Recognizing malicious code and knowing how to respond appropriately

✓ Understanding how easy social engineering has become

✓ Learning the concepts of proper auditing

The challenge of working in a mixed operating system environment becomes a factor when trying to secure your resources. It has become very common for servers to be subject to a myriad of attacks through services, protocols, and open ports.

The Security+ exam requires that you understand that eliminating nonessential services can thwart many would-be attackers and that you understand the different types of attacks that can happen.

Understanding and Identifying Common Services and Nonessential Services Posing Possible Security Threats

It is an IT professional's responsibility to be sure that the network is secure and safe from attacks. This is an enormous undertaking. Most servers come with a wide range of services and protocols, many of which are turned on by default. The first step in securing your environment is to formulate a plan. The plan should include the following:

➤ The role of each server along with its current configuration

➤ The services, protocols, and applications required to meet the business needs

➤ Any configuration changes that should be made to the existing servers, such as additions and the removal of nonessential server services that don't meet business needs

Overlooking the planning phase can spell disaster. Many times though, this phase is skipped because the server has to be put in place right away or its original role has been changed without any reconfiguration. The technology world is changing constantly, and your network needs to change along with it to accommodate new ways of doing business while protecting yourself from new vulnerabilities. It is dangerous to sit down at a server and try to configure it without a plan. Each operating system has its own set of protocols, scripting languages, and tools. You could not possibly cover all bases efficiently and effectively without proper planning. Your plan should also be reevaluated on a regular basis. What is a viable solution now might not work in the future.

Establishing a Server Role

By identifying the role that each server plays, it can more easily be determined which services and protocols are required or needed. Common roles for servers include the following:

➤ *Logon server*—These servers authenticate users when they log on to their workstations. These servers can also function as other types of servers.

➤ *Network services server*—These servers host services that are required for the network to function as per the configuration. These include Dynamic Host Configuration Protocol (DHCP), Domain Name System (DNS), Windows Internet Name Service (WINS), and Simple Network Management Protocol (SNMP).

➤ *Application server*—Used for hosting applications such as custom accounting packages and office suites.

➤ *File server*—Used for access to common user files and home directories.

➤ *Print server*—Used for access to the network shared printers.

➤ *Web server*—Used to host Web-based applications and internal or external Web sites.

➤ *FTP server*—Used to store files that are downloaded or uploaded. These can be internal as well as external.

➤ *Email server*—Used for email but can also be used to host public folders and groupware applications.

➤ *News/Usenet (NNTP) server*—Used as a newsgroup server where users can post and retrieve messages in a common location.

It should also be determined whether the server will be accessed from the internal network, from the external world, or both. This helps identify the services and protocols you need on your server. In the following sections, we discuss how to determine which protocols and services you need on your server as well as the benefits of removing unnecessary protocols and services.

Required and Critical Services

Every operating system requires different services for it to operate properly. Ideally, the configuration process should start with installing only the services necessary for the server to function. The manufacturer should have these services listed in the documentation. If not, a wealth of information on hardening servers can be found in books and on the Web. Using documentation to standardize the methods used to set up servers will make new deployments easier and more secure.

The best way to ensure that only necessary services are running is to do a clean install. When a computer system is shipped to you, there is usually additional software, such as the manufacturer's tools, or additional configuration changes that have been made. The only way to be sure the machine meets the specifications of the plan is to perform a clean installation using predetermined checklists or policies. This task is very time consuming but in the long run is worth it. An additional benefit is that it ensures you have all the software and skills required to rebuild the server should this ever need to be done. Taking the time to do it right the first time saves you many headaches down the road.

Determining Required Protocols

Some administrators install unnecessary protocols because they either misunderstand the protocols' function or think they may need them later. Protocols, like services, should not be installed unless required. When looking at your network environment, the following should be determined:

➤ Whether the protocol(s) is required for desktop-to–server communication

➤ Whether the protocol(s) is required for server-to-server communication

➤ Whether the protocol(s) is required for remote access–to-server communication

➤ Whether the protocol(s) chosen requires additional services

➤ Whether there are any known security issues associated with the protocol(s) chosen

Many networks consist of a mixed Windows and Unix operating system environment. Hypothetically, you have decided to use TCP/IP as the communications protocol. Next, you need to determine whether to implement TCP/IP statically or dynamically through DHCP.

If you decide that TCP/IP is to be deployed dynamically, you need to use an additional service (DHCP). Although DHCP can ease administration costs, it is less secure because unknown users can plug into your network and receive a TCP/IP address. This is especially true on unsecured wireless networks, where someone can be in the parking lot with a laptop attached to your network via a wireless connection.

TCP/IP also requires that you have a DNS server deployed for proper name resolution. In the hypothetical network, both Unix and Windows operating systems are running, and depending on whether Windows NT 4.0 or Windows 2000 is used, both DNS and WINS may be needed.

You must consider the implications in security planning. Weighing the factors helps you make wise choices in deploying services and protocols. The risks associated with running each choice of service and protocol should be researched and documented. It would be great to eliminate the associated risks altogether, but this is virtually impossible in today's world. However, being able to come up with possible solutions to reduce the risks associated with each service and protocol is a step in the right direction.

Benefits of Removing Protocols and Services

Deploying a server out of the box may have services installed that actually pose security risks. An unconfigured server is a server looking to be hacked. Therefore, you need to determine which services can be uninstalled or disabled. It is not wise to run services that aren't going to be used. If they are left installed and improperly configured, someone else may use them to do harm to the network. This can happen from inside the network as well as from the outside. These days, more harm is done by disgruntled and curious employees than from outside hackers.

Remember that secure networks require planning time. Companies have a tendency to want to deploy new technology as fast as they can to take advantage of what it can do for them. The number of configuration options offered in each new operating system increases faster than we can imagine. Being able to identify and implement only the necessary services and protocols required is a skill that must be learned. This approach helps reduce the attacks that affect every network.

Attacks

Due to the anonymity of networks and the Internet, we are seeing an increase in attacks on all types of servers. The reasons for such attacks can be attributed to anything from simple curiosity to malicious intent.

In an effort to prevent your network from becoming part of the growing number of statistics, you need to recognize when an attack is happening and take the proper steps to end it. Learning to identify which types of attacks you might be subject to and how to implement proper security to protect your environment are important functions of your position. Some of the more common attacks are listed in this section.

Denial of Service (DoS) and Distributed Denial of Service (DDoS) Attacks

The purpose of a denial of service (DoS) attack is to disrupt the resources or services that a user would expect to have access to. These types of attacks are executed by manipulating protocols and can happen without the need to be validated by the network.

Many of the tools used to produce this type of attack are readily available on the Internet. Administrators use them to test connectivity and troubleshoot problems on the network, whereas malicious users use them to cause connectivity issues.

Here are some examples of DoS attacks:

➤ *Smurf/smurfing*—This attack is based on the Internet Control Message Protocol (ICMP) echo reply function. It is more commonly known as *ping*, which is the command-line tool used to invoke this function. In this attack, the attacker sends ping packets to the broadcast address of the network, replacing the original source address in the ping packets with the source address of the victim, thus causing a flood of traffic to be sent to the unsuspecting network device.

➤ *Fraggle*—This attack is similar to a Smurf attack. The difference is that it uses the User Datagram Protocol (UDP) instead of ICMP. The attacker sends spoofed UDP packets to broadcast addresses as in the Smurf attack. These UDP packets are directed to port 7 (echo) or port 19 (chargen). When connected to port 19, a character generator attack can be run. Table 3.1 lists the most commonly exploited ports.

➤ *Ping flood*—This attack attempts to block service or reduce activity on a host by sending ping requests directly to the victim. A variation of this type of attack is the ping of death, in which the packet size is too large and the system doesn't know how to handle the packets.

➤ *SYN flood*—This attack takes advantage of the TCP three-way hand-shake. The source system sends a flood of synchronization (SYN) requests and never sends the final acknowledgment (ACK), thus creating half-open TCP sessions. Because the TCP stack waits before resetting the port, the attack overflows the destination computer's connection buffer, making it impossible to service connection requests from valid users.

➤ *Land*—This attack exploits a behavior in the operating systems of several versions of Windows, Unix, Macintosh OS, and Cisco IOS with respect to their TCP/IP stacks. The attacker spoofs a TCP/IP synchronization (SYN) packet to the victim system with the same source and destination IP address and the same source and destination ports. This confuses the system as it tries to respond to the packet.

➤ *Teardrop*—This form of attack targets a known behavior of UDP in the TCP/IP stack of some operating systems. The Teardrop attack sends fragmented UDP packets to the victim with odd offset values in subse-quent packets. When the operating system attempts to rebuild the origi-nal packets from the fragments, the fragments overwrite each other, causing confusion. Because some operating systems cannot gracefully handle the error, the system will most likely crash or reboot.

➤ *Bonk*—This attack affects mostly Windows machines by sending corrupt UDP packets to DNS port 53. This causes confusion, and the system crashes.

➤ *Boink*—This is a Bonk attack that targets multiple ports instead of just port 53.

You should know the difference between the various types of attacks and the ports they are executed on.

Table 3.1	Commonly Exploited Ports
Port	**Service**
7	Echo
11	Systat
15	Netstat
19	Chargen
20	FTP-Data
21	FTP
22	SSH
23	Telnet
25	SMTP
49	TACACS
53	DNS
80	HTTP
110	POP3
111	Portmap
161/162	SNMP
443	HTTPS
1812	RADIUS

Another form of attack is a simple expansion of a DoS attack, referred to as a Distributed DoS (DDoS) attack. There is already downloadable software that allows DDoS attacks to be generated from inside the network. This will allow disgruntled or malicious users to disrupt services without any outside influence. The attacker distributes zombie software that allows the attacker partial or full control of the infected computer system. Once an attacker has enough systems compromised with the installed zombie software, he can initiate an attack against a victim from a wide variety of hosts. The attacks come in the form of the standard DoS attacks, but the effects are multiplied by the total number of zombie machines under the control of the attacker.

To help protect your network, you can set up filters on external routers to drop packets involved in these types of attacks. You should also set up another filter that denies traffic originating from the Internet that shows an internal network address. When you do this, the loss of ping and some services and utilities for testing network connectivity will be incurred, but this is a small price to pay for network protection. If the operating system allows it, you should reduce the amount of time before the reset of an unfinished TCP connection. This will make it harder to keep resources unavailable for extended periods of time.

 In the case of a DDoS attack, your best weapon is to get in touch quickly with your upstream ISP and see whether it can divert traffic or block the traffic at a higher level.

Subscribing to newsgroups and checking security Web sites daily ensures that you keep up with the latest attacks and exploits. Applying the manufacturer's latest operating system patches or fixes can also help prevent attacks.

Back Door

A back door is a program that allows access to a system without using security checks. Usually programmers put back doors in programs so they can debug and change code during test deployments of software. Because many of these back doors are undocumented, they may get left in, causing security risks.

Some of the better-known software programs that can be used as back doors include the following:

➤ *Back Orifice*—This is a remote administration tool that allows system administrators to control a computer from a remote location (that is, across the Internet). It is construed as a dangerous back door designed by a group called the Cult of the Dead Cow Communications. Back Orifice consists of two main pieces: a client application and a server application. The client application, running on one machine, can be used to monitor and control a second machine running the server application.

➤ *NetBus*—Like Back Orifice, NetBus allows a remote user to access and control a machine via the Internet. NetBus runs under the Windows NT operating system as well as Windows 95/98. NetBus also has two essential parts: a server (the part that resides on the victim's system) and a client (the application used to find and control the server). Features and functions vary, but the result is much the same—loss of privacy and security on a computer anytime it is connected to the Internet.

➤ *Sub7 (or SubSeven)*—This is a Windows 9X Internet backdoor Trojan similar to Back Orifice and NetBus. When it is running, anyone running the appropriate client software has unlimited access to the system while it is connected to the Internet.

The following are legitimate products that may be installed by malicious users to cause harm:

➤ *Virtual Network Computing (VNC)*—This is remote control software by AT&T labs that allows you to view a desktop environment from anywhere on the Internet and from a wide variety of machine architectures.

➤ *PCAnywhere*—This product is produced by Symantec. It is remote control software with encryption and authentication. It is used by many companies in their help desk departments for resolving user issues.

➤ *Terminal Services*—This application is used by Microsoft operating systems for remote control. It delivers the Windows desktop and applications by means of terminal emulation.

Back Orifice, NetBus, and Sub7 have two essential parts: a server and client. The server is the infected machine and the client is used for remote-controlling the server. These programs are known as illicit servers.

As with most utilities, the software in the preceding list can be used with good intent or maliciousness. The best ways to prevent backdoor attacks are user education and software monitoring. Users should be instructed to only download software off the Internet that has been approved by network or security administration and from approved sites. Installation and use of software such as antivirus packages can catch many of these backdoor applications, including Back Orifice, NetBus, and Sub7. Be sure your antivirus software is scheduled to download the latest virus definitions at least weekly.

Another type of back door comes in the form of a privileged user account. An existing user who already has privileges often creates the backdoor account. This account is set up to look like a normal user's account and given a high-level privilege. This allows the user or an attacker to come in under an alias. To prevent this situation, you need to set proper access so users will not have the right or privilege to alter operating system files—know who has administrative rights. Auditing, covered in the last section of this chapter, can help detect the creation and use of backdoor accounts by tracking the creation of these accounts and their frequency of use.

Spoofing

Spoofing is making data appear to come from somewhere other than where it really originated. This is accomplished by modifying the source address of traffic or source of information. Spoofing seeks to bypass IP address filters by setting up a connection from a client and sourcing the packets with an IP address that is allowed through the filter.

Services such as email, Hypertext Transfer Protocol (HTTP), and File Transfer Protocol (FTP) can also be spoofed. Web spoofing happens when an attacker creates a convincing but false copy of an entire World Wide Web. The false Web looks just like the real one: It has all the same pages and links. However, the attacker controls the false Web so that all network traffic between the victim's browser and the Web goes through the attacker. In email spoofing, a spammer or a computer virus can forge the email packet information in an email so that it appears the email is coming from a trusted host, from one of your friends, or even from your own email address. If you leave your email address at some Internet site or exchange email with other people, a spoofer may be able to use your email address as the sender address to send spam. These forms of attacks are often used to get additional information from network users in order to complete a more aggressive attack.

As mentioned earlier, you should set up a filter that denies traffic originating from the Internet that shows an internal network address. Using the signing capabilities of certificates on servers and clients allows Web and email services to be more secure. The use of IPSec can secure transmissions between critical servers and clients. This will help prevent these types of attacks from taking place.

Man in the Middle

The man-in-the-middle attack takes place when an attacker intercepts traffic and then tricks the parties at both ends into believing that they are communicating with each other. The attacker can also choose to alter the data or merely eavesdrop and pass it along. This attack is common in Telnet and wireless technologies. It is also generally difficult to implement because of physical routing issues, TCP sequence numbers, and speed. Because the hacker has to be able to sniff both sides of the connection simultaneously, programs such as Juggernaut, T-Sight, and Hunt have been developed to help make the process easier.

If the attack is attempted on an internal network, physical access to the network will be required. Be sure that access to wiring closets and switches is restricted—if possible, the area should be locked. After you have secured the physical aspect, the services and resources that allow a system to be inserted into a session should be protected. DNS can be compromised and used to redirect the initial request for service, providing an opportunity to execute a man-in-the-middle attack. DNS access to should be restricted to read-only for everyone except the administrator. The best way to prevent these types of attacks is to use encryption and secure protocols.

 A man-in-the-middle attack takes place when a computer intercepts traffic and either eavesdrops on the traffic or alters it.

Replay

In a replay attack, packets are captured by using sniffers. After the pertinent information is extracted, the packets are placed back on the network. This type of attack can be used to replay bank transactions or other similar types of data transfer in the hopes of replicating or changing activities, such as deposits or transfers.

Protecting yourself against replay attacks involves some type of timestamp associated with the packets or time-valued, nonrepeating serial numbers. Secure protocols such as IPSec prevent replays of data traffic in addition to providing authentication and data encryption.

TCP/IP Hijacking

Hijacking is the term used when an attack takes control of a session between the server and a client. This starts as a man-in-the-middle attack and then adds a reset request to the client. The result is that the client gets kicked off the session, while the rogue machine still communicates with the server. This commonly happens during Telnet and Web sessions where security is lacking or when session timeouts aren't configured properly.

Forcing a user to reauthenticate before allowing transactions to occur could help prevent this type of attack. Other protection mechanisms include the use of unique initial sequence numbers (ISNs) and Web session cookies.

Weak Keys

Weak keys generally denote a weak choice in the number of combinations during encryption. This is usually found in the block cipher method used in 40-bit and 56-bit encryption, whereby the messages are broken into blocks that are independent of each other.

Mathematical

A mathematical attack on an algorithm uses the mathematical properties of the algorithm to decrypt data using computations that are more efficient than guessing. They can come in the form of ciphertext-only, plaintext, or chosen plaintext attacks. These concepts are explained in greater detail in Chapter 8, "Basics of Cryptography."

The best way to avoid weak key, birthday (discussed later), and mathematical attacks is to use 128-bit encryption. Both 40-bit and 56-bit encryption have already been broken—40-bit in less than four hours. Keep in mind that export laws prohibit strong encryption from being exported, resulting in many vulnerable servers.

Password Guessing

Allowing users to choose their own passwords produces an unsecure environment because users typically choose passwords that are easy-to-remember words. On the other end of the spectrum, if the passwords are too difficult to remember, users will write them down and post them on monitors, keyboards, and any number of easy-to-find places. Secure passwords should consist of uppercase and lowercase letters, numbers, and special characters. The two basic types of attacks on passwords are brute-force and dictionary attacks. Passwords can also be guessed by *shoulder surfing*, which is looking over a person's shoulder and watching as she types.

 When allowing users to choose their own passwords, you might to have them combine the first letters and dates of important events. An example would be "My daughter Diane was born on Jan 1, 1976." The password would be MdDwbJ11976.

Brute Force

Brute force is a term used to describe a way of cracking a cryptographic key or password. It involves systematically trying every conceivable combination until a password is found, or until all possible combinations have been exhausted. The more complex the password is, the longer it takes to crack. Many programs exist that try to guess passwords or decipher password files.

Dictionary

We tend to choose passwords that have special meaning to us or relate to our everyday lives. This makes them easy to crack because they are usually found in the dictionary. A dictionary attack is the first step of a brute-force attack. This type of attack checks through known words in a dictionary data file trying to match the password.

Birthday

Birthday attacks are a type of brute-force technique that uses hash functions. It gets its name from the probability that two or more people in a group of 23 sharing the same birthday is greater than 50%.

Some of the more popular password guessing programs include:

➤ *Crack*—A password-cracking program designed to quickly locate insecurities in Unix (or other) password files by scanning the contents of a password file.

➤ *John the Ripper*—A password cracker currently available for Unix, DOS, and Windows NT/95. It has its own modules for different ciphertext formats and architectures.

➤ *L0phtCrack*—A Windows and Unix password-auditing tool that produces user passwords from the cryptographic hashes that are stored by the operating system.

The following are measures you can use to help reduce the use of brute-force password-guessing tools:

➤ Make the password length at least eight characters and require the use of uppercase and lowercase letters, numbers, and special characters.

➤ Lock user accounts out after three to five failed logon attempts. This stops programs from deciphering the passwords on locked accounts.

➤ Monitor the network for the use of questionable tools. If password files can be captured, they can be run though password-guessing programs on another machine.

 Passwords should be at least eight characters in length and possess a combination of uppercase and lowercase letters, numbers, and special characters.

Software Exploitation

Software exploitation takes advantage of a program's flawed code. One of the most used flaws is the buffer overflow. When more data is sent to a buffer than it is able to handle, it doesn't know how to react to the extra data.

Usually this crashes the system and leaves it in a state where arbitrary code can be executed or an intruder can function as an administrator.

In the case of buffer overflow, good quality assurance and secure programming practices would definitely thwart this type of attack. The most effective way to prevent an attacker from exploiting software bugs is to keep the manufacturer's latest patches and service packs applied as well as monitor the Web for newly discovered vulnerabilities.

Malicious Code

In today's network environment, malicious code (or *malware*) has become a serious problem. The target is not only the information stored on local computers, but also other resources and computers. As a security professional, part of your responsibility is to recognize malicious code and know how to respond appropriately. This section covers the various types of malicious code you might encounter, including viruses, Trojan horses, logic bombs, and worms.

Viruses

A program or piece of code that runs on your computer without your knowledge is a virus. It is designed to attach itself to other code and replicate. It replicates when an infected file is executed or launched. At this point, it attaches to other files, adds its code to the application's code, and continues to spread. Even a simple virus is dangerous because it can use all available resources and bring the system to a halt. Many viruses can replicate themselves across networks and bypass security systems. There are several types of viruses:

➤ *Boot-sector*—This type of virus is placed into the first sector of the hard drive so when the computer boots, the virus loads into memory.

➤ *Polymorphic*—This type of virus can change form each time it is executed. It was developed to avoid detection by antivirus software.

➤ *Macro*—This type of virus is inserted into a Microsoft Office document and emailed to unsuspecting users.

Viruses have to be executed by some type of action, such as running a program.

Here are some common viruses:

➤ *Stoned*—The Stoned virus was first reported in New Zealand in early 1988. All known variants are capable of infecting the hard disk Master Boot Record (MBR), and some may damage directories or the File Allocation Table (FAT). It is transmitted via floppy from one computer system to another.

➤ *Michelangelo*—Michelangelo is a Master Boot Record virus. It is based on the Stoned virus, although it is different in its behavior. The Michelangelo virus erases the contents of the infected drive on March 6th (the birth date of the virus' namesake) of the current year.

➤ *Melissa*—Melissa first appeared in March 1999. It is a macro virus that is received by email and is embedded in a Microsoft Word document. When the recipient of the email opens the document, the virus sends email to the first 50 addresses in the victim's address book and attaches itself to each email.

➤ *I Love You*—A variant of the Melissa virus that emails itself to all addresses in the address book. It also infects the `Normal.dot` template in Microsoft Word, causing all new documents created to be infected as well.

The viruses listed are a very small number of the total population of computer viruses. Viruses are growing at an alarming rate, and newer ones do more damage as virus writers get more sophisticated. In any case, viruses cost you money due to the time it takes to clean the software and recover lost data.

Virus Hoaxes

A virus hoax uses system resources and consumes users' time. Many times, they come in the form of a chain letter bragging of free money. There also have been hoaxes sent telling users to delete files from their systems or informing them a certain program has a logic bomb. If there is any doubt as to whether the virus threat is real, you should do a little investigative work. Many good Web sites list these hoaxes. Check out the following sites for more virus information:

➤ Symantec's Antivirus Web site—`www.symantec.com/avcenter/index.html`

➤ McAfee Security Antivirus Web site—`vil.mcafee.com/`

➤ Sophos Antivirus Web site—`www.sophos.com/`

Trojan Horses

Trojan horses are programs disguised as useful applications. Trojan horses do not replicate themselves like viruses but they can be just as destructive. Code is hidden inside the application that can attack your system directly or allow the system to be compromised by the code's originator. The Trojan horse is typically hidden so its ability to spread is dependent on the popularity of the software and a user's willingness to download and install the software.

Some Trojan horses include the following:

➤ *Acid Rain*—This is an old DOS Trojan horse that, when run, deletes system files, renames folders, and creates many empty folders.

➤ *Trojan.W32.Nuker*—This is a Trojan horse designed to function as a denial of service (DoS) attack against a workstation connected to the Internet.

➤ *Simpsons*—The user is tricked into running a file that deletes files on selected drives via an extracted BAT file. This Trojan horse uses the program `deltree.exe` found on Windows 9*X* systems.

As with viruses, Trojan horses can do a significant amount of damage to a system or network of systems.

Logic Bombs

A logic bomb is a virus or Trojan horse that is built to go off when a certain event occurs or a period of time goes by. For example, a programmer might create a logic bomb to delete all his code from the server on a future date, most likely after he has left the company. In several cases recently, ex-employees have been prosecuted for their role in this type of destruction. During software development, it is a good idea to bring in a consultant to evaluate the code to keep logic bombs from being inserted. Although this is a preventative measure, it will not guarantee a logic bomb won't be inserted after the programming has been completed.

Worms

Worms are similar in function and behavior to a virus, Trojan horse, or logic bomb, with the exception that worms are self-replicating. A worm is built to take advantage of a security hole in an existing application or operating system and then find other systems running the same software and automatically replicate itself to the new host. This process repeats with no user intervention. After the worm is running on a system, it checks for Internet connectivity. If it exists, the worm then tries to replicate from one system to the next.

Some examples of worms include the following:

➤ *Morris*—This is probably the most famous worm of all. It took advantage of a Sendmail vulnerability and shut down the entire Internet in 1988.

➤ *Badtrans*—This mass-mailing worm attempts to send itself using Microsoft Outlook by replying to unread email messages. It also drops a remote access Trojan horse.

➤ *Nimda*—This worm virus infects using several methods, including mass mailing, network share propagation, and several Microsoft vulnerabilities. Its name is *admin* spelled backward.

➤ *Code Red*—A buffer overflow exploit is used to spread this worm. This threat only affects Web servers running Microsoft Windows 2000.

Many variants exist to each of these worms. Many times they are quite difficult to remove, so antivirus companies have downloadable tools available to remove them.

 A worm is similar to a virus or Trojan horse, except that it replicates by itself, without any user interaction.

You can take several steps to protect your network from malicious code:

➤ Install antivirus software and update the files on a regular basis. Antivirus software doesn't do a company any good if it is not updated often.

➤ Only open attachments sent to you by people you know. Many viruses infect user address books, so even if you know who the attachment is from, be sure to scan it before you open it.

➤ Do not use any type of removable media from another user without first scanning the disk.

➤ Perform backups on a daily basis.

➤ Install firewalls or intrusion-prevention systems on client machines.

➤ Subscribe to newsgroups and check antivirus Web sites on a regular basis.

Social Engineering

The last attack that needs to be addressed can be one of the easiest and most productive attacks of all—*social engineering*. It plays on human behavior and how we interact with one another. The attack doesn't feel like an attack at all. As a matter of fact, we teach our employees to be customer service oriented, so many times they think they are being helpful and doing the right thing. It is imperative that you understand how easy social engineering has become. Some scenarios of social engineering attacks are provided in the following list:

➤ A vice president calls you and states that she's in real trouble. She's attempting to do a presentation for a very important client and has forgotten her password. She just changed it yesterday and can't remember what it is. She needs to have it right away because she has a room full of clients waiting and she's starting to look incompetent. This is a really big client and means a lot of money to the company.

➤ Someone you have never seen before approaches you as you are entering a secured building. She has her hands full carrying coffee and doughnuts. She smiles and says she just doesn't seem to have an extra hand to grab the door. She asks that you please hold it for her.

➤ You receive a call from the corporate office saying that they are putting a new mail server into place and need to verify current user accounts and passwords. You are told that it is not good to send this information via email, so please print it and fax it directly to a number given to you that is a direct line for the person putting the new server into place.

 Social engineering is an attack that plays upon human behavior.

In each of these situations, an attacker tries to manipulate corporate users to gain access or knowledge that will allow him entry into either the building or the network. Empathy and urgency are played upon in the first two scenarios. This makes users feel that it is okay to give out information or allow access to the building. In the third scenario, the user is made to feel that the use of email will be affected if she doesn't comply. Each attack plays on human behavior and our willingness to help and trust others.

The best defense against social engineering is a combination of operational/administrative, technical, and environmental control. It comes down to technology, policies, education, awareness, and training.

Now that we've completed our overviews of the different types of attacks and viruses, you need to understand the auditing process so you can track users' actions on the network to prevent these attacks and viruses from occurring.

Auditing

Auditing is the process of tracking users and their actions on the network. Learning the concepts of proper auditing will be a valuable asset.

The types of activities that can be audited include the following:

➤ Network logons and logoffs

➤ File access

➤ Printer access

➤ Remote access services

➤ Network services

➤ Application usage

Auditing should be built around security goals and policies. Effective planning and well-defined structure must be a part of an audit policy for it to work properly. You should not monitor everything; otherwise, you will stress system resources, fill up the hard drive and log files, and never be able to weed through the mounds of data that has accumulated. Therefore, monitor what is really important. If you aren't sure what is important, many recommendations can be found on the Internet. Microsoft has an area devoted to securing its operating systems that also contains auditing information. In the end, auditing should be a policy determined to meet the specific needs of the company.

Here are the steps to take when initiating an audit policy:

1. Identify potential resources at risk within your networking environment. This may include files and services that should be protected from unauthorized access.

2. After the resources are identified, set up the actual audit policy. Each operating system will have its own tools for tracking and logging access. If the policy stipulates auditing large amounts of data, be sure

that the hardware can handle the load. Auditing can easily add 20% to 30% additional load onto a server.

3. Make time to view the log files generated after auditing is turned on. If your network is compromised and the intrusion was recorded in your log files six months ago, what good is that? If possible, import these files into a database and view the data graphically or query for abnormalities.

Along with auditing, establish a baseline of normal activity. Then the network behavior can be monitored against the baseline. As you begin to understand the patterns of your users and the network, it will be much easier to identify odd or suspicious behaviors.

System Scanning

Scanning is a process used to probe ports. Scanning programs keep track of those ports that are receptive listeners, and they also analyze weaknesses. Many vulnerability scanners are available for download on the Internet. These tools can be extremely useful in determining how vulnerable your network is. However, you should not try these tools without an administrator's permission. The following list names some of the most commonly used tools:

➤ *Nessus*—Provides a free, powerful, up-to-date and easy-to-use remote security scanner. Nessus is fast, reliable and has a modular architecture that allows you to fit it to your needs.

➤ *NetRecon*—Helps organizations secure their Windows NT networks by scanning systems and services on the network and simulating intrusion or attack scenarios.

➤ *Nmap*—Nmap (network mapper) is a Linux open-source utility for network exploration or security auditing. It was designed to scan large networks but also works fine on single hosts.

➤ *SAFEsuite*—This suite can scan a TCP/IP network, look for problems in a Web server, and test both proxy-based and packet filter–based firewalls. It can be used on Windows NT, Solaris, and Linux platforms.

➤ *Security Administrator's Tool for Analyzing Networks (SATAN)*—An administrative tool that recognizes several common security problems and for each one found offers a tutorial that explains the problem, what its impact could be, and how to correct it.

➤ *Security Administrator's Integrated Network Tool (SAINT)*—An enhanced version of SATAN, SAINT is used for evaluating the security of networks.

➤ *Tiger Tools TigerSuite*—Includes modules for remote scanning, service detection, and penetration testing. Also, tools are available for the PocketPC and Windows CE handhelds.

Although network administrators can find these tools very useful, there can be serious consequences for using them in a malicious way. These days, the members of the Board of Directors can be held responsible should data be compromised. For example, you work for a financial institution. You do business with other financial institutions. The help desk employees use PCAnywhere to help users resolve issues. Last week you hired a new technician. Yesterday, you found out that one of the companies you do business with has called about some odd behavior on its network. You find out that the new technician has been running a utility and scanning all the networks of the clients he has dialed into since he started. You, your company, and the Board of Directors can be held responsible for his actions.

Practice Questions

Question 1

> Unauthorized access has been detected on the network. Someone had been log-
> ging in as one of the help desk technicians during off hours. Later you find out
> he received an email from the network administrator asking him to supply his
> password so that he could make changes to his profile. What types of attacks
> have been executed? [Choose the two best answers.]
>
> ❑ A. Spoofing
> ❑ B. Man in the middle
> ❑ C. Replay
> ❑ D. Social engineering

Answers A and D are correct. Spoofing involves modifying the source
address of traffic or source of information. In this instance, the email was
spoofed to make the user think it came from the administrator. By replying
to the request, the user was tricked into supplying compromising information, which is a classic sign of social engineering. Answer B is incorrect
because a man-in-the-middle attack is commonly used to gather information
in transit between two hosts. In a replay attack, an attacker intercepts traffic
between two endpoints and retransmits (or *replays*) it later; therefore, answer
C is incorrect.

Question 2

> You're the security administrator for a bank. The users are complaining about
> the network being slow. However, it is not a particularly busy time of the day.
> You capture network packets and discover that hundreds of ICMP packets have
> been sent to the host. What type of attack is likely being executed against your
> network?
>
> ○ A. Spoofing
> ○ B. Man-in-the-middle
> ○ C. Worm
> ○ D. Denial of service

Answer D is correct. A ping flood is a DoS attack that attempts to block service or reduce activity on a host by sending ping requests directly to the victim. Answer A is incorrect because spoofing involves modifying the source

address of traffic or source of information. Answer B is incorrect because a man-in-the middle attack is commonly used to gather information in transit between two hosts. Answer C is incorrect because a worm is a form of malicious code.

Question 3

Which of the following is a correct definition of a Trojan horse?

○ A. It needs no user intervention to replicate.

○ B. It sends messages to a computer with an IP address indicating that the message is coming from a trusted host.

○ C. It is open-source code and attacks only open-source software.

○ D. It buries itself in the operating system software and infects other systems only after a user executes the application that it is buried in.

Answer D is correct. A Trojan horse appears to be useful software but has code hidden inside that will attack your system directly or allow the system to be infiltrated by the originator of the code once it is executed. Answers A is incorrect because a Trojan horse is not self-executing. Answer B is incorrect because it is the description of spoofing. Answer C is incorrect because viruses are based on exploits of Microsoft Visual Basic, not Trojan horses.

Question 4

You are checking your network to ensure users are conforming to a new password security policy that requires them to use complex passwords. You plan on using a password-cracking program. Which of the following programs can you use? [Choose all correct answers.]

❑ A. John the Ripper

❑ B. SATAN

❑ C. L0phtCrack

❑ D. SAINT

Answers A and C are correct. John the Ripper and L0phtCrack are both used to crack passwords. Answers B and D are incorrect because both SATAN and SAINT are vulnerability-testing tools.

Question 5

> Back Orifice is considered a(n) _____.
>
> ○ A. Virus
> ○ B. Illicit server
> ○ C. Worm
> ○ D. Trojan horse

Answer B is correct. Back Orifice, NetBus, and Sub7 have two essential parts: a server and client. These programs are known as *illicit servers*. Answer A is incorrect because a software virus is a small chunk of code designed to attach to other code. Answer C is incorrect because a worm is a form of malicious code. Answer D is incorrect because a Trojan horse appears to be useful software but has code hidden inside that will attack your system directly or allow the system to be infiltrated by the originator of the code once it is executed.

Question 6

> You have created a utility for defragmenting hard drives. You have hidden code inside the utility that will install itself and cause the infected system to erase the hard drive's contents on April 1, 2004. Which of the following attacks has been used in your code?
>
> ○ A. Virus
> ○ B. Spoofing
> ○ C. Logic bomb
> ○ D. Trojan horse

Answer C is correct. A logic bomb is a virus or Trojan horse that is built to go off when a certain event occurs or a period of time goes by. Answers A and D are incorrect because a specified time element is involved. Answer B is incorrect because spoofing involves modifying the source address of traffic or the source of information.

Question 7

Your network is under attack. Traffic patterns indicate that an unauthorized service is relaying information to a source outside the network. What type of attack
is being executed against you?

○ A. Spoofing

○ B. Man-in-the-middle

○ C. Replay

○ D. Denial of service

Answer B is correct. A man-in-the-middle attack is commonly used to gather information in transit between two hosts Answer A is incorrect because
spoofing involves modifying the source address of traffic or source of information. In a replay, an attacker intercepts traffic between two endpoints and
retransmits or replays it later; therefore, answer C is incorrect. Because the
purpose of a DoS attack is to deny use of resources or services to legitimate
users, answer D is incorrect.

Question 8

Your new server is preinstalled with a suite of manufacturer tools and the following components:

Web server

FTP server

Telnet server

TCP/IP

NetBEUI

IPX/SPX

NNTP server

This machine is to be configured as a Novell application server. What is the best
way to be sure the server is secure as possible?

○ A. Remove everything except NetBEUI.

○ B. Remove everything except IPX/SPX.

○ C. Reformat the machine and start from scratch.

○ D. Remove everything except TCP/IP.

Answer C is correct. Because a suite of tools from the manufacturer is
installed, it may not be possible to determine what services these tools use;
therefore, reformatting the machine would be the best way to ensure

security. Be sure you have all the drivers and manufacturer software handy so you can reinstall everything you need. Answers A, B, and D are incorrect because these do not take into account the manufacturers tools.

Question 9

You have been assigned the task of setting auditing on the network. What is the first action you should take?

- ○ A. Determine where the log files will be stored.
- ○ B. Start auditing resources immediately.
- ○ C. Use a vulnerability scanner to see which resources are poorly protected.
- ○ D. Plan.

Answer D is correct. Planning is always the first step in implementing an audit policy. Answers A and C are incorrect because these steps follow the planning stage. Answer B is an unwise move—auditing without planning first can tax system resources and fill up the log files quickly.

Question 10

Due to a previous IP spoofing attack, you want to make some changes to the network to prevent future attacks. Which of following actions should you take?

- ○ A. Install antivirus software.
- ○ B. Set up IP address filters.
- ○ C. Install certificates on clients and servers.
- ○ D. Block all ports on the router.

Answer B is correct. By setting up filters to drop external packets with internal source addresses, you can help prevent this type of attack. Answers A and C are incorrect because antivirus software and certificates will not prevent IP address spoofing. Blocking all ports on the router will not allow any traffic in or out; therefore, answer D is incorrect.

Need to Know More?

 Chirillo, John. *Hack Attacks Denied: A Complete Guide to Network Lockdown for UNIX, Windows, and Linux, Second Edition.* John Wiley & Sons. Indianapolis, IN, 2002. ISBN 0471232831.

Refer to Chapter 1, "Common Ports and Services," and Chapter 4, "Safeguarding Against Penetration Attacks."

 Chirillo, John. *Hack Attacks Revealed: A Complete Reference for UNIX, Windows, and Linux with Custom Security Toolkit, Second Edition.* John Wiley & Sons. Indianapolis, IN, 2002. ISBN 0471232823.

Refer to Chapter 4, "Well-Known Ports and Their Services," and Chapter 5, "Discovery and Scanning Techniques."

 McClure, Stuart, Joel Scambray, and George Kurtz. *Hacking Exposed: Network Security Secrets and Solutions, Third Edition.* McGraw-Hill. New York, NY, 2001. ISBN 0072193816.

Refer to Chapter 12, "Denial of Service Attacks."

Virus Bulletin Web site: `http://www.virusbtn.com`

The Twenty Most Critical Internet Security Vulnerabilities list (SANS): `http://www.sans.org/top20/`

The CERT Coordination Center (CERT/CC): `http://www.cert.org`

4

Communication Security

Terms you'll need to understand:

✓ Virtual Private Network (VPN)
✓ Layer 2 Tunneling Protocol (L2TP)
✓ Point-to-Point Tunneling Protocol (PPTP)
✓ Terminal Access Controller Access Control System (TACACS)
✓ Remote Authentication Dial-In User Service (RADIUS)
✓ Secure Sockets Layer (SSL)
✓ Internet Protocol Security (IPSec)
✓ Secure Shell (SSH)
✓ Open Systems Interconnection (OSI) model
✓ Pretty Good Privacy (PGP)
✓ Secure Multipurpose Internet Mail Extension (S/MIME)
✓ Hypertext Transport Protocol over Secure Sockets (HTTPS)
✓ Transport Layer Security (TLS)

Techniques you'll need to master:

✓ Understanding the use of encapsulating protocols in the creation of a Virtual Private Network over a public network
✓ Recognizing the use of IPSec to create a secured encapsulation of client and server data
✓ Being able to identify the use of HTTP and HTTPS protocol connections over ports 80 and 443

The hallmark of modern computer use involves network connectivity over many local area network (LAN) and wide area network (WAN) protocols. A wide variety of solutions for connectivity are available, although the most universally available addressing scheme involves the TCP/IP-based global network commonly referred to as the *Internet*.

This connectivity creates the need for many security considerations, including encapsulation and authentication mechanisms, internetworking communications (such as email and Web-based connectivity), and issues surrounding the transfer of data across distributed public networks. In this chapter, we discuss the security-related issues surrounding communications through modern network technologies.

 If you are following along with CompTIA's objective list for this exam, note that several topics listed in the objectives under Communication Security are covered in Chapter 5, "Online Vulnerabilities." The domain 2.0 sections "1.3.4. Vulnerabilities," "1.4. Directory—Recognition not administration," "1.5. File transfer," and "1.6. Wireless" have been moved to Chapter 5 for organizational purposes.

Remote Access

The first area of focus within the communications security realm involves providing remote or mobile clients the ability to connect to necessary resources. Remote access might include a wireless fidelity (Wi-Fi) link supporting a small office or home office network using modern 802.11-compliant wireless networking equipment, or perhaps allowing employees in a mobile sales force to be authenticated as they dial in to a central office using telephony carriers.

We focus on several specific areas of concern regarding remote access, including the following:

➤ 802.11*x* wireless networking

➤ Virtual Private Network (VPN) connections using Layer 2 Tunneling Protocol (L2TP) or Point-to-Point Tunneling Protocol (PPTP) connections

➤ Dial-up authentication using the Remote Authentication Dial-In User Service (RADIUS) or the Terminal Access Controller Access Control System (TACACS and TACACS+)

➤ Secure terminal connections using the Secure Sockets Layer (SSL) interface

➤ Packet-level authentication of VPN connections using the Internet Protocol Security (IPSec) standard

The exam contains many acronyms specifying security terminology. Make sure you are comfortable with the common acronyms, and pay particular attention to similar acronyms, such as PPP (Point-to-Point Protocol), which is used by L2TP, and PPTP (Point-to-Point Tunneling Protocol), which is an alternative to L2TP connectivity.

802.11x Wireless Networking

The 802.11x specification establishes standards for wireless network connectivity. When an 802.11x-compliant connection is attempted, a wireless client tries to contact a wireless access point (WAP), which then authenticates the client through a basic challenge/response method and opens ports allowed for a wireless connection to the network. This one-way authentication process, broadcast using radio waves, is susceptible to several security concerns:

➤ *Radio traffic detection*—802.11x transmissions generate detectable radio-frequency traffic in all directions. Although intervening material and walls may affect the functional distance, these radio-frequencies may be used for normal network connectivity. Someone can "sniff" the data transmitted over the network using many solutions to increase the distance over which detection is possible, including the use of reflective tube waveguides (such as the popular Pringles can) flying overhead to increase detection range without interference from building structures.

➤ *Clear data*—Without the use of some type of encryption standard, data transacted over an 802.11x wireless link is passed in clear-text form. Additional forms of encryption are being integrated, such as the Wired Equivalent Privacy (WEP) and Advanced Encryption Standard (AES), but current implementations suffer from the fact that a determined listener can easily obtain enough traffic data to calculate the encoding key in use. New standards that involve time-changing encryption keys may help with this, such as the Temporal Key Integrity Protocol (TKIP) standard.

➤ *Session hijacking*—Because the authentication mechanism is one-way, it is easy for a hijacker to wait until the authentication cycle is completed and then generate a signal to the client that causes the client to think it has been disconnected from the access point, while at the same time beginning to transact data traffic, pretending to be the original client.

➤ *Man-in-the-middle attacks*—Because the request for connection by the client is an omnidirectional open broadcast, it is possible for a hijacker to act as an access point to the client, and as a client to the true network access point, thus allowing the hijacker to follow all data transactions and modify, insert, or delete packets at will.

➤ *War-driving and war-chalking*—Coordinated efforts are underway aimed at the identification of existing wireless networks, the SSIDs used to identify these wireless networks, and any known WEP keys. A popular pastime known as *war-driving* involves driving around with a laptop system configured to listen for open 802.11x access points. Several Web sites provide central repositories for identified networks to be collected, graphed, and even generated against city maps for the convenience of others looking for open access links to the Internet. A modification of early "hobo signs" is also being used to mark buildings, curbs, and other landmarks indicating the presence of available access points and their connection details. This so-called *war-chalking* utilizes a set of symbols and shorthand details to provide the specifics needed to connect using these access points.

Virtual Private Network (VPN) Connections

When data must pass across a public or unsecured network, one popular method of securing the data involves the use of a Virtual Private Network (VPN) connection. VPN connections provide a mechanism for the creation of a secured tunnel through a public network such as the Internet, which then encapsulates data packets to prevent sniffing over the public network.

This technology allows for a secure, authenticated connection between a remote user and the internal private network of an organization. Additional security may be gained through the use of encryption protocols and authentication methods, such as using the IPSec protocol over the VPN connection. VPN connections may be used to create secured connections between remote offices to allow replication traffic and other forms of intersite communication to occur, without incurring the cost of expensive, dedicated leased circuits or modem bank solutions. Two of the more common protocols used in VPN solutions are PPTP and L2TP. You will learn more about these protocols next.

 VPN connections are also used to connect Remote Access Service (RAS) servers located within an organization's demilitarized zone (DMZ) through a secure conduit to a Remote Authentication Dial-In User Service (RADIUS) server. The RADIUS server is located within an organization's private network and provides a secured channel for the authentication of dial-in users connecting to RAS servers located within the semi-private DMZ.

Point-to-Point Tunneling Protocol (PPTP) Connections

One common Virtual Private Network encapsulation protocol, proposed initially by a group of companies including Microsoft, is the Point-to-Point

Tunneling Protocol (PPTP). Connections between remote users and sites may be made using this encapsulation protocol, which creates a secured "tunnel" through which other data can be transferred.

Layer 2 Tunneling Protocol (L2TP) Connections

The Layer 2 Tunneling Protocol (L2TP) is an extension of the earlier PPTP and Layer 2 Forwarding (L2F) standards. Proposed by the Cisco Corporation and its partners, this protocol is rapidly replacing PPTP as the standard encapsulation protocol used for VPN connections. L2TP connections are created by first allowing a client to connect to an L2TP access concentrator, which then tunnels individual Point-to-Point Protocol (PPP) frames through a public network to the network access server (NAS), where the frames may then be processed as if generated locally.

 Remember that the L2TP protocol is gaining widespread acknowledgement as the successor to the more obsolete PPTP-based VPN connection.

Dial-Up User Access

Although broadband solutions such as cable modems and Digital Subscriber Line (DSL) connections are becoming increasingly available, the use of an acoustic modem (short for modulator/demodulator) over normal telephone lines remains a common means of remote connectivity. Client systems equipped with a modem can connect using normal dial-up acoustic connections to a properly equipped RAS server, which then functions as a gateway through which the remote user may access local resources or gain connectivity to the Internet.

Most Internet Service Providers (ISPs) still offer dial-up network connectivity for their users, although many organizations still maintain the use of RAS servers to provide direct connectivity for remote users or administrators and to provide failover fault-tolerant communications in the event of WAN connectivity loss. Demand-dial solutions involving the use of modem technology may even provide on-demand intersite connectivity for replication or communications, without requiring a continuous form of connection between the remote sites.

The authentication protocols often found in dial-up infrastructures are TACACS, RADIUS, and TACACS+. The authentication and/or transport services that these protocols offer are discussed in more depth next.

Terminal Access Controller Access Control System (TACACS)

The Terminal Access Controller Access Control System (TACACS) protocol is an early authentication mechanism used by Unix-based RAS servers to forward dial-up user logon and password values to an authentication server. TACACS does not provide authentication itself but rather is an encryption protocol used to send the logon information to a separate authentication service.

Remote Authentication Dial-In User Service (RADIUS) and TACACS+

Modern solutions, including the Remote Authentication Dial-In User Service (RADIUS) and TACACS+ protocols, provide for both user authentication and authorization. A RADIUS server functions to authenticate dial-in users using a symmetric key (private key) method and provides authorization settings through a stored user profile.

Authentication is managed through a client/server configuration in which the RAS server functions as a client of the RADIUS server, passing dial-in user access information to the RADIUS server, often through a VPN connection between the two systems.

 Remember that in RADIUS-based authentication, the RAS server is the RADIUS client, not the system initiating the dial-up connection to the RAS server.

The TACACS+ protocol is an extension of the earlier TACACS form, adding authentication and authorization capabilities similar to the RADIUS authentication method. One important difference between these two is that the TACACS+ protocol relies on Transmission Control Protocol (TCP) connectivity, whereas RADIUS uses the User Datagram Protocol (UDP).

Secure Shell (SSH) Connections

As a more secure replacement for the common command-line terminal utility `telnet`, the Secure Shell (SSH) utility establishes a session between the client and host computers using an authenticated and encrypted connection. SSH utilizes the asymmetric (public key) Rivest-Shamir-Adleman (RSA) cryptography method to provide both connection and authentication.

Data encryption is accomplished using one of the following algorithms:

➤ *International Data Encryption Algorithm (IDEA)*—The default encryption algorithm used by SSH, which uses a 128-bit symmetric key block cipher.

➤ *Blowfish*—A symmetric (private key) encryption algorithm that uses a variable 32- to 448-bit secret key.

➤ *Data Encryption Standard (DES)*—A symmetric key encryption algorithm that uses a random key selected from a large number of shared keys. Most forms of this algorithm cannot be used in products meant for export.

The Secure Shell suite encapsulates three secure utilities: slogin, ssh, and scp, derived from the earlier nonsecure Unix utilities rlogin, rsh, and rcp. SSH provides a large number of available options that you may be at least somewhat familiar with (see Figure 4.1).

Figure 4.1   A Linux version of the **ssh** utility showing available options.

Like telnet, SSH provides a command-line connection through which an administrator may input commands on a remote server. SSH provides an authenticated and encrypted data stream, as opposed to the cleartext communications of a telnet session. The three utilities within the Secure Shell suite provide the following functionalities:

➤ *Secure Login (slogin)*—A secure version of the Unix Remote Login (rlogin) service, which allows a user to connect to a remote server and interact with the system as if directly connected

> *Secure Shell* (ssh)—A secure version of the Unix Remote Shell (rsh) environment interface protocol

> *Secure Copy* (scp)—A secure version of the Unix Remote Copy (rcp) utility, which allows for the transfer of files in a manner similar to the File Transfer Protocol (FTP)

Some versions of SSH, including the Secure Shell for Windows Server, include a secure version of the File Transfer Protocol (SFTP) along with the other common SSH utilities.

Internet Protocol Security (IPSec)

The Internet Protocol Security (IPSec) authentication and encapsulation standard is widely used to establish secure Virtual Private Network communications. Unlike most security systems that function within the Application layer of the Open Systems Interconnection (OSI) model, the IPSec protocol functions within the Network layer.

The OSI model is a logically structured model that encompasses the translation of data entered at the Application layer through increasingly more abstracted layers of data, resulting in the actual binary bits passed at the Physical layer. This process of adding data at different layers is referred to as *encapsulation*. At the other end of a data transfer, the individual packets of data are ordered and reassembled by passing back through the layers of operation of the OSI model until the original data is reproduced at the Application layer on the receiving system.

Here are the layers of the OSI model:

7. Application layer

6. Presentation layer

5. Session layer

4. Transport layer

3. Network layer

2. Data Link layer

1. Physical layer

You should be thoroughly familiar with the OSI model as well as the common protocols and network hardware that function within each level.

IPSec provides authentication services as well as encapsulation of data through support of the Internet Key Exchange (IKE) protocol.

IPSec Services

The asymmetric key standard defining IPSec provides two primary security services:

> ➤ *Authentication Header (AH)*—Provides authentication of the data's sender

> ➤ *Encapsulating Security Payload (ESP)*—Supports authentication of the data's sender as well as encryption of the data being transferred

Internet Key Exchange (IKE) Protocol

IPSec supports the Internet Key Exchange (IKE) protocol, which is a key-management standard used to specify separate key protocols to be used during data encryption. IKE functions within the Internet Security Association and Key Management Protocol (ISAKMP), which defines the payloads used to exchange key and authentication data appended to each packet.

 Be sure you are familiar with common key-exchange protocols such as Oakley and SKEME; standard encryption algorithms, including asymmetric key solutions such as the Diffie-Hellman Key Agreement and the Rivest-Shamir-Adleman (RSA) standards; symmetric key solutions such as the International Data Encryption Algorithm (IDEA) and the Digital Encryption Standard (DES); and hashing algorithms such as Message Digest 5 (MD5) and Secure Hash Algorithm (SHA).

Securing Email

One of the most fundamental changes wrought by the global interconnectivity of networked computers has been the rise of what has come to be known as *electronic mail (email)*. Originally used to send messages between systems operators on the early Bitnet and other pre-Internet networks, email is a widespread method of communication between individuals and business partners. It is also used to facilitate financial transactions and electronic commerce. Email has been used successfully as evidence in several court trials, and it now forms the fundamental method of communication within many organizations.

The global nature of email distribution and the speed of delivery (often only seconds separate transmission and receipt, even between users on separate continents) make email a valuable tool. However, the speed and accessibility of this technology also carry several security considerations. Public transfer of sensitive information could potentially expose this information to undesired recipients. In addition, undesired and often unsolicited email can require a significant amount of time to review and discard. Email messages may also contain any number of hazardous programmatic file attachments directed at unsuspecting users. In the following sections, we cover S/MIME, PGP, and other email vulnerabilities such as Spam and email hoaxes.

 We do not focus on potentially hazardous payloads here, beyond mentioning that many viruses, Trojan horses, worms, and other forms of viral programming agents transmit themselves using electronic mail as their carrier. A detailed discussion of viral programming agents is provided in Chapter 3, "Nonessential Services and Attacks."

Secure Multipurpose Internet Mail Extension (S/MIME)

The Multipurpose Internet Mail Extension (MIME) protocol extends the original Simple Mail Transfer Protocol (SMTP) to allow the inclusion of nontextual data within an email message. Embedding data within an email message allows for a simple method of transferring and receiving images, audio and video files, application programs, and many other types of non-ASCII text.

To provide a secure method of transmission, the Secure Multipurpose Internet Mail Extension (S/MIME) standard was developed. S/MIME uses the RSA asymmetric encryption scheme to encrypt email transmissions over public networks. Modern versions of Netscape and Internet Explorer include S/MIME support in their role as email clients.

Pretty Good Privacy (PGP)

An alternative to the use of S/MIME is the proposed PGP/MIME standard, derived from the Pretty Good Privacy application program developed by Phillip R. Zimmerman in 1991. This program encrypts and decrypts email messages using either the RSA or the Diffie-Hellman asymmetric encryption schemes. The PGP application must be purchased and is available for individual and corporate use.

One useful feature of the PGP program is that it can include a digital signature, which validates an email to its recipient. This calculated hash value can be used by the recipient to verify that the received email has not been tampered with.

Undesirable Email

One of the strengths of email is its capability to be rapidly transmitted to one or many recipients, who rapidly receive the directed message, generally without per-item charges (in contrast to surface mail, which requires a stamp for each item). This allows small organizations to rapidly reach a tremendously large potential base of consumers—whether with a possible item for sale, a request for donation, a notice of service, or any other manner of information. Unfortunately, this very strength of email can result in undesirable email such as spam and hoax messages, as described in the following sections.

Spam

Obviously, with the entire world only a single click of the Send button away, the volume of messages a user may receive can become too great to manage quickly and easily. Undesired or unsolicited email has gained the nickname *spam* (derived from an amalgamated meat product of the same name). These electronic "junk mail" messages can rapidly overtax the capacity of email servers and consume a large amount of user time in order for the user to review, respond to, or discard each item.

Many solutions are available to attempt to halt the rising tide of spam messages flowing into users' inboxes, such as subscriptions to email blacklists, which register known spam senders so that email matching a sender's address can be discarded before any messages are received by an organization's clients. Most email clients allow you to configure automatic rules that can handle many types of spam, discarding items from particular senders or items that contain a particular set of words or phrases.

Obviously, the subjective nature of any type of email filtering can be problematic to implement, especially when it is critical that messages are received from clients or vendors who might inadvertently put the wrong words or phrases within the body of an important message.

Hoaxes

Another form of problematic email includes messages that contain incorrect or misleading information. These hoax messages may warn of pending legislation that does not exist or instruct users to delete certain files to ensure their security against a new virus while actually only rendering the system more susceptible to later viral agents.

Hoaxes might offer users great sums of money if they will simply provide all their personal and financial information to the source, or they might even tell of an expensive cookie recipe that the sender will be glad to make available for only a fraction of the price. These and many more hoax items circulate in a growing thread of tales and ideas that encapsulates everything from urban myths to detailed instructions that can result in a loss of functionality, damage to the user's computer, or some other later security vulnerability.

Instant Messaging

One alternative to the asynchronous form of communication of email is the growing use of instant messaging (IM) software solutions, such as the MSN Messenger, ICQ, and AOL Instant Messenger products that link to a central server when the software is opened and provide a continuously available means of communications with other users of the same system. Also, file-sharing solutions that use both client/server and peer-to-peer network connectivity (such as the Napster and Gnutella products that have been the subject of many items of legislation recently) are included in this category.

Instant messaging solutions pose many of the same vulnerabilities as email, in that they are readily accessible to a broad audience and may receive a high volume of spam, hoaxes, and unwanted viral programs. In addition, IM communications are sent in cleartext by default. This leaves the communications vulnerable to packet sniffing. Another potential hazard of IM is the fact that many IM clients now include file-transfer capabilities. Because the IM client application might not integrate strongly with the operating system, file-transfer capabilities could be used to transmit viral agents that bypass some forms of antivirus protection.

Because some file-sharing systems only advertise the platform-independent short name form of a file's name, which specifies only an eight-character filename and a three-character file extension (often written as *8.3 naming*), it is possible to receive and automatically process improperly named executable files that perform unexpected and often undesirable actions.

Open file shares inadvertently advertised by file-sharing systems can generate a tremendous load on the network bandwidth used by others connecting to the shared system, potentially exposing many forms of sensitive information. Additionally, because many IM clients transmit data in plaintext, user conversations along with any sensitive information transferred can be sniffed and later used for nefarious purposes.

Web Connectivity

The Internet allows users to connect to millions of sources of information, services, products, and other functionality through what has come to be known as the *World Wide Web* (or simply, the *Web*). Business transactions, membership information, vendor/client communications, and even distributed business logic transactions can all occur using the basic connectivity of the Web, which uses the Hypertext Transport Protocol (HTTP) on TCP port 80.

Chapter 5 deals with the vulnerabilities of many Web-based technologies. In this chapter, we focus only on the protocols SSL, TLS, and HTTPS, which are used to secure basic communications with a Web server.

Secure Sockets Layer (SSL)

Secure Sockets Layer (SSL) protocol communications occur between the HTTP (Application) and TCP (Transport) layers of Internet communications. SSL establishes a stateful connection negotiated by a handshaking procedure between client and server. During this handshake, the client and server exchange the specifications for the cipher that will be used for that session. SSL communicates using an asymmetric key with a cipher strength of 40 or 128 bits.

Transport Layer Security (TLS)

Another asymmetric key encapsulation, currently considered the successor to SSL transport, is the Transport Layer Security (TLS) protocol, which is based on Netscape's Secure Sockets Layer 3.0 (SSL3) transport protocol. TLS provides encryption using stronger methods, such as the Data Encryption Standard (DES), or it may be used without encryption altogether, if desired, for authentication only.

TLS has two layers of operation:

➤ *TLS Record Protocol*—This protocol allows the client and server to communicate using some form of encryption algorithm or without encryption if desired.

➤ *TLS Handshake Protocol*—This protocol allows the client and server to authenticate one another and exchange encryption keys to be used during the session.

SSL transport and TLS transport are similar but not entirely interoperable.

Hypertext Transport Protocol over Secure Sockets Layer (HTTPS)

Basic Web connectivity using HTTP occurs over TCP port 80. An alternative to this involves the use of SSL transport protocols operating on port 443. To differentiate a call to port 80 (http://servername/, where servername is the name of your server), HTTP over SSL makes calls on port 443 to utilize HTTPS as the URL port designator (https://servername/).

HTTPS was created by the Netscape Corporation and originally used a 40-bit RC4 stream encryption algorithm to establish a secured connection encapsulating data transferred between the client and Web server, although it can also support the use of X.509 digital certificates to allow the user to authenticate the sender. Now, 128-bit encryption keys are available, which have become the accepted level of secure connectivity for online banking and electronic commerce transactions.

Practice Questions

Question 1

> Between which layers of the OSI model does the SSL protocol function?
> [Choose the two best answers.]
>
> ❏ A. Application layer
>
> ❏ B. Presentation layer
>
> ❏ C. Session layer
>
> ❏ D. Transport layer
>
> ❏ E. Network layer
>
> ❏ F. Data Link layer
>
> ❏ G. Physical layer

Answers A and D are correct. SSL connections occur between the Application and Transport layers. Answers B and C are incorrect because the SSL transport effectively fills the same role as these OSI model layers. Answers E, F, and G are incorrect because the data has been abstracted (encapsulated) beyond the level at which SSL operates.

Question 2

> Which of the following encryption protocols are used in Secure Shell connections? [Choose the three best answers.]
>
> ❏ A. International Data Encryption Algorithm (IDEA)
>
> ❏ B. Blowfish
>
> ❏ C. Rivest Cipher 4 (RC4)
>
> ❏ D. Digital Encryption Standard (DES)
>
> ❏ E. Message Digest 5 (MD5)

Answers A, B, and D are correct. SSH connections can use the IDEA, Blowfish, and DES encryption methods. Answer C is incorrect because the RC4 protocol is used by the SSL protocol. Answer E is incorrect because the MD5 hashing algorithm is not used by SSH connectivity.

Question 3

> Which term best describes email that is received without the desire or request of the recipient?
>
> O A. Hoax
>
> O B. Virus
>
> O C. Trojan horse
>
> O D. Spam

Answer D is correct. Spam is the name given to electronic junk mail and includes any items not requested or desired by the receiver. A hoax is email that includes messages that contain incorrect or misleading information; therefore, answer A is incorrect. A virus is a small chunk of code designed to attach to other code; therefore, answer B is incorrect. A Trojan horse appears to be useful software but has code hidden inside it that will attack your system directly or allow the system to be infiltrated by the originator of the code once it is executed; therefore, answer C is incorrect.

Question 4

> Which of the following encryption methods are available when using Pretty Good Privacy? [Choose the two best answers.]
>
> ❏ A. International Data Encryption Algorithm (IDEA)
>
> ❏ B. Blowfish
>
> ❏ C. Diffie-Hellman
>
> ❏ D. Digital Encryption Standard (DES)
>
> ❏ E. Rivest-Shamir-Adleman (RSA)

Answers C and E are correct. PGP can use either the Diffie-Hellman or the RSA public key encryption method. Answers A, B, and D are incorrect because these protocols are not available within PGP.

Question 5

Which standard port is used to establish a Web connection using the 40-bit RC4 encryption protocol?

○ A. 21

○ B. 80

○ C. 443

○ D. 8250

Answer C is correct. A connection using the HTTP protocol over SSL (HTTPS) is made using the RC4 cipher and port 443. Answer A is incorrect because port 21 is used for FTP connections. Answer B is incorrect because port 80 is used for unsecure plaintext HTTP communications. Answer D is incorrect because port 8250 is not designated to a particular TCP/IP protocol.

Question 6

Which of the Secure Shell utilities is used to establish a secure command-line connection to a remote server?

○ A. **rlogin**

○ B. **slogin**

○ C. **rsh**

○ D. **ssh**

○ E. **rcp**

○ F. **scp**

Answer B is correct. The slogin SSH utility provides secured command-line connections to a remote server. Answers A, C, and E are incorrect because rlogin, rsh, and rcp do not use secured connections. Answer D is incorrect because the ssh utility is used to establish a secured environment link to a remote server, whereas answer F is incorrect because the scp utility is used for secure file copying.

Question 7

When RADIUS is used to authenticate a dial-in user, which of the following is the RADIUS client?

- ○ A. Dial-in user's computer
- ○ B. RAS server
- ○ C. RADIUS server
- ○ D. Client's ISP
- ○ E. VPN

Answer B is correct. The RAS server functions as the RADIUS client, authenticating dial-in user attempts against the RADIUS server. Answer A is incorrect because the dial-in user does not directly contact the RADIUS server. Answer C is incorrect because the RADIUS server would not be its own client. Answer D is incorrect because a client dialing in to an RAS server would not connect through a separate ISP. Answer E is incorrect because a VPN connection establishes a secured tunnel between two systems and is not involved in RADIUS authentication.

Question 8

Which of the following is true of TACACS?

- ○ A. It is an advanced protocol that allows for both authentication and authorization.
- ○ B. It is an advanced protocol used to encrypt data sent by VPN clients.
- ○ C. It is an older protocol used to pass authentication requests sent by dial-up clients.
- ○ D. It is a protocol used for authorizing dial-in clients and setting access control.

Answer C is correct. TACACS is an older protocol that forwards logon information to an authentication server but cannot provide authentication by itself. Answers A and D are incorrect because they describe RADIUS. Answer B is a made up statement; therefore, it is incorrect.

Question 9

> At which layer of the OSI model does the IPSec protocol function?
>
> ○ A. Application layer
> ○ B. Presentation layer
> ○ C. Session layer
> ○ D. Transport layer
> ○ E. Network layer
> ○ F. Data Link layer
> ○ G. Physical layer

Answer E is correct. IPSec validation and encryption function at the Network layer of the OSI model. Answers A, B, C, and D are incorrect because IPSec functions at a lower level of the OSI model. Answers F and G are incorrect because they define a more abstracted level of data manipulation than is managed by the IPSec standard.

Question 10

> Which of the following are possible dangers of using instant messaging clients? [Choose the best answers.]
>
> ❑ A. Spam
> ❑ B. Hoaxes
> ❑ C. Viruses
> ❑ D. File-sharing
> ❑ E. File execution

Answers A, B, C, D, and E are all correct. IM solutions have many potential security problems, including the receipt of spam and hoax messages, the possible execution of files and viruses bypassing operating system protections, and the possible exposure of file shares to public access.

Question 11

> Which of the following are asymmetric encryption standards? [Choose the two
> best answers.]
>
> ❏ A. IDEA
>
> ❏ B. MD5
>
> ❏ C. RSA
>
> ❏ D. SHA
>
> ❏ E. Diffie-Hellman
>
> ❏ F. DES

Answers C and E are correct. The Rivest-Shamir-Adleman and Diffie-Hellman encryption standards specify public key (asymmetric) encryption methods. Answers A and F are incorrect because the Digital Encryption Standard and International Data Encryption Algorithm standards specify private key (symmetric) encryption methods. Answers B and D are incorrect because the Message Digest 5 and Secure Hash Algorithm standards specify hashing algorithms.

Need to Know More?

 Allen, Julia H. *The CERT Guide to System and Network Security Practices*. Addison-Wesley. Upper Saddle River, NJ, 2001. ISBN 020173723X.

 SANS Information Security Reading Room: `rr.sans.org/ index.php`

Online Vulnerabilities

Terms you'll need to understand:

✓ Java
✓ JavaScript
✓ ActiveX
✓ Cookies
✓ CGI scripts
✓ SMTP Relay
✓ Lightweight Directory Access Protocol (LDAP)
✓ S/FTP
✓ Anonymous
✓ WTLS
✓ WLAN
✓ 802.11
✓ WEP/WAP
✓ Site survey

Techniques you'll need to master:

✓ Understanding the common vulnerabilities present in browser-based technologies
✓ Understanding the common vulnerabilities in LDAP services
✓ Understanding the common vulnerabilities in FTP services
✓ Knowing the common vulnerabilities in present wireless technologies
✓ Recognizing the more common considerations in performing a site survey

A common saying about the only truly secure computer is that it is one left in its box and connected to nothing. Although this may be an oversimplification, it is true that the moment a computer is connected to a network, the requirements for securing against unwanted intrusion multiply. In this chapter, we will examine vulnerabilities common to many standard technologies that may be exposed by connecting to a networked system.

Web Vulnerabilities

One primary area of network security involves the use of a public Web server. Web security includes client-side vulnerabilities presented by ActiveX or JavaScript code running within the client's browser, server-side vulnerabilities, such as CGI scripting exploits as well as buffer overflows used to run undesirable code on the server, and other forms of Web-related security vulnerabilities, such as those involving the transfer of cookies or unsigned applets.

NOTE: Although this section focuses on Web-based vulnerabilities, it should be noted that many of these vulnerabilities also affect HTML-enabled clients of other types, including many modern email clients.

Java and JavaScript

Many Web sites utilize a scripting language created originally by the Netscape Corporation known as JavaScript. JavaScript code is transferred to the client's browser, where it is interpreted and used to control and manipulate many browser settings. Java, on the other hand, is a server-side compilation language created by Sun Microsystems. We discuss Java and JavaScript in more detail in the following sections.

Java Vulnerabilities

Because Java is a precompiled language, a Java-based mini-program, called an *applet*, may present many security risks to the client, including those identified in Table 5.1.

Table 5.1 Identified Java Vulnerabilities	
Vulnerability	**Description**
Buffer overflow in the Java Virtual Machine (JVM)	The client-side environment supporting Java applets is referred to as the *JVM*. Improperly created applets can potentially generate a buffer overflow condition, crashing the client system.
Ability to execute instructions	Early versions of the JVM could be used to issue commands to the client system, allowing the manipulation of the file system and data files at will.
Resource monopolization	Improperly designed Java applets can easily consume all available system resources on the client system. It is possible to create applets that continue running within the JVM even after the applet is closed.
Unexpected redirection	Early JVM versions allowed Java applets to redirect the browser and create connections to other hosts without user interaction.

JavaScript Vulnerabilities

Unlike precompiled Java applets, JavaScript is interpreted within the client's browser environment. Because it must be compiled and executed within the client's environment, JavaScript vulnerabilities must be addressed based on the operating system and browser version used on each client. Although new JavaScript vulnerabilities are regularly discovered, many of the more common ones are identified in Table 5.2.

Table 5.2 Identified JavaScript Vulnerabilities	
Vulnerability	**Description**
File access	JavaScript code may be used on unsecured systems to access any file on the client computer that the current user can access. These files may then be sent elsewhere, manipulated, or deleted.
Cache access	Properly designed JavaScript code can be used to read the URLs within a browser's cache, allowing the code to examine the user's browsing habits, preferences, email settings, site cookies, and information entered in Web forms.
File upload	It is possible to create JavaScript code that will cause access of a Web page to upload files from the client's system without the user's knowledge or input. The name of the file must be known for this to occur.
Email exposure	Early browser versions allowed JavaScript to send emails as if sent by the user.

Remember that Java is a compiled language that can lead to the execution of arbitrary commands or direct manipulation of data, whereas JavaScript is a client-side interpreted language that mainly poses privacy-related vulnerability issues.

ActiveX Controls

Microsoft developed a precompiled application technology that can be embedded in a Web page in the same way as Java applets. This technology is called ActiveX, and its controls share many of the same vulnerabilities present in embedded Java applets.

ActiveX controls may be digitally signed using an Authenticode signature, which is verified by its issuing Certificate Authority (CA). Unlike Java applets, where browser configuration settings control the possible behavior of the applet, ActiveX controls are restricted based on whether they are signed. ActiveX controls do not have restrictions on what forms of action they may enact.

If a user configures her browser to allow the execution of unsigned ActiveX controls, controls from any source performing any action may be enacted by visiting a Web site hosting such a control embedded within an HTML page.

Buffer Overflows

A *buffer overflow* condition occurs when the data presented to an application or service exceeds the storage space allocation that has been reserved in memory for that application or service. Poor application design might allow the input of 100 characters into a field linked to a variable only capable of holding 50 characters. Basically what happens is that the application doesn't know how to handle the extra data and becomes unstable. Because the overflow portion of the input data must be discarded or otherwise handled by the application, it could create undesirable results. This can be likened to cramming for an exam: If you give your brain more information than it can process, it will shut down! Buffer overflow attacks are often waged against applications such as Microsoft Outlook and against Internet-accessible services such as ToolTalk, Linuxconf, and many types of Web servers.

A buffer overflow could result in the following:

➤ An overwrite of data or memory storage

➤ A denial of service due to overloading the input buffer's ability to cope with the additional data

➤ The originator being allowed to execute arbitrary code, often at a privileged level

The reason buffer overflows are so prevalent throughout so many types of programming is that programmers often assume that presented data will conform to expectations. It is important for developers to plan for attempted or accidental overflows and set up preprocessing restrictions on data input to block this form of attack.

Cookies

To overcome the limitations of a stateful connection when scaled to global Web site deployments, the Netscape Corporation created a technology that uses temporary files stored in the client's browser cache to maintain settings across multiple pages, servers, or sites. These small files are known as *cookies*, and they may be used to maintain data (such as user settings between visits to the same site on multiple days) or to track user browsing habits (such as those used by sites hosting DoubleClick banner advertisements).

Privacy Issues

Many sites require that browsing clients be configured to accept cookies to store information such as configuration settings or shopping cart data for electronic commerce (e-commerce) sites. Cookies can be used to track information such as the name and IP address of the client system as well as the operating system and browser client being used. Additional information includes the name of the target and previous URLs, along with any specific settings specified within the cookie by the host Web site.

If cookies are accessed across many sites, they may be used to track the user's browsing habits and present the user with targeted advertising or content. Many users feel this is a violation of their privacy.

Session Values

Cookies may also be used to store session settings across multiple, actual connections to a Web server. This is very helpful when connecting to a distributed server farm, where each page access might be handled by a separate physical server, preventing the use of session variables to maintain details from one page to another.

This is very useful in e-commerce sites where a shopping cart application might add items from multiple pages to a growing total invoice before transferring it to a billing application. These cookies are also useful to provide custom user configuration settings on subsequent entries to Web portals whose content is presented in a dynamic manner.

The danger in maintaining session information is that sites may access cookies stored in the browser's cache that may contain details on the user's e-commerce shopping habits. In addition, these cookies may include many user details that could possibly contain sensitive information identifying the user or allowing access to secured sites.

Signed Applets

Java applets are popular for presenting textual, formatting, and graphical elements within Web pages. These small programs operate within the Java Virtual Machine (JVM), encapsulating their operation and limiting access to system resources. Applets may be digitally signed so that the client system can verify their origin and ensure that the applets have not been modified since being signed. If the local security policy allows it, a signed applet may then access resources such as the local file system and system variables.

To digitally sign an applet, a public/private key pair is obtained from a Certificate Authority (CA) such as VeriSign or Thawte. The private key is used to encrypt the hashed value of the applet's code, and the resulting digital signature is included with the applet along with the public key. When a client attempts to execute the signed applet, it uses the public key to decrypt the hashed value and compare this to a calculated hash of the applet to ensure that the code has not been modified. The client can also contact the CA to verify that the key and signature come from the proper origin and remain unchanged. If the signature is validated and the local security policy allows it, the applet can then access additional resources.

It is also possible for a user to configure his browser client to allow the execution of unsigned applets, which can result in the execution of many types of undesired code capable of accessing system resources. System administrators should prevent users from allowing the execution of unsigned applets by default.

Common Gateway Interface (CGI) Vulnerabilities

A server-side interpretation option includes the use of Common Gateway Interface (CGI) script, often written in the Perl language. Because these scripts are interpreted on the server system, generally utilizing user input values, they are highly subject to exploitation in many ways. Most exploits can be grouped into two general categories:

➤ CGI scripts may leak information about the server.

➤ CGI scripts used to process user input data may be exploited to execute unwanted commands on the server.

Because CGI scripts are executed on the server, they are particularly susceptible to exploit through user input. These exploits may allow the identification of server-configuration details that might be helpful to later unauthorized access attempts—a process often referred to as *profiling*.

Because any process that can execute functionality on the server has inherent access rights, improperly formed CGI scripts could be used to execute arbitrary commands on the server, change server-configuration settings, and even create unauthorized user accounts on the server that could later be used to gain greater control over the server. It is vital that an exposed service such as a Web server not run under a privileged account.

Buffer overflow and script abuse will execute in the same context as the Web server. CGI scripts used to present such items as Web site guest books or display counters can use an account that has very little privileges; therefore, it is possible to cause a buffer overflow or to run a script using an account that has very few privileges. To protect the server, you may want to disable scripting of objects marked as safe. Another option is to implement a proxy server along with a content-filtering solution to rid the network of unsafe coding embedded in Web pages.

Some processes constantly run on a system to provide access or monitoring of many types. These processes are called *services* in the Windows environment and *daemons* in the Unix environment.

CGI script creation requires many considerations for security, including the following:

➤ Poorly written CGI scripts may leak information about the server, such as the directory structure and any running applications and daemons.

➤ Data input should always include a default value and character limitations to avoid buffer overflow exploitation.

➤ Many standard scripts are installed in default Web server installations. These are in known folder locations and often contain sample code that is not designed for security and may include well-known exploits.

➤ It is possible for poorly written CGI scripts to pass user input data directly to the shell environment, which could allow a properly formatted input value to execute arbitrary commands on the Web server.

Simple Mail Transport Protocol (SMTP) Relay

Although not specifically a Web-related problem, the possible exploitation of Simple Mail Transport Protocol (SMTP) Relay agents to send large numbers of spam email messages is included in our list of vulnerabilities. This is because many Web servers include a local SMTP service utilized by server-side processes to perform mailto functions needed in the Web site.

The purpose of SMTP Relay is for a SMTP server to accept user connections to deliver email. The email, once received, is then sent or relayed until it reaches the intended recipient. The issue with this is that user connections are not authenticated with the SMTP server. This allows spammers to connect and send thousands of emails using someone else's server, thereby concealing their identity.

Most servers can block connections that are not warranted. SMTP servers that are not configured to check addresses within their domain are called *open relays*. Having an open-relay SMTP server can present huge consequences. Besides the fact that spammers can send thousands of unsolicited emails through your server, many companies maintain a list of servers from which spam originates. Those companies then refuse to accept mail from these servers. When this occurs, your capability to send mail becomes severely affected. As if this isn't bad enough, you also end up on a spammers' list. To be removed from the list, you have to prove that the open relay has been remedied. After this is done, the repair is tested. If it's satisfactory, you are removed from the list, and only then will your email be able to be sent to its final destination. Sometimes, by the time this occurs, the damage done to the company has become extremely costly. Many companies post addresses on their spammers' lists. The following links are worth looking at to get an idea of the scope of spam-related sites:

➤ mail-abuse.org

➤ www.spamprimer.com

➤ abl.v6net.org

➤ www.dgraph.com/spammers.html

Because spammers search for unprotected SMTP Relay services running on public servers—these services can be used to resend SMTP messages to obscure their true source—it is extremely important that the SMTP server is properly secured.

Protocol Vulnerabilities

Many protocols contain common vulnerabilities that may be exploited, including Secure Sockets Layer (SSL) connections and Lightweight Directory Access Protocol (LDAP).

SSL/TLS

Transport Layer Security (TLS) including SSL-encapsulated data transfer may be exploited in many ways. The encapsulated data stream could potentially be compromised through cryptographic identification of the key, although modern 128-bit keys are considered to be beyond a reasonable level of encryption.

SSL connections are also particularly vulnerable during the handshake process, where the client and server exchange details of the shared encryption keys to be used. Malformed certificates may be used to exploit the parsing libraries used by SSL agents to compromise security details and possibly execute code on the compromised system. In addition, many forms of buffer overrun may also be used during the SSL handshake process to compromise the secured connection.

In the fall of 2002, the Linux Slapper worm infected about 7,000 servers. The worm exploited a flaw in SSL on Linux-based Web servers. To read more on this, go to `www.cert.org/advisories/CA-2002-27.html` or `news.com.com/2100-1001-958758.html`.

The premise behind this vulnerability is that the handshake process during an SSL server connection can cause a buffer overflow by a client using a malformed key.

LDAP

Lightweight Directory Access Protocol (LDAP) provides access to directory services, including the one used by Microsoft's Active Directory. Exploits against variations of this protocol share many common vulnerabilities, including the following:

➤ Buffer overflow vulnerabilities may be used to enact arbitrary commands on the LDAP server. For example, an LDAP advisory was issued in 1999 for an exploit in Microsoft's Directory Services. This was a buffer overflow exploit that occurred during the LDAP binding process. For more information, visit ciac.llnl.gov/ciac/bulletins/j-036.shtml.

➤ Format string vulnerabilities may result in unauthorized access to enact commands on the LDAP server or impair its normal operation.

➤ Improperly formatted requests may be used to create an effective denial of service (DoS) attack against the LDAP server, preventing it from responding to normal requests. For example, Cisco's Call Manager had a security advisory notice posted in early 2002. There was a memory leak associated with systems integrated with customer directories that did not validate passwords. For more information on this, go to www.cisco.com/warp/public/707/callmanager-ctifw-leak-pub.shtml.

> LDAP utilizes an object-oriented access model defined by the Directory Enabled Networking (DEN) standard, which is based on the Common Information Model (CIM) standard.

File Transfer Protocol (FTP) Vulnerabilities

Another common, publicly exposed service involves the File Transfer Protocol (FTP) defined within the TCP/IP suite. FTP allows users to upload or download files between client systems and a networked FTP server. FTP servers include many potential security issues, such as anonymous file access and unencrypted authentication.

As with SMTP and LDAP, FTP servers can incorrectly manage buffers and allow rogue code to be run on them. In early 2001, the CERT coordination center issued an advisory in regard to one of these exploits. Details can be found at www.cert.org/advisories/CA-2001-07.html. The Security Administrator's Integrated Network Tool (SAINT) Web site has a great tutorial on FTP vulnerabilities as well.

Anonymous Access

Many FTP servers include the capability for anonymous access in their default installation configuration. Anonymous access is a popular method to provide general access to publicly available downloads such as a mirror site that contains a new open-access license (OAL) software distribution—perhaps the newest version of Linux. Here, it is unnecessary and even undesirable to require every possible user to first obtain an account and password to access the download area, so an option is provided to allow anonymous access.

The problem with this form of access is that any user may download (and potentially upload) any file desired. This may rapidly result in a server's available file storage and network access bandwidth being consumed for purposes other than those intended by the server's administrator. If unauthorized file upload is allowed along with download, illegal file content could be placed on the server for download without the knowledge of the system's administrator.

Unencrypted Authentication

Even when user authentication is required, protocols such as FTP and Telnet pass the username, password, and even transacted data in an unencrypted form (cleartext), allowing packet sniffing of the network traffic to read these values, which may then be used for unauthorized access to the server. A *packet sniffer* is a software agent capable of monitoring all data traffic through a network interface card (NIC) running in promiscuous mode. Sniffers listen to all traffic on a local subnet and then filter what particular information is requested. Because most sniffers allow the data to be modified and retransmitted, man-in-the-middle and spoofing attacks can occur if network wiring is not properly secured and access to workstations is not restricted. Products such as Snort, Sniffit, and even Microsoft's integrated Network Monitor can provide a detailed analysis of the protocols and data being transmitted.

Besides protecting access to LAN segments, routers should be secured too. A common way to access routers is through the use of Telnet, which passes passwords in cleartext. Cisco has some excellent informative papers on its Web site in regard to router security and how to apply access control lists (ACLs) to a Telnet connection.

A more secure version of FTP (S/FTP) has been developed that includes Secure Sockets Layer (SSL) encapsulation. RFC 2228 defines several security extensions to the FTP specification (RFC 959), including support for security issues such as authentication (AUTH), data channel protection (PROT), integrity protection (MIC), and confidentiality (CONF).

The preferred alternative to the Telnet protocol is the Secure Shell (SSH) protocol, which is intended as a replacement for **telnet**, **rlogin**, **rsh**, and **rcp**. Currently, two forms of the SSH protocol are in use: SSH1 and SSH2. These forms are not directly compatible. For more information on the working group involved with the SSH specifications, visit **www.ssh.com**.

Blind Access

Many public and semiprivate FTP sites may be configured for blind access. A blind FTP server is configured to allow uploads to folders that do not allow FTP users to view their contents, making the actual filenames secret. One potential problem with this setting is that a new file of exactly the same name as another file can potentially overwrite that other file if the operating system does not support file versioning.

Blind FTP sites may also be used for download if an additional layer of security over the file contents in a directory is desired. Users can be given the name of the file to download and are unable to see other files, thus preventing access to those files. If this solution is used, it is important to avoid naming all files using a standard naming scheme that might be guessed by a user seeking unauthorized access to files within the blind FTP site.

File Sharing

Publicly accessible FTP sites are very popular within file-sharing groups, particularly with individuals seeking locations through which they may anonymously share Warez (cracked commercial programs), MPEG Layer-3 (MP3) audio files, and many other types of file content that may be considered undesirable or even illegal. Sites that are not properly protected can be rapidly identified and exploited for this purpose. In fact, many newsgroup lists identify current FTP hosts that can be used for unauthorized file swapping.

The default installation of many FTP servers includes anonymous (public) access and may rely on the configuration of an additional file, such as the ftpusers file, to specify those accounts that do not have access to the FTP site. Coupled with the ability for the FTP service to operate on any port (21 by default), this functionality makes protecting FTP sites and completely securing them against undesirable file sharing very difficult.

Wireless Network Vulnerabilities

Many new technological solutions being embraced by the mobile workforce include the use of mobile data-connected equipment such as cell phones, text pagers, and personal digital assistants (PDAs). Mobile equipment may use many different communications standards, including long-range mobile communications using the Wireless Application Protocol (WAP) or i-Mode standards, as well as wireless local area network (WLAN) communications using the 802.11 wireless fidelity (Wi-Fi) or Bluetooth standards.

Wireless Transport Layer Security (WTLS)

Wireless Transport Layer Security (WTLS) is the security level for the Wireless Application Protocol (WAP). Its objective is to provide reliability and privacy for wireless applications. The basis for WTLS is Transport Layer Security (TLS). WTLS was developed because most wireless devices have limited memory and processing power as well as operate in limited-bandwidth environments.

In a wireless environment, the client communicates directly with a gateway. The gateway translates the request to communicate with a server. WTLS encrypts the communication between the client and the gateway. The gateway then decrypts the message and reencrypts it using SSL.

WTLS presents several security issues. It allows for weak algorithms, and there is a possibility that the gateway could be compromised if it is not properly protected. For more information on security and WTLS, see `www.hut.fi/~jtlaine2/wtls/#chap4.3`.

 WTLS is continually being developed, and future versions may address some of the current vulnerabilities.

Wireless Local Area Networks (WLANs) Using 802.11x or Bluetooth Standards

New technologies using radio frequency transmissions are beginning to replace wired office networks and provide network support for mobile Bluetooth- or 802.11x-enabled devices. Popular coffee house chains, college campuses, apartment complexes, and home users are taking advantage of the rapid proliferation of 802.11b technology using the 2.4GHz unregulated range of frequencies made popular by many vendors producing Wi-Fi network equipment.

The 802.11 specifications extend the Carrier Sense Multiple Access with Collision Avoidance (CSMA/CA) method of connectivity specified within the Ethernet protocol to provide wireless network access.

There are currently four 802.11x specifications:

➤ *802.11*—This specification was released in 1997. It has a data rate of 1 to 2Mbps in the 2.4GHz band.

➤ *802.11a*—This specification is an extension to 802.11. It provides up to 54Mbps in the 5GHz band.

➤ *802.11b*—Adopted in 1999, this specification provides 11Mbps (with fallback to 5.5, 2, and 1) in the 2.4GHz band.

➤ *802.11g*—This specification provides 20+ Mbps in the 2.4GHz band.

The Bluetooth wireless specification operates under the 802.11b specification at 1MHz in the 2.4GHz band. It uses frequency-hopping techniques to keep noise out of communications. Its distance is currently limited to about 10 meters. Each Bluetooth network can support eight devices, and many networks can operate in the same area. Its premise is communications in personal space or *personal area networks (PANs)*.

WAP and i-Mode

Wireless technologies such as mobile data cell phones can present Web content in textual format using either the Compact Wireless Application Protocol (CWAP) over Japan's i-Mode standard or the Wireless Markup Language (WML) supported by the WAP standard. Both standards also provide the capability to access email, instant messaging, newsgroups, and other types of data.

NOTE
The Wireless Application Protocol (WAP) forum is working with many standards organizations, including the Internet Engineering Task Force (IETF) and the World Wide Web Consortium (W3C), to develop the official standard.

The WAP standard includes several other standard specifications:

➤ *Wireless Application Environment (WAE)*—Specifies the framework used to develop applications for mobile devices, including cell phones, data pagers, and PDAs.

➤ *Wireless Session Layer (WSL)*—Equivalent to the Session layer of the Open Systems Interconnection (OSI) model.

➤ *Wireless Transport Layer (WTL)*—Equivalent to the Transport layer of the OSI model.

➤ *Wireless Transport Layer Security (WTLS)*—Specifies a WTL security standard based on the Transport Layer Security (TLS) standard. WTLS is optimized for low-bandwidth communications with possible lengthy delays between packet transmission and receipt, which is referred to as *latency*.

WAP uses WTLS, which must be decrypted when it gets to the gateway and then reencrypted to be forwarded on to the Web under the SSL protocol. WAP does not offer end to end security. The information flows in cleartext during this process, which is often referred to as the *gap in the WAP*. i-Mode, on the other hand, does not have these limitations.

Wired Equivalent Privacy (WEP)

Specifications for the Wired Equivalent Privacy (WEP) standard are detailed in the 802.11b (Wi-Fi) specification. This specification details a method of data encryption and authentication that may be used to establish a more secured wireless connection.

 Recent developments in cryptography have revealed the WEP encryption method to be less secure than originally intended and vulnerable to cryptographic analysis of network traffic. Current recommendations for a more secure wireless network include the use of IPSec and VPN connectivity to tunnel data communications through a secured connection.

Site Surveys

A site survey is necessary before implementing any WLAN solution to optimize network layout within each unique location. This is particularly important in distributed wireless network configurations spanning multiple buildings or open natural areas, where imposing structures and tree growth may affect network access in key areas.

A site survey should include a review of the desired physical and logical structure of the network, selection of possible technologies, and several other factors, including the following:

➤ Federal, state, and local laws and regulations relating to the proposed network solution.

➤ Potential sources of radio frequency (RF) interference, including local broadcast systems as well as motors, fans, and other types of equipment that generate radio frequency interference. This includes an analysis of potential channel overlap between wireless access point hardware.

➤ Available locations for WAP hardware installation and physical network integration connectivity.

➤ Any special requirements of users, applications, and network equipment that must function over the proposed wireless network solution.

➤ Whether a point-to-point (ad-hoc or wireless bridge) or multipoint wireless solution is required. In most solutions, point-to-multipoint connectivity will be required to support multiple wireless clients from each wireless access point connected to the physical network.

All wireless networks share several common security vulnerabilities related to their use of radio frequency broadcasts, which may potentially be detected and compromised without the knowledge of the network administrator. Data transported over this medium is available to anyone with the proper equipment; therefore, it must be secured through encryption and encapsulation mechanisms not subject to public compromise.

Wireless solutions are susceptible to interception and sniffing because installing a wireless device is relatively easy to do, and many wireless devices are set up without any encryption. In addition, wireless communication takes place over airwaves; therefore, it is possible for hackers to access the network without any physical access. This is known as *war-driving*. A hacker can sit in the parking lot and access the network via unsecured wireless devices, especially because most networks use DHCP. The devices the hacker uses can easily obtain a network address because wireless access points advertise their presence and service set identifier (SSID).

You can use encryption on a wireless network, but the encryption (RC4) is weak. The RC4 keyspace is small; therefore, a hacker can use a sniffer to collect all the keys in a relatively short time. After the keys are collected, the encrypted text can be broken. Because so many networks are unprotected, if a hacker finds a network using encryption, he may move on, but if there is information on the network he wants to access, he may spend the additional time to hack the network.

To protect your wireless network, be sure that WEP is enabled, change the default SSIDs of access points, disable the SSID broadcast, and, if possible, use static addresses instead of DHCP. You may also want to put wireless access points in a DMZ and use a VPN for the wireless users or place them on a separate subnet. You should also use a program from outside of your building to check for rogue access points. Airsnort is a Linux program that can take advantage of the weakness in the key-scheduling algorithm of RC4. It can determine a WEP key in seconds. NetStumbler is shareware program that logs an exceptional amount of data and also allows you to discover key details.

Practice Questions

Question 1

Which of the following are client-side Web technologies? [Choose the four best answers.]

- ❏ A. ActiveX controls
- ❏ B. JavaScript
- ❏ C. CGI scripts
- ❏ D. Cookies
- ❏ E. Java applets

Answers A, B, D, and E are correct. Client-side Web technologies include ActiveX controls, JavaScript interpreted code, cookies, and Java applets. Cookies might also be considered a server-side technology because the Web server may access them and store information within the cookies; however, they reside in the client system's browser cache or in a small text file on the client computer. Answer C is incorrect because CGI scripts are stored and interpreted on the Web server.

Question 2

Which of the following is a common bandwidth for 802.11b communications?

- ○ A. 19.2Kbps
- ○ B. 64Kbps
- ○ C. 1.5Mbps
- ○ D. 10Mbps
- ○ E. 11Mbps
- ○ F. 100Mbps

Answer E is correct. The 802.11b WLAN specification allows up to 11Mbps wireless connectivity. Answers A and B are incorrect because they specify common modem bandwidth limits. Answer C is incorrect because 1.5Mbps is a common speed for T1 connectivity. Answers D and F are incorrect because 10Mbps and 100Mbps are common wired LAN data-transfer rates.

Question 3

Unsecured SMTP servers are an asset to spammers because
_____.

- ○ A. They can use these servers to hide the origin of their transmissions
- ○ B. They can plant viruses and rogue code on these servers
- ○ C. These servers store information in cleartext and can be easily compromised
- ○ D. They can use these servers send company email without putting up their own mail server

Answer A is correct. Spammers use SMTP Relay agents that are not properly secured to relay their SMTP email spam messages, hiding the true origin of the email messages. Answer B is incorrect because the purpose of an email server is to relay email messages. Rogue code and viruses are usually planted on file or application servers. Answer C is incorrect because FTP and Telnet are associated with cleartext messages; the purpose of exploiting SMTP Relay is to send mass emails while disguising one's identity, not to capture messages. Answer D is incorrect because it is a bogus answer.

Question 4

Which of the following are good uses for cookies? [Choose the two best answers.]

- ❏ A. Maintaining user portal settings between sessions
- ❏ B. Storing credit card and user identification data
- ❏ C. Storing a listing of items within a shopping cart application
- ❏ D. Maintaining password and logon information for easy return to visited secured sites
- ❏ E. Providing details regarding the network settings in use by the client, like its IP address

Answers A and C are correct. Cookies are well suited for maintaining user portal settings between sessions and storing a list of items within a shopping cart application. Answers B and D are incorrect because cookies that store user identification data, credit card information, or password and logon details could be exploited to allow others to use this information by mining the client's cache. Answer E is incorrect because cookies are used to store session information between pages or servers, rather than to store information that the server can obtain for itself, such as the IP address used by the client.

Question 5

> Which of the following are potential exploits for CGI scripts? [Choose the four best answers.]
>
> ❑ A. Providing information on processes running on the server.
>
> ❑ B. Executing arbitrary commands on the client.
>
> ❑ C. Samples may not include proper security.
>
> ❑ D. Buffer overflows may occur.
>
> ❑ E. Arbitrary commands may be executed on the server.

Answers A, C, D, and E are correct. CGI scripts may be exploited to leak information such as details on running server processes and daemons. Also, samples included in some default installations are not intended for security and include well-known exploits, and buffer overflows may allow arbitrary commands to be executed on the server. Answer B is incorrect because CGI scripts do not run on the client system.

Question 6

> Which of the following is a WLAN technology that uses the Ethernet protocols?
>
> ○ A. Bluetooth
>
> ○ B. IETF
>
> ○ C. WAP
>
> ○ D. i-Mode
>
> ○ E. Wi-Fi

Answer E is correct. The 802.11b (Wi-Fi) standard uses the CSMA/CA connectivity methods commonly found in Ethernet. Answer A is incorrect because Bluetooth is based on a differing transmission protocol. Answer B is incorrect because the Internet Engineering Task Force (IETF) is a standards organization and not a communications protocol. Answers C and D are incorrect because both WAP and i-Mode are standards used by mobile devices such as cell phones, pagers, and PDAs and are not used to specify WLAN standards.

Question 7

Which of the following is not an LDAP vulnerability?

○ A. Buffer overflow vulnerabilities

○ B. Format string vulnerabilities

○ C. Incorrect handling of requests

○ D. Information passed in cleartext

Answer D is correct. Information passed in cleartext is associated with FTP and Telnet, not LDAP. Answers A, B, and C are incorrect because they are all LDAP vulnerabilities.

Question 8

Which of the following is not a potential vulnerability of the FTP service?

○ A. Buffer overflow

○ B. Execution of arbitrary commands

○ C. Anonymous access

○ D. Unencrypted credentials

○ E. Cache mining

Answers E is correct. The FTP service does not provide access to the browser's cache. Answers A, B, C, and D are incorrect because FTP servers may be exposed to anonymous access and transfer logon credentials in clear form. The FTP service is also known for common vulnerabilities that may be exploited using buffer overflows to execute arbitrary commands on the server.

Question 9

The Wired Equivalent Privacy (WEP) standard uses which encryption scheme?

○ A. Blowfish

○ B. RC4

○ C. El Gamal

○ D. Diffie-Hellman

Answer B is correct. WEP is based on the RC4 encryption scheme. Answer A is incorrect because Blowfish is a block cipher based on 64-bit blocks of data. Answer C is incorrect because El Gamal is a public key algorithm used for digital signatures and key exchange. Answer D is incorrect because Diffie-Hellman is a key exchange algorithm.

Question 10

Which of the following statements about Java and JavaScript is true?

- ○ A. Java applets can be used to execute arbitrary instructions on the server.
- ○ B. JavaScript code can continue running even after the applet is closed.
- ○ C. JavaScript can provide access to files of a known name and path.
- ○ D. Java applets can be used to send email as the user.
- ○ E. Java applets allow access to cache information.

Answer C is correct. An early exploit of JavaScript allowed access to files located on the client's system if the name and path were known. Answers A, D, and E are incorrect because JavaScript, not Java, can be used to execute arbitrary instructions on the server, send email as the user, and allow access to cache information. Answer B is incorrect because Java, not JavaScript, can continue running even after the applet has been closed.

Need to Know More?

 Allen, Julia H. *The CERT Guide to System and Network Security Practices*. Addison-Wesley. Upper Saddle River, NJ, 2001. ISBN 020173723X.

 The World Wide Web Security FAQ: www.w3.org/Security/Faq/

 The SANS Information Security Reading Room: rr.sans.org/index.php

 The IEEE Standards Association: standards.ieee.org

Infrastructure Security

Terms you'll need to understand:

✓ Firewalls, routers, and switches
✓ Wireless
✓ Modem
✓ RAS
✓ Telecom/PBX
✓ VPN
✓ IDS
✓ Network Monitoring/Diagnostics
✓ Workstations, servers, and mobile devices
✓ Coaxial, UTP/STP, and fiber cable
✓ Removable media
✓ Security zones
✓ VLAN
✓ NAT
✓ Tunneling

Techniques you'll need to master:

✓ Understanding the basic security concepts of communication and network devices
✓ Being familiar with the basic security concepts of media
✓ Understanding the basic security concepts of network and storage media devices
✓ Knowing the basic security concepts, strengths, and vulnerabilities of security topologies
✓ Being able to explain the strengths and vulnerabilities of various security zones and devices

Understanding the Basic Security Concepts of Communication and Network Devices

The easiest way to keep a computer safe is by physically isolating it from outside contact. Because of the way most companies currently do business, this is virtually impossible. Securing the devices on the network is imperative to protecting the environment. To secure devices, you have to understand the basic security concepts of communication and network devices. This section introduces security concepts as they apply to physical devices found on most networks.

Firewalls

A firewall is a component placed between computers and networks to help eliminate undesired access by the outside world. It can be comprised of hardware, software, or a combination of both. A firewall is the first line of defense for the network. How firewalls are configured is important—especially for large companies where a compromised firewall may spell disaster in the form of bad publicity or a lawsuit, not only for the company, but also for the companies it does business with. For smaller companies, a firewall is an excellent investment because most small companies don't have a full-time technology staff, and an intrusion could easily put them out of business. All things considered, a firewall is an important part of your defense, but you should not rely on it exclusively for network protection. See Figure 6.1 for an example of a firewall.

There are three main types of firewalls:

➤ Packet-filtering firewall

➤ Proxy-service firewall

    ➤ Circuit-level gateway

    ➤ Application-level gateway

➤ Stateful-inspection firewall

Packet-Filtering Firewall

A packet-filtering firewall is typically a router. Packets can be filtered based on IP addresses, ports, or protocols. They operate at the Network layer

(layer 3) of the Open System Interconnection (OSI) model. Packet-filtering solutions are generally considered less secure firewalls because they still allow packets inside the network, regardless of communication pattern within the session. This leaves the system open to denial of services (DoS) attacks. Even though they are the simplest and least secure, they are a good first line of defense. Their main advantage is speed, which is why they are sometimes used before other types of firewalls to perform the first filtering pass.

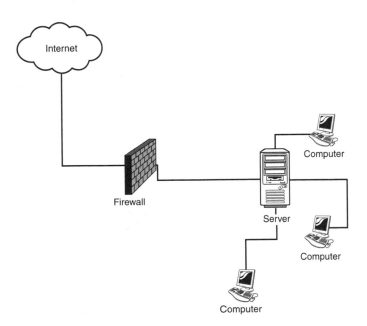

Figure 6.1   A network with a firewall.

Proxy Service Firewall

Proxy service firewalls are go-betweens for the network and the Internet. They hide the internal addresses from the outside world and don't allow the computers on the network to directly access the Internet. This type of firewall has a set of rules that the packets must pass to get in or out. It receives all packets and replaces the IP address on the packets going out with its own address and then changes the address of the packets coming in to the destination address. Proxy service firewalls can also serve as caching servers. In this capacity, these firewalls hold frequently visited Web pages in cache to reduce the time it takes to get a response from the Internet. Here are the two basic types of proxies:

➤ *Circuit-level gateway*—Operates at the OSI Session layer (layer 5) by monitoring the TCP packet flow to determine whether the session requested is a legitimate one. DoS attacks are detected and prevented in circuit-level architecture where a security device discards suspicious requests.

➤ *Application-level gateway*—All traffic is examined to check for OSI Application layer (layer 7) protocols that are allowed. Examples of this type of traffic are File Transfer Protocol (FTP), Simple Mail Transfer Protocol (SMTP), and Hypertext Transfer Protocol (HTTP). Because the filtering is application specific, it adds overhead to the transmissions but is more secure than packet filtering.

Stateful-Inspection Firewall

This is a combination of all types of firewalls. This firewall relies on algorithms to process Application layer data. Because it knows the connection status, it can protect against IP spoofing. It has better security controls than packet filtering, but because it has more security controls and features, it increases the attack surface and is more complicated to maintain.

Other Firewall Considerations

In addition to the core firewall components, other elements are involved in designing a firewall solution that administrators should consider. These include network, remote access, and authentication policies. Firewalls can also provide access control, logging, and intrusion notification. Firewall architecture is covered later in this chapter in the "Basic Security Concepts, Strengths, and Vulnerabilities of Security Topologies" section.

Routers

Routers operate at the Network layer of the OSI model. They are the items that receive information from a host and forward that information to its destination on the network or the Internet. Routers maintain tables that are checked each time a packet needs to be redirected from one interface to another. The tables inside the router help speed up request resolution so packets can reach their destination quicker. The routes may be added manually to the routing table or may be updated automatically using the following protocols:

➤ Routing Information Protocol (RIP/RIPv2)

➤ Interior Gateway Routing Protocol (IGRP)

➤ Enhanced Interior Gateway Routing Protocol (EIGRP)

➤ Open Shortest Path First (OSPF)

➤ Border Gateway Protocol (BGP)

➤ Exterior Gateway Protocol (EGP)

➤ Intermediate System–Intermediate System (IS-IS)

Although routers are primarily used to segment traffic, they have some good security features. One of the best features of a router is its ability to filter packets, either by source address, destination address, protocol, or port. These filters are referred to as access control lists (ACLs). Routers can also be configured to help prevent spoofing by using strong protocol authentication.

 Remember, no matter how secure the routing protocol of choice is, if you never change the default password on the router, you have left yourself wide open to attacks.

Switches

Switches are rapidly becoming more popular than hubs when it comes to connecting desktops to the wiring closet. Switches operate at the Data Link layer (layer 2) of the OSI model. Their packet-forwarding decisions are based on MAC addresses. They allow LANs to be segmented, thus increasing the amount of bandwidth that goes to each device. Each segment is a separate collision domain, but all segments are in the same broadcast domain. Here are the basic functions of a switch:

➤ Filtering and forwarding frames

➤ Learning Media Access Control (MAC) addresses

➤ Preventing loops

Because most switches are configurable, implementing sound security with your switches can be done very similarly to configuring security on a firewall or a router. Physical and virtual security controls must be in place. Switches should be placed in a physically secured area if possible. Be sure that strong authentication and password policies are in place to secure access to the operating system and configuration files.

Wireless

Wireless devices have become extremely popular because of the mobility they provide. However, wireless devices are not really considered secure yet.

There are all kinds of stories about war-driving, war-chalking, and making wireless antennas out of Pringles cans.

War-driving is the practice of using a laptop computer with a wireless network card to locate unsecured wireless networks. A hacker can drive around and see where he can gain network access. This is mostly done in business districts but can also be done in residential neighborhoods. From the parking lot or street the unsecured network is accessed without the company's permission or knowledge.

War-chalking is the practice of marking the buildings of unsecured wireless networks so other hackers will know they can gain access. Several Web sites list the coordinates of unsecured networks using a GPS.

The current Institute of Electrical and Electronics Engineers (IEEE) standards for wireless are 802.11a and 802.11b. There are plans to implement 802.11e, f, g, and i in 2003. These standards operate on radio frequencies. One of the issues with the current wireless technology is that it is a broadcast signal. This basically means that a wireless device advertises that it is out there and open, making it easy for an intruder to pick up and monitor.

Wired Equivalent Privacy (WEP) is an IEEE Wireless Fidelity security protocol. It is defined in the 802.11b standard and is an encryption algorithm that can be used to secure a wireless environment when it is enabled. WEP can have trouble exchanging public and private keys between wireless hosts, but a WEP-enabled network is more secure than a wireless network without it.

Several tools exist to help you monitor wireless networks. The following are some tools that can check the security of a wireless LAN (WLAN):

➤ Kismet

➤ NetStumbler

➤ Airopeek NX

➤ Sniffer Wireless

Wireless LANs can be subject to session hijacking and man-in-the-middle attacks. Using WEP is better than leaving your network unprotected, but it can lead to a false sense of security. WEP works by using the RC4 encryption scheme. The 802.11 design uses a shared key. (Refer to Chapter 8, "Basics of Cryptography," for more information.) Additional risks remain because anyone can purchase an access point and set it up, and access points are small enough to be attractive to thieves. Access points are devices that allow wireless networks to connect to wired networks. As with firewalls, routers, and switches, great care needs to be taken to configure wireless devices for tight security because these devices have distinct potentials to leave large holes open on a corporate network.

 Wireless LANs can be subject to session hijacking and man-in-the-middle attacks.

Modems

Modems are used via the phone line to dial in to a server or computer. They are gradually being replaced by high-speed cable and Digital Subscriber Line (DSL) solutions, which are faster than dial-up access.

Most companies use modems for employees to dial in to the network and work from home. The modems on network computers or servers are usually configured to take incoming calls. Leaving modems open for incoming calls with little to no authentication for users dialing in can be a clear security vulnerability in the network. For example, war-dialing attacks take advantage of this situation. War-dialing is the process by which an automated software application is used to dial numbers in a given range to determine whether any of the numbers are serviced by modems that accept dial-in requests. This attack can be set to target connected modems that are set to receive calls without any authentication, thus allowing attackers an easy path into the network. There are several ways to resolve this:

➤ Set the callback features to have the modem call the user back at a preset number.

➤ Make sure authentication is required using strong passwords.

➤ Be sure employees have not set up modems at their workstations with remote control software installed.

As mentioned, cable and DSL modems are more popular these days. They act more like routers than modems. Although these devices are not prone to war-dialing attacks, they do present a certain amount of danger by maintaining an always-on connection. By leaving the connection on all the time, a hacker has ample time to get into the machine and the network. The use of encryption and firewall solutions will help keep the environment safe from attacks.

RAS

Remote Access Service (RAS) allows a user to dial in to the network via a modem or modem pool while providing the user with secure access during the time he is connected. Many controls may be used to protect the RAS entry point. Here are some examples:

➤ Providing strong authentication

➤ Allowing dial-in only with callback to a preset number

➤ Restricting dial-in hours and user access

➤ Using account lockout and strict password policies

These are just a few of the controls that can be set. In addition, the physical area where the modems or modem pools are located should be secure. Once the physical and logical environments are safe, it is possible they will still be susceptible to DoS attacks, buffer overflows, social engineering, and PBX vulnerabilities, so be sure auditing is implemented.

Telecom/PBX

The telecommunications (telecom) system and Private Branch Exchange (PBX) are a vital part of an organization's infrastructure. Besides the standard block, there are also PBX servers, where the PBX board plugs into the server and is configured through software on the computer. Many companies have moved to Voice over IP (VoIP) to integrate computer telephony, video-conferencing, and document sharing.

For years PBX-type systems have been targeted by hackers, mainly to get free long-distance service. The vulnerabilities that phone networks are subject to include social engineering, long-distance toll fraud, and breach of data privacy.

To protect your network, make sure the PBX is in a secure area, any default passwords have been changed, and only authorized maintenance is done. Many times hackers can gain access to the phone system via social engineering because this device is usually serviced through a remote maintenance port.

VPN

A Virtual Private Network (VPN) is a network connection that allows you access via a secure tunnel created through an Internet connection. VPNs are very popular for several reasons:

> Users in an organization can dial a local Internet access number and connect to the corporate network for the cost of a local phone call.

> Administrative overhead is reduced with a VPN because the Internet Service Provider (ISP) is responsible for maintaining the connectivity once the user is connected to the Internet.

> There are various security advantages to using a VPN, including encryption, encapsulation, and authentication.

In a VPN, encryption/decryption takes quite a bit of CPU cycles and memory usage, so be prepared to factor dedicated hardware or existing hardware upgrades into the costs of proposed solutions.

IDS

IDS stands for *intrusion-detection system*. Intrusion-detection systems are designed to analyze data, identify attacks, and respond to the intrusion. They are different from firewalls in that firewalls control the information that gets in and out of the network, whereas IDSs can identify unauthorized activity. Intrusion-detection systems are also designed to catch attacks in progress within the network, not just on the boundary between private and public networks. The two basic types of intrusion-detection systems are *network based* and *host based*. As the names suggest, network-based IDSs look at the information exchanged between machines, and host-based IDSs look at information that originates on the individual machines. Here are some specifics:

> Network-based IDSs monitor the packet flow and try to locate packets that may have gotten through the firewall and are not allowed for one reason or another. They are best at detecting DoS attacks and unauthorized user access.

> Host-based IDSs monitor communications on a host-by-host basis and try to filter malicious data. These types of IDSs are good at detecting unauthorized file modifications and user activity.

 Network-based IDSs try to locate packets not allowed on the network that the firewall missed. Host-based IDSs collect and analyze data that originates on the local machine or a computer hosting a service. Network-based IDSs tend to be more distributed.

Network-based IDSs and host-based IDSs should be used together to ensure a truly secure environment. IDSs can be located anywhere on the network. They can be placed internally or between firewalls. Many different types of IDSs are available, all with different capabilities, so make sure they meet the needs of your company before committing to using them. Chapter 7, "Intrusion Detection and Security Baselines," covers IDSs in more detail.

Intrusion Prevention Systems

Intrusion-prevention software differs from intrusion-detection software in that it actually prevents attacks rather than only detecting the occurrence of an attack. Intrusion-detection software is reactive, scanning for configuration weaknesses and detecting attacks after they occur. By the time an alert has been issued, the attack has usually occurred and has damaged the network or desktop. Intrusion-prevention security systems are the next generation in network security software. These systems proactively protect machines against damage from attacks that signature-based technologies cannot detect.

Network Monitoring/Diagnostics

Most organizations use monitoring and diagnostic tools to help manage their networks. Diagnostic tools can be actual tools, such as cable testers and loopback connectors, or software programs and utilities. Some of the more common network diagnostic tools include the following:

➤ *Ping*—Packet Internet Grouper (ping) is a utility that tests network connectivity by sending an Internet Control Message Protocol (ICMP) echo request to a host. It is a good troubleshooting tool to tell whether a route is available to a host.

➤ *Tracert/traceroute*—This utility traces the route a packet takes and records the hops along the way. This is a good tool to use to find out where a packet is getting hung up.

➤ *Nslookup*—This is a command-line utility used to troubleshoot a Domain Name Server (DNS) database. It queries the DNS server to check whether the correct information is in the zone database.

➤ *Netstat*—Netstat displays all the ports on which the computer is listening. It can also be used to display the routing table and pre-protocol statistics.

➤ *IPConfig/Ifconfig*—IPConfig is used to display the TCP/IP settings on a Windows machine. It can display the IP address, subnet mask, default gateway, Windows Internet Naming Service (WINS), DNS, and MAC information. This is useful in verifying that the Transmission Control Protocol/Internet Protocol (TCP/IP) configuration is correct if connectivity issues arise.

➤ *Telnet*—Telnet is a terminal emulation program used to access remote routers and Unix systems. This is an excellent tool to use to determine whether the port on a host computer is working properly.

 Know the different utilities that are used to troubleshoot networks and what they are used for.

Port scanners, vulnerability scanners, and intrusion-detection systems are also used in network monitoring. Port and vulnerability scanners were discussed in Chapter 3, "Nonessential Services and Attacks," and intrusion-detection systems were discussed earlier in this chapter. If these tools are used on the network, be sure the information they gather is protected as well.

SNMP

Simple Network Management Protocol (SNMP) is an Application layer protocol whose purpose is to collect statistics from TCP/IP devices. Its management infrastructure consists of three components:

➤ SNMP managed node

➤ SNMP agent

➤ SNMP network management station

The device loads the agent, which in turn collects the information and forwards it to the management station. Network management stations collect a massive amount of critical network information and are likely targets of intruders because SNMPv1 is insecure. The only security measure it has in place is its community name, which is similar to a password. By default, this is "public" and many times is not changed, thus leaving the information wide open to intruders. SNMPv2 uses Message Digest Version 5 (MD5) for authentication. The transmissions can also be encrypted. SNMPv3 is the current standard, but most devices are likely to still be using SNMPv1 or SNMPv2.

SNMP is often overlooked when checking for vulnerabilities because it uses User Datagram Protocol (UDP) ports 161 and 162. Make sure network management stations are secure physically and secure on the network. You might even consider using a separate management subnet and protecting it using a router with an access list.

Workstations

Workstation security is often overlooked, yet this is one of the areas that can attract intruders the most because it is the path of least resistance to deploying an attack. This mostly happens because users are unaware of the dangers they put themselves and the company in by doing some of the following:

➤ Installing unauthorized software

➤ Downloading infected music and movie files

➤ Opening email that has a virus

➤ Forwarding email hoaxes

➤ Sharing their C: drive with full access, no password

➤ Using weak passwords

➤ Not logging off the network when leaving the building

This by no means covers all the possible situations users get into. There is also theft and lost equipment, failed components, and physical access by visitors to consider.

In the area of physical theft, the most obvious solution is security locks. Every laptop comes with a hook for a security lock that can be used to discourage theft attempts. Similar locks exist for desktop workstations as well. In addition to physical locks, educate your employees to always log off or lock their workstations while they are unattended.

To protect the information on stolen or lost equipment, use encryption to make it impossible to read this information without appropriate login credentials.

Should a component in a workstation fail, such as a hard drive, running nightly backups will be instrumental in making sure the data can be recovered. You may also want to consider removing floppy drives or disabling devices that aren't absolutely necessary. This prevents visitors and users from bringing in infected files.

Antivirus software can be used to scan email and for downloadable malicious code. Be sure that the definitions are updated on a regular basis; the software alone will not do the job. Again, user education and training will help ensure that the updates are timely.

User education in company security policies and the scope of their responsibilities is the ultimate key to success in keeping the workstations secure.

Servers

As you learned in Chapter 3, servers can serve a variety of functions and their vulnerabilities are determined by their use. Servers are more sensitive to attacks than workstations, and these attacks can be more costly. Therefore, all network servers should be isolated in a server room and locked to prevent any kind of unauthorized physical access. Visitors to these premises must be justified and supervised. Besides having physical controls, availability must also be ensured. This can be accomplished via Redundant Array of Inexpensive Disks (RAID), uninterruptible power supply (UPS) equipment, and clustering. We already discussed ways to make the server environment safer in Chapter 3, the server hardening is discussed in Chapter 7.

Mobile Devices

Laptops, personal digital assistants (PDAs), Palm Pilots, and PocketPCs are all mobile devices. They are very susceptible to theft because they are small, valuable, and many times contain important information about a company. They use wireless or infrared technology, and as you saw in an earlier discussion, you need to be sure that encryption is enabled to keep their data safe. If possible, you should protect these devices with passwords so there is at least an initial deterrent.

We have covered basic security concepts as they apply to physical devices. These devices all use some type of media to communicate with each other. With that in mind, let's move to the next section.

Understanding the Basic Security Concepts of Media

If an attack is launched against the signal on the wire, hackers may be able to copy information as the bits flow across the wire. This may not be as dangerous if the data is encrypted, but depending on the communication medium, it may be possible for hackers to at least steal the service. Being familiar with the basic security concepts of media will help you recognize attacks and how to keep them from happening.

Coax

Coaxial cable was the first type of cable used to network computers and was instrumental in forming the basis of the Ethernet standard. Coaxial cables are made of a thick copper core with an outer metallic shield used to reduce interference. Often, the shield is made of woven cooper mesh or aluminum. The cable is then surrounded by a plastic covering, called a *sheath*. Although coaxial cables are no longer deployed, they may still be found in legacy environments. Here are the two main types of coax cables used:

> ➤ *10Base2*—Also known as *thinnet*, 10Base2 has a communication speed of 10Mbps, uses baseband signaling, and is limited in length to 185 meters per segment. It uses BNC connectors to attach segments to each other. Terminators are required at both ends of each segment to prevent signal echo.

> ➤ *10Base5*—Also known as *thicknet*, 10Base5 has a communication speed of 10Mbps, uses baseband signaling, and is limited in length to 500 meters per segment. 10Base5 uses attachment unit interface (AUI) external transceivers connected to each NIC by a vampire tap that allows access to the network by piercing the cable.

Coax cables have no physical transmission security and are very simple to tap without interrupting regular transmissions or being noticed. The electric signal, conducted by a single core wire, can easily be tapped by piercing the sheath. It would then be possible to eavesdrop on the conversations of all hosts attached to the segment because coax cabling implements broadband transmission technology and assumes many hosts connected to the same wire. Another security concern of coax cable is reliability. Because no focal point is involved, a faulty cable can bring the whole network down. Missing terminators or improperly functioning transceivers can cause poor network performance and transmission errors. If you are using coax cable, be sure to have proper cable testing equipment available and periodically scan the network for unfamiliar devices.

UTP/STP

Twisted-pair cable is used in most of today's network topologies. Twisted-pair cabling is either unshielded (UTP) or shielded (STP). Plenum cable is also available; this is a grade that complies with fire codes. The outer casing is more fire resistant than regular twisted pair cable. Ethernet networks have typically used UTP, and STP is mostly used for AppleTalk and Token Ring networks.

UTP is popular because it is inexpensive and easy to install. There are seven types of UTP cable, the most popular being Category 5 (or Cat5). Before Cat5, Cat3-type cable was used on Ethernet networks, and some networks may still have it in place. Cat3 is the lowest category that meets standards for a 10BaseT network. Here are the speeds and cable lengths for both:

➤ *Cat3*—Speed capability of 10Mbps, with cable segments up to 100 meters

➤ *Cat5*—Speed capability of 1Gbps, with cable segments up to 100 meters

UTP is eight wires twisted into four pairs. The design cancels much of the overflow and interference from one wire to the next, but UTP is subject to interference from outside electromagnetic sources and is prone to radio frequency interference (RFI) and electromagnetic interference (EMI) as well as crosstalk.

STP is different from UTP in that it has shielding surrounding the cable's wires. Some STP has shielding around the individual wires, which helps prevent crosstalk. STP is more resistant to EMI and is considered a bit more secure because the shielding makes wire tapping more difficult.

Both UTP and STP are possible to tap, although it is physically a little trickier than tapping coax cable because of the physical structure of STP and UTP cable. With UTP and STP, a more inherent danger lies in the fact that it is easy to add devices to the network via open ports on unsecured hubs and switches. These devices should be secured from unauthorized access, and cables should be clearly marked so a visual inspection can let you know whether something is awry. Also, software programs are available that can help detect unauthorized devices.

Fiber

Fiber was designed for transmissions at higher speeds over longer distances. It uses light pulses for signal transmission, making it immune to RFI, EMI, and eavesdropping. Fiber optic has a plastic or glass center, surrounded by another layer of plastic or glass with a protective outer coating. Data-transmission speed ranges from 100Mbps to 2Gbps and can be sent a distance of 2 kilometers per segment.

On the downside, fiber is still quite expensive compared to more traditional cabling, it is more difficult to install, and fixing breaks can be costly.

As far as security is concerned, fiber cabling eliminates the signal tapping that is possible with coax. It is impossible to tap fiber without interrupting the service and using specially constructed equipment. This makes it more difficult to eavesdrop or steal service.

Removable Media

Removable media poses a security risk to a company for the following reasons:

> ➤ The theft of classified or confidential information can destroy the business if this information ends up in the hands of competitors.

> ➤ The reputation of the business may become permanently damaged if information belonging to customers or vendors is posted publicly.

> ➤ Information in the hands of an intruder can give her enough ammunition to mount successful attacks at any given time.

The most likely reason for a company to have removable media is for offsite storage of backups. The data should be protected by at least a password and possibly encryption. It is also common in military environments to have removable storage media that is locked in a proper safe or container at the end of the day.

Tape

Tape devices use magnetic storage media and are extremely popular backup technologies because of the amount of data that can fit on a small amount of space. Tape backups are widely used to back up system configurations, mission-critical systems, and system account information, which means they often may contain system Registry information, network user account databases, sensitive customer information, and files.

Several types of magnetic media can be used to back up important data, including the following:

> ➤ *4mm DAT (Digital Audio Tape)*—DAT technology involves 4mm tape that employs helical scan recording.

> ➤ *8mm DAT*—This 8mm tape technology is similar to 4mm DAT but with greater capacities.

> ➤ *QIC (Quarter Inch Cartridge)*—QIC cartridges look much like audiotape cassettes.

> ➤ *Travan*—The Travan standard, developed by Imation, was introduced 1997. It has built-in tape alignment and tensioning, thereby reducing the amount of hardware needed in the drive itself. Bulk erasing (degaussing) renders the cartridge unusable.

➤ *AIT (Advanced Intelligent Tape)*—Developed by Sony, AIT is an 8mm technology that includes stronger, thinner media that is more stable and has better coatings than previously available.

➤ *DLT (Digital Linear Tape)*—DLT is an adaptation of reel-to-reel magnetic recording, where the tape cartridge performs as one reel and the tape drive as the other.

➤ *Super DLT (Digital Linear Tape)*—The next generation of Digital Linear Tape. The expected capacity is up to 1.2TB of uncompressed data.

When using any of these types of tape, be sure it fits the storage requirements of your company and check the specifications of the drive before ordering tapes. Many come in different variations; for example, not all QIC and Travan tapes can be used in all QIC and Travan drives. They may fit into the drive, but if the tape isn't designed for the drive, the drive won't record on the media. Another consideration is shelf life. If a DLT has a shelf life of 40 years, and 25 years from now you have to retrieve data, will there be equipment that can still read that type of data? With technology advancing rapidly, chance are that unless accommodations are made to be sure that the equipment is available to read the media, you will be out of luck.

To minimize chances of theft, tapes must be stored in a secure environment, and employees who are not responsible for doing backups should not know where the tapes are stored. In smaller companies, fireproof safes can be used to store the tapes. In larger environments, tape libraries can be implemented for remote tape rotation and backup device administration. Tapes that are going out of rotation and into an archive should be stored offsite, in safety deposit boxes or similar secure environments. Offsite storage ensures business continuity in unforeseeable or unfortunate situations.

Backup Strategies and Security Concerns for Tape Media

Several backup methods can be employed in disaster-recovery strategies, and they are not specific to tape devices. The most popular backup strategies are as follows:

➤ *Full backup*—Copies all selected files and resets the archive bit. This method allows you to restore using just one tape. In case of theft, this poses the most risk since all data is on one tape.

➤ *Incremental backup*—Contains all the information that was modified since the last incremental backup and resets the archive bit. If there is a need to restore, the number of tapes will include the last full backup and all incremental tapes. For example, if the server dies on Thursday, four tapes will be needed: the full from Friday and the incremental tapes from Monday, Tuesday, and Wednesday. If any incremental tape is stolen, it may or may not be of value to the offender, but it still represents risk to the company.

▶ *Differential backup*—Copies all information changed since the last full backup, regardless of if or when the last differential backup was made because it doesn't reset the archive bit. If there is a need to restore, the number of tapes will include the last full backup and one differential tapes. For example, if the server dies on Thursday, two tapes will be needed, the full from Friday and the differential from Wednesday. Theft of a differential tape is more risky than an incremental as larger chunks of sequential data may be stored on tape the further away from the last full backup it gets.

▶ *Copy backup*—Very similar to full backup in that it copies all selected files but doesn't reset the archive bit. From the security perspective, the loss of a tape with a copy backup is the same as losing a tape with a full backup.

In addition to these backup strategies, companies employ tape rotation and retention policies. The various methods of tape rotation include the grandfather, Tower of Hanoi, and 10-tape rotation. Backup tapes should be tested regularly. Many companies think they are backing up their data, and find out that the tapes are blank, or the tape heads have become worn or dirty and now they can't restore their data. After the backups are complete, they must be clearly marked or labeled so they can be properly safeguarded.

Backup is just one small part of the overall disaster recovery planning. Despite obvious security threats, backups must be done on a regular basis on every server or computer, based on whether physical failure would cause any amount of inconvenience.

An incremental backup resets the archive bit, a differential does not.

Every company should determine its own backup policy, depending on the needs and the nature of information to be protected. The policy should be determined by the amount and type of data to be backed up, how far back data might be needed, and whether the back up type can be offline or online storage. Remember, proper planning and testing can help divert potential disaster.

CDR

Recordable or rewritable compact discs (CD-Rs or CD-RWs) have become relatively inexpensive and, as a result, can be used as an alternative to magnetic media for backups.

A writable CD (CD-R) is a solid disk of clear plastic that has etching within it to act as a guide for the laser. Then comes the reflective layer, made of aluminum or gold foil. This is followed by a layer of organic dye. Listed here are the common dyes used today:

➤ Cyanine (blue-green) is used in many less-expensive CD-Rs. These CDs have a lifespan of between 10 and 75 years.

➤ Phthalocyanine (golden colored) is the longest-lasting dye, producing CD-R disks that have a shelf life of close to 100 years.

➤ Formazan (greenish gold) produces CD-Rs with a somewhat better lifetime than cyanine.

➤ Metallized azo (dark blue) produces CD-Rs a lifetime more toward the higher end of the scale.

If a CD is no longer useful or is not working correctly, it must be made safe to discard. Formal as well as physical processes can be used to do this. The formal processes will be discussed after the section on diskettes. CDs can be destroyed by breaking or scratching them. Some companies now make CD shredders, which would also serve the purpose. The destruction should be done by authorized personnel and the remains disposed of as per company policy.

Hard Drives

The cost of hard drives has come down considerably in the last few years. Besides being cheaper, hard drives can now store over 100GB of data, making them an easy choice for backup or redundant data. Removable hard drives should be handled carefully; if dropped, they may not work correctly. Proper storage is also a consideration. Be sure they are placed in a secure environment where they are safe from Electro Magnetic Field (EMF), high temperatures, and theft. If you choose to overwrite the data, pay particular attention to the section on proper sanitization.

Diskettes

Floppy disks are still used in many environments. They are magnetic media that store 1.44MB of data. They are sensitive to heat, EMF, and can be easily stolen due to their small size. If they are to be stored, be sure they are in an environment similar to that described for hard drives.

Discarding Information on Removable Media

Before we discuss flashcards and smartcards, let's go over some concepts in regard to the proper way to handle removable media when either the data should be overwritten or is no longer useful or pertinent to the company. The following choices apply to all removable media units:

➤ *Declassification*—A formal process of assessing the risk involved in discarding particular information. All possible considerations should be assessed. What if this information ends up in the wrong hands? What is the worst that can happen? If no threat is posed, the information can be declassified.

➤ *Sanitization*—The process of removing the contents from the media as fully as possible, making it extremely difficult to restore it even for data-recovery specialists. The processes employed by sanitization include degaussing and overwriting:

   ➤ *Degaussing*—This method uses an electrical device to reduce the magnetic flux density of the storage media to zero. This method is considered very safe.

   ➤ *Overwriting*—This method is applicable to magnetic storage devices. Be cautious about slack space on hard drives. When data is overwritten, it is still possible to recover data that was there previously.

➤ *Destruction*—The process of physically destroying the media and the information stored on it. Destruction is the only safe method of completely removing all traces of information stored on a removable media device.

Because CDs and CD-Rs are optical media, sanitization is not applicable to them, so either declassification or destruction should be used. Hard drives and diskettes are magnetic media, and any of the methods can be used.

Flashcards

Flashcards are most often used in digital cameras, MP3 players, and PDAs. These cards store a good amount of information in a relatively small space.

Data transferred via flashcards many times is stored unencrypted. If the device used supports encryption, it would be wise to use it, because these devices are small and easy to steal. Because flashcards may contain traces of classified or confidential information, such as customer data, companies should consider sanitizing or destroying these components when upgrading or discarding the outdated equipment.

Smartcards

Smartcards are devices that contain memory and sometimes embedded chips. They are used in cell phones and mobile devices to store customer ID information, personal data, and employee credentials. They are inserted into a smartcard reader that reads the data embedded on them. There are two basic types of smartcards:

➤ *Stored value*—This type of card only holds data and is similar to magnetic strip cards used by banks.

➤ *Integrated circuit cards (ICCs)*—This type of card can perform tasks such as key exchanges.

These cards are not easy to tamper with, but because they are small, they can be easily lost or stolen.

Companies must institute and enforce strict smartcard policies because theft is a big risk associated with the use of this type of device. They should be guarded, and lost or stolen cards should be reported immediately. On the upside, administrators can revoke issued certificates or disable user accounts, making the smartcard basically a piece of useless plastic.

So far, we have covered the basic security concepts of media, which should help you recognize some of the vulnerabilities they present. The area we will cover next is security topology, which deals with how devices are arranged on the network and how they communicate with each other.

Basic Security Concepts, Strengths, and Vulnerabilities of Security Topologies

The concepts of security topologies are based on securing the communication between devices on the network. Topologies consist of security zones that are created using hardware devices. This section provides an overview of how firewalls are used to segment the network into security zones and create various security topologies. It will also help you understand basic security concepts, strengths, and vulnerabilities of security topologies and be able to explain the strengths and vulnerabilities of these topologies.

Security Zones

To understand security zones, we must first discuss the major types of firewall architectures or security topologies. They are as follows:

➤ Bastion host

➤ Screened host gateway

➤ Screened subnet gateway

Bastion Host

A bastion host is the first line of security that a company allows to be addressed directly from the Internet. Figure 6.2 shows how a bastion host works. It is designed to screen the rest of its network from security exposure. It is the device that the firewall software is installed on, and it supports packet filtering, proxy, and hybrid firewall applications, such as a dual-homed host, where there are two NICs. A bastion host can be a router running access lists or a PC running an operating system that supports some kind of routing rules definition or traffic-filtering mechanism. Bastion hosts can also be used for Web, email, FTP, or DNS servers.

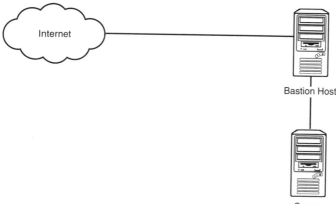

Figure 6.2 A bastion host.

Bastion host solutions are most common to small networks or remote locations. Because each host has a specific role, all unnecessary services and protocols should be uninstalled. The server's operating system and software also needs to be hardened. This process is discussed in Chapter 7.

Screened Host Gateway

A screened host gateway is implemented using a screening router and a bastion host. The bastion host is on the private network and communicates directly with a border router. The screening router blocks traffic by packet filtering; it may also block traffic on specific ports, as shown in Figure 6.3. The bastion host serves as a choke point through which all traffic flows. This network design includes an application gateway. Traffic coming in from the Internet gets filtered through the router based on what is allowed. If it is allowed, the traffic gets forwarded to the application gateway. The application gateway then redirects it to the appropriate server or a workstation. The process works essentially backwards for outgoing communications.

Screened Host

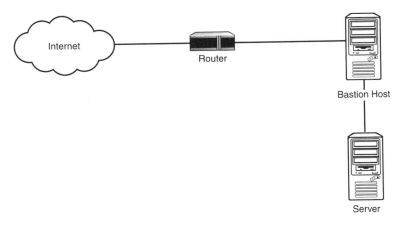

Figure 6.3   A screened host gateway.

Compared to bastion host, the screened host gateway is more likely to let certain types of offending traffic in. In the case of a bastion host, all rules are configured on one device. With application gateways, two devices need to be configured. This leaves room for error. Another reason why this could be less secure is because the packet filter is configured quite liberally, usually allowing "all or none." The requests are then forwarded to the application gateway, where the majority of the filtering is done. If configured properly, this is a good solution because two devices would have to be compromised.

Screened Subnet Gateway

The third type is called a *screened subnet gateway*. Screened subnet gateway architecture includes two screened host gateway devices that isolate the LAN from the Internet. Essentially, this is an isolated subnet between the Internet and the internal network, as shown in Figure 6.4.

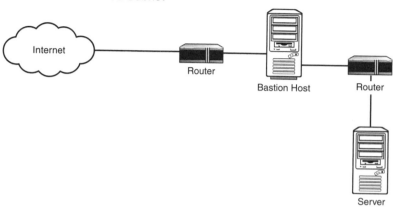

Figure 6.4   A screened subnet gateway.

With a screened subnet, two local subnet IP addresses are needed. Both the Internet and the private network have access to the screened subnet, but neither can access each other. Therefore, one subnet is needed for the internal network and one is needed for the screened subnet. This type of setup is recommended because traffic is controlled more finely and it isolates the internal network by more than one layer of security. Public inbound traffic is allowed only in the DMZ subnet. Outbound traffic flows through the DMZ, which creates anonymity for the requesting clients on the LAN.

Disadvantages of this architecture are complex implementation and possible breaches when packets are allowed from the borderline firewall through the DMZ and into the internal network. This topology is by far the most flexible and secure, where one can completely eliminate direct outside-to-inside communications and conduct everything through a strictly controlled area called a DMZ.

DMZ

A *demilitarized zone* (DMZ) is a small network between the internal network and the Internet that provides a layer of security and privacy. This configuration is described in the previous screened subnet gateway section. Both internal and external users have limited access to the servers in this area. Often Web and mail servers are placed in the DMZ. Because these devices are exposed to the Internet, it is important that they are hardened and patches are kept current. See Table 6.1 for a list of the most common services and ports that are run on servers inside the DMZ.

You should know the various types of services and the ports they are executed on.

Table 6.1	Commonly Used Ports
Port	**Service**
21	FTP
22	SSH
25	SMTP
53	DNS
80	HTTP
110	POP3
443	HTTPS

Intranet

An intranet is a portion of the internal network that uses Web-based technologies. The information is stored on Web servers and accessed using browsers. Although Web servers are used, they don't necessarily have to be accessible to the outside world. This is possible because the IP addresses of the servers are reserved for private, internal use. We will go over private IP addresses in the "NAT" section, later in this chapter. If the intranet can be accessed from public networks, it should be through a VPN for security reasons.

Extranet

An extranet is the public portion of the company's IT infrastructure that allows resources to be used by authorized partners and resellers that have proper authorization and authentication. This type of arrangement is commonly used for business-to-business relationships. Because an extranet can provide liability for a company, care must be taken to ensure that VPNs and firewalls are configured properly and that security policies are strictly enforced.

VLANs

VLAN is short for *virtual local area network*, and its purpose is to unite network nodes logically into the same broadcast domain regardless of their physical attachment to the network. VLANs provide a way to limit broadcast traffic in a switched network. This creates a boundary and, in essence, creates multiple, isolated LANs on one switch. Because switches operate on layer 2 of the OSI model, if data is to be passed from one VLAN to another, a router is required.

 The purpose of a VLAN is to logically group network nodes regardless of their physical location.

Frame tagging is the technology used for VLANs. The 802.1Q standard defines a mechanism that encapsulates the frames with headers, which then tags them with a VLAN ID. VLAN-aware network devices look for these tags in frames and make appropriate forwarding decisions. A VLAN is basically a software solution that allows creating unique tag identifiers to be assigned to different ports on the switch. For more information on frame tagging and VLANs, see the "Need to Know More?" section at the end of the chapter.

The most notable benefit of using a VLAN is that it can span multiple switches. Because users on the same VLAN don't have to be associated by physical location, they can be grouped by department or function. Here are the benefits that VLANs provide:

➤ Users can be grouped by department rather than physical location.

➤ Moving and adding users is simplified. No matter where a user physically moves, changes are made to the software configuration changes in the switch.

➤ Because VLANs allow users to be grouped, applying security policies becomes easier.

Keep in mind that using a VLAN is not to be considered an absolute safeguard against security infringements. It does not provide the same level of security as a router. A VLAN is a software solution and cannot take the place of a well-subnetted or routed network. It is possible to make frames hop from one VLAN to another. This takes skill and knowledge on the part of an attacker, but it is possible.

NAT

Network Address Translation (NAT) acts as a liaison between an internal network and the Internet. It allows multiple computers to connect to the Internet using one IP address. In this situation, the internal network uses a private IP address. Special ranges in each IP class are used specifically for private addressing. These addresses are considered nonroutable on the Internet.

Here are the private address ranges:

➤ *Class A*—10.0.0.0 network. Valid host IDs are from 10.0.0.1 to 10.255.255.254.

➤ *Class B*—172.16.0.0 through 172.31.0.0 networks. Valid host IDs are from 172.16.0.1 through 172.31.255.254.

➤ *Class C*—192.168.0.0 network. Valid host IDs are from 192.168.0.1 to 192.168.255.254.

For smaller companies, NAT can be used in the form of Windows Internet Connection Sharing (ICS), where all machines share one Internet connection, such as a dial-up modem. NAT can also be used for address translation between multiple protocols, which improves security and provides for more interoperability in heterogeneous networks.

 Keep in mind that NAT and IPSec do not work well together. NAT has to replace the headers of the incoming packet with its own headers before sending the packet. This may not possible because IPSec information is encrypted.

 Another address range to keep in mind when designing IP address space is Automatic Private IP Addressing (APIPA). Microsoft implemented this in Windows 98 and 2000 clients. In the event that no Dynamic Host Configuration Protocol (DHCP) server is available at the time that the client issues a DHCP lease request, it will be automatically configured with an address from the 169.254.0.1 through 169.254.255.254 range.

IP Classes

In case you are unclear about IP classes, the following information will help you review or learn about the different classes. IP address space is divided into five classes: A, B, C, D, and E. The first byte of the address determines which class an address belongs to:

➤ Network addresses with the first byte between 1 and 126 are Class A and can have about 17 million hosts each.

➤ Network addresses with the first byte between 128 and 191 are Class B and can have about 65,000 hosts each.

➤ Network addresses with the first byte between 192 and 223 are Class C and can have about 250 hosts.

> ➤ Network addresses with the first byte between 224 and 239 are Class D and are used for multicasting.

> ➤ Network addresses with the first byte between 240 and 255 are Class E and are used as experimental addresses.

Tunneling

Tunneling involves one network sending its data through the connection of another network. It works by encapsulating a network protocol within packets carried by the public network. A common approach to tunneling is Point-to-Point Tunneling Protocol (PPTP) technology, which embeds its own network protocol within the TCP/IP packets carried by the Internet. Layer 2 Tunneling Protocol (L2TP) can also be used. Tunneling should not be used as a substitute for encryption. The strongest level of encryption possible needs to be used within the VPN.

The downside of tunneling is that for the firewall to establish the tunnel, a set of rules needs to be configured to permit such activity. Once the VPN tunnel is created, it is considered a channel that has already passed security checks. In addition, when encryption is used within a tunnel, it is not possible to filter the packets because the firewall does not see the encrypted contents.

Practice Questions

Question 1

> Your company is in the process of setting up a DMZ segment. You have to allow email traffic in the DMZ segment. Which TCP ports do you have to open? [Check all correct answers.]
>
> ❑ A. 110
> ❑ B. 139
> ❑ C. 25
> ❑ D. 443

Answers A and C are correct. Port 110 is used for POP3 incoming mail, and port 25 is used for SMTP outgoing mail. POP3 delivers mail only and SMTP transfers mail between servers. Answer B is incorrect because UDP uses port 139 for network sharing. Port 443 is used by HTTPS; therefore, answer D is incorrect.

Question 2

> The main fan in your server died on Wednesday morning. It will be at least two days before it can be replaced. You decide to use another server instead but need to restore the data from the dead one. You have been doing incremental backups and the last full backup was performed on Friday evening. The backup doesn't run on weekends. How many backup tapes will you need to restore the data?
>
> ○ A. Two
> ○ B. Four
> ○ C. One
> ○ D. Three

Answer D is correct. You will need the full backup from Friday, the incremental tape from Monday, and the incremental from Tuesday. Answer A is incorrect because two tapes would be needed if the backup type was differential. Answer B is incorrect because Wednesday's backup hasn't happened yet. Answer C is incorrect because one tape would be enough only if full backups were done daily.

Question 3

Your company is in the process of setting up a management system on your network, and you want to use SNMP. You have to allow this traffic through the router. Which UDP ports do you have to open? [Check all correct answers.]

- ❏ A. 161
- ❏ B. 139
- ❏ C. 138
- ❏ D. 162

Answers A and D are correct. UDP ports 161 and 162 are used by SNMP. Answer B is incorrect because UDP uses port 139 for network sharing. Answer C is incorrect because port 138 is used to allow NetBIOS traffic for name resolution.

Question 4

You are having problems with your email server. No one seems to be receiving any mail. You're not exactly sure where the problem lies. You go to a remote office, open a DOS prompt, and type which command?

- ○ A. **netstat**
- ○ B. **tracert**
- ○ C. **ipconfig**
- ○ D. **nslookup**

Answer B is correct. Tracert traces the route a packet takes and records the hops along the way. This is a good tool to use to find out where a packet is getting hung up. Netstat displays all the ports on which the computer is listening; therefore, answer A is incorrect. Answer C is incorrect because IPConfig is used to display the TCP/IP settings on a Windows machine. Answer D is also incorrect because Nslookup is a command-line utility used to troubleshoot a Domain Name Server (DNS) database

Question 5

You have implemented a proxy firewall technology that can distinguish between an FTP **get** command and an FTP **put** command. What type of firewall are you using?

○ A. Proxy gateway

○ B. Circuit-level gateway

○ C. Application-level gateway

○ D. SOCKS proxy

Answer C is correct. An application-level gateway understands services and protocols. Answer A is too generic to be a proper answer. Answer B is incorrect because a circuit-level gateway's decisions are based on source and destination addresses. Answer D is incorrect because SOCKS proxy is an example of a circuit-level gateway.

Question 6

You want to use NAT on your network, and you have received a Class C address from your ISP. What range of addresses should you use?

○ A. 10.x.x.x

○ B. 172.16.x.x

○ C. 172.31.x.x

○ D. 192.168.x.x

Answer D is correct. In a Class C network, valid host IDs are from 192.168.0.1 to 192.168.255.254. Answer A is incorrect because it is a Class A address. Valid host IDs are from 10.0.0.1 to 10.255.255.254. Answers B and C are incorrect because they are both Class B addresses; valid host IDs are from 172.16.0.1 through 172.31.255.254.

Question 7

> You are setting up a switched network and want to group users by department. Which technology would you implement?
>
> ○ A. DMZ
> ○ B. VPN
> ○ C. VLAN
> ○ D. NAT

Answer C is correct. The purpose of a VLAN is to unite network nodes logically into the same broadcast domain regardless of their physical attachment to the network. Answer A is incorrect because a DMZ is a small network between the internal network and the Internet that provides a layer of security and privacy. Answer B is incorrect because a Virtual Private Network (VPN) is a network connection that allows you access via a secure tunnel created through an Internet connection. Answer D is incorrect because NAT acts as a liaison between an internal network and the Internet.

Question 8

> You have a Web server that needs to be accessed by both the employees and by external customers. What type of architecture should be implemented?
>
> ○ A. Bastion host
> ○ B. Screened subnet
> ○ C. Screened host
> ○ D. Bastion subnet

Answer B is correct. A screened subnet is an isolated subnet between the Internet and the internal network. A bastion host is the first line of security that a company allows to be addressed directly from the Internet; therefore, answer A is incorrect. A bastion host on the private network communicating directly with a border router is a screened host; therefore, answer C incorrect. Answer D is fictitious and therefore incorrect as well.

Question 9

An exposed device that's the foundation for firewall software to operate on is called a _____.

○ A. Bastion host

○ B. Screened subnet

○ C. Screened host

○ D. Bastion subnet

Answer A is correct. A bastion host is the first line of security that a company allows to be addressed directly from the Internet. Answer B is incorrect because a screened subnet is an isolated subnet between the Internet and the internal network. A bastion host on the private network communicating directly with a border router is a screened host; therefore, answer C is incorrect. Answer D is fictitious and therefore incorrect as well.

Question 10

You have recently had some security breaches in the network. You suspect it may be a small group of employees. You want to implement a solution that will monitor the internal network as well as external traffic. Which of the following devices would you use? [Check all correct answers.]

❏ A. A router

❏ B. A network-based IDS

❏ C. A firewall

❏ D. A host-based IDS

Answers B and D are correct. Because you want to monitor both types of traffic, the IDSs should be used together. Network-based intrusion-detection systems monitor the packet flow and try to locate packets that are not allowed for one reason or another and may have gotten through the firewall. Host-based intrusion-detection systems monitor communications on a host-by-host basis and try to filter malicious data. These types of IDSs are good at detecting unauthorized file modifications and user activity. Answer A is incorrect because a router forwards information to its destination on the network or the Internet. A firewall protects computers and networks from undesired access by the outside world; therefore, answer C is incorrect.

Need to Know More?

 Bragg, Roberta. *CISSP Training Guide*. Que. Indianapolis, IN, 2002. ISBN 078972801X.

Refer to Chapter 2, "Telecommunications and Network Security."

 Lammle, Todd. *CCNA Cisco Certified Network Associate Study Guide, Second Edition*. Sybex. Alameda, CA, 2000. ISBN 0782126472.

Refer to Chapter 6, "Virtual LANs (VLANs)."

 Maufer, Thomas A. *IP Fundamentals: What Everyone Needs to Know About Addressing & Routing*. Prentice Hall PTR. Upper Saddle River, NJ, 1999. ISBN 0139754830.

Refer to Chapter 12, "Introduction to Routing."

 Firewall architectures: www.invir.com/int-sec-firearc.html

 Introduction to the Internet and Internet security: csrc.nist.gov/publications/nistpubs/800-10/node1.html

 IP in IP Tunneling (RFC 1853): www.faqs.org/rfcs/rfc1853.html

VLAN information: net21.ucdavis.edu/newvlan.htm

Intrusion Detection and Security Baselines

Terms you'll need to understand:

✓ Intrusion
✓ Misuse
✓ Knowledge-based IDS
✓ Behavior-based IDS
✓ Network-based IDS
✓ Host-based IDS
✓ Honeypot
✓ Deflection
✓ Countermeasures
✓ Baseline
✓ Hardening

Techniques you'll need to master:

✓ Understanding the use of host- and network-based IDS solutions and how they may be used together to secure a network
✓ Understanding the purpose behind establishing security baselines
✓ Recognizing common considerations in planning for operating system, network, and application hardening

To secure a network, it is important to identify the normal operating parameters and be able to identify atypical variations from this baseline operational level. The first step toward minimizing the potential damage that may result from unauthorized access attempts is the detection and identification of an unauthorized intrusion.

Intrusion detection requires a detailed understanding of all operational aspects of the network, along with a means to identify variations and bring these changes to the attention of the proper responsible parties. In this chapter, we will examine several forms of intrusion-detection solutions and review the requirements for establishing reasonable baseline standards.

Intrusion Detection

Although it is possible for human monitoring to identify real-time intrusion events within small, tightly controlled networks, it is more likely that a human administrator will monitor alerts and notifications generated by intrusion-detection systems (IDSs). These software and hardware agents can monitor network traffic for patterns that may indicate an attempt at intrusion, called an *attack signature*, or can monitor server-side logs for improper activity or unauthorized access.

Intrusion generally refers to unauthorized access by outside parties, whereas *misuse* is typically used to refer to unauthorized access by internal parties.

Methods of Intrusion Detection

Intrusion detection may be managed by two basic methods: *knowledge-based* and *behavior-based detection*. Knowledge-based detection relies on the identification of known attack signatures and events that should never occur within a network. Behavior-based detection involves the use of established usage patterns and baseline operation to identify variations that may pinpoint unauthorized access attempts.

Knowledge-Based IDS

The most common form of IDS detection involves knowledge-based identification of improper, unauthorized, or incorrect access and use of network resources. The identification of known attack signatures allows for few false alarms—a known attack pattern is almost always a good sign of a danger to the network. Because the signature identifies a known method of attack, you can use detailed planning to counter and recover from the attack.

Internet Control Message Protocol (ICMP) abuse and port scans represent known attack signatures. The Ping utility uses ICMP and is often used as a probing utility prior to an attack or may be the attack itself. If a host is being bombarded with ICMP echo requests or other ICMP traffic, this behavior should set off the IDS. Port scans are a more devious form of attack/reconnaissance used to discover information about a system. Port scanning is not an attack but is often a precursor to such activity. Port scans can be sequential, starting with port 1 and scanning to port 65535, or random. A knowledge-based IDS should recognize either type of scan and send an alert.

Knowledge-based IDS may also monitor for patterns of access that have been established as never being appropriate within the monitored network (for example, communications directed at common ports used by services, such as unauthorized FTP or Web servers running on local systems).

Knowledge-based IDS has several limitations, including the following:

➤ The maintenance of the knowledge library to include newly identified signatures can become a complex and time-consuming task.

➤ Knowledge-based detection of internal misuse is difficult because most misuse involves an improper utilization of a normal form of access or privilege.

➤ As new exploits are identified, it will take some time before an identified signature for the attack can be prepared and distributed. During this time, knowledge-based IDS cannot identify attacks of the new type.

➤ Knowledge-based IDS is closely tied to the technologies used within a particular network. As new technologies are integrated, or evolutionary changes are made to the network environment, knowledge-based systems may be unable to provide support for all potential avenues of attack created by the changes.

Behavior-Based IDS

One of the most common workstation-level compromise-detection methods involves a user noticing an unusual pattern of behavior, such as a continually operating hard drive or a significantly slowed level of performance. The ability to detect anomalies from normal patterns of operation makes it possible to identify new threats that may bypass knowledge-based IDS. Highly secure environments may use complex patterns of behavior analysis, in some cases, learning individual usage patterns of each user profile so that variations can be identified.

Here are some common features of behavior-based IDS solutions:

➤ They can identify new forms of vulnerability.

➤ They are more flexible as networks evolve.

➤ They can be used to identify internal misuse through the recognition of actions outside of the normal patterns of access or authorized events outside of normal profile usage, such as the access of protected files during off-business hours.

Although more flexible than knowledge-based IDS, behavior-based detection has several limitations, including the following:

➤ The most common drawback to behavior-based IDS is the high incidence of false alarms. Because anything falling outside of the established behavior profile is considered a potential sign of attack, any action that varies from the norm may generate an alert.

➤ Behavior profiles must be regularly updated to include changes in technology, changes in network configuration, and changes to business practices that may affect the normal order of operations. In systems that maintain detailed user access profiles, even a simple promotion within the business structure might require administrative action to update the usage profile of the user involved.

➤ Because of the need for periodic updates to behavior profiles, behavior-based IDS might not provide identification of threats during the update cycle and may even identify an ongoing attack pattern as part of the normal pattern of use, thus creating a potential area for later exploitation.

Intrusion-Detection Sources

Whether knowledge based or behavior based, intrusion detection relies in the capability to monitor activity, identify potential risks, and alert the appropriate responsible parties. Monitoring may be performed on the network itself or on a host system, based on the security needs mandated by business requirements.

Network-Based IDS

Network-based IDS solutions monitor all network traffic to identify signatures within the network packets that may indicate an attack. The types of signatures include the following:

➤ *String signatures*—Identify text strings used in common attacks, such as the code transmitted by Code Red–infected systems.

➤ *Port signatures*—Used to identify traffic directed to ports of common services not running on the identified host as well as ports used by well-known exploits such as the Blade Runner and SubSeven Trojan horse services.

➤ *Header signatures*—Used to detect the presence of conflicting or inappropriate packet headers, such as the SYN packets that might indicate a flood attack.

Figure 7.1 details a simplified network-based IDS solution monitoring traffic that passes through an organization's firewall to the systems within the protected network.

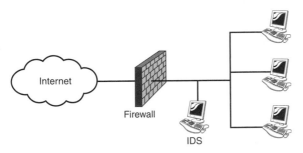

Figure 7.1 An idealized example displaying a network-based IDS solution.

 During normal operation, a network interface card (NIC) will only register packets that are directed to its address. To capture raw packets directed at any host within a network, you must have a NIC that supports promiscuous mode.

Table 7.1 details some of the strengths of network-based IDS solutions.

Table 7.1 Strengths of Network-Based IDS	
Strength	**Description**
Low cost of ownership	Because a single network-based IDS can be used to monitor traffic passing through the entire network, the number of systems required remains small while providing adequate network coverage.
Pre-host detection	Network-based IDS solutions can be used to detect attacks that cannot be easily identified by the host, such as denial of service (DoS) attacks that target the host's ability to connect to a network. An IDS placed outside of a firewall or within a DMZ can identify patterns of failed attempts as well as successful intrusions.
Real-time detection	Network-based IDS solutions analyze network traffic as it occurs, allowing alerts to be generated while the attack is underway. This also makes it harder for an attacker to cover his tracks, because network monitoring can capture not only the packets detailing the access attempt, but also those that detail the attacker's attempts to remove evidence of the attack.
Environment independent	Because network-based IDS solutions analyze raw data packets, they are more adaptable to a wide variety of network and technology configurations.

Host-Based IDS

Host-based IDS solutions involve processes running on a host that monitor event and applications logs, port access, and other running processes in order to identify signatures or behaviors that indicate an attack or unauthorized access attempt. Some host-based IDS solutions involve the deployment of individual client applications on each host, which relay their findings to a central IDS server responsible for compiling the data to identify distributed trends.

Table 7.2 details some of the strengths of host-based IDS solutions.

Table 7.2 Strengths of Host-Based IDS	
Strength	**Description**
Low number of false positives	Because host-based IDS solutions analyze logged events, both success and failure events may be monitored and alerts generated only after a proper threshold has been achieved.

(continued)

Table 7.2 Strengths of Host-Based IDS *(continued)*	
Strength	**Description**
Auditing change monitoring	Host-based IDS solutions can monitor individual processes on each host, including changes to the auditing process itself.
Non-network attack detection	Host-based IDS solutions can be used to monitor events on standalone systems, including access from the keyboard.
Encrypted communication monitoring	Some attacks use encrypted or encapsulated data communications, bypassing network-based IDS.
Cost savings by directed monitoring	Unlike network-based IDSs, which must observe all data traffic across the monitored network, host-based solutions require no additional hardware purchasing and may be deployed on just those systems that require ID.
Single-point monitoring	Within large, switched networks, network-based IDS solutions may be inadvertently or purposefully bypassed by using a secondary access route. Host-based IDS solutions are not limited to a particular communications path for detection.

Layered Intrusion Detection

In most network-deployment scenarios, a layered intrusion-detection approach is required to provide protection against all forms of attack. Through user training, host-based and network-based IDS solutions, and the hardening of services and systems to exclude known vulnerabilities, a unified solution to many developing security requirements can be formed.

Honeypots and Honeynets

Honeypots are systems configured to simulate one or more services within an organization's network, and they are intentionally left exposed to network access as a means to attract would-be attackers. For instance, a honeypot can be used to identify the level of aggressive attention directed at a network should an administrator suspect an attack or potential attack. Honeypots are also used to study and learn from an attacker's common methods of attack. When an attacker accesses a honeypot system, her activities are logged and monitored by other processes so that the attacker's actions and methods may be later reviewed in detail. The honeypot system also serves to distract the attacker from valid network resources. This is important information that is used for legal action as well as to gain knowledge of method attacks that can be used in later attack situations.

Honeynets are collections of honeypot systems interconnected to create functional-appearing networks that may be used to study an attacker's behavior within the network. Honeynets use specialized software agents that create normal-seeming network traffic. Honeynets and honeypots can be used to distract attackers from valid network content, to study the attacker's methods, and to provide an early warning of attack attempts that may later be waged against the more secured portions of the network. See www.honeynet.org for more information.

An exposed server that provides public access to a critical service, such as a Web or email server, may be configured to isolate it from an organization's network and to report attack attempts to the network administrator. Such an isolated server is referred to as a *bastion host*, named for the isolated towers that were used to provide castles of advanced notice of pending assault.

Incident Handling

When IDS solutions alert responsible parties of a successful or ongoing attack attempt, it is important to have previously documented plans for responding to incidents. Several forms of response can be derived from the analysis and identification of attack attempts, including the following:

➤ *Deflection*—Redirecting or misdirecting an attacker to secured segmented areas, allowing them to assume they have been successful while preventing access to secured resources. Honeypots and honeynets are examples of deflection solutions.

➤ *Countermeasures*—Intrusion Countermeasure Equipment (ICE) can be used in some scenarios to provide automatic response in the event of intrusion detection. ICE agents may automatically lock down a network or increase access security to critical resources in the event of an alert; however, false positives could create problems for legitimate users in such a scenario.

➤ *Detection*—After identification of an attack, forensic analysis of affected systems can yield information about the identity of the attacker. This information may then be used to direct the attention of the proper authorities to the source of the attack.

Post-attack analysis of successful intrusions should be used to harden systems against further intrusion attempts that use the same methodology. Via honeypot systems, planning can be used to configure access restrictions as well as modify the network to make it appear less desirable to potential attackers.

Security Baselines

To identify atypical behavior, it is necessary first to identify typical behavior of both network and application processes. The measure of normal activity is known as a *baseline*. Baselines must be regularly updated as networks and deployed technologies change. What was once a normal pattern of behavior is likely to change over time.

It is important that solid, closely watched security monitoring occur while you're establishing a baseline for network and application performance. Security monitoring during baselining is important because an ongoing attack during the baselining process could be registered as the normal level of activity. Obviously, this type of situation, as well as any other situation that will skew baseline readings, must be thought out and averted to establish true baseline data.

When establishing operational baselines, it is important to harden all technologies against as many possible avenues of attack as possible. The three basic areas of hardening are as follows:

➤ *Operating system*—Security of the operating system, including domain architecture and user logon access planning

➤ *Network*—Security of the network through hardware implementations, such as firewall and NAT devices, as well as logical security involving access control over distributed resources

➤ *Application*—Security of applications and services, such as Domain Name Service (DNS), Dynamic Host Configuration Protocol (DHCP), and Web servers, as well as client-side user applications and integration suites

Operating System Hardening

Hardening of the operating system includes planning against both accidental and directed attacks, such as the use of fault-tolerant hardware and software solutions. Additionally, it is important to implement an effective system for file-level security, including encrypted file support and secured file system selection that allows for the proper level of access control. For example,

Microsoft's New Technology File System (NTFS) allows for file-level access control, whereas most File Allocation Table–based (FAT-based) systems allow for only share-level access control.

It is also imperative to include regular update reviews for all deployed operating systems in order to address newly identified exploits and apply security hotfixes, patches, and service packs. Many automated attacks use common vulnerabilities, often ones for which patches and hotfixes are already available. Failure to include planning for application updates on a regular basis, along with update auditing, can result in an unsecure solution that provides an attacker access to additional resources throughout an organization's network.

IP Security (IPSec) and PKI implementations must also be properly configured and updated to maintain key and ticket stores. Some systems may be hardened to include specific levels of access (for example, hardening a system to gain the C2 security rating required by many government deployment scenarios).

Operating system hardening also includes configuring log files and auditing, changing default administrator account names and default passwords, and instituting account lockout and password policies to guarantee strong passwords that will be resistant to brute-force attacks.

Network Hardening

Network hardening involves access restrictions to network shares and services, updates to security hardware and software, and disabling unnecessary protocol support and services.

Restricting Access to the Network

Firewall and Network Address Translation (NAT) software and hardware solutions provide the first layer of defense against unauthorized access attempts.

Mapping avenues of access is also critical in hardening a network. This process is a part of the site survey that should be performed for any network, especially those that involve public areas where a simple connection through a workstation might link the protected internal network directly to a public broadband connection.

Wireless networks also create significant avenues for unsecure access to a secured network. A user who configures a PC card on her workstation to allow for the synchronization of her 802.11-compliant wireless PDA may have inadvertently bypassed all security surrounding an organization's network.

 A popular pastime for potential attackers involves the process of *war-driving*, which involves driving around with a Wi-Fi device configured in promiscuous mode to identify open wireless access points to the Internet in public areas or target locations. See Chapter 4, "Communication Security," for more information.

If a centralized access control system is used, such as those found in Windows and Novell networks, resource access and restrictions may be assigned to groups, and users can be granted membership to those groups. Properly configured access control lists help provide resource access to authorized parties and also limit potential avenues of unauthorized access.

Updating Security Hardware and Software

As with operating system hardening, default configurations and passwords must be changed in network hardware such as routers and managed network devices. Routing hardware must also be maintained in a current state by regularly reviewing applied firmware updates and applying updates that are required for the network configuration and hardware solutions used.

Security software packages need to be updated with as much vigilance as hardware. New tools, better protection, and up-to-date virus and attack definition files become available on almost a daily basis. A regular schedule should be identified and followed for proper update procedures for both security hardware and software.

Disabling Unnecessary Protocols and Services

Leaving protocols and services open and unconfigured when they are not necessary for your network can be a dangerous situation. When you install items on your network, we suggest that you do not accept default configurations because the defaults offered may not meet the business and security requirements of your network.

For example, in a homogenous network such as an all–Windows 2000 network, it might be possible to terminate support for AppleTalk, Internetwork Packet Exchange/Sequenced Packet Exchange (IPX/SPX), or other forms of unused network communications protocols. Because you don't have any Macintosh clients or Novell systems on the network, you don't need the services and protocols associated with these systems. By eliminating services such as these, you are closing holes that can potentially be exploited by attackers.

Application Hardening

Each application and service that may be installed within a network must also be considered when planning security for an organization. Applications must be maintained in an updated state through the regular review of hotfixes, patches, and service packs. Many applications, such as antivirus software, require regular updates to provide protection against newly emerging threats. Default application-administration accounts, standard passwords, and common services installed by default should also be reviewed and changed or disabled as required.

Web Servers

Access restrictions to Internet and intranet Web services may be required to ensure proper authentication for nonpublic sites, whereas anonymous access may be required for other sites. Access control may be accomplished at the operating system or application level, with many sites requiring regular updates of Secure Sockets Layer (SSL) certifications for secured communications.

Regular log review is critical for Web servers to ensure that submitted URL values are not used to exploit unpatched buffer overruns or other forms of common exploits. Many Web servers may also include security add-ins, provided to restrict those URLs that may be meaningfully submitted, filtering out any that do not meet the defined criteria. Microsoft's URLScan for the Internet Information Services (IIS) Web service is one such filtering add-in.

Email Services

Email servers require network access to transfer Simple Mail Transfer Protocol (SMTP) traffic. Email is often used to transport executable agents, including Trojan horses and other forms of viral software. Email servers may require transport through firewall solutions to allow remote Post Office Protocol version 3 (POP3) or Internet Message Access Protocol (IMAP) access, or they may require integration with VPN solutions to provide secure connections for remote users. User authentication is also of key importance, especially when email and calendaring solutions allow delegated review and manipulation. Inadequate hardware may be attacked through mail bombs and other types of attacks meant to overwhelm the server's ability to transact email messages.

FTP Servers

File Transfer Protocol (FTP) servers are used to provide file upload and download capabilities to users, whether through anonymous or authenticated connections. Because of limitations in the protocol, unless an encapsulation scheme is used between the client and host systems, the logon and password details are passed in cleartext and may be subject to interception via packet sniffing. Unauthorized parties may also use FTP servers that allow anonymous access to share files of questionable or undesirable content while also consuming network bandwidth and server processing resources.

DNS Servers

DNS servers are responsible for name resolution and may be subject to many forms of attack, including attempts at denial of service (DoS) attacks intended to prevent proper name resolution for key corporate holdings. Hardening DNS server solutions should include planning for redundant hardware and software solutions, along with regular backups to protect against loss of name registrations. Technologies that allow dynamic updates must also include access control and authentication to ensure that registrations are valid.

NNTP Servers

Network News Transfer Protocol (NNTP) servers provide user access to newsgroup posts and share many of the same security considerations that email servers generate. Access control for newsgroups may be somewhat more complex, with moderated groups allowing public anonymous submission with authenticated access required for post approval. Heavily loaded servers may be attacked to perform a denial of service, and detailed user account information in public newsgroup posting stores, such as those of the AOL and MSN communities, may be exploited in many ways.

File and Print Servers

User file storage solutions often come under attack when unauthorized access attempts provide avenues for manipulation. Files may be corrupted, modified, deleted, or manipulated in many ways. Access control through proper restriction of file and share permissions is necessary, coupled with access auditing and user-authentication schemes to ensure proper access. Removal of default access permissions, such as the automatic granting of Allow access to the Everyone group in Windows systems, must be done before network file shares can be secured.

Distributed file system and encrypted file system solutions may require bandwidth planning and proper user authentication to allow even basic access. Security planning for these solutions may also include placing user-access authenticating servers close to the file servers to decrease delays created by authentication traffic.

Print servers also pose several risks, including possible security breaches in the event that unauthorized parties may access cached print jobs. Denial of service attacks may be used to disrupt normal methods of business. Network connected printers require authentication of access to prevent attackers from generating printed memos, invoices, or any other manner of printed materials as desired.

DHCP Servers

DHCP servers share many of the same security problems associated with other network services, such as DNS servers. DHCP servers may be overwhelmed by lease requests if bandwidth and processing resources are insufficient. This can be worsened by the use of DHCP proxy systems relaying lease requests from widely deployed subnets. Scope address pools may also be overcome if lease duration is insufficient, and short lease duration may increase request traffic. If the operating system in use does not support DHCP server authentication, attackers may also configure their own DHCP servers within a subnet, taking control of the network settings of clients obtaining leases from the rogue servers. Planning for DHCP security must include regular review of networks for unauthorized DHCP servers.

Data Repositories

Data repositories of any type may require specialized security considerations based on the following:

> The bandwidth and processing resource requirements that are needed to prevent denial of service attacks

> The removal of default password and administration accounts (such as the SQL default "sa" account)

> Security of replication traffic to prevent exposure of access credentials to packet sniffing

Placement of authentication, name resolution, and data stores within secured and partially secured zones, such as an organization's DMZ, may require the use of secured VPN connections or the establishment of highly secured bastion hosts. Role-Based Access Control (RBAC) may be used to improve security, and the elimination of unneeded connection libraries and character sets may help to alleviate common exploits.

Practice Questions

Question 1

> Which of the following IDS forms uses known attack signatures to identify unauthorized access attempts?
>
> ○ A. Knowledge-based IDS
> ○ B. Behavior-based IDS
> ○ C. Network-based IDS
> ○ D. Host-based IDS

Answer A is correct. Knowledge-based IDS solutions use known attack signatures to identify network attacks. Answer B is incorrect because behavior-based IDS solutions measure access patterns against known baselines to identify attacks. Answers C and D are incorrect because either might include knowledge-based or behavior-based IDS solutions, so neither one is the best answer here.

Question 2

> Which of the following IDS forms is subject to common false positive attack indications?
>
> ○ A. Knowledge-based IDS
> ○ B. Behavior-based IDS
> ○ C. Network-based IDS
> ○ D. Host-based IDS

Answer B is correct. Behavior-based IDS solutions measure patterns of access against known security baselines. As a result, any variation from the previous baseline may be detected as a possible attack. Answer A is incorrect because knowledge-based IDS solutions use known attack signatures to identify attacks and therefore are not often subject to false positives. Answers C and D are incorrect because either might include knowledge-based or behavior-based IDS solutions, so neither one is the best answer here.

Question 3

> Which type of IDS is slow to identify new forms of attack?
> ○ A. Network-based IDS
> ○ B. Knowledge-based IDS
> ○ C. Client-based IDS
> ○ D. Behavior-based IDS

Answer B is correct. Because knowledge-based IDS solutions require identification of known attack signatures, new forms of attack may go undetected until the new attack signatures are added to the IDS's library. Answers A and C are incorrect because they are IDS configurations, not behaviors. Answer D is incorrect because behavior-based IDS looks for anything out of the baseline norm. New attacks are likely to be outside the norm, so behavior-based IDS finds these fairly easily.

Question 4

> Which of the following IDS forms are relatively platform independent? [Choose the two best answers.]
> ❑ A. Knowledge-based IDS
> ❑ B. Behavior-based IDS
> ❑ C. Network-based IDS
> ❑ D. Host-based IDS

Answers B and C are correct. Behavior-based IDS solutions and network-based solutions operate on patterns of access and data packet transfer to identify attacks. As a result, both are able to evolve to meet changes in the network technologies in use. Answers A and D are incorrect because knowledge-based IDS solutions must be able to identify known attack signatures directed at the protected technologies, whereas host-based IDS solutions involve client agents running on the monitored hosts; therefore, both are strongly affected by changes to the protected technologies.

Question 5

> You have deployed a packet-monitoring system to sniff packets passing through
> your organization's DMZ. Which of the following types of IDS is this solution?
>
> ○ A. Knowledge-based IDS
>
> ○ B. Behavior-based IDS
>
> ○ C. Network-based IDS
>
> ○ D. Host-based IDS

Answer C is correct. This is a common network-based IDS solution, where
packet data is monitored for unauthorized access patterns. Answers A and B
are incorrect because the proposed solution might use either knowledge-
based or behavior-based IDS, so neither is the best answer here. Answer D
is incorrect because a host-based IDS solution would utilize client agents
operating on the monitored hosts rather than sniffing the network traffic.

Question 6

> You have installed a custom monitoring service on a Web server that reviews
> Web service logs to watch for the URLs used by the Code Red worm to propa-
> gate itself. When this custom service detects an attack, it raises an alert via
> email. Which of the following types of IDS is this solution? [Choose the two best
> answers.]
>
> ❑ A. Knowledge-based IDS
>
> ❑ B. Behavior-based IDS
>
> ❑ C. Network-based IDS
>
> ❑ D. Host-based IDS

Answers A and D are correct. This scenario describes a host-based solution
identifying a known attack signature. Answer B is incorrect because no
baselining is required for this solution. Answer C is incorrect because the
agent does not attempt to capture packet data—it only reviews the Web service logs on the local system.

Question 7

Which of the following terms describes a host configured to expose a specific service to a public network while hardening all other resource access to restrict access within an organization's secure network?

- ○ A. Honeypot
- ○ B. Honeynet
- ○ C. Bastion
- ○ D. War-driving

Answer C is correct. A bastion host exposes a service or port while protecting against other forms of exploit. Answers A and B are incorrect because honeypots and honeynets are used to distract attackers or to monitor their access methods. Answer D is incorrect because the process of war-driving involves driving around with a wireless card in promiscuous mode, attempting to detect open wireless access points.

Question 8

Monitoring a network during the creation of a new performance baseline is critical because _____.

- ○ A. new systems being added may generate false positives
- ○ B. false positives are less likely to occur later if monitoring is on during the baseline process
- ○ C. you must ensure that an attack is not made part of the baseline
- ○ D. monitoring allows you to set the traffic patterns that are considered normal

Answer C is correct. It is most important to monitor for attacks during regular baseline update cycles to avoid an attacker's actions being considered typical behavior within the network. Adding new workstations won't generate false positives; therefore, answer A is incorrect. The IDS is looking at the network traffic, but the monitoring station is not doing anything; therefore, answer B is incorrect. Setting the baselines is the job of the IDS, and a monitoring application would have nothing to do with the IDS baseline; therefore, answer D is incorrect.

Question 9

> You have configured your Web server to use Windows NTFS partitions and the Microsoft System Update Service (SUS) to regularly apply new Windows 2000 hotfixes and patches. Which of the following forms of hardening are specified in this solution?
>
> ○ A. Application
> ○ B. Baseline
> ○ C. Operating system
> ○ D. Network

Answer C is correct. The tasks of selecting a secure file system, such as NTFS, and regularly applying operating system updates fall within the considerations for operating system hardening. Answer A is incorrect because application hardening involves the security of user applications and services. Answer B is incorrect because a baseline establishes the normal operating levels of a network and is not itself hardened. Answer D is incorrect because network hardening involves the security of network access.

Question 10

> Which of the following servers may be overcome by a denial of service (DoS) type of attack? [Choose the best answers.]
>
> ❏ A. Web servers
> ❏ B. FTP servers
> ❏ C. DNS servers
> ❏ D. NNTP servers

Answers A, B, C, and D, are correct. All these services may be overcome by a DoS-style attack if the attacker can overload the available processing and bandwidth resources available to each service. When multiple services are loaded onto a single system, this problem can be compounded.

Need to Know More?

 Shipley, Greg. *Maximum Security, Third Edition*. Sams Publishing. Indianapolis, IN. 2001. ISBN 0-672-31871-7.

 The World Wide Web Security FAQ: `www.w3.org/Security/Faq/`

 SANS Information Security Reading Room: `rr.sans.org/index.php`

 CERT Incident Reporting Guidelines: `www.cert.org/tech_tips/incident_reporting.html`

Basics of Cryptography

Terms you'll need to understand:

✓ Cryptography
✓ Algorithm
✓ Asymmetric key
✓ Symmetric key
✓ Block cipher
✓ Stream cipher
✓ Confidentiality
✓ Integrity
✓ Authentication
✓ Digital signature
✓ Nonrepudiation
✓ Private key
✓ Public key
✓ Hashing
✓ Public Key Infrastructure (PKI)
✓ CertIflcate Authority (CA)
✓ Certificate Revocation List (CRL)
✓ Digital certificates
✓ Certificate policies
✓ Certificate Practice Statement (CPS)

Techniques you'll need to master:

✓ Identifying and understanding cryptography algorithms and how they can be used to help improve security
✓ Understanding the concepts of using cryptography in a secure environment
✓ Understanding the role and components of Public Key Infrastructure as well as the roles and policies in creating a PKI

A cryptosystem or cipher system provides a method for protecting information by encrypting (disguising) it into a format that can be read only by authorized systems or individuals. The use and creation of such systems is called *cryptography*—often considered both an art and a science.

Cryptography dates back to the ancient Assyrians and Egyptians. In the beginning, the systems of cryptography were manually performed, but during the twentieth century, mechanical cryptography was born. The cryptography that is the focus of this chapter as well as the exam is modern cryptography, which began with the advent of the computer.

Recently, modern cryptography has become increasingly important and ubiquitous. There have been growing concerns over the security of sensitive data with the growing capabilities of hackers and the proliferation of business networks connected to the Internet. One very practical method of securing this data is through the use of cryptography in the form of *encryption algorithms* applied to data that is passed around networks or even stored on hard drives.

This chapter discusses the concepts of cryptography as well as many popular encryption methods. You will begin to understand how cryptography can be used as a tool to protect and authenticate all types of information, as well as protect the computers and networks in information security systems.

Algorithms

In broad terms, an *algorithm* is a step-by-step procedure for solving a problem. For example, suppose your problem is that you are unable to bake cookies that are exactly like Grandma's. What is needed is an algorithm—her secret recipe. With the recipe card in hand, you have the ingredients and the sequence of events that are required to achieve the desired result.

In encryption, the algorithm is what is used to define how the encryption will be applied, how the data held inside is encrypted, and how the data is unencrypted on the other end. Think of the algorithm as the guidebook to how any particular encryption method is applied.

Most people wouldn't understand or don't really need to know the internal details of how an encryption algorithm works. However, knowing the fundamental design of any given encryption algorithm can provide insights into how it will perform as well as how secure it is. With this information you can select which algorithm is going to do the job for your given situation, because some algorithms are better suited than others, given different tasks.

The three different types of cryptographic algorithms include the following:

➤ Hashing algorithms

➤ Symmetric key-based algorithms

➤ Asymmetric key-based algorithms

Each of these algorithms is discussed in further detail in the following sections.

Hashing

A *hash* is a generated summary from a mathematical rule or algorithm and is used to verify the integrity of files. In other words, hashing algorithms are not encryption methods but provide added security to systems to ensure that data has not been tampered with.

Keep in mind that hashing is one-way. Although you can create a hash from a document, you cannot re-create the document from the hash. If this all sounds confusing, the following example should help clear things up. Suppose you want to send an email to a friend, and you also want to ensure that during transit, it cannot be read or unknowingly altered. You would first utilize software that generates a hash (a summary or tag) of the message to accompany the email and then encrypt both the hash and the message. After receiving the email, the recipient's software decrypts the message and the hash and then produces another hash from the received email. The two hashes are then compared, and a match would indicate that the message was not tampered with. Alternatively, any change in the original message would produce a change in the hash on the recipient's machine.

Common hash algorithms include the following:

➤ *Secure Hash Algorithm (SHA, SHA-1)*—Hash algorithms pioneered by the National Security Agency and widely used in the U.S. government. SHA-1 can generate a 160-bit hash from any variable-length string of data, making it very secure but also resource intensive.

➤ *Message Digest Series Algorithm (MD2, MD4, MD5)*—A series of encryption algorithms designed to be fast, simple, and secure. The MD series generates a hash of up to 128-bit strength out of any length of data.

Both SHA and the MD series are similar in design; however, keep in mind that because of the higher bit strength of the SHA-1 algorithm, it will be in the range of 20% to 30% slower to process than the MD family of algorithms.

Hashing within security systems is used to ensure that transmitted messages have not been altered. Be able to identify the common types of hash algorithms.

As you can determine from the different versions of Message Digest listed, there has been some refinements to the algorithm over the years. The most commonly used are MD4 and MD5, which are both faster than MD2. Both MD4 and MD5 produce a 128-bit hash; however, the hash used in MD4 was successfully broken a while back. This spurred the development of MD5, which features a redeveloped cipher that makes it stronger than the MD4 algorithm while still featuring a 128-bit hash. Although MD5 is the more common hashing algorithm, SHA-1 is quickly being embraced by those outside of the U.S. government.

It's worth noting that an alternative to the hash algorithms just mentioned is RIPEMD-160, which has been placed in the public domain by its designers. RIPEMD-160 is a cryptographic hash function designed to replace MD4 and MD5. More information on this algorithm can be found on the RIPEMD-160 home page at **www.esat. kuleuven.ac.be/~bosselae/ripemd160.html**.

Symmetric Algorithms

Symmetric key algorithms and *asymmetric key algorithms* (discussed in the following section) are the two fundamental types of encryption algorithms. Symmetric key algorithms use the same key to encrypt and decrypt a message. A drawback of this particular situation is that every party participating in communications must have the exact same key on the other end to compare the information. If the key is compromised at any point, it is impossible to guarantee that a secure connection has commenced. Additionally, to use symmetric key algorithms, two parties must first exchange the encryption key, which can present difficulties in doing so securely. Despite these drawbacks however, symmetric key algorithms are easier to implement over other methods and are typically faster.

Discussions of cryptography use the term *key*, which does not denote the traditional metal object used with a physical locking device. Instead, the term is analogous, and a cryptography key actually describes a string of bits used for encrypting and decrypting data. These keys can also be thought of as a password or table.

Symmetric key algorithms are often referred to as *secret key algorithms* and *private key algorithms*.

Even given the possible risks involved with symmetric key encryption, the method is used quite often in today's society mainly for its simplicity and ease of deployment. On top of that, it is generally considered very strong as long as the source and destination that house the key information are kept secure.

Symmetric key encryption can be divided into the following two categories:

➤ *Block ciphers* take a number of bits (usually 64 bits) and encrypt them as a single unit.

➤ *Stream ciphers* encrypt a single bit of plaintext at a time—that is, each binary digit in a data stream is encrypted one bit at a time.

It's difficult to discuss encryption methods without using the term *bit strength*. This term is used to indicate the strength of a particular encryption method or hash. The longer the hash used (measured in bits), the more secure it is. In addition, the more processing time the hash takes to generate, the larger it will be when passing information over a network. A strong encryption is typically 128 bit. Before recent changes to encryption export controls in 2002, anything this level or higher typically saw limited use outside of North America, with exceptions for some trusted countries around the world. The recently relaxed laws however still limit the export of software using strong encryption to specific foreign countries that perhaps may have a more nefarious use for keeping data or communications locked away.

A multitude of symmetric key algorithms are used today. The more commonly used algorithms include the following:

➤ *Data Encryption Standard (DES)*—DES was adopted for use by the National Institute of Standards and Technology in 1977. DES is a block cipher that uses a 56-bit key on each 64-bit chuck of data, and it is limited in use because of its relatively short key length limit.

➤ *Triple Data Encryption Standard (3DES)*—3DES, also known as *Triple-DES*, dramatically improves upon DES by using the DES algorithm three times with three distinct keys. This provides a total bit strength of 168 bits.

➤ *Advanced Encryption Standard (AES)*—Also called *Rijndael*, this block cipher has been chosen by the National Institute of Standards and Technology (NIST) to be the successor to DES as the United States' new Advanced Encryption Standard. AES is similar to DES in that it can create keys from 128-bit to 256-bit in length and can perform the encryption and decryption of data up to 128-bit chunks of data (in comparison to the 64-bit chunks of the original DES). And similar to 3DES, the data is passed through three layers, each with a specific task, such as generating random keys based on the data and the bit strength being used. The data is then encrypted with the keys through multiple encryption rounds, like DES, and then the final key is applied to the data.

➤ *Blowfish Encryption Algorithm*—Blowfish is a block cipher that can encrypt using any size chunk of data; in addition, Blowfish can also perform encryption with any length encryption key up to 448 bits, making it a very flexible and secure symmetric encryption algorithm.

➤ *International Data Encryption Algorithm (IDEA)*— Originally created around 1990, IDEA went through several variations before arriving at its final acronym. Originally called the Proposed Encryption Standard (PES), it was later renamed and refined to the Improved Proposed Encryption Standard (IPES). After even more refinement, it was ultimately named IDEA in 1992. In its final form, IDEA is capable of encrypting 64-bit blocks of data at a time and uses a 128-bit strength encryption key. The use of IDEA has been limited primarily because of software patents on the algorithm, which many feel hinder development, research, and education.

➤ *Rivest Cipher (RC2, RC4, RC5, RC6)*—As far as widely available commercial applications go, the Rivest Cipher (RC) series of encryption algorithms comprises the most commonly implemented ciphers for encryption security. The RC series (RC2, RC4, RC5, and RC6) are all similarly designed; yet, each version has its own take on the block cipher design, as well as its own capabilities.

Table 8.1 provides a comparison of the algorithms just mentioned, as well as some lesser-known ones. Additionally, notice the differences between the various types of RC algorithms.

Be sure you understand the differences between various symmetric key algorithms. Note that these are symmetric, and not asymmetric, and be sure to differentiate between stream ciphers and block ciphers.

Table 8.1 A Comparison of Symmetric Key Algorithms		
Algorithm	**Cipher Type**	**Key Length**
DES	Block	56 bits
Triple-DES (3DES)	Block	168 bits
AES (Rijndael)	Block	128–256 bits
Blowfish	Block	1–448 bits
IDEA	Block	128 bits
RC2	Block	1–2048 bits
RC4	Stream	1–2048 bits
RC5	Block	128–256 bits
RC6	Block	128–256 bits
CAST	Block	128–256 bits
MARS	Block	128–256 bits
Serpent	Block	128–256 bits
Twofish	Block	128–256 bits

Asymmetric Algorithms

As mentioned earlier in this chapter, two major types of algorithms are used today: symmetric, which has one key kept private at all times, and asymmetric, which has two keys (a public one and a private one). Both the public key and private key are mathematically related, yet it is computationally infeasible to try and determine the private key based on the information from the public key. In the asymmetric algorithm, there is always a public key that is made available to whoever is going to encrypt the data sent to the holder of the private key. The private key is maintained on the host system or application. Quite often, the public encryption key is made available in a number of fashions, such as via email or centralized servers that host a pseudo address book of published public encryption keys. Figure 8.1 illustrates the asymmetric encryption process.

Asymmetric algorithms are often referred to as *public key algorithms* because of their use of the public key as the focal point for the algorithm.

As an example of asymmetric encryption, we'll use the secure exchange of an email. When someone wants to send a secure email to another, he or she obtains the target user's public encryption key and encrypts the message using this key. Because the message can only be unencrypted with the private key, only the target user can read the information held within. Ideally, for this system to work well, everyone should have access to everyone else's public keys.

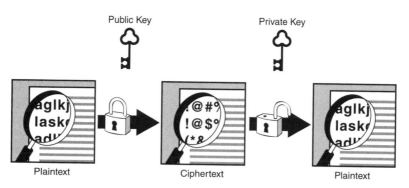

Public Key   Private Key

Plaintext   Ciphertext   Plaintext

Figure 8.1 An example of asymmetric encryption.

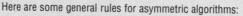

TIP

Here are some general rules for asymmetric algorithms:

➤ The public key can never decrypt a message that it was used to encrypt.

➤ Private keys should never be able to be determined through the public key (if it is designed properly).

➤ Each key should be able to decrypt a message made with the other. For instance, if a message is encrypted with the private key, the public key should be able to decrypt it.

Wide arrays of asymmetric algorithms have been designed; however, very few have gained the widespread acceptance as seen with symmetric algorithms. Some things to keep in mind while reading about the following few asymmetric algorithms are that some have unique features, including built-in digital signatures (which you will learn more about later). Also, because of the additional computational overhead generated by using a public and private key for encryption/decryption, far more resources are required to use asymmetric algorithms.

The one environment where public key encryption has proven very useful is on networks such as the Internet. This is primarily because the public key is all that needs to be distributed. Because nothing harmful can be done with the public key, it is useful over unsecured networks where data can pass through many hands and is vulnerable to interception and abuse. Symmetric encryption works fine over the Internet as well, but the limitations on providing the key securely to everyone who requires it can be difficult. The following are some of the more popular asymmetric encryption algorithms:

> *Rivest, Shamir & Adleman Encryption Algorithm (RSA)*—RSA, named after the three men who developed it, is a well-known cryptography system used for encryption and digital signatures. The RSA key may be of any length, and it works by multiplying two large prime numbers. In addition, through other operations in the algorithm, it derives a set of numbers—one for the public key and the other for the private key.

> *Diffie-Hellman Key Exchange*—The Diffie-Hellman Key Exchange (also called *exponential key agreement*) is an early key exchange design whereby two parties, without prior arrangements, can agree upon a secret key that is known only to them. The keys are passed in a way that they are not compromised using encryption algorithms to verify that the data is arriving at its intended recipient.

> *El Gamal Encryption Algorithm*—As an extension to the Diffie-Hellman design, in 1985, Dr. El Gamal took to task the design requirements of utilizing encryption to develop digital signatures. Rather than focusing just on the key design, El Gamal designed a complete public key encryption algorithm using some of the key exchange elements from Diffie-Hellman and incorporating encryption on those keys. The resultant encrypted keys reinforced the security and authenticity of public key encryption design and also helped lead to future advances in asymmetric encryption technology.

> *Elliptic Curve Cryptography (ECC)*—Elliptic Curve Cryptography (ECC) utilizes a method in which elliptic curves can be used to calculate simple but very-difficult-to-break encryption keys to use in general-purpose encryption. One of the key benefits of ECC encryption algorithms is that they have a very compact design because of the advanced mathematics involved in ECC. For instance, an ECC encryption key of 160-bit strength would, in actuality, be equal in strength to a 1024-bit RSA encryption key.

Throughout this section on different encryption algorithms, you have learned how each type performs. One thing you haven't seen yet is how bit strengths compare to each other when looking at asymmetric and symmetric algorithms in general. The following list reveals why symmetric algorithms are favored for most applications and why asymmetric algorithms are widely considered very secure but often too complex and resource intensive for every environment.

➤ 64-bit symmetric key strength equals 512-bit asymmetric key strength.

➤ 112-bit symmetric key strength equals 1792-bit asymmetric key strength.

➤ 128-bit symmetric key strength equals 2304-bit asymmetric key strength.

As you can see, there is a dramatic difference in the strength and, consequently, the overall size of asymmetric encryption keys. For most environments today, 128-bit strength is considered adequate; therefore, symmetric encryption may often suffice. If you want to simplify how you distribute keys, however, asymmetric encryption may be the better choice.

As you can imagine, you will have to look at many aspects to determine which method or combination of methods should be used. The following sections of this chapter reveal how encryption can help augment security.

Concepts of Using Cryptography

In many situations, using encryption can make a huge difference in how secure your environment is. This is true from the workstation level, to the server level, to even how data is transferred to and from your business partners. Encryption is continuously becoming more and more important. This situation is amplified when you take into account the increasing sophistication of users and available tools, as well as the propensity for mischief that these users may possess.

As it stands today, encryption still requires a lot of thought and preparation prior to implementation. More often than not, careful consideration should be given to answer many different questions, which could include the following:

➤ How will encryption affect the performance on my network as well as my servers and workstations attached to that network?

➤ In what way will my end users interact with encryption? What type of encryption will they experience on an end-user level? Will server or simply network encryption be all that is needed?

➤ What additional costs will encryption bring to my organization and, in particular, the department that manages it? Will we need additional hardware, software, and training?

➤ What real, tangible benefits will encryption bring to my organization? Can this be tempered against the costs to make encryption worthwhile?

➤ Do the business partners or other organizations we communicate with use encryption? If so, what do they use and how do we integrate with them?

➤ How will the encryption algorithm, software, and other methods we implement today scale with what we want to do tomorrow as well as the long-term IT and business goals of our organization?

As you can see from the preceding questions, a great deal of consideration and research needs to be done before you can even start to think about implementing encryption in an organization. The following subsections discuss and examine how encryption can work within environments to promote confidentiality of sensitive data, integrity of data and authentication, as well as digital signatures and access control.

Confidentiality

One of the key benefits that implementing encryption can bring to an organization is the promise of *confidentiality*. Confidentiality describes the act of limiting disclosure of private information. In fact, the ability of encryption to provide confidentiality is important to today's companies as well as to individuals in countries that restrict free speech and monitor the messages and emails sent and received over the Internet.

Like any open environment where sensitive information is shared, the most important thing to most people is keeping the information secret and not letting anyone know you are sending the data. It is not unheard of to have large corporations hire people as spies who try to capture competitors' sensitive data being transmitted on their networks as a means to gain an edge.

Now think of the individual sitting in an Internet café in a foreign country (often the only way these people can access the Internet). You have governments so afraid of what their citizens may see from the outside world that they restrict what people can see in addition to recording and monitoring what information they post. Encryption enables people to take this control away from the government. So, you can imagine that publicly available, strong encryption isn't very popular with these types of governments unless it's for their own use.

Pretty Good Privacy (PGP)

In the early 90s, the U.S. Government tried to suppress the use of Pretty Good Privacy (PGP), which was gaining popularity and exposure in the media. The government tried to force the software to be taken down and made unavailable to public consumption. (PGP is an email program that uses encryption and is available to anyone who wanted to download it within North America.)

Part of the government's argument against PGP was that it could not control the information people were sending. In cases where criminals were involved, they could use encryption and seemingly be able to hide their online activities and data from the prying eyes of the government. Eventually, the public's right to use encryption (and PGP, in particular) won out, but you can be sure the government has been busy working on ways to get around the problem of encryption.

Integrity

Ensuring that the data you send arrives at its intended destination unmodified is one of those things you take for granted in most cases. If you have sensitive data or you need to ensure that the recipient is assured that the data being delivered is actually what was sent from you, you will likely want to look into one of the other major benefits of encryption—*integrity*.

Integrity is the assurance that data and information can only be modified by those authorized to do so. Integrity can take on many forms. On the one hand, integrity can be provided using encryption, assuming you have a secure algorithm. After the data arrives at the destination, it can be decrypted. If the key has been changed or the data modified, the recipient may not be able to open or decrypt the data, depending on the encryption algorithm used.

In the case of digital signatures (which you will learn about shortly), you can also provide verification that the data is in fact from you. Once again, if the digital signature on the data being sent can't be unencrypted, it may have been modified, and the recipient will know it is not from who it says it is from. This allows the recipient to either discard the data or possibly request another copy or confirmation directly with the sender.

Like confidentiality, integrity is certainly a huge aspect of what corporate America and other organizations around the world require when dealing with transferring data over unsecured networks. In many cases, contractors that deal with the U.S. Government (in particular, the armed forces) have to run a minimum specified level of encryption before they are even allowed to do any kind of work. This is because of the sensitive nature of the information transmitted. For some contractors, there must be a minimum level of overall security compliance that encompasses not only encryption but also certain security practices.

By selecting the right encryption algorithm or the right combination of algorithms and digital signature schemes, you can increase both the confidentiality and integrity of your data.

Digital Signatures

Digital signatures attempt to guarantee the identity of the person sending the data from one point to another. The digital signature acts as an electronic signature that is used to authenticate the identity of the sender as well as to ensure that the original content sent has not been changed.

 Do not confuse a digital signature with a digital certificate (to be discussed later). Additionally, do not confuse digital signatures with encryption. Although digital signatures and encryption use related concepts, their intentions and operations are quite different. Finally, do not confuse a digital signature with the block of identification information, such as the sender's name and telephone number or the digitally created image often appended to the end of an email.

Digital signatures can easily be transported and are designed so they cannot be copied by anyone else. This ensures that something signed cannot be repudiated (nonrepudiation and digital signatures are discussed in further detail later).

 A digital signature does not have to accompany an encrypted message. It can simply be used to assure the receiver of the sender's identity and that the message's integrity was maintained. The digital signature contains the digital signature of the Certificate Authority (CA) that issued the certificate for verification.

The point of this verification is to prevent or alert the recipient to any data tampering. Ideally, if a packet of data is digitally signed, it can only bear the original mark of the sender. If this mark is different, the receiver would know that the packet is different from what it is supposed to be and then the packet either is not unencrypted or is dropped altogether. This works based on the encryption algorithm principles you learned previously. If the receiver can't determine what the original data was in the encrypted packet (in this case, the signature), it becomes much harder to fake the data and actually get it past the receiver as legitimate data.

For example, assume you need to digitally sign a document sent to your stockbroker. You need to guarantee the integrity of the message and assure the stockbroker that the message is really from you. The exchange would occur as follows:

1. You type the email.

2. Using software built in to your email client, you obtain a hash of the message.

3. You use your private key to encrypt the hash. This encrypted hash is your digital signature for the message.

4. You send the message to your stockbroker.

5. Your stockbroker receives the message and, using his software, makes a hash of the received message.

6. The stockbroker uses your public key to decrypt the message hash.

7. A match of the hashes proves that the message is valid.

Authentication

Today, encryption has an increasing role in securing the authentication of users to workstations and networks. Authentication is a verification process that ensures the identity of a user or system. The digital signatures discussed previously are often used for authentication (for example, to identify the author of an email or to identify a Web transaction). Authentication and encryption each has its own responsibilities; however, by combining the two, one achieves maximum security.

Nonrepudiation

Nonrepudiation is intended to provide, through encryption, a method in which there is no refute from where data has come. It guarantees that the sender cannot later refute having been the sender and that the recipient cannot refute having been the receiver. This definition, however, does not take into account the possible compromise of the workstation or system used to create the private key and the encrypted digital signature. The following list outlines four of the key elements that nonrepudiation services provide on a typical client/server connection:

➤ *Proof of origin*—The host gets proof that the client is the originator of particular data or an authentication request from a particular time and location.

➤ *Proof of submission*—The client gets proof that the data (or authentication, in this case) has been sent.

➤ *Proof of delivery*—The client gets proof that the data (or authentication, in this case) has been received.

➤ *Proof of receipt*—The client gets proof that the data (or authentication, in this case) has been received correctly.

Digital Signatures and Nonrepudiation

Earlier in this chapter, we discussed digital signatures and how they provide integrity and authentication. However, digital signatures also provide nonrepudiation with proof of origin. Although authentication and nonrepudiation may appear to be similar, the difference is that with nonrepudiation, proof can be demonstrated to a third party.

A sender of a message signs a message using her private key. This provides unforgeable proof that the sender did indeed generate the message. Nonrepudiation is unique to asymmetric systems because the private (secret) key is not shared. Remember that in a symmetric system, both parties involved would share the secret key. Therefore, any party can deny sending a message by claiming the other party was the originator.

Access Control

Access control in an organization can take on many different forms. In most environments today, access control can encompass something as simple as limiting the directories to which the users have access as well as something as involved as defining what content users can and cannot view on the Internet. Access control can be an important aspect to implement in an organization when you want to have the best possible control over what your users can see and, potentially, what they can send from and bring into the network. The less potentially dangerous the data and connections coming in and out of your network are, the less chance there is of there being a security issue (in particular viruses). It makes sense that the less you let in or out, the less you worry about.

NOTE

Access control is typically most effective when you combine it with encryption—for example, in Windows 2000, using Kerberos to encrypt the authentication process or using Public Key Infrastructure (PKI) to secure remote connections to a server. Any way of controlling access (using a password, setting rights, establishing user policies, and so on) will help augment security; however, when you combine it with encryption, you get the benefits of confidentiality and integrity as well.

A newer and more popular way of implementing access control is the Extensible Markup Language (XML). XML documents can be written to provide a wide variety of services and are particularly useful in company intranets where having centralized services accessible through the Web is quite handy. Another version of XML that is specifically designed for access control is XML Access Control Language (XACL).

XACL is a newer development that allows granular access control using XML. The ability to control what the end user sees and can use makes XACL a very powerful tool and could prove to be something that extends to the Internet for companies providing services over the Web to customers of their sites or products. XML was designed to allow developers to take advantage of today's strong encryption algorithms. Therefore, any XML document created can use encryption to provide more robust access control as well as data integrity and confidentiality.

Public Key Infrastructure (PKI)

Public Key Infrastructure provides the system for the secure exchange of data over a network through the use of an asymmetric key system. This system, for the most part, consists of digital certificates and the Certificate Authorities (CAs) that issue the certificates. These certificates identify individuals, systems, and organizations that have been verified as authentic and trustworthy.

One of the best-known companies currently involved with PKI and providing PKI solutions is VeriSign, which is perhaps the leading Certificate Authority today.

PKI has far reaches because it provides the secure infrastructure for applications and networks, which includes access control to resources from Web browsers, secure email, and much more. PKI protects information by providing the following:

➤ Identity authentication

➤ Integrity verification

➤ Privacy assurance

➤ Access authorization

➤ Transaction authorization

➤ Nonrepudiation support

Public Key Infrastructure is a vast collection of varying technologies and policies for the creation and use of digital certificates. PKI encompasses Certificate Authorities, digital certificates, as well as tools and systems used to bring them all together.

Certificate Authorities (CAs) are the trusted entities—an important concept within PKI. Aside from the third-party CAs, such as Entrust and VeriSign, an organization may establish its own CA, typically to be used only within the organization. The CA's job is to verify the holder of a digital certificate and ensure that the holder of the certificate is who he claims to be. A common analogy used is to compare a CA to a passport-issuing authority. To obtain a passport, you need the assistance of another (for example, a customs office) to verify your identity. Passports are trusted, because the issuing authority is trusted.

You have learned about various components and terms that make up PKI, such as digital signatures, public key encryption, confidentiality, integrity, authentication, access control, and nonrepudiation. In the following sections, you'll learn more about the digital certificates and trust hierarchies involved in PKI.

 You often hear PKI referred to as a *trust hierarchy*.

Certificates

A *digital certificate* is a digitally signed block of data that allows public key cryptography to be used for identification purposes. Certification Authorities issue these certificates, which are signed using the CA's private key. Most certificates contain the following information:

➤ CA's name

➤ CA's digital signature

➤ Serial number

➤ Issued date

➤ Period of validity

➤ Version

➤ Subject or owner

➤ Subject or owner's public key

Although most certificates follow the X.509 v3 hierarchical PKI standard, the PGP key system uses its own certificate format.

The most common application of digital certificates that you have likely used involves Web sites. Web sites that ask for personal information, especially credit card information, use digital certificates (not necessarily all do; however, they should). The traffic from your computer to the Web site is secured via a protocol called Secure Sockets Layer (SSL), and the Web server uses a digital certificate for the secure exchange of information. This is easily identified by a small padlock located in the bottom status bar of most browsers. By clicking this icon, you can view the digital certificate. Figure 8.2 shows the digital certificate for www.castadream.com, as viewed through Microsoft Internet Explorer.

Figure 8.2 The digital certificate for a Web site.

Certificate Policies

A *certificate policy* indicates specific uses applied to a digital certificate, as well as other technical details. Not all certificates are created equal—digital certificates are issued often following different practices and procedures, and they are issued for different purposes. Thus, the certificate policy provides the rules that indicate the purpose and use of an assigned digital certificate. For example, one certificate may have a policy indicating its use for electronic data interchange to conduct e-commerce, whereas another may be issued to only digitally sign documents.

You need to remember that a certificate policy identifies the purpose for which the certificate can be used, but you should also be able to identify the other types of information that can be included within a certificate policy, which include the following:

➤ Legal issues often used to protect the CA

➤ Mechanisms for how users will be authenticated by the CA

➤ Key management requirements

➤ Instructions for what to do if the private key is compromised

➤ Lifetime of the certificate

➤ Certificate enrollment and renewal

➤ Rules regarding exporting the private key

➤ Private and public key minimum lengths

Certificate Practice Statements

A *Certificate Practice Statement* (CPS) is a legal document created and published by a CA for the purpose of conveying information to those depending on the CA's issued certificates. The information within a CPS provides for the general practices followed by the CA in issuing certificates as well as information relating to the customers in regard to certificates, responsibilities, and problem management. It is important to understand that these statements are described in the context of operating procedures and systems architecture, as opposed to certificate policies (discussed previously), which indicate the rules that apply to an issued certificate. A CPS includes the following items:

➤ Identification of the CA

➤ Types of certificates issued as well as applicable certificate policies

➤ Operating procedures for issuing and renewing certificates as well as revocation of certificates

➤ Technical and physical security controls used by the CA

A Certificate Practice Statement (CPS) is a written statement of the practices for the CA relating to how the CA manages the certificates it issues.

Revocation

Just as digital certificates are issued, they can also be revoked. Revoking a certificate invalidates a certificate before its expiration date; typically, because the certificate is considered no longer trustworthy. For example, if a certificate holder's private key is compromised, the certificate is likely to be revoked. Other examples include fraudulently obtained certificates and a change in the holder's status, which may indicate less trustworthiness.

A component of PKI includes a mechanism for distributing certificate revocation information, called a *Certificate Revocation List* (CRL). A CRL is used when verification of a digital certificate takes place to ensure the validity of the digital certificate.

 A newer mechanism for identifying revoked certificates is the Online Certificate Status Protocol (OCSP). A limitation of CRLs is that they must be constantly updated; otherwise, certificates may be accepted despite the fact they were recently revoked. The OCSP, however, checks certificate status in real time rather than relying on the end user to have a current copy of the CRL.

Trust Models

There are several models or architectures that arrange Certificate Authorities within a PKI. The simplest model consists of a single CA. In the single-CA architecture, only one CA exists to issue and maintain certificates. Although this model may be beneficial to smaller organizations because of its administrative simplicity, it has the potential to present many problems. For example, if the CA fails, there is no other CA that can quickly take its place. Another problem can exist if a private key becomes compromised, because all the issued certificates from that CA would then be invalid. A new CA would have to be created, which, in turn, would need to reissue all the certificates.

A more common model, and one that reduces the risks imposed by a single CA, is the hierarchical CA model. In this model, an initial root CA exists at the top of the hierarchy and subordinate CAs exist beneath the root. The subordinate CAs provide redundancy and load balancing should any of the other CAs fail or be taken offline.

A root CA differs from subordinate CAs in that the root CA is usually offline. Remember, if the root CA is compromised, the entire architecture is compromised. If, however, a subordinate CA is compromised, the root CA can revoke the subordinate CA.

An alternative to this hierarchical model is the *cross-certification model*, often referred to as a *web of trust*. In this model, CAs are considered peers to each other. Such configuration, for example, may exist at a small company that started with a single-CA model. Then, as the company grew, it continued to implement other single-CA models and then decided that each division of the company needed to communicate with each other and ensure secure exchange of information across the company. To enable this, each of the CAs establishes a peer-to-peer trust relationship with the others. As you might imagine, such a configuration could become difficult to manage over time.

The root CA should be taken offline and only be made available to create and revoke certificates for subordinate CAs.

A solution to the complexity of a large cross-certification model is to implement what is known as a *bridge CA model*. Remember that in the cross-certification model, each CA must trust the others; however, by implementing bridging, it is possible to have a single CA, known as the *bridge CA*, be the central point of trust and act as the coordinator for the other participating CAs (known as *principals*).

Three primary models define the organization of Certificate Authorities: single CA, hierarchical CA, and the bridge CA.

Practice Questions

Question 1

What type of algorithm does the MD series of encryption algorithms use?

○ A. Asymmetric encryption algorithm

○ B. Digital signature

○ C. Hashing algorithm

○ D. All of the above

Answer C is correct. Although the Message Digest series of algorithms is classified globally as a symmetric key encryption algorithm, the correct answer is hashing algorithm, which is the method that the algorithm uses to encrypt data. Answer A is incorrect because this is an algorithm that uses a public and private key pair and is not associated with the MD series of encryption. Answer B is incorrect because a digital signature is not an encryption algorithm. Answer D is an incorrect choice because there's only one correct answer.

Question 2

In encryption, when data is broken into single units of varying sizes (dependant on algorithm) and the encryption is applied to those chunks of data, what type of algorithm is that called?

○ A. Symmetric encryption algorithm

○ B. Elliptic curve

○ C. Block cipher

○ D. All of the above

Answer C is correct. When data that is going to be encrypted is broken into chunks of data and then encrypted, the type of encryption is called a *block cipher*. Although many symmetric algorithms use a block cipher, answer A is incorrect because a block cipher is a more precise and accurate term for the given question. Answer B is incorrect because an elliptic curve is an asymmetric algorithm, and block ciphers aren't even used. Answer D is incorrect because there is only one correct answer.

Question 3

The National Institute of Standards and Technology (NIST) put out a call to have a new algorithm replace the aging DES as the standard encryption algorithm. Which algorithm was eventually selected as the Advanced Encryption Standard?

○ A. Rijndael

○ B. 3DES

○ C. RC6

○ D. Twofish

○ E. CAST

Answer A is correct. Rijndael was the winner of the new AES standard. Although RC6 and Twofish competed for selection, they were not chosen; therefore, answers C and D are incorrect. 3DES and CAST did not participate; therefore, answers B and E are incorrect.

Question 4

Which type of algorithm generates a key pair of a public key and a private key that is then used to encrypt and decrypt data and messages sent and received?

○ A. Elliptic curve

○ B. Symmetric encryption algorithm

○ C. Asymmetric encryption algorithm

○ D. Paired algorithm

Answer C is correct. Although many different types of algorithms use public and private keys to apply their encryption algorithms in varying methods, the type of algorithms that perform this way are called *asymmetric encryption algorithms* (or *public key encryption*). Answer A is incorrect because this is only a type of asymmetric encryption algorithm. Answer B is incorrect because symmetric algorithms use a single key. Paired algorithm is not a type of algorithm; therefore, answer D is incorrect.

Question 5

Which of the following algorithms are examples of a symmetric encryption algorithm? [Check all correct answers.]

❏ A. Rijndael

❏ B. Diffie-Hellman

❏ C. RC6

❏ D. AES

Answers A, C, and D are correct. Because Rijndael and AES are now one in the same, they both can be called symmetric encryption algorithms. RC6 is symmetric as well. Answer B is incorrect because Diffie-Hellman uses public and private keys, so it is considered an asymmetric encryption algorithm.

Question 6

Which of the following algorithms are examples of an asymmetric encryption algorithm? [Check all correct answers.]

❏ A. Elliptic curve

❏ B. 3DES

❏ C. CAST

❏ D. RSA

❏ E. AES

Answers A and D are correct. In this case, both elliptic curve and RSA are types of asymmetric encryption algorithms. Although the elliptic curve algorithm is typically incorporated into other algorithms, it falls into the asymmetric family of algorithms because of its use of public and private keys, just like the RSA algorithm. Answers B, C, and E are all incorrect because 3DES, CAST, and AES are symmetric encryption algorithms.

Question 7

When encrypting and decrypting data using an asymmetric encryption algorithm, you _____.

- ○ A. use only the private key to encrypt and only the public key to decrypt
- ○ B. use only the public key to encrypt and only the private key to decrypt
- ○ C. can use the public key to either encrypt or decrypt
- ○ D. use only the private key to decrypt data encrypted with the public key

Answer D is correct. Answer D provides the only valid statement to complete the sentence. Answers A and B are both incorrect because in public key encryption, if one key is used to encrypt, you can use the other to decrypt the data. Answer C is incorrect because the public key cannot decrypt the same data it encrypted.

Question 8

Which one of the following best identifies the system of digital certificates and Certificate Authorities used in public key technology?

- ○ A. Certificate Practice System (CPS)
- ○ B. Public Key Exchange (PKE)
- ○ C. Certificate Practice Statement (CPS)
- ○ D. Public Key Infrastructure (PKI)

Answer D is correct. PKI represents the system of digital certificates and Certificate Authorities. Certificate Practice System (CPS) and Public Key Exchange (PKE) are both fictitious terms. Therefore, answers A and B are incorrect. A CPS is a document created and published by a CA that provides for the general practices followed by the CA. Therefore, answer C is incorrect.

Question 9

> Which of the following is *not* an architectural model for the arranging of Certificate Authorities?
>
> ○ A. Bridge CA architecture
>
> ○ B. Sub-CA architecture
>
> ○ C. Single-CA architecture
>
> ○ D. Hierarchical CA architecture

Answer B is correct. Answer B is correct because it does not represent a valid trust model. Answers A, C, and D, however, all represent legitimate trust models. Another common model also exists, called cross-certification. However, it usually makes more sense to implement a bridge architecture over this type of model.

Question 10

> When a Certificate Authority revokes a certificate, notice of the revocation is distributed via a _____.
>
> ○ A. Certificate Revocation List
>
> ○ B. Certificate policy
>
> ○ C. Digital signature
>
> ○ D. Certificate Practice Statement

Answer A is correct. Certificate Revocation Lists are used to identify revoked certificates. However, they are being replaced by the Online Certificate Status Protocol (OCSP), which provides certificate status in real time. Answers B and D are both incorrect because these terms relate to the polices and practices of certificates and the issuing authorities. Answer C is incorrect because a digital signature is an electronic signature used for identity authentication.

Need to Know More?

 Krutz, Ronald, and Russell Dean Vines. *The CISSP Prep Guide: Mastering the Ten Domains of Computer Security.* John Wiley & Sons. Indianapolis, IN, 2001. ISBN 0471413569.

Refer to Chapter 4, "Cryptography."

 The How Encryption Works reference Web site: www.howstuffworks.com/encryption.htm

 The RSA-based Cryptographic Schemes Web site: www.rsasecurity.com/rsalabs/rsa_algorithm/

 The W3C XML Encryption Working Group Web site: www.w3.org/Encryption/2001/

 The National Institute of Standards and Technology Web site: www.nist.gov

 The Rijndael Web site: www.esat.kuleuven.ac.be/~rijmen/rijndael/

 The Request for Comments (RFC) 2527, "Internet X.509 Public Key Infrastructure Certificate Policy and Certification Practices Framework" on the Internet Engineering Task Force (IETF) Web site: www.ietf.org/rfc/rfc2527.txt

The Microsoft Kerberos deployment Web page: www.microsoft.com/technet/treeview/default.asp?url=/TechNet/prodtechnol/windows2000serv/deploy/kerberos.asp

The Security books, journals, bibliographies, and publications listing Web site: www.cs.auckland.ac.nz/~pgut001/links/books.html

Deploying Cryptography

Terms you'll need to understand:

- ✓ Public Key Infrastructure (PKI)
- ✓ Certificate Authority (CA)
- ✓ X.509
- ✓ Public Key Infrastructure based on X.509 certificates (PKIX)
- ✓ Public Key Cryptography Standards (PKCS)
- ✓ Secure Sockets Layer (SSL)
- ✓ Transport Layer Security (TLS)
- ✓ Internet Security Associate and Key Management Protocol (ISAKMP)
- ✓ Certificate Management Protocol (CMP)
- ✓ XML Key Management Specification (XKMS)
- ✓ Secure Multipurpose Internet Mail Extensions (S/MIME)
- ✓ Pretty Good Privacy (PGP)
- ✓ Hypertext Transfer Protocol over Secure Sockets Layer (HTTPS)
- ✓ Internet Protocol Security (IPSec)
- ✓ Certificate Enrollment Protocol (CEP)
- ✓ Federal Information Processing Standard (FIPS)
- ✓ Common Criteria (CC)
- ✓ Wireless Transport Layer Security (WTLS)
- ✓ Wired Equivalent Privacy (WEP)
- ✓ ISO 17799
- ✓ Key management
- ✓ Certificate lifecycle

Techniques you'll need to master:

✓ Understanding the basic security features and operational concepts involved with digital certificates

✓ Recognizing and understanding the essential standards and protocols associated with a Public Key Infrastructure (PKI)

✓ Understanding the concepts involved in key management and the digital certificate lifecycle

Standards and Protocols

Public Key Infrastructure (PKI) is composed of several standards and protocols. These standards and protocols are necessary to allow for interoperability among security products offered by different vendors. Keep in mind that digital certificates, for example, may be issued by different Certificate Authorities (CAs); therefore, a common language or protocol must exist.

X.509-Based Public Key Infrastructure

PKI based on X.509 certificates (PKIX) is the Internet Engineering Task Force (IETF) working group established for the development of Internet standards for X.509-based PKI. The group's focus includes the following:

➤ Profiles of X.509 version 3 Public Key Certificates and X.509 version 2 Certificate Revocation Lists (CRLs)

➤ PKI management protocols

➤ Operational protocols

➤ Certificate policies and Certificate Practice Statements (CPS)

➤ Timestamping and data-certification services as well as validation services

Public Key Cryptography Standards (PKCS)

Whereas PKIX describes the development of Internet standards for X.509-based PKI, the Public Key Cryptography Standards (PKCS) are the *de facto* cryptographic message standards developed and maintained by RSA Laboratories, a division of the RSA Security Corporation. PKCS provides a basic and widely accepted framework for the development of PKI solutions. There were recently 15 documents in the PKCS specification library;

however, two of the documents have been incorporated into another. These documents include the following:

➤ *PKCS #1: RSA Cryptography Standard*—Provides recommendations for the implementation of public key cryptography based on the RSA algorithm.

➤ *PKCS #2*—No longer exists and has been integrated into PKCS #1.

➤ *PKCS #3: Diffie-Hellman Key Agreement Standard*—Describes a method for using the Diffie-Hellman key agreement.

➤ *PKCS #4*—No longer exists and has been integrated into PKCS #1.

➤ *PKCS #5: Password-Based Cryptography Standard*—Provides recommendations for encrypting a data string, such as a private key, with a secret key that has been derived from a password.

➤ *PKCS #6: Extended-Certificate Syntax Standard*—Provides a method for certifying additional information about a given entity beyond just the public key by describing the syntax of a certificate's attributes.

➤ *PKCS #7: Cryptographic Message Syntax Standard*—Describes the syntax for data streams, such as digital signatures, that may have cryptography applied to them.

➤ *PKCS #8: Private Key Information Syntax Standard*—Describes a syntax for private key information, including the private key of a public key cryptographic algorithm.

➤ *PKCS #9: Selected Attribute Types*—Defines certain attribute types of use in PKCS #6, PKCS #7, PKCS #9, and PKCS #10.

➤ *PKCS #10: Certification Request Syntax Standard*—Describes the syntax for a certification request to include a distinguished name, a public key, and an optional set of attributes.

➤ *PKCS #11: Cryptographic Token Interface Standard*—Defines an application programming interface (API) named Cryptoki for devices holding cryptographic information.

➤ *PKCS #12: Personal Information Exchange Syntax Standard*—Specifies a format for storing and/or transporting a user's private key, digital certificate, and attribute information.

➤ *PKCS #13: Elliptic Curve Cryptography Standard*—Addresses Elliptic Curve Cryptography (ECC) as related to PKI. As of this writing, PKCS #13 is still under development.

➤ *PKCS #14: Pseudo Random Number Generation*—Addresses pseudo random number generation (PRNG), which produces a sequence of bits that has a random-looking distribution. As of this writing, PKCS #14 is still under development.

➤ *PKCS #15: Cryptographic Token Information Format Standard*—Establishes a standard for the format of cryptographic information on cryptographic tokens.

Each of the preceding standards documents may be revised and amended as changes in cryptography occur, and they are always accessible from RSA Security's Web site (www.rsasecurity.com) or anonymous FTP server.

X.509 Standards

It was stated earlier that PKIX is an IETF working group established to create standards for X.509 PKI. X.509 has been an International Telecommunications Union (ITU) recommendation since implemented as a *de facto* standard. X.509 defines a framework for authentication services by a directory.

 X.509 was first published as part of the ITU's X.500 directory service standard. X.500 is similar to a telephone book in that it is a database of names. This directory may include people, computers, and printers, for example. Although X.500 has not become an accepted standard like its slimmer cousin, Lightweight Directory Access Protocol (LDAP), X.509 has become the Internet's PKI standard for digital certificates.

The X.509 standard additionally defines the format of required data for digital certificates. In the previous chapter, you were briefly introduced to the contents of a digital certificate; however, it is worth reiterating some of these fields in more detail, which include those required to be compliant with the X.509 standard:

➤ *Version*—Identifies the version of the X.509 standard for which the certificate is compliant.

➤ *Serial Number*—The Certificate Authority (CA) that creates the certificate is responsible for assigning a unique serial number.

➤ *Signature Algorithm Identifier*—Identifies the cryptographic algorithm used by the CA to sign the certificate.

➤ *Issuer*—Identifies the directory name of the entity signing the certificate, which is typically a CA.

➤ *Validity Period*—Identifies the time frame for which the private key is valid, if the private key has not been compromised. This period is indicated with both a start and an end time and may be of any duration, but it is often set to one year.

➤ *Subject Name*—The name of the entity that is identified in the public key associated with the certificate. This name uses the X.500 standard for globally unique naming and is often called the *Distinguished Name (DN)*—for example, CN=Michael Dalton, OU=Security Architecture Division, O=Castadream Inc, and C=US.

➤ *Subject Public Key Information*—Includes the public key of the entity named in the certificate as well as a cryptographic algorithm identifier and optional key parameters associated with the key.

There are currently three versions of X.509:

➤ *Version 1*—This version has been around since 1988, and although it is the most generic, it is also the most ubiquitous.

➤ *Version 2*—This version is not widely used. It introduced the idea of unique identifiers for the issuing entity and the subject.

➤ *Version 3*—This version was introduced in 1996. It supports an optional extension field to provide for more informational fields. Therefore, an extension can be defined by an entity and included in the certificate.

Other Standards and Protocols

So far we have provided a good foundation of knowledge covering the standards for the deployment of cryptography and a Public Key Infrastructure. However, many other standards and protocols still need to be considered. The following list touches on many of the additional acronyms you should understand:

➤ *Secure Sockets Layer (SSL)*—SSL is the most widely used protocol for managing secure communication between a client and server over the Web. It provides for client- and server-side authentication as well as an encrypted connection between the two. SSL operates at the Session layer of the OSI model.

➤ *Transport Layer Security (TLS)*—TLS is the successor to SSL and similar to SSL in that it ensures secure communication between two parties on the Internet. TLS consists of two additional protocols: TLS Record

Protocol and TLS Handshake Protocol. The TLS Handshake Protocol allows the client and server to authenticate to one another, and the TLS Record Protocol provides connection security.

➤ *Internet Security Association and Key Management Protocol (ISAKMP)*— This protocol defines a common framework for the creation, negotiation, modification, and deletion of security associations in Virtual Private Networks (VPNs). ISAKMP is quite flexible in that it may be implemented over any transport protocol.

➤ *Certificate Management Protocol (CMP)*—This protocol provides a mechanism for advanced management functions associated with the use of digital certificates, such as certificate issuance, exchange, invalidation, revocation, and key commission. CMP is also capable of operating over any transport protocol.

➤ *XML Key Management Specification (XKMS)*—This specification defines protocols for distributing and registering public key information for use with XML signatures and is composed of the XML Key Information Service Specification (X-KISS) and the XML Key Registration Service Specification (X-KRSS). X-KISS is designed to minimize the complexity of applications using XML signatures, and X-KRSS allows key owners to register their key information for use in X-KISS.

➤ *Secure Multipurpose Internet Mail Extensions (S/MIME)*—This specification provides email privacy using encryption and authentication via digital signatures. It is a new and secure version of the popular Multi-Purpose Internet Mail Extensions (MIME). S/MIME supports the DES, 3DES, and RC2 encryption algorithms and is integrated in many email products, thus allowing for easy interoperability among different clients.

➤ *Pretty Good Privacy (PGP)*—Like S/MIME, PGP is based on public key encryption and is used for encrypting email messages. Not only is PGP a specification, but it is also an application available from the PGP Corporation, which has integrated it into popular email packages.

➤ *Hypertext Transfer Protocol over Secure Sockets Layer (HTTPS)*—As opposed to SSL, HTTPS is used specifically for HTTP data communication. HTTPS is essentially the transmission of data using HTTP over SSL. Web addresses using HTTP over SSL start with `https://` instead of `http://`.

➤ *Internet Protocol Security (IPSec)*—IPSec is a set of protocols widely implemented to support VPNs. It provides for the secure exchange of packets at the IP layer; therefore, organizations can leverage IPSec to exchange private information over public networks such as the Internet. IPSec achieves this higher level of assurance for data transport through the use of multiple protocols, including Authentication Header (AH), Encapsulated Secure Payload (ESP), and Internet Key Exchange (IKE). The AH protocol provides data integrity, authentication, and, optionally, anti-replay capabilities for packets. ESP provides for confidentiality of the data being transmitted and also includes authentication capabilities. Although IPSec can be implemented with IKE, IKE provides for additional features and ease of configuration. IKE specifically provides authentication for IPSec peers and negotiates IPSec keys and security associations.

➤ *Certificate Enrollment Protocol (CEP)*—A proprietary protocol developed by Cisco, CEP allows Cisco devices to acquire and utilize digital certificates from CAs. CEP is primarily used for the deployment of IPSec VPNs when using Cisco devices and digital certificate authentication.

➤ *Federal Information Processing Standard (FIPS)*—FIPS includes standards issued by the United States government for the evaluation of cryptographic modules, such as hardware, firmware, or software using cryptography that will be used in solutions for the U.S. government. FIPS 140-2 is the specific standard typically associated with PKI, and it specifies four levels of security with specific requirements, where level one provides for the lowest level of security and level four provides for the highest.

➤ *Common Criteria (CC)*—CC is a specification designed to set a baseline for security evaluations of security devices and solutions beyond United States standards. It is also referred to as the *Common Criteria for Information Technology Security Evaluation*.

➤ *Wireless Transport Layer Security (WTLS)*—WTLS is the security layer for the Wireless Application Protocol (WAP) and is used to establish secure communication channels between WAP-enabled devices (for example, mobile phones and personal digital assistants) and WAP-enabled servers. Although it is similar in function to SSL and TLS, WTLS is optimized for use with mobile devices.

➤ *Wired Equivalent Privacy (WEP)*—WEP is a standard used in 802.11 wireless networks and is designed to protect wireless local area network connections from eavesdropping. WEP does not provide end-to-end security because it only operates at the lower two levels of the OSI model—the Physical and Data Link layers.

➤ *ISO 17799*—This detailed, internationally recognized security standard provides a comprehensive set of controls comprising best practices in information security. This standard is rapidly gaining popularity and is composed of 10 broad sections.

 IPSec can achieve greater levels of assurance for data transport through the use of additional protocols, two of which you should remember include the *Authentication Header* and the *Encapsulated Secure Payload*. The AH protocol provides data integrity, authentication, and, optionally, anti-replay capabilities for data packets. ESP provides confidentiality of the data being transmitted and also includes authentication capabilities.

ISO 17799

It is worth discussing ISO 17799 in further detail because it deals with many of the important security topics pertinent to many security professionals. ISO 17799, also known as the *Code of Practice for Information Security Management*, is composed of 10 major sections, each covering an information security topic. The sections and their purposes as defined by the standard are as follows:

➤ *Business Continuity Planning*—Used to counteract interruptions to business activities and to critical business processes from the effects of major failures or disasters.

➤ *System Access Control*—Used to (1) control access to information; (2) prevent unauthorized access to information systems; (3) ensure the protection of networked services; (4) prevent unauthorized computer access; (5) detect unauthorized activities; and (6) ensure information security when using mobile computing and telenetworking facilities.

➤ *System Development and Maintenance*—Used to (1) ensure security is built in to operational systems; (2) prevent loss, modification, or misuse of user data in application systems; (3) protect the confidentiality, authenticity, and integrity of information; (4) ensure IT projects and support activities are conducted in a secure manner; and (5) maintain the security of application system software and data.

➤ *Physical and Environmental Security*—Used to (1) prevent unauthorized access, damage, and interference to business premises and information; (2) prevent loss, damage, or compromise of assets and interruption to business activities; and (3) prevent compromise or theft of information and information-processing facilities.

➤ *Compliance*—Used to (1) avoid breaches of any criminal or civil law, statutory, regulatory, or contractual obligations, and of any security requirements; (2) ensure compliance of systems with organizational security policies and standards; and (3) maximize the effectiveness of and minimize interference to/from the system-audit process.

➤ *Personnel Security*—Used to (1) reduce the risks of human error, theft, fraud, or misuse of facilities; (2) ensure that users are aware of information security threats and concerns and are equipped to support the corporate security policy in the course of their normal work; and (3) minimize the damage from security incidents and malfunctions and learn from such incidents.

➤ *Security Organization*—Used to (1) manage information security within the company; (2) maintain the security of organizational information-processing facilities and information assets accessed by third parties; and (3) maintain the security of information when the responsibility for information processing has been outsourced to another organization.

➤ *Computer and Operations Management*—Used to (1) ensure the correct and secure operation of information-processing facilities; (2) minimize the risk of systems failures; (3) protect the integrity of software and information; (4) maintain the integrity and availability of information processing and communication; (5) ensure the safeguarding of information in networks and the protection of the supporting infrastructure; (6) prevent damage to assets and interruptions to business activities; and (7) prevent loss, modification, or misuse of information exchanged between organizations.

➤ *Asset Classification and Control*—Used to maintain appropriate protection of corporate assets and ensure that information assets receive an appropriate level of protection.

➤ *Security Policy*—Used to provide management direction and support for information security.

In the previous chapter, we discussed the management structure for digital certificates. In this chapter, we've discussed the standards and protocols available to utilize them. In the following section, we'll discuss the management structure for the keys themselves. This includes the critical elements that must be taken into account to properly protect and account for the private key material, which is the most important element of a PKI solution.

Key Management and the Certificate Lifecycle

Being able to manage the digital certificates and key pairs used is a critical component to any PKI solution. A method of management involves the use of a *lifecycle* for digital certificates and their keys. The lifecycle is typically based on two documents discussed in the previous chapter—these include the *certificate policy* and the *Certificate Practice Statement (CPS)*. The lifecycle is a perpetual set of events required for creating, using, and destroying public keys and the digital certificates with which they are associated. The certificate lifecycle is composed of the following events:

➤ *Key generation*—A generator creates a public key pair. Although the CA may generate the key pair, the requesting entity may also generate the pair and provide the public key with the submission of identity in the next step.

➤ *Identity submission*—The requesting entity submits its identify information to the CA.

➤ *Registration*—The CA registers the request for a certificate and ensures the accuracy of the submission of identity.

➤ *Certification*—If the identity is validated, the CA creates a certificate and then digitally signs the certificate with its own digital signature.

➤ *Distribution*—The CA distributes and/or publishes the digital certificate.

➤ *Usage*—The entity receiving the certificate is authorized to use the certificate only for the certificate's intended use.

➤ *Revocation and expiration*—The certificate will typically expire and must be withdrawn. Alternatively, the certificate may need to be revoked for various reasons prior to expiration (for example, if the owner's private key becomes compromised).

➤ *Renewal*—A certificate can be renewed if requested, provided that a new key pair is generated.

➤ *Recovery*—Recovery may become necessary if a certifying key is compromised, yet the certificate holder is still considered valid and trusted.

➤ *Archiving*—This event involves storing the certificates' records and their uses.

The preceding list offers a broad view of the certificate lifecycle; however, in the following sections, we will go into more detail about important topics you should understand in regard to key management and the digital certificate lifecycle.

Centralized Versus Decentralized

Alternative methods exist for creating and managing digital certificates. These operations may either be centralized or decentralized, depending on the organization's security policy.

Centralized key management allows the issuing authority to have complete control over the process. Although this provides for a high level of control, many do not like the idea of a centralized system having a copy of the private key. Whereas the benefit of central control may be seen as an advantage, a centralized system also has other disadvantages, which include additional required infrastructure, a need to positively authenticate the end entity prior to transmitting the private key, as well as the need for a secure channel to transmit the private key.

Decentralized key management allows the requesting entity to generate the key pair and only submit the public key to the CA. Although the CA can still take on the role of distributing and publishing the digital certificate, it can no longer store the private key. As a result, the entity must maintain complete control over the private key, which is considered one of the most sensitive portions of the PKI solution. This, however, creates the added burden for the CA to ensure that the keys were generated properly and all the policies where adhered to in regard to the generation of the key pair.

Storage

Once the key pairs are generated and the CA has issued a digital certificate, both keys must be stored appropriately to ensure their integrity is maintained and that they are still easy and efficient to use. The methods used to store the keys may either be hardware or software based.

Hardware storage is typically associated with higher levels of security and assurance than software because hardware can have specialized components and physical encasements to protect the integrity of the data stored within. In addition to being more secure, hardware devices are more efficient because they provide dedicated resources to PKI functions. Naturally, however, hardware solutions often have a higher cost than software solutions.

Although software solutions do not have the same level of security as their hardware counterparts, software storage solutions are less complicated to distribute and provide for easier administration and transportability as well as lower costs.

Because the private key is so sensitive, it requires a higher level of protection than the public key. As a result, special care needs to be taken to protect private keys, especially the root key for a CA. Remember that if the private key is compromised, the public key and the associated certificate are also compromised and should no longer be valid. In the case of the CA's root key, if it becomes compromised, all active keys generated using the CA are also compromised and should be revoked and reissued. As a result of this need for increased security over the private keys, hardware solutions are often used to protect them.

Even a private key in the possession of an end user should be carefully guarded. At a minimum, this key is protected via a password. An additional safeguard may be to provide another layer of security by storing the private key on a portable device such as a smartcard; therefore, possession of the card, as well as knowledge of the password, is required.

Escrow

Key escrow occurs when a CA or other entity maintains a copy of the private key associated with the public key signed by the CA. This allows the CA or escrow agent to have access to all information that is encrypted using the public key from a user's certificate as well as to create digital signatures on behalf of the user. As a result, key escrow is a sensitive topic within the PKI community, because there could be harmful results if the private key is misused. Because of this issue, key escrow is not a favorable public PKI solution.

Contrary to the preceding paragraph, key escrow is often seen as a *good* idea in corporate PKI environments. In most cases, an employee of an organization is bound by the information security policies of the organization that mandate that the organization have access to all intellectual property generated by a user as well as access to any data an employee generates. Additionally, key escrow enables an organization to overcome the large problem of forgotten passwords. Rather than revoke and reissue new keys, an organization can instead generate a new certificate using the private key stored in escrow.

Expiration

When digital certificates are issued, they are given an issued date and an expiration date. This period is indicated in a specific field within the certificate. Many certificates are set to expire after one year; however, the time period may be shorter or longer depending on the needs. In Figure 9.1, note the "Valid to" and "Valid from" fields within the certificate.

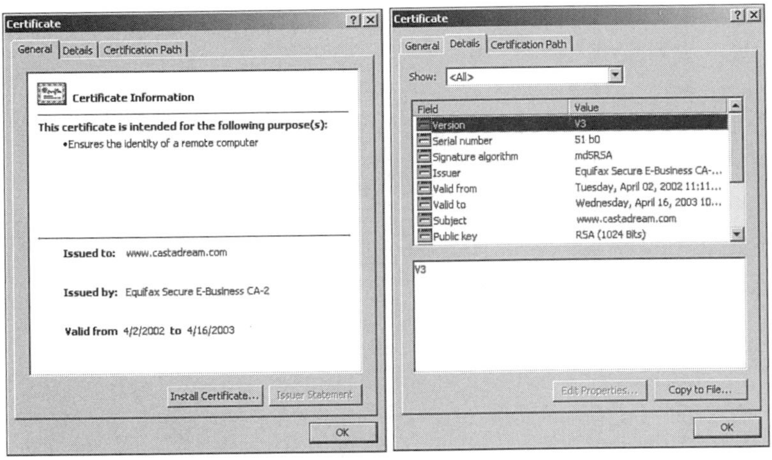

Figure 9.1 The digital certificate for a Web site.

You might recall several years ago the issue with older Web browsers as the year 2000 approached. VeriSign's root certificate, embedded into Web browsers, had an expiration date of December 31, 1999. After the certificate expired, many browsers, if they weren't updated, were unable to correctly verify certificates issued or signed by VeriSign. As a result, many certificates are given expiration dates further out. For example, a recent check of the certificates installed in one of our Web browsers shows certificates from VeriSign and Microsoft not expiring until the year 2028—we sure hope we've upgraded beyond Internet Explorer version 6 before the year 2028 rolls around.

Revocation

After a certificate is no longer valid, *certificate revocation* occurs. There are many reasons why this may occur—for example, a private key becomes compromised, the private key is lost, or the identifying credentials are no longer valid. Revoking a certificate, however, is simply not enough. The community that trusts this certificate must be notified that the certificate is no longer valid. This is accomplished via a Certificate Revocation List (CRL) or the Online Certificate Status Protocol (OCSP), both of which were discussed in the Chapter 8, "Basics of Cryptography."

Status Checking

Both OCSP and CRLs are used to verify the status of a certificate. Most PKI solutions have three basic status levels: valid, suspended, and revoked. The status of a certificate can be checked by going to the CA that issued the certificate or to an agreed upon directory server that maintains a database indicating the status level for a set of certificates. In most cases, however, the application (such as a Web browser) has a function available that initiates a check for certificates. For example, Microsoft introduced automated status checking for users of Internet Explorer 3.0 with the download of its Authenticode 2.0.

Suspension

Certificate suspension occurs when a certificate is under investigation to determine whether it should be revoked. This mechanism allows a certificate to stay in place, but it is not valid for any type of use. Like the status checking that occurs with revoked certificates, users and systems are notified of suspended certificates in the same way. The primary difference is that new credentials will not need to be retrieved—it is only necessary to be notified that current credentials have had a change in status and are temporarily invalid.

Recovery

Key recovery is the process of restoring a key pair from a backup and re-creating a digital certificate using the recovered keys. Unlike in the case of a key compromise, this should only be done if the key pair becomes corrupted but is still considered valid and trusted. Although it is beneficial to back up an individual user's key pair, it is even more important to back up the CA's keys in a secured location for business continuity and recovery purposes.

M of N Control

M of N control, in regard to PKI, relates to the concept of backing up the public and private keys across multiple systems. This provides a protective measure to ensure that people cannot re-create their key pairs from the backup. The backup process involves a mathematical function to distribute that data across a number of systems. A typical setup includes multiple personnel with unique job functions who are from different parts of the organization to circumvent collusion among the individuals for the purpose of recovering the keys without proper authority. The mathematical equation involved can support up to 255 individuals to perform such an event; however, in most cases, no more than five are used.

Renewal

As mentioned previously, every certificate is issued with the date through which it is valid. Once the certificate expires, a new certificate needs to be reissued. Provided that the certificate holder's needs or identity information has not changed, the process is relatively simple. Once the issuing CA validates the entity identity, a new certificate can be generated based on the current public key.

Destruction

Destruction of a key pair and certificate typically occurs when the materials are no longer valid. There are, however, some precautions that should be followed in regard to destruction. If the key pair to be destroyed is used for digital signatures, the private key portion should be destroyed first to prevent future signing activities with the key. If, however, the materials were used for privacy purposes only, it may be necessary to archive a copy of the private key, because it may be needed later to decrypt archived data that was encrypted using the key. Additionally, a digital certificate associated with a key that is no longer valid should be added to the CRL regardless of whether the key is actually destroyed or archived for possible future use.

Key Usage

Digital certificates and key pairs can be used for multiple purposes, including privacy and authentication. The security policy of the organization using the key and/or the CA defines the purposes and capabilities for the certificates issued.

To achieve privacy, a user requires the public key of the individual or entity he would like to communicate with securely. This public key is used to encrypt the data transmitted, thus the corresponding private key is used on the other end to decrypt the message.

Authentication is achieved by digitally signing the message being transmitted. To digitally sign a message, the signing entity requires access to the private key.

In short, the key usage defines how the private key can be used—either to enable the exchange of sensitive information or to create digital signatures. In addition, the key usage can define that an entity can use the key for both the exchange of sensitive information and for signature purposes.

Multiple Key Pairs

There might be circumstances that require dual or multiple key pairs to be used to support distinct and separate services. For example, an individual in a corporate environment may require one key pair to be used only for signing, yet require another for encrypting messages. Another example might be the reorder associate who has one key pair to use for signing and sending encrypted messages and another that is restricted to ordering equipment worth no more than a specific dollar amount. Multiple key pairs will also require multiple certificates because the X.509 certificate format does not support multiple keys.

Practice Questions

Question 1

> Which of the following are included within a digital certificate? [Choose the three best answers.]
>
> ❏ A. User's public key
>
> ❏ B. User's private key
>
> ❏ C. Information about the user
>
> ❏ D. Digital signature of the issuing CA

Answers A, C, and D are correct. The user's public key, information about the user, and the digital signature of the issuing CA are all included within a digital certificate. A user's private key should never be contained within the digital certificate and should remain under tight control; therefore, answer B is incorrect.

Question 2

> Which of the following are associated with the secure exchange of email? [Choose the two best answers.]
>
> ❏ A. S/MIME
>
> ❏ B. HTTPS
>
> ❏ C. PGP
>
> ❏ D. M of N

Answers A and C are correct. Both S/MIME and PGP are used for the secure transmission of email messages. HTTPS is used on the Web for HTTP over SSL; therefore, answer B is incorrect. M of N describes a mathematical function; therefore, answer D is incorrect.

Question 3

> What part of the IPSec protocol provides authentication and integrity but not privacy?
>
> ○ A. Encapsulated Security Payload
>
> ○ B. Sans-Privacy Protocol
>
> ○ C. Authentication Header
>
> ○ D. Virtual Private Network

Answer C is correct. The Authentication Header (AH) provides authentication so the receiver can be confident of the source of the data. It does not utilize encryption to scramble the data, so it cannot provide privacy. Encapsulate Security Payload provides for confidentiality of the data being transmitted and also includes authentication capabilities; therefore, answer A is incorrect. Answer B is incorrect because it does not exist. A Virtual Private Network uses the IPSec protocol and secures communications over public networks; therefore, answer D is incorrect.

Question 4

> In a decentralized key-management system, the user is responsible for which one of the following functions?
>
> ○ A. Creation of the private and public keys
>
> ○ B. Creation of the digital certificate
>
> ○ C. Creation of the CRL
>
> ○ D. Revocation of the digital certificate

Answer A is correct. In a decentralized key-management system, the end user will generate his own key pair. The other functions, such as the creation of the certificate and the CRL as well as the revocation of the certificate, are still handled by the Certificate Authority; therefore, answers B, C, and D are incorrect.

Question 5

> To check the validity of a digital certificate, which one of the following would be used?
>
> ○ A. Corporate security policy
>
> ○ B. Certificate policy
>
> ○ C. Certificate Revocation List
>
> ○ D. Expired domain names

Answer C is correct. A Certificate Revocation List (CRL) provides a detailed list of certificates that are no longer valid. A corporate security policy would not provide current information on the validity of issued certificates; therefore, answer A is incorrect. A certificate policy also does not provide information on invalid issued certificates; therefore, answer B is incorrect. Finally, an expired domain name has no bearing on the validity of a digital certificate; therefore, answer D is incorrect.

Question 6

> What is the acronym for the *de facto* cryptographic message standards developed by RSA Laboratories?
>
> ○ A. PKIX
>
> ○ B. X.509
>
> ○ C. PKCS
>
> ○ D. Both A and C

Answer C is correct. The Public Key Cryptography Standards (PKCS) are the *de facto* cryptographic message standards developed and maintained by RSA Laboratories, a division of the RSA Security Corporation. PKIX describes the development of Internet standards for X.509-based digital certificates; therefore, answers A, B, and D are incorrect.

Question 7

> Which one of the following defines APIs for devices such as smartcards that will contain cryptographic information?
>
> ○ A. PKCS #11
>
> ○ B. PKCS #13
>
> ○ C. PKCS #4
>
> ○ D. PKCS #2

Answer A is correct. PKCS #11, the Cryptographic Token Interface Standard, defines an application programming interface (API) named Cryptoki for devices holding cryptographic information. Answer B is incorrect because PKCS #13 is the Elliptic Curve Cryptography Standard. Both C and D are incorrect because PKCS #2 and PKCS #4 no longer exist and have been integrated into PKCS #1, the RSA Cryptography Standard.

Question 8

> What is the Public Key Cryptography Standard for the Diffie-Hellman Key Agreement Standard?
>
> ○ A. PKCS #12
>
> ○ B. PKCS #5
>
> ○ C. PKCS #3
>
> ○ D. None of the above

Answer C is correct. PKCS #3, the Diffie-Hellman Key Agreement Standard, describes a method for using the Diffie-Hellman key agreement. Answer A is incorrect, because PKCS #12 is the Personal Information Exchange Syntax Standard. Answer B is incorrect because PKCS #5 is the Password-Based Cryptography Standard. Because answer C is correct, answer D is incorrect.

Question 9

Which of the fields included within a digital certificate identifies the directory name of the entity signing the certificate?

- ◯ A. Signature Algorithm Identifier
- ◯ B. Issuer
- ◯ C. Subject Name
- ◯ D. Subject Public Key Information

Answer B is correct. The Issuer field identifies the name of the entity signing the certificate, which is usually a Certificate Authority. The Signature Algorithm Identifier identifies the cryptographic algorithm used by the CA to sign the certificate; therefore, answer A is incorrect. The Subject Name is the name of the end entity identified in the public key associated with the certificate; therefore, answer C is incorrect. The Subject Public Key Information field includes the public key of the entity named in the certificate, including a cryptographic algorithm identifier; therefore, answer D is incorrect.

Question 10

Which version of X.509 supports an optional extension field?

- ◯ A. Version 1
- ◯ B. Version 2
- ◯ C. Version 3
- ◯ D. Answers B and C

Answer C is correct. Version 3 of X.509, which was introduced in 1996, supports an optional extension field used to provide more informational fields. Version 1 was the most generic version and did not incorporate this feature; therefore, answer A is incorrect. Version 2 introduced the idea of unique identifiers, but not the optional extension field; therefore, answers B and D are incorrect.

Question 11

Which of the following protocols are used to manage secure communication between a client and a server over the Web? [Choose the two best answers.]

❑ A.   Secure Sockets Layer

❑ B.   Internet Security Association and Key Management Protocol

❑ C.   Pretty Good Privacy

❑ D.   Transport Layer Security

Answers A and D are correct. Secure Sockets Layer is the most widely used protocol for managing secure communication between clients and servers on the Web, and the Transport Layer Security protocol is similar, and it is considered the successor to SSL. Answer B is incorrect because ISAKMP is a protocol common to Virtual Private Networks. Answer C is incorrect because Pretty Good Privacy is used for the encryption of email.

Question 12

Which of the following are typically associated with Virtual Private Networks (VPNs)? [Choose the two best answers.]

❑ A.   IPSec

❑ B.   ISAKMP

❑ C.   S/MIME

❑ D.   PGP

Answers A and B are correct. Both IPSec and ISAKMP are used in the creation of VPNs. IPSec provides for the secure exchange of packets at the IP layer, and ISAKMP defines a common framework for the creation, negotiation, modification, and deletion of security associations in VPNs. S/MIME and PGP are used for secure email transfer; therefore, answers C and D are incorrect.

Question 13

Where is ISO 17799 recognized?

○ A. In the United States only

○ B. In Europe and the United States only

○ C. Internationally

○ D. In Europe and Southwest Asian countries only

Answer C is correct. ISO 17799 is a detailed and internationally recognized security standard comprising best practices in information security. Because it is internationally recognized, answers A, B, and D are incorrect.

Question 14

Which of the following is not true regarding expiration dates of certificates?

○ A. Certificates may be issued for a week.

○ B. Certificates are only issued at yearly intervals.

○ C. Certificates may be issued for 20 years.

○ D. Certificates must always have an expiration date.

Answer B is correct. Digital certificates contain a field indicating the date through which the certificate is valid. This date is mandatory and can be for a very short period of time or for a number of years; therefore, answers A, C and D are incorrect.

Question 15

Which of the following are used to verify the status of a certificate? [Choose the two best answers.]

❑ A. OCSP

❑ B. CRL

❑ C. OSPF

❑ D. ACL

Answers A and B are correct. The Online Certificate Status Protocol (OCSP) and the Certificate Revocation List (CRL) are used to verify the status of digital certificates. OSPF is a routing protocol; therefore, answer C is incorrect. An ACL is used to define access control; therefore, answer D is incorrect.

Need to Know More?

 Krutz, Ronald, and Russell Dean Vines. *The CISSP Prep Guide: Mastering the Ten Domains of Computer Security*. John Wiley & Sons. Indianapolis, IN, 2001. ISBN 0471413569.

 Housley, Russ, and Tim Polk. *Planning for PKI*. John Wiley & Sons. New York, NY, 2001. ISBN 0471397024.

 The PKI X. 509 PKIX Charter Web page: `www.ietf.org/html.charters/pkix-charter.html`

 The International Telecommunications Union Web site: `www.itu.int/rec/recommendation.asp?type=products&lang=e&parent=T-REC-X`

 The RSA Corporation "Public Key Cryptography Standards" Web page: `www.rsasecurity.com/rsalabs/pkcs/`

 The National Institute of Standards and Technology "Security Requirements for Cryptographic Modules" Web page: `csrc.nist.gov/cyrptval/140-1.htm`

Organizational Security

Terms you'll need to understand:

✓ Access control
✓ Social engineering
✓ Business continuity
✓ Disaster recovery
✓ Security policies
✓ Acceptable use
✓ Due care
✓ Separation of duties

Techniques you'll need to master:

✓ Knowing the common areas of concern when planning for physical security of network resources
✓ Understanding how social engineering may be used to obtain unauthorized access
✓ Recognizing the more common security policy planning categories

Network security and system hardening provide the strongest possible levels of security against directed attacks, but organizational security must also be considered when planning an organization's data security. This chapter examines the issues surrounding physical security, disaster recovery, and security policies that improve network security to those areas "beyond the wire."

Physical Security

When planning security for network scenarios, many organizations overlook physical security. In many smaller organizations, the servers, routers, and patch panels are placed as a matter of convenience due to space restrictions. This can cause security issues. Speaking from experience, this equipment ends up in the oddest places, such as in the coat closet by the receptionist's desk in the lobby, in the room with the copy machine, or in a storage room with a backdoor exit that's unlocked most of the time. Securing physical access and ensuring that access requires proper authentication is necessary to avoid accidental exposure of sensitive data to attackers performing physical profiling of a target organization.

When planning physical security, you must take into consideration events such as natural and man-made disasters. If you have space constraints and put the servers in a room with the hot-water heater, how will you deal with the consequences when the hot-water heater springs a leak? How soon will your network be back up and running? If your building is in a flood zone and the most important equipment is in the lowest spot in the building, you need to be prepared when heavy rains come. Man-made disasters can be as simple as a clumsy technician spilling his soda into the most important piece of equipment you have. Many times these types of scenarios are overlooked until it is too late.

 Be familiar with physical security descriptions indicating potential security flaws. Watch for descriptions that include physical details or organizational processes.

Physical access to a system creates many avenues for a breach in security, for several reasons. Many tools may be used to extract password and account information that can then be used to access secured network resources. Given the ability to reboot a system and load software from a floppy disk, attackers may be able to access data or implant Trojan horses and other applications intended to weaken or compromise network security. Unsecured equipment is also vulnerable to social engineering attacks. It is much easier for an attacker to walk into a reception area, say she is here to do some work on the server, and get access to that server in the closet in the front lobby than to get into a physically secured area with a guest sign-in and sign-out sheet. As shown earlier, weak physical controls can also amplify the effects of natural and man-made disasters.

In this next section, we cover physical access control, including barriers, facilities, and environments, as well as the different types of social engineering and how to educate your users concerning them.

Access Control

Physical security controls parallel the data controls we discussed in Chapter 2, "General Security Practices." Mandatory physical access controls are commonly found in government facilities and military installations where users are closely monitored and very restricted. Users cannot modify entry methods or let others in because they are being monitored by security personnel. Discretionary physical control to a building or room is delegated to parties responsible for that building or room. In role-based access methods for physical control, groups of people who have common access needs are predetermined, and access to different locations is allowed with the same key or swipe card. Users in this model generally have some security training and are often allowed to grant access to others by serving as an escort or by issuing a guest badge. The security department coordinates the secure setup of the facility and surrounding areas, identifies the groups allowed to enter various areas, and allows them access based on their group membership.

When physical security is examined, the most obvious consideration to control is physical access to systems and resources. Your goal is to allow only trusted use of these resources via positive identification that the entity accessing the systems is someone or something that has permission to do so based on the security model you have chosen. When planning for access control, you pay attention not only to direct physical contact with hosts and network hardware but also to *line-of-sight access*, which means you need to place systems in such a way that you don't allow an attacker with a telescope or binoculars to spy on typed passwords. You also need to consider areas covered by wireless device transmissions, which may be detected at far greater distances than are useful for two-way network connectivity. Even the location of systems in low-traffic, public, or unmonitored areas may pose security risks.

You should consider controlling direct access to computer equipment and facilities as well as the computer environment, as discussed in the following sections.

Physical Barriers

Access might be controlled by physically securing a system within a locked room or cabinet, attaching the system to fixed, nonmovable furniture using locking cables or restraints, and locking the case itself to prevent the removal of key components. Nonstandard case screws are also available to add another layer of security for publicly accessible terminals. Other secured area considerations include ensuring that air ducts, drop ceilings, and raised floors do not provide unauthorized avenues for physical access. You can have the most secure lock on the door with biometric devices for identification, but if the walls don't go up all the way and ceiling tiles can be removed to access rooms with sensitive equipment in them, someone can easily walk off with equipment and sensitive data.

Frosted or painted glass can be used to eliminate direct visual observation of user actions, and very high security scenarios may mandate the use of electromagnetic shielding to prevent remote monitoring of emissions generated by video monitors, network switching, and system operation. Additionally, many modems and network hardware solutions use raw, transmitted data to illuminate activity indicator lights. Direct observation of these may allow an attacker to remotely eavesdrop on transmitted data using a telescope.

Security guards, surveillance cameras, motion detectors, limited-access zones, token-based and biometric access requirements for restricted areas, and many other considerations may be involved in access control planning. Additionally, users must be educated in the need for each measure taken to prevent circumvention to improve ease of normal access. A single propped-open door, a system left logged in when the administrator is away from her desk, or a paper with sensitive data on it thrown in the garbage could undo many layers of protection.

Facilities

Because a physical security plan should start with examining the perimeter of the building first, this section discusses the various methods used to secure your facilities from the outside of the building.

Buildings that house sensitive information and systems usually have an area of cleared land surrounding them. This area is referred to as *no-man's land*. The purpose of this area is to eliminate the possibility of an intruder hiding in the bushes or behind another building. Intruders often *piggyback* their way into a building, meaning they wait for someone with proper access to enter the building and then enter behind them before the door closes. Depending on the company policy, the time of day, or the employee, these intruders may never be questioned or escorted out. Having a clear area in the main facility can keep this from happening.

The next common deterrent is a fence or similar device that surrounds the entire building. A fence keeps out unwanted vehicles and people. One factor to consider in fencing is the height. The higher the fence, the harder it is to get over. Another factor to consider is the material the fence is made of. It is much easier to remove wooden slats or cut a chain link fence with bolt cutters than it is to drill through concrete or block. One final note: If the fence isn't maintained or the area around it isn't well lit, the fence can easily be compromised.

The last physical barrier is a *moat*. Moats surround part or all of a facility and are excellent physical barriers because they have a low profile and are not as obtrusive as fencing. In this instance, the consideration would be the depth and width. As with all physical barriers, the moat must be well maintained.

Here are some additional security measures that can be implemented to help deter unauthorized access:

➤ *Security guards and dogs*—Security guards and dogs can be great deterrents to intruders. It is imperative that they are trained properly. They are often used in combination with other measures.

➤ *External lighting and cameras*—If areas are brightly lit and have cameras, they are less likely to have unauthorized access attempts.

➤ *External motion detectors*—Motion detectors can alert security personnel of intruders or suspicious activity on the company's premises. They can be based on light, sound, infrared, or ultrasonic technology.

➤ *External doors and windows*—Steel doors are the best deterrent, but steel-reinforced wooden doors work as well. Windows should have locking mechanisms, and building security alarms should monitor the open/closed position of all windows that could pose an entry risk.

➤ *Mantraps*—A mantrap is a holding area between two entry points that gives security personnel time to view a person before allowing him into the internal building. Figure 10.1 shows a revolving door, which is an example of a mantrap.

Figure 10.1 An example of a mantrap.

➤ *Internal motion detectors*—As mentioned earlier, the four common motion detectors are light, sound, infrared, and ultrasonic. These can be deployed inside a building as well as outside. These devices must be properly configured because they are extremely sensitive and can issue false alarms if set too stringently.

➤ *Locks*—Locks must be easy to operate yet deter intruders. Besides the normal key locks, several different types can be considered. A cipher lock has a punch code entry system. A wireless lock is opened by a receiver mechanism that reads the card when it is held close to the receiver. A swipe card lock requires a card to be inserted into the lock (many hotels use these). The factors to consider are strength, material, and cost.

➤ *Biometrics*—Physical security can also integrate biometric methods into a door-lock mechanism. Biometrics can use a variety of methods. See Table 10.1 for a review of these technologies. When using biometrics, remember that each method has its own degree of error ratios, and some methods may seem invasive to the users and may not be accepted gracefully.

Table 10.1	Biometric Technologies
Method	**Description**
Fingerprint	Scans and matches a thumbprint or fingerprint to a reference file.
Hand/palm geometry	Uses a person's palm or hand profile, which includes the length and width of the hand and fingers.
Voiceprint	Identifies a person by having her speak into a microphone to measure speech patterns.
Facial geometry	Identifies a user based on the profile and characteristics of his face. This includes bone structure, chin shape, and forehead size.
Iris profile	Identifies an individual by using the colored part of the eye that surrounds the pupil.
Retina scan	Identifies an individual by using the blood vessel pattern at the back of the eyeball.
Signature	Matches an individual's electronic signature to a database by comparing electronic signals created by the speed and manner in which a document is signed.

Because a physical security plan should start with examining the perimeter of the building first, it might also be wise to discuss what happens when an evacuation is necessary. You don't want intruders plundering the building while employees are haphazardly running all over the place. The evacuation process could be a part of the disaster recovery plan and should include some of the following items:

➤ A map of the internal building and all exit areas

➤ What departments will exit through which doors

➤ What equipment will be shut down and by whom

➤ Who will do a final inspection of each area and make sure it is secure

➤ Where each department, once evacuated, will go and how far away from the building they will be located

➤ Who will notify the proper authorities or agencies of the incident

Make sure that all users understand how these plans function and practice orderly evacuation procedures so that an emergency situation does not leave critical systems unguarded or unsecured. Smoke from a cigarette or a purposefully set flame could create an opportunity for an attacker to gain access to highly secure areas if evacuation planning does not include security considerations.

Social Engineering

One area of security planning that is often considered the most difficult to adequately secure is the legitimate user. *Social engineering* is a process by which an attacker may extract useful information from users who are often simply tricked into helping the attacker. It is extremely successful because it relies on human emotions. Common examples of social engineering attacks include the following:

➤ An attacker calls a valid user pretending to be a guest, temp agent, or new user asking for assistance in accessing the network or details involving the business processes of the organization.

➤ An attacker contacts a legitimate user, posing as a technical aide attempting to update some type of information, and asks for identifying user details that may then be used to gain access.

➤ An attacker poses as a network administrator, directing the legitimate user to reset his password to a specific value so an imaginary update may be applied.

➤ An attacker provides the user with a "helpful" program or agent, through email, a Web site, or other means of distribution. This program may require the user to enter logon details or personal information useful to the attacker, or it may install other programs that compromise the system's security.

Reverse Social Engineering

Another form of social engineering has come to be known as *reverse social engineering*. Here, an attacker provides information to the legitimate user that causes the user to believe the attacker is an authorized technical assistant. This may be accomplished by obtaining an IT support badge or logo-bearing shirt that validates the attacker's legitimacy, by inserting the attacker's contact information for technical support in a secretary's Rolodex, or by making himself known for his technical skills by helping people around the office.

Many users would rather ask assistance of a known nontechnical person who they know to be skilled in computer support rather than contact a legitimate technical staff person, who may be perceived as busy with more important matters. An attacker who can plan and cause a minor problem will then be able to easily correct this problem, gaining the confidence of the legitimate user while being able to observe operational and network configuration details as well as logon information, and potentially being left alone with an authorized account logged in to the network.

Training

Users must be trained to avoid falling victim to social engineering attacks. This should be an ongoing process. Human behavior is difficult, if not impossible, to predict. Some guidelines for information to be included in user training may consist of the following points:

➤ How to address someone who has her hands full and asks for help getting into a secure area

➤ How to react to someone who has piggybacked into the building

➤ What procedure should be followed when a vendor comes in to work on the servers

➤ What to say to a sales representative who is at a customer site doing a demonstration and has forgotten the Web site password

➤ What to say to a vice president who has forgotten his password and needs it right away

➤ What items can and cannot go in the trash or recycle bin and what paperwork must be shredded

➤ What to do when an administrator calls and asks for a user's password

As new methods of social engineering come out, so must new training methods. The scope of the training should be done so that management has a different type of training than the users. Management training should focus on the ramifications of social engineering, such as the liability of the company when a breach happens, the financial damage that can happen, and how this can affect the reputation or credibility of the company.

Security reviews involving tiger team assessments often begin with many types of social engineering attacks to locate vulnerable areas and to identify common business practices that may be exploited by an attacker. The U.S. Air Force used special groups of security experts to test for vulnerabilities at its bases. This is where the "tiger team" concept originated. The Department of Defense documented the first use of tiger teams to assess computer security in 1973. During the 1980s and early 1990s, tiger teams were used by large companies with complex networks. Since then, tiger teams have evolved into groups that mimic intruders and hackers. They are given permission to target a company's vulnerabilities by a management member, without any notification given to the network administrators or security personnel. This can be a very useful way of assessing vulnerabilities. Speaking from personal experience, it can be real eye-opener.

 Planning, training, regular reminders, and firm and clear security policies are important when you're attempting to minimize vulnerabilities created by social engineering.

Environment

Users should not be allowed to smoke, eat, or drink around critical hardware to prevent potential damage. Fluids, particulate matter, and smoke should not be allowed to enter keyboards, mice, power supplies, or other forms of hardware. Additionally, food trash can attract vermin and pests that may enter or damage equipment and wiring.

Other environmental factors should be considered to protect key systems, including protection from strong magnetic fields near motors and generators as well as isolation from vibration or earth tremors. Extreme cold, high or low humidity, very dusty areas, and even lint in clothing may need to be considered when planning environmental security.

Wireless Cells

Cell phones have become a very important part of our technological lives. Their advances should raise concern for network administrators. Mobile phones now have the capability to allow users to access their desktop systems and download unread email. An intruder with an AC adapter and a PCS phone with unlimited data usage could leak sensitive email to virtually any location in the world. Phones called *IP phones* operate within a network on an IP address by using *Voice over IP (VoIP)* technology. The IP address is relatively easy to set up, posing a huge security risk. A policy should be in place in regard to the use of these devices in the workplace.

Location

The location of everything from the actual building to wireless antennas affects security. When picking a location for a building, an organization should investigate the type of neighborhood, population, crime rate, and emergency response times. This will help in the planning of the physical barriers needed, such as fencing, lighting, and security personnel. An organization must also analyze the potential dangers from natural disasters and plan to reduce their impact when possible.

When protecting computers, wiring closets, and other devices from physical damage due to either natural or man-made disasters, you must select their locations carefully. Proper placement of the equipment should cost a company little money upfront yet provide significant protection from possible loss of data due to flooding, fire, or theft.

Shielding

One risk that can often be overlooked is that of electronic emissions. Electrical equipment generally gives off electrical signals. Monitors, printers, fax machines, and even keyboards use electricity. These electronic signals are said to "leak" from computer and electronic equipment. *Shielding* seeks to reduce this output. The shielding can be local, cover an entire room, or cover a whole building, depending on the perceived threat. We're going to look at two types of shielding: TEMPEST and Faraday cages.

TEMPEST is a code word developed by the U.S. government in the 1950s. It is an acronym built from the Transient Electromagnetic Pulse Emanation Standard. It describes standards used to limit or block electromagnetic emanation (radiation) from electronic equipment. TEMPEST has since grown in its definition to include the study of this radiation. Individual pieces of equipment are protected through extra shielding that helps prevent electrical signals from emanating. This extra shielding is a metallic sheath surrounding connection wires for mouse, keyboard, and video monitor connectors. It can also be a completely shielded case for the motherboard, CPU, hard drive, and video display system. This protection prevents the transfer of signals through the air or nearby conductors, such as copper pipes, electrical wires, and phone wires. You are most likely to find TEMPEST equipment in government, military, and corporate environments that process government/military classified information. Because this can be costly to implement, protecting an area within a building makes more sense than protecting individual pieces of equipment.

A more efficient way to protect a large quantity of equipment from electronic eavesdropping is to place the equipment into a well-grounded metal box called a *Faraday cage*, which is named after its inventor, Dr. Michael Faraday. The box can be small enough for a cell phone or can encompass an entire building. The idea behind the cage is to protect its contents from electromagnetic fields. Two examples of Faraday cages are shown in Figures 10.2 and 10.3.

The cage surrounds an object with interconnected and well-grounded metal. The metal used is typically a copper mesh that is attached to the walls and covered with plaster or drywall. The wire mesh acts as a net for stray electric signals, either inside or outside the box.

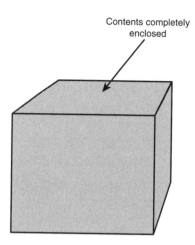

Figure 10.2 Configuration of a Faraday cage that completely encloses the contents.

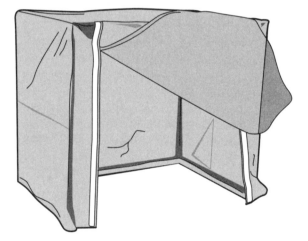

Figure 10.3 Alternate configuration of a Faraday cage.

Fire Suppression

Fire is a danger common to all business environments and one that must be planned for well in advance of any possible occurrence. The first step in a fire safety program is fire prevention.

The best way to prevent fires is to train employees to recognize dangerous situations and report these situations immediately. Knowing where a fire extinguisher is and how to use it can stop a small fire from becoming a major catastrophe. Many of the newer motion- and ultrasonic-detection systems also include heat and smoke detection for fire prevention. These systems alert the monitoring station of smoke or a rapid increase in temperature. If a fire does break out somewhere within the facility, a proper fire-suppression system can avert major damage. Keep in mind that laws and ordinances apply to the deployment and monitoring of a fire-suppression system. It is your responsibility to ensure that these codes are properly met.

Fire requires three main components to exist: heat, oxygen, and fuel. Eliminate any of these components and the fire goes out. A common way to fight fire is with water. Water attempts to take away oxygen and heat. A wet-pipe fire-suppression system is the one that most people think of when discussing an indoor sprinkler system. The term *wet* is used to describe the state of the pipe during normal operations. The pipe in the wet-pipe system has water under pressure in it at all times. The pipes are interconnected and have sprinkler heads attached at regularly spaced intervals. The sprinkler heads have a stopper held in place with a bonding agent that is designed to melt at an appropriate temperature. After the stopper melts, it opens the valve and allows water to flow from the sprinkler head and extinguish the fire. Keep in mind that electronic equipment and water don't get along well. Fires that start outside electrical areas are well served by water-based sprinkler systems. Also keep in mind that all these systems should have both manual activation and manual shutoff capabilities. You want to be able to turn off a sprinkler system to prevent potential water damage. Most systems are designed to activate only one head at a time. This works effectively to put out fires in the early stages.

Dry-pipe systems work in exactly the same fashion as wet-pipe systems, except that the pipes are filled with pressurized air instead of water. The stoppers work on the same principle. When the stopper melts, the air pressure is released and a valve in the system opens. One of the reasons for using a dry-pipe system is that when the outside temperature drops below freezing, any water in the pipes will freeze, causing them to burst. Another reason for justifying a dry-pipe system is the delay associated between the system activation and the actual water deployment. Because some laws require a sprinkler system even in areas of the building that house electrical equipment, there is enough of a delay that it is feasible for someone to manually deactivate the system before water starts to flow. In such a case, a company could deploy a dry-pipe system and a chemical system together. The delay in the dry-pipe system can be used to deploy the chemical system first and avoid serious damage to the running equipment from a water-based sprinkler system.

Know the difference between the different types of fire-suppression systems.

Chemical systems can be wet or dry and have the capability to put out fires more quickly than straight water-based systems. Chemical systems have the added benefit of being able to put out fires involving many types of fuel, including wood, oil, metal, fabric, chemical, and electrical.

Disaster Recovery

After the events surrounding September 11th, 2001, many companies became aware that disaster recovery planning is of critical importance. Events such as natural disasters and terrorist activity can bypass even the most rigorous physical security measures, and common hardware failures and even accidental deletions may require some form of recovery capability.

Backup and Recovery Planning

Fundamental to any disaster recovery plan is the need to provide for regular backups of key information, including user file and email storage, database stores, event logs, and security principal details such as user logons, passwords, and group membership assignments. Without a regular backup process, loss of data through accidents or directed attack could severely impair business processes.

Any backup and recovery plan must include regular testing of the restoration process to ensure that backup media and procedures are adequate to restore lost functionality.

The form of backup in use may also affect what may be recovered following a disaster. Disaster recovery planning should include identification of the type and regularity of the backup process to be used. The following sections cover the different types of backups you can employ.

Full Backup

This is a complete backup of all data and is the most time-intensive and resource-intensive form of backup, requiring the largest amount of data storage. Restoration from a complete backup will be faster than other methods in the event of a total loss of data. A full backup copies all selected files and resets the archive bit. This method allows you to restore using just one tape. In case of theft, this poses the most risk because all data is on one tape.

Differential Backup

A differential backup includes all data that has changed since the last full backup, regardless of if or when the last differential backup was made because it doesn't reset the archive bit. This form of backup is incomplete for full recovery without a valid full backup. For example, if the server dies on Thursday, two tapes will be needed—the full from Friday and the differential from Wednesday. Differential backups require a variable amount of storage, depending on the regularity of normal backups and the number of changes that occur during the period between full backups. Theft of a differential tape is more risky than an incremental tape because larger chunks of sequential data may be stored on the tape the further away it is from the last full backup.

Incremental Backup

An incremental backup includes all data that has changed since the last incremental backup, and it resets the archive bit. An incremental backup is incomplete for full recovery without a valid full backup and all incremental backups since the last full backup. For example, if the server dies on Thursday, four tapes will be needed—the full from Friday and the incremental tapes from Monday, Tuesday, and Wednesday. Incremental backups require the smallest amount of data storage and require the least amount of backup time, but they can take the most time during restoration. If an incremental tape is stolen, it might not be of value to the offender, but it still represents risk to the company.

Copy Backup

A copy backup is very similar to a full backup in that it copies all selected files. However, it doesn't reset the archive bit. From a security perspective, the loss of a tape with a copy backup is the same as losing a tape with a full backup.

Choosing a Backup Strategy

When choosing a backup strategy, a company should look at the following factors:

➤ *How often it needs to restore files*—As a matter of convenience, if files are restored regularly, a full backup may be decided upon because it can be done with one tape.

➤ *How fast the data needs to be restored*—If large amounts of data are backed up, the incremental backup method may work best.

➤ *How long the data needs to be kept before being overwritten*—If used in a development arena where data is constantly changing, a differential backup method may be the best choice.

After the backups are complete, they must be clearly marked or labeled so they can be properly safeguarded. In addition to these backup strategies, companies employ tape rotation and retention policies. The various methods of tape rotation include the grandfather, Tower of Hanoi, and 10-tape rotation schemes.

One final note in this area: In some instances, it may be more beneficial to copy or image a hard drive for backup purposes. For example, in a development office, where there may be large amounts of data that changes constantly, instead of spending money on a complex backup system to back up all the developers' data, it may be less expensive and more efficient to buy another hard drive for each developer and have him back up his data that way. If the drive is imaged, it ensures that if a machine has a hard drive failure, a swift way of getting it back up and running again is available.

Restoration Procedures

Disaster recovery planning should include detailed restoration procedures. This planning should explain any needed configuration details that may be required to restore access and network function. These may include items that can either be general or very specific.

The policy for restoring a server hardware failure, for example, is as follows:

1. Upon discovery, the on-duty IT manager must be notified. If not on the premises, she should be paged or reached on her cell phone.

2. The IT manager assesses the damage to determine whether the machine can survive on the UPS. If so, for how long? If not, what data must be protected before the machine shuts down.

3. Because all equipment is under warranty, no cases should be opened without the consent of the proper vendor.

4. The IT manager will assign a technician to contact the vendor for instructions and a date when a replacement part can be expected.

5. A determination will be made by the IT manager as to whether the company can survive without the machine until the replacement part is received.

6. If the machine is a vital part of the business, the IT manager must then notify the head of the department affected by the situation and give him an assessment of how and when it will be remedied.

7. The IT manager will then find another machine with similar hardware to replace the damaged server.

8. The damaged machine will be shut down properly if possible, unplugged from the network, and placed in the vendor-assigned work area.

9. The replacement machine will be configured by an assigned technician to ensure it meets the specifications listed in the IT department's server-configuration manual.

10. The most recent backup will be checked out of the tape library by the IT manager. The data will then be restored by the assigned technician.

11. When the technician has determined that the machine is ready to be placed online, the IT manager will evaluate it to be sure it meets the specifications.

12. The replacement server is put in place by the IT manager. Connectivity must be verified and then the appropriate department head can be notified that the situation has been remedied.

Also, a restoration plan should include contingency planning to recover systems and data even in the event of administration personnel loss or lack of availability. This plan should include procedures on what to do if a disgruntled employee changes an administrative password before leaving. Statistics show that more damage to a network comes from inside than outside. Therefore, any key root-level account passwords and critical procedures should be properly documented so another equally trained individual can manage the restoration process.

Secure Recovery

Recovery planning documentation and backup media obviously contain many details that could be exploited by an attacker seeking access to an organization's network or data. As a result, planning documentation, backup scheduling, and backup media must include protections against unauthorized access or potential damage. The data should be protected by at least a password and possibly encryption. Once the backups are complete, they must be clearly marked or labeled so they can be properly safeguarded. Imagine having to perform a restore for an organization that stores its backup tapes in a plastic bin in the server room. The rotation is supposed to be on a two-week basis. When you go to get the needed tape, you discover that the tapes are not marked, nor are they in any particular order. How much time will be spent just trying to find the proper tape? Also, is it a good practice to keep backup tapes in the same room with the servers? What happens if there is a fire? How backup media is handled is just as important as how it is marked. You certainly don't want to store CDs in a place where they can easily be scratched or store tapes in an area that reaches 110 degrees during the day.

Both documentation and media should be stored in an offsite location, protected from unauthorized access as well as fire, flood, and other forms of environmental hazard. It is also common in military environments to have removable storage media that is locked in a proper safe or container at the end of the day.

During the process of recovery, attackers may also attempt to obtain details through packet sniffing of traffic between silo backup servers and deployed network servers. Therefore, planning should include protections against network exploit during the actual restoration.

In Chapter 6, "Infrastructure Security," we covered the proper way to handle removable media when either the data should be overwritten or is no longer useful or pertinent to the company. Here's a quick review of the choices that apply to all removable media units:

➤ *Declassification*—A formal process of assessing the risk involved in discarding particular information.

➤ *Sanitization*—The process of removing the contents from the media as fully as possible, making it extremely difficult to restore.

➤ *Degaussing*—This method uses an electrical device to reduce the magnetic flux density of the storage media to zero.

➤ *Overwriting*—This method is applicable to magnetic storage devices.

➤ *Destruction*—The process of physically destroying the media and the information stored on it.

Disaster Recovery Plan

A detailed disaster recovery plan should be created to provide structure to the process of backup, data security, and recovery. Disaster recovery planning may involve many aspects, including the following:

➤ *Impact and risk assessment*—It is important to determine the magnitude and criticality of service and data failure so you can figure out what forms of recovery planning and preparations must be implemented. In addition, you need to establish the order of recovery in the event of a catastrophic failure.

➤ *Disaster recovery plan*—A detailed disaster recovery plan should be created, including details for contingency planning in the event that catastrophic events preclude the use of previous network resources.

➤ *Disaster recovery policies*—These policies detail responsibilities and procedures to follow during disaster recovery events, including how to contact key employees, vendors, customers, and the press. They should also include instructions for situations in which it may be necessary to bypass the normal chain of command to minimize damage or the effects of a disaster.

➤ *Service-level agreements (SLAs)*—Contracts with Internet Service Providers (ISPs), utilities, facilities managers, and other types of suppliers that detail minimum levels of support that must be provided in the event of failure or disaster.

Business Continuity Planning

Beyond backup and restoration of data, disaster recovery planning must also include a detailed analysis of underlying business practices and support requirements needed to ensure that business continuity can be maintained in the event of failure. Business continuity planning should include an analysis of any required services, such as network access and utility agreements, along with planning for automatic failover of critical services to redundant offsite systems.

Some considerations that may be included in continuity planning include the following:

➤ *Network connectivity*—In the event that a disaster is widespread or targeted at an ISP or key routing hardware point, an organization's continuity plan should include options for alternate network access, including dedicated administrative connections that may be required for recovery to occur.

➤ *Facilities*—Continuity planning should include considerations for recovery in the event that existing hardware and facilities are rendered inaccessible or unrecoverable. Hardware configuration details, network requirements, and utilities agreements for alternate sites (that is, warm and cold sites) should be included in this area.

➤ *Clustering*—To provide load-balancing to avoid loss of functionality through directed attacks meant to prevent valid access, continuity planning may include the use of clustering solutions that allow multiple nodes to perform support while transparently acting as a single host to the user. High-availability clustering may also be used to ensure that automatic failover will occur in the event that hardware failure renders the primary node unable to provide normal service.

➤ *Fault tolerance*—Cross-site replication between hot and cold backup servers may be included for high-availability solutions requiring high levels of fault tolerance. Individual servers may also be configured to allow for the continued function of key services even in the case of hardware failure. Common fault-tolerant solutions include Redundant Arrays of Inexpensive Disks (RAID) solutions, which maintain duplicated data across multiple disks so that the loss of one disk will not cause the loss of data. Many of these solutions may also support hot-swapping of failed drives so that replacement hardware may be installed without ever taking the server offline.

Security Policies and Procedures

To ensure that disaster recovery planning is managed and maintained, it is important to establish clear and detailed security policies that are ratified by an organization's management and brought to the attention of its users. Policies of which the users have no knowledge are rarely effective, whereas those that lack management support may prove to be unenforceable. Security policy planning details many areas, including the following:

➤ *Risk assessment*—The security policy team must perform a detailed risk assessment to determine the scope of assets to be protected by the policies, along with the identification of users and vendors who must abide by these policies.

➤ *Security*—Considerations must include the specification of physical security requirements, network security planning details such as equipment and protocol specifications, and a detailed agreement of approved software that may be installed within the network, including provisions for testing and approving new software packages.

➤ *Acceptable use*—Details must be provided that specify what users may do with their network access, from email and instant messaging usage for personal purposes through limitations on access times and the storage space available to each user. It is important to provide users the least possible access rights while allowing them to fulfill legitimate actions.

➤ *Compliance*—Policy planning must include detailed sanctions that may be imposed in the event of a violation of each security policy. Sanctions must have management approval and support and may include measures ranging from loss of network privileges to legal action, depending on the severity of the breach.

Additional considerations that may be required by security policy planning might include the following:

➤ *Due care*—Due care is based on best practices and what a prudent organization would do in a similar case. In other words, it involves doing the right thing and acting responsibly.

➤ *Privacy*—Users and administrators must be made aware of privacy issues that may arise, including adequate notice of access rights claimed by the organization over file, email, and instant messaging traffic within the organization's network.

➤ *Separation of duties*—It is important to include a separation of duties when planning for security policy compliance. Without a clear separation between review tasks, all areas of access control and compliance review may be left in the hands of a single individual for whom the check-and-balance process has not applied. The loss of a key individual may also pose difficulties if planning for assumption of duties is not performed. This policy might include such details as the identification of which group is responsible for updating security hotfixes and which is responsible for updating data records in an organization's database. Another method used to separate duties is *data aggregation*, which is the process of combining separate pieces of data that by themselves may be of no use, but when they're combined with other bits of data, they provide greater understanding.

➤ *Need to know*—The nature of network data access includes the possibility for broad distribution of all possible data, which may place an organization's data and trade secrets at risk. Users should only have access to the resources and information necessary to perform their roles. Any request to access information must be justified. Just because the information is there doesn't necessarily mean a user should have access to it; he should only have access to the information he needs to know.

➤ *Password management*—Weak passwords pose many security risks that may be exploited by an attacker. It is important that password duration and complexity requirements are established and that users are made aware of these requirements along with the reasons why they exist. Regular review of existing passwords using auditing tools is also important in order to ensure that users are in compliance with these policies.

➤ *Disposal and destruction*—Outdated or failed hardware and discarded reporting may often be exploited by attackers to obtain access to a network. Dumpster-diving and other forms of access to discarded materials are common during tiger team assessments to identify user account details, potential security flaws, and details of backup and recovery planning. Many businesses require shredding of all documents and security-erasure of storage media before they may be discarded.

➤ *Human Resource policies*—Security planning must include procedures for the creation and authorization of accounts for newly hired personnel as well as the planned removal of privileges following employment termination. When termination involves power users who enjoy high levels of access rights or knowledge of service administration account passwords, it is critical to institute password and security updates to exclude known avenues of access while also increasing security monitoring for possible reprisals against the organization. The hiring process should also include provisions for making new employees aware of acceptable use and disposal policies, along with the sanctions that may be enacted if violations occur. An organization should also institute a formal code of ethics to which all employees should subscribe—particularly power users with broad administrative rights.

➤ *Incident response*—Incident response planning policies should be documented, including the identification of required forensic and data-gathering procedures along with proper reporting and recovery procedures for each type of security-related incident.

Users must be made aware of security policies, potential methods of social engineering attacks, and expectations for disposal and proper use to minimize potential weaknesses in network security. Without this education and regular testing and reminders, users may fail to perform simple tasks that can be exploited to grant an attacker access to your network.

Practice Questions

Question 1

Which of the following security policies would identify that a user may be fined for using email to run a personal business?

- ○ A. Acceptable use
- ○ B. Privacy
- ○ C. Due care
- ○ D. Compliance
- ○ E. Separation of duties
- ○ F. Need to know

Answer D is correct. Security policy compliance statements detail the sanctions that may result from violations of acceptable use policies. Answer A is incorrect because although this appears to be a violation of acceptable use, details of the sanctions resulting from the violation are detailed within the compliance policy. Answers B, C, E, and F are also incorrect because they detail individual policies for which the compliance policy may detail sanctions if violated, but they would not be used to detail these sanctions individually.

Question 2

Which of the following environmental considerations would be of the greatest concern when planning to perform in-place hardware upgrades?

- ○ A. Temperature control
- ○ B. Humidity control
- ○ C. Static dissipation
- ○ D. Vibration isolation

Answer C is correct. When planning to perform hardware maintenance, it is important to remember to plan for dissipation of static through the use of grounding wrist straps and antistatic pads. Answers A and B are incorrect because, although both temperature and humidity may play a role in antistatic planning, they are not directly applicable here because an in-place upgrade does not involve a significant change from the normal operating environment of the system. Answer D is incorrect because vibration is not directly of concern during a normal upgrade scenario, although care to avoid breakage is important.

Question 3

An attacker offers her business card as an IT solution provider and then later causes a user's computer to appear to fail. What is this an example of?

○ A. Reverse social engineering

○ B. Social engineering

○ C. Separation of duties

○ D. Inverse social engineering

Answer A is correct. Reverse social engineering involves an attacker convincing the user that she is a legitimate IT authority, causing the user to solicit her assistance. Answer B is incorrect because social engineering is when an intruder tricks a user into giving him private information. Answer C is incorrect because separation of duties is when two users are assigned a part of a task that both of them need to complete. Answer D is incorrect because it is a bogus answer.

Question 4

Why is it important to protect systems from line-of-sight monitoring? [Choose the three best answers.]

❑ A. Remote monitoring may allow an attacker to observe standard operational routines.

❑ B. An attacker may learn a user's logon credentials.

❑ C. Data may be directly observed through a telescope.

❑ D. Electromagnetic detection of wireless signals could compromise sensitive data.

Answers A, B, and C are correct. Attackers with direct line-of-sight access may observe operational routines, user logon and password keystrokes, or raw data used to illuminate data transmission status readouts. Answer D is incorrect because electromagnetic remote monitoring of wireless signals is not limited to the line of sight.

Question 5

What is the difference between a wet-pipe and a dry-pipe fire-suppression system?

- ○ A. A dry-pipe system uses air to suppress fire, whereas a wet-pipe system uses water.
- ○ B. A dry-pipe system uses dry chemicals, whereas a wet-pipe system uses wet chemicals.
- ○ C. A wet-pipe system has water in the pipe at all times, whereas in a dry-pipe system water is used but is held back by a valve until a certain temperature is reached.
- ○ D. A wet-pipe system uses wet chemicals that deploy after the pipe loses air pressure, whereas a dry-pipe system uses dry chemicals that deploy before the pipe loses air pressure.

Answer C is correct. A wet-pipe system constantly has water in it. In dry pipe systems, water is used but is held back by a valve until a certain temperature is reached. Therefore, answers A, B, and D are incorrect.

Question 6

Which of the following aspects of disaster recovery planning details how fast an ISP must have a new Frame Relay connection configured to an alternate site?

- ○ A. Impact and risk assessment
- ○ B. Disaster recovery plan
- ○ C. Disaster recovery policies
- ○ D. Service-level agreement

Answer D is correct. Service-level agreements establish the contracted requirements for service through utilities, facility management, and ISPs. Answer A is incorrect because risk assessment is used to identify areas that must be addressed in disaster recovery provisions. Answers B and C are incorrect because, although the disaster recovery plan and its policies may include details of the service-level agreement's implementation, neither is the best answer in this case.

Question 7

Which type of backup requires the least amount of time to restore in the event of a total loss?

- ○ A. Full
- ○ B. Daily
- ○ C. Differential
- ○ D. Incremental

Answer A is correct. A full backup includes a copy of all data, so it may be used to directly restore all data and settings as of the time of the last backup. Answers B, C, and D are incorrect because daily, differential, and incremental backups all require a full backup as well as additional backup files to restore from a total loss of data.

Question 8

Which of the following statements best describes a disaster recovery plan (DRP)?

- ○ A. A DRP reduces the impact of a hurricane on a facility.
- ○ B. A DRP is an immediate action plan used to bring a business back online immediately after a disaster has struck.
- ○ C. A DRP attempts to manage risks associated with theft of equipment.
- ○ D. A DRP plans for automatic failover of critical services to redundant off-site systems.

Answer B is correct. A DRP is an immediate action plan to be implemented after a disaster. Answer A is incorrect because it describes physical disasters. Answer C is incorrect because it describes loss prevention. Answer D is incorrect because it describes a business continuity plan.

Question 9

Which of the following are examples of social engineering? [Choose the two best answers.]

- ❏ A. An attacker configures a packet sniffer to monitor user logon credentials.
- ❏ B. An attacker sets off a fire alarm so that he can access a secured area when the legitimate employees are evacuated.
- ❏ C. An attacker waits until legitimate users have left and sneaks into the server room through the raised floor.
- ❏ D. An attacker unplugs a user's network connection and then offers to help try to correct the problem.
- ❏ E. An attacker obtains an IT office T-shirt from a local thrift store and takes a user's computer for service.

Answers D and E are correct. Social engineering attacks involve tricking a user into providing the attacker with access rights or operational details. Answer A is incorrect because packet sniffing is a form of a network security threat. Answers B and C are incorrect because they involve physical access control risks rather than social engineering.

Question 10

Full backups are made weekly on Sunday at 1:00 a.m., and incremental backups are made on weekdays at 1:00 a.m. If a drive failure causes a total loss of data at 8:00 a.m. on Tuesday morning, what is the minimum number of backup files that must be used to restore the lost data?

- ○ A. One
- ○ B. Two
- ○ C. Three
- ○ D. Four
- ○ E. Five

Answer C is correct. Sunday's full backup must be installed, followed by Monday's incremental backup and finally Tuesday morning's incremental backup. This will recover all data as of 1:00 a.m. Tuesday morning. Answers A and B are incorrect because a full backup Tuesday morning would be required to allow a single-file recovery of all data, whereas a differential backup on Tuesday morning would be required so that only two backup files would be needed. Answers D and E are incorrect because no files from before the last full backup would be required.

Need to Know More?

 Chirillo, John. *Hack Attacks Denied*. John Wiley & Sons. New York, NY, 2001. ISBN 0471416258.

 Shipley, Greg. *Maximum Security, Third Edition*. Sams Publishing. Indianapolis, IN, 2001. ISBN 0672318717.

 SANS Information Security Reading Room: `rr.sans.org/index.php`

 CERT Incident Reporting Guidelines: `www.cert.org/tech_tips/incident_reporting.html`

Privilege Management, Forensics, Risk Identification, Education, and Documentation

Terms you'll need to understand:

✓ Privilege management
✓ Access control
✓ Mandatory Access Control (MAC)
✓ Discretionary Access Control (DAC)
✓ Role-Based Access Control (RBAC)
✓ Risk assessment
✓ Vulncrabilities
✓ Acceptable use
✓ Forensics

Techniques you'll need to master:

✓ Knowing the differences between user-based, group-based, and Role-Based Access Control models
✓ Understanding the basic steps involved in performing a risk assessment for an organization
✓ Understanding the steps involved in forensic analysis of data

After securing both physical and network access, as discussed in Chapter 10, "Organizational Security," it is necessary to plan for proper privilege management over network resource access as well as to plan for later security auditing and incident-response standards. This chapter will look at models of privilege management and basic details relating to risk identification, education, documentation, and post-incident forensics. This chapter will not attempt to cover all possible avenues of risk assessment and response management but will provide you with the necessary details for the exam. Additional resources are detailed at the end of the chapter.

Understanding Privilege Management

The concept of *privilege* refers to levels of access authority over resources and actions within your network. The level at which privileges may be managed is often referred to as the *granularity of access control*. Several levels of granular access control are possible:

➤ *User based*—Within a user-based model, permissions and access denials are uniquely assigned to each account. Within a peer-to-peer network, such as a workgroup, this is the form of access control used.

➤ *Group based*—In group-based access control schemes, permissions and access denials are assigned to groups, and user accounts are made members of these groups to control aggregate access permissions for each account based on the combined permissions inherited from its group memberships. Access control over large numbers of user accounts may be easily accomplished by managing the access permissions on each group, which are then inherited by the group's members.

➤ *Role based*—Role-Based Access Control (RBAC) involves a variation of the group-based access control method. Each defined role is given the proper access permissions necessary for the defined role, and then roles are assigned to the appropriate user accounts. Access control is accomplished by assigning roles to the proper accounts and changing permissions on each role as required.

Single Sign-On

For a long time, it was thought that for each server on the network to remain secure, users should maintain a different user account and password for each server. The premise being that if a user's account was compromised, it would only allow access to one server and therefore would reduce the impact of the compromise. This concept worked well when networks were small and servers were few. But what happens when users have to access 10, 20, or even 100 different servers? Maintaining a separate username and password for each server becomes unmanageable. This is mostly because users now write down their passwords because they can't remember so many different ones, and the whole purpose of multiple user accounts and passwords becomes a security risk. Thus single sign-on (SSO) came into being. Users sign on or log on to a network once and can access any desired network resource, regardless of the operating system managing it. SSO is designed to make the life of both users and administrators easier. Network administrators benefit by being able to have a single set of users to track and grant privilege to. In addition, help desk calls are reduced because account lockouts and password resets won't occur as frequently.

 One benefit to an authentication database–supported method of access control is that an account may be granted privileges over resources located throughout an enterprise scenario. A single sign-on (SSO) solution allows users to authenticate once and then access resources throughout a network based on the account's access control list (ACL).

Centralized Versus Decentralized

Security management is based on one of two models: centralized or decentralized. Both the group-based and role-based methods of access control require a *centralized* database of accounts and roles or groups to which these are assigned. This database may be maintained on a single, central server that must then be contacted by servers providing resources when an account's proper ACL must be verified for access to a resource. Centralized privilege management is more secure because all privilege assignments and changes made to existing accounts are done through one department or group. The drawback to the centralized model of privilege management is the ability to scale. As the company and network grow, it becomes more and more difficult to keep up with the tasks of assigning and managing network resource access and privileges.

Decentralized security management is less secure but more scalable. Responsibilities are delegated, and employees at different locations are made responsible for managing privileges within their administrative areas. Decentralized management is less secure because more people are involved in the process, and a greater possibility for errors exists.

Most companies use a hybrid network-management approach. Management may decide to centralize the creation of user accounts while decentralizing resource access and privilege assignment to the owners of the servers and data.

Managing Access Control

Access control may be managed in several ways, depending on whether access rights must be strictly enforced for all accounts or they may reflect changes in the network environment. Some of the more common access control configurations include the following:

➤ *Mandatory Access Control (MAC)*—Control is determined by the security policy of the system. The system makes access determinations by comparing the labels of the user and the object. Users have little control or influence over the data or the environment. The object owner cannot override the security.

➤ *Discretionary Access Control (DAC)*—Control is determined by the data owner. The creator/owner of a file can determine who has access to the file. The basis of DAC is the use of ACLs. These lists are enforced by the operating system but are determined by the owners and set by the network administrator.

➤ *Role-Based Access Control (RBAC)*—In this type of access control, it is determined what job functions each employee performs and then access is assigned based on those functions. Role-Based Access Control is also known as *nondiscretionary access control*. Users are assigned roles and then permissions are assigned to the roles.

Monitoring Access Use

After you have established the proper access control scheme, it is important to monitor changes in access rights. Auditing user privileges is generally a two-step process that involves turning auditing on within the operating system and then specifying the resources to be audited. After enabling auditing, you also need to monitor the logs that are generated. Auditing should include both privilege and usage. Auditing of access use and rights changes should be implemented to prevent unauthorized or unintentional access or escalation of privileges, which might allow a guest or restricted user account access to sensitive or protected resources. Figure 11.1 provides an example of an auditing policy configured to log privilege use and account management.

```
Local Security Settings                                              _ □ x
File   Action   View   Help

Security Settings                  Policy                          Security Setting
  Account Policies                  Audit account logon events       Success, Failure
    Password Policy                 Audit account management         Success, Failure
    Account Lockout Policy          Audit directory service access   No auditing
  Local Policies                    Audit logon events               Success, Failure
    Audit Policy                    Audit object access              Failure
    User Rights Assignment          Audit policy change              Success, Failure
    Security Options                Audit privilege use              Success, Failure
  Public Key Policies               Audit process tracking           No auditing
  Software Restriction Policies     Audit system events              No auditing
  IP Security Policies on Local Computer
```

Figure 11.1   An example of a Windows audit policy configured for the monitoring of privilege use and account management.

When configuring an audit policy, it is important to monitor successful as well as failed access attempts. Failure events allow you to identify unauthorized access attempts; successful events can reveal an accidental or intentional escalation of access rights.

Understanding Computer Forensics

When a potential security breach must be reviewed, the computer forensics process comes into play. Similar to other forms of legal forensics, this process requires a vast knowledge of computer hardware and software in order to protect the chain of custody over the evidence, avoid accidental invalidation or destruction of evidence, and preserve the evidence for future analysis. Computer forensic review involves the application of investigative and analytical techniques to acquire and protect potential legal evidence. Therefore, a professional within this field needs a detailed understanding of the local, regional, national, and even international laws affecting the process of evidence collection and retention—especially in cases involving attacks that may be waged from widely distributed systems located in many separate regions.

Chain of Custody

Forensic analysis first involves establishing a clear *chain of custody* over the evidence, which is the documentation of all transfers of evidence from one person to another, showing the date, time, and reason for transfer as well as the signatures of both parties involved in the transfer. In other words, it tells how the evidence made it from the crime scene to the courtroom, including documentation of how the evidence was collected, preserved, and analyzed. If you are asked to testify regarding data that has been recovered or preserved, it is critical that you, as the investigating security administrator, be able to prove that no other individuals or agents could have tampered with or modified the evidence. This requires careful collection and preservation of all evidence, including the detailed logging of investigative access and the scope of the investigation. Definition of the scope is crucial to ensure that accidental privacy violations or unrelated exposure will not contaminate the evidence trail. After data is collected, it must be secured in such a manner that you, as the investigating official, can state with certainty that the evidence could not have been accessed or modified during your custodial term.

Preservation of Evidence

After the evidence has been identified, it must be properly collected and preserved to be used in court. If the evidence is not preserved properly, it may be inadmissible. The forensic process is built around the fact that computer evidence can be altered, lost, or destroyed. Preserving evidence is difficult in computers because the data itself is not physical; instead it resides on physical devices. Information obtained from a computer will generally fall under the category of hearsay. Hearsay is considered secondhand evidence and is not normally admissible in court.

Any affected system should be immediately imaged before any other investigative tools are used. This ensures that data is preserved in its current state. If this step is not followed, timestamps may be inadvertently changed or files may be modified. Worse yet, because criminals have become more sophisticated, viruses or logic bombs may be set off. After the image is captured, it should be written to nonerasable media and documented according to local laws. If memory and cache are to be examined, the proper tools for capturing and reading these hardware devices should be used before imaging. Because imaging requires the computer to be rebooted, it would destroy data located in RAM and cache devices.

During each of the steps, logs should be kept. If the data is accessed as a part of the investigation, all activity should be logged. If the evidence is moved, the reason for the move and the procedures used should be documented. This may sound like a lot of unnecessary work, but it is critical to preserving the trustworthiness of the data so that it can be presented in court. Remember that evidence should be labeled and stored properly in an area that is secure.

Collection of Evidence

As mentioned in the preceding section, hearsay is generally inadmissible. Computer evidence can be admissible if it can be shown that it was collected under defined procedures and as part of a routine business practice. These procedures must be established before the incident and collection occur in order for the evidence to be admissible.

An investigating administrator must take many steps during the process of evidence acquisition, including the following:

➤ *Protection*—It is important to protect the subject computer system or systems against alteration, physical damage, data corruption, or viral incursion.

➤ *Discovery*—Investigations must include existing files, deleted files, slack space (where unallocated space may retain valuable evidence), hidden files, encrypted files, and details regarding file ownership, file access, and file modification. This includes temporary file stores, pagefiles, and swap areas.

➤ *Analysis*—An analysis of the information should include details of any assumptions made during the course of the investigation, along with the results generated based on these assumptions. It is critical to include both successful and failed assumptions.

➤ *Documentation*—Documentation should include printouts, file listings, system and network layouts, file structures and file system details, discovered data and file ownership information, and any other details that might indicate the events that may have occurred. It is recommended that a detailed log of all access attempts and assumptions be included to prove that changes made during the investigative process were valid and not corruptive.

➤ *Preservation*—It is vital to preserve all documentation, data, and related items until such time as a properly designated and authorized agent of the court or the organization's legal staff is able to take possession. A signed document detailing the transfer should also be included in the documentation to provide clear tracking from the moment of the investigation's initiation to its conclusion.

➤ *Testimony*—An investigator should be prepared to provide expert analysis, consultation, and testimony if required. In many cases, the time between an investigation and its resolution may be significant, causing the documentation to become more important if the investigator is asked to testify or provide later analysis.

The practice of forensic analysis is a detailed and exacting one. The information provided in this chapter allows an entering professional to recognize the actions that will be taken during an investigation. It is crucial that you do not attempt to perform these tasks without detailed training in the hardware, software, network, and legal issues involved in forensic analysis.

Forensic software is available for collecting data properly. Forensic software allows you to collect and digitally sign a container that electronically stores evidence. After evidence is placed inside a digital bag, it is signed with a certificate to prove that no tampering has occurred since it was collected. Evidence gathered properly in this manner has already withstood the rigors of court and has been successful.

Another form of collecting data involves the imaging of the system or systems compromised. This can be done by copying the entire drive at the binary level, or the data can be copied into a digital evidence bag. After a complete copy is made, it should be sealed as read-only. After that complete copy of the data is collected and stored, it must be secured from tampering or alteration to meet the necessary chain of custody rules. If the chain of custody is broken at any point, the court will simply throw out the evidence.

Identifying Risks

Because security resources will always be limited in some manner, it is important to determine what resources are present that may need securing. Then you need to determine the threat level of exposure that each resource creates and plan your network defenses accordingly. Previously, we discussed how to protect resources and assets; now we'll look at how to identify the risks that affect them. In this section, we cover the following methods of identifying risks: asset identification, risk and threat assessment, and vulnerabilities.

Asset Identification

Before you can determine which resources are most in need of protection, it is important to properly document all available resources. For the purpose of our discussion, the term *resource* can refer to a physical item (such as a server or piece of networking equipment), a logical object (such as a Web site or financial report), or even a business procedure (such as a distribution strategy or marketing scheme). Sales demographics, trade secrets, customer data, and even payroll information could be considered sensitive resources within an organization.

Risk Assessment

After assets have been identified, you need to determine which of these assets are more important than the others and which assets pose significant security risks. During the process of risk assessment, it is necessary to review many areas, such as the following:

➤ Methods of access

➤ Authentication schemes

➤ Audit policies

➤ Hiring and release procedures

➤ Isolated services that may provide a single point of failure or avenue of compromise

➤ Data or services requiring special backup or automatic failover support

 Risk assessment should include planning against both external and internal threats. An insider familiar with an organization's procedures can pose a very dangerous risk to network security.

Threat Assessment

During a risk assessment, it is important to identify potential threats and document standard response policies for each. Threats may include the following:

➤ Direct access attempts

➤ Automated cracking agents

➤ Viral agents, including worms and Trojan horses

➤ Released or dissatisfied employees

➤ Denial of service attacks or overloaded capacity on critical services

➤ Hardware or software failure, including facility-related issues such as power or plumbing failures

Vulnerabilities

After you have identified all sensitive assets and performed a detailed risk assessment, it is necessary to review potential vulnerabilities and take actions to harden each based on its relative worth and level of exposure. Evaluations should include an assessment of the relative risk to an organization's operations, the ease of defense or recovery, and the relative popularity and complexity of the potential form of attack.

Many automated vulnerability-scanning tools are available for various platforms. These may be used to perform regular assessments of your network; however, because of the constant discovery of new vulnerabilities, it is also very important to include a review of newly discovered vulnerabilities as part of your standard operating procedures.

 Online resources such as those provided by the SANS Institute and the BUGTRAQ lists are good examples of the resources available to network administrators responsible for watching for new vulnerabilities.

When you're performing an analysis of potential vulnerabilities, several possible steps may be taken:

➤ *Blind testing*—Performing an audit from outside using no prior knowledge of an organization's network or procedures.

➤ *Knowledgeable testing*—Performing an audit using known details on the infrastructure and current business practices.

➤ *Internet service testing*—Attempting penetration using common exploits accessible through the Internet.

➤ *Dial-up service testing*—Performing a penetration attempt against an organization's remote access servers through war-dialing and other modes of dial-up access attempts.

➤ *Infrastructure testing*—Evaluating protocols used as well as the subjective user perception of operational parameters. Users may sometimes note obscure or unnecessarily complex configurations that might be exploited.

➤ *Network testing*—Evaluating distributed resources, replication architecture, and critical services, such as DNS or DHCP, along with firewall and IDS configuration settings.

➤ *Application testing*—Evaluating homegrown and store-bought applications. This is necessary to ensure end-to-end security.

Implementing User Education

One of the most powerful tools available to a security administrator is the body of network users, who may notice and draw attention to unusual access methods or unexpected changes. This same body of users also creates the greatest number of potential security holes, because each user may be unaware of newly emerging vulnerabilities, threats, or required standards of action and access that must be followed. Like a chain, a network is only as secure as its weakest link—and users present a wide variety of bad habits, a vast range of knowledge, and varying intent in access.

When planning for user notification of new threats, such as a virus or an email-distributed agent of mischief, it is crucial that your solution includes a means of communication other than that affected by the potential threat. For example, it will do little good to warn users of a new email bomb via email if the bomb has already affected your avenue of distribution.

User education is mandatory to ensure that users are made aware of expectations, options, and requirements relating to secure access within an organization's network. Education may include many different forms of communication, including the following:

➤ New employees and contract agents should be provided education in security requirements as a part of the hiring process.

➤ Reminders and security-awareness newsletters, emails, and flyers should be provided to raise general security awareness.

➤ General security policies must be defined, documented, and distributed to employees.

➤ Regular focus group sessions and on-the-job training should be provided for users regarding changes to the user interface, application suites, and general policies.

➤ General online security-related resources should be made available to users through a simple, concise, and easily navigable interface.

It is important to locate a suitable upper-level sponsor for security initiatives to ensure that published security training and other requirements are applied to all users equally. Hackers, crackers, and other agents seeking unauthorized access often search for highly placed users within an organization who have exempted themselves from standard security policies.

Understanding Security Documentation

Vulnerability assessments, change-management procedures, incident-response guidelines, security procedures, logs, and many other security-related factors may require extensive documentation. In addition, you should plan for the proper storage and disposal of these documents to prevent accidental exposure of sensitive information. Because security audit documentation provides focused information detailing vulnerabilities and risks, these documents should always be kept in a sealed, limited-access location.

Security Policies

Security policy documentation is often the most extensive in terms of variety, rapidity of change, and requirements for retention and disposal. Possible security policies include the following:

➤ *Acceptable use policy*—Specifies the acceptable use of equipment and resources as well as the expected security measures users should follow. This may include a more detailed email use policy.

➤ *Antivirus policy*—Specifies requirements for antivirus software, definitions update procedures, and computer use expectations involving potential avenues for viral incursion.

➤ *Audit policy*—Specifies details to authorize, conduct, and investigate audits, security risk assessments, and user compliance. This may also include authorization for incident response and reporting, along with limitations on what data may be logged and how long it may be stored during client monitoring.

➤ *Nondisclosure agreement*—Documents the user's agreement to avoid disclosing sensitive information. This may include specific details regarding the level of access granted to a particular user and should be maintained in a secured, limited-access, fireproof location.

➤ *Password policy*—Specifies password requirements, including length, strength, history, and required rate of change. This may include details on regular security reviews of password settings.

➤ *Remote access policy*—Specifies access requirements and methods used during the remote access of an organization's resources, such as dial-up or VPN connections.

➤ *Server security policy*—Specifies the minimum security required of servers operating within an organization's protected network. This may include additional details specific to DMZ or bastion servers.

➤ *Wireless network policy*—Specifies the standards, WEP keys, and other configuration settings used in WLAN solutions.

Architecture Documentation

Following the discovery and profiling phases of your asset-identification and risk assessments, you need to produce detailed documentation on the system's architecture. This documentation includes hardware and software inventories, as well as specifications on logical replication paths and protocols in use. Security architectural documentation should include remote access, VPN, firewall, and IDS systems. Obviously, these documents should be carefully protected to avoid accidental exposure.

Because the network architecture will continue to evolve, it is critical to plan for change management. Change-management policies should include specifications for change authorization, documentation, and notification, along with inventory-control procedures and retirement procedures to be used when hardware, software, or storage media is replaced or discarded.

An organization's information sensitivity policy will define requirements for the classification and security of data and hardware resources based on their relative level of sensitivity. Some resources, such as hard drives, might require very extensive preparations before they may be discarded.

Change Documentation

All changes should be documented. Many companies are lacking in this area. We are often in a hurry to make changes and say we will do the documentation later—most of the time, that doesn't happen. You should realize that documentation is critical. It eliminates misunderstandings and serves as a trail if something goes awry down the road. Change documentation should include the following:

➤ Specific details, such as the files being replaced, the configuration being changed, the machines or operating systems affected, and so on

➤ The name of the authority who approved the changes

➤ A list of the departments that will be involved in performing the changes and the names of their supervisors

➤ What the immediate effect of the change will be

➤ What the long-term effect of the change will be

➤ The date and time the change will occur

After the change has occurred, the following should be added to the documentation:

➤ Specific problems and issues that occurred during the process

➤ Any known workarounds if issues have occurred

➤ Recommendations and notes on the event

After the change has been requested, documented, and approved, you should then send out notification. Notification is discussed a little bit later.

Logs and Inventories

The log files themselves are documentation, but how do you set up a log properly? Standards should be developed for each platform, application, and server type to make this a checklist or monitoring function. When choosing what to audit, be sure you choose carefully. Audit logs take up space and use system resources. They also have to be read, and if you audit too much, the system will bog down and it will take a long time to weed through the log files to determine what is important. A common storage location for all logs should be mandated, and documentation should state proper methods for archiving and reviewing logs.

Classification

The last area of documentation we'll discuss is the classification of data. You should set standards for how information is evaluated and classified. The standards for data classification can be taken directly from standards published by the U.S. government, or you can come up with your own model. After that is accomplished, you can then document how to store the data. There should also be a policy in place for the destruction of data. Many criminals have found valuable data by "dumpster diving," and many companies have been embarrassed by the media, conducting their own investigations, using information these companies do not destroy properly.

Retention and storage documentation should outline the standards for storing each classification level of data. Take, for example, the military levels of data classification. Their documentation would include directions on handling and storing the following types of data:

➤ Unclassified

➤ Sensitive

➤ Confidential

➤ Secret

➤ Top secret

Documentation for data should include how to classify, handle, store, and destroy it. The important thing to remember here is to document your security objectives. Then change and adjust that documentation when and as needed (with emphasis on *when and as needed*). There may be a reason to make new classifications as business goals change, but make sure this gets into your documentation. This is an ongoing, ever-changing process.

Notification

Change notification should be distributed to those possibly affected by the change. The notification process should include a feedback option in the event that someone finds a step or detail that was overlooked in the original submission. Before you actually deploy the change, an impact assessment should be conducted.

An impact assessment or test phase should be conducted on nonproduction equipment in a test lab and evaluated without affecting user productivity. The most effective way is to create a mockup of the production environment and deploy changes there first. Deployment on lab equipment may uncover immediate problems and allow you time to adjust the process to overcome the issues. A good example would be a software patch. Many vendors release security patches for their software. By testing the patch in a lab environment, you may help avert a disaster later on, when the patch adversely affects another security issue. Impact testing should be well documented and should involve simulated end-user activity on the system. You never know the true impact of a change until you take the final step and upgrade your production systems. So what happens if disaster strikes? How do you remove the changes?

A rollback strategy should be part of *every* change operation. You need to remember that you are making changes that may impact productivity and the ability of the company to conduct business. Something as simple as upgrading a video driver can turn into a nightmare if you can't find a copy of the old driver when the new one fails. You need to protect yourself from such scenarios. Make sure you have a rollback plan in place before any changes are made.

Retention and Disposal

Log files, physical records, security evaluations, and other operational documentation should be managed within an organization's retention and disposal policies. These should include specifications for access authorization, term of retention, and requirements for disposal. Depending on the relative level of data sensitivity, retention and disposal requirements may become extensive and detailed.

Practice Questions

Question 1

Why is it important to audit both failed events and successful events?

- ○ A. It's not. You only need to audit failed events.
- ○ B. Because they will reveal unauthorized access attempts.
- ○ C. Because you can't just audit one. Both have to be activated.
- ○ D. It's not. You only need to audit successful events.

Answer B is correct. It is equally important to audit both failed and successful events because both may reveal unauthorized access or an unexpected escalation of access rights. Answer A and D are incorrect because it is important to audit both types of events. Answer C is incorrect because you can audit either successful or failed events if you choose.

Question 2

In which of the following vulnerability assessment tests would you evaluate a user's ability to connect to a RAS server via telephony?

- ○ A. Blind testing
- ○ B. Knowledgeable testing
- ○ C. Internet service testing
- ○ D. Dial-up service testing
- ○ E. Infrastructure testing

Answer D is correct. Dial-up service testing involves attempting to penetrate a network's security through telephonic connectivity to a RAS server supporting modem dial-in access. Answers A and B are incorrect because they involve a general audit either with or without prior knowledge of the network, and they do not target remote access servers specifically. Answer C is incorrect because an Internet service test focuses on Internet-accessible avenues of penetration rather than dial-up access. Answer E is incorrect because an infrastructure test involves the analysis of networking, protocols, and distributed resources and services, without focusing specifically on RAS services.

Question 3

In which of the following policies would you detail what type of authorization is needed to perform a port scan of an organization's network?

- ○ A. Acceptable use policy
- ○ B. Audit policy
- ○ C. Nondisclosure agreement
- ○ D. Remote access policy
- ○ E. Server security policy

Answer B is correct. The audit policy includes specifications for external auditing and profiling, such as performing a port scan. Answer A is incorrect because the acceptable use policy details what constitutes acceptable use of computer equipment and resources. Answer C is incorrect because the NDA is used to obtain a user's agreement to not disclose sensitive information. This should be required of any agent performing an audit, but it does not directly provide the method for audit authorization. Answers D and E are incorrect because they specify access restrictions and minimum security configurations required for servers, including RAS servers.

Question 4

You are the primary investigator on a team that is investigating the theft of some important information from your network. You have collected and analyzed data and are preparing to present your information in court. What is the process called when presenting the path that the evidence took to the courtroom?

- ○ A. Evidenced path
- ○ B. Chain of custody
- ○ C. Forensics
- ○ D. Chain of evidence

Answer B is correct. Verifying the path of evidence from the crime scene to the courtroom is called the *chain of custody*. Answers A and D are incorrect because they are made-up terms. Answer C is incorrect because forensics is the study of evidence.

Question 5

With Discretionary Access Control (DAC), what determines access rights to resources?

- ○ A. Roles
- ○ B. Rules
- ○ C. Owner discretion
- ○ D. Security labels

Answer C is correct. DAC enables the owner of the resources to specify who can access those resources. Answer A is incorrect because roles are used to group access rights by role name; the use of resources is restricted to those associated with an authorized role. Answer B is incorrect because rules are part of Mandatory Access Control. Answer D is incorrect because security labels are also used in Mandatory Access Control.

Question 6

In which of the following models would you require a centralized database of user accounts? [Choose the two best answers.]

- ❑ A. User based
- ❑ B. Group based
- ❑ C. Role based
- ❑ D. Risk based

Answers B and C are correct. Both group-based and Role-Based Access Control models require a centralized database of user accounts and groups or roles through which permissions may be inherited. Answer A is incorrect because it is possible to have a user-based access control scenario within a peer-to-peer network. Answer D is not a valid model and is therefore incorrect.

Question 7

> What is the name given to the activity that involves collecting information that will later be used for monitoring and review purposes?
>
> ○ A. Logging
> ○ B. Auditing
> ○ C. Inspecting
> ○ D. Vetting

Answer A is correct. Logging is the process of collecting data to be used for monitoring and auditing purposes. Auditing is the process of verification that normally involves going through log files; therefore, answer B is incorrect. Typically, the log files are frequently inspected, and inspection is not the process of collecting the data; therefore, answer C is incorrect. Vetting is the process of thorough examination or evaluation; therefore, answer D is incorrect.

Question 8

> Which of the following are important steps toward the education of users regarding security requirements? [Choose all correct answers.]
>
> ❏ A. New employee training
> ❏ B. Security flyers
> ❏ C. On-the-job training
> ❏ D. Infrastructure documentation
> ❏ E. Security policy documentation

Answers A, B, C, and E are correct. Education of users about security requirements may be performed during new employee orientation and on-the-job training sessions as well as through security flyers and published security policies. Answer D is incorrect because the documentation created during an infrastructure audit is not generally useful to most users.

Question 9

Risk is made up of which of the following components? [Choose the three best answers.]

- ❑ A. Vulnerability
- ❑ B. Threat
- ❑ C. Probability
- ❑ D. Value

Answers A, B, and C are correct. Risk can be defined as the probability of a threat exploiting a vulnerability. Answer D is incorrect because value is not a component of risk; however, value may affect your decision of whether to accept a risk.

Question 10

Your manager wants you to investigate a client/server system that allows your company's users to be able to log in to a central server to authenticate and then access other servers without having to authenticate again. What type of system should you research?

- ○ A. Single sign-on
- ○ B. RAS servers
- ○ C. RADIUS
- ○ D. PPTP

Answer A is correct. Single sign-on provides the mechanism whereby a user only needs to authenticate to a system one time and can then access multiple systems without reauthenticating or maintaining separate usernames and passwords. Answer B is incorrect because Remote Access Server (RAS) is the system used to handle remote user access, and your manager wants a central server to communicate with these servers. Answer C is incorrect because Remote Authentication Dial-In User Service (RADIUS) is a client/server system that facilitates the communication between remote access servers and a central server. The central server will authenticate the dial-in users and authorize their access. Answer D is incorrect because PPTP is a tunneling protocol.

Need to Know More?

 Chirillo, John. *Hack Attacks Denied: A Complete Guide to Network Lockdown for UNIX, Windows, and Linux, Second Edition.* John Wiley & Sons. Indianapolis, IN, 2001. ISBN: 0471232831.

Refer to Chapter 4, "Security Policies."

 Cole, Eric. *Hackers Beware*. Pearson Education. Indianapolis, IN, 2001. ISBN 0735710090.

See Chapter 18, "Covering the Tracks."

 "An Explanation of Computer Forensics," by Judd Robbins: www.computerforensics.net/forensics.htm

 CERT Incident Reporting Guidelines: www.cert.org/tech_tips/incident_reporting.html

Sample Test #1

The best way to prepare for the test, after you have studied, is to take several practice exams. We've included two in this book for that reason. The answers to the following questions are in a separate chapter immediately following the test. Pay special attention to the explanations for the incorrect answers. Understanding why answers are incorrect will help you eliminate some of the answer choices, and this can be very valuable when taking the actual test.

Question 1

Which of the following are architectural models for the arranging of Certificate Authorities? [Check all correct answers.]

❑ A. Bridge CA architecture

❑ B. Sub CA architecture

❑ C. Single CA architecture

❑ D. Hierarchical CA architecture

Question 2

Sub7 is considered a(n) _____.

○ A. virus

○ B. illicit server

○ C. worm

○ D. Trojan horse

Question 3

You are in sales and you receive an email telling you about an easy way to make money. The email instructs you to open the attached letter of intent, read it carefully, and then reply to the email. Which of the following should you do?

○ A. Open the letter of intent, read it, and reply to the email.

○ B. Forward this great offer to your friends and coworkers.

○ C. Notify your system administrator of the email.

○ D. Delete the email and reboot your computer.

Question 4

You have an FTP server that needs to be accessed by both employees and external customers. What type of architecture should be implemented?

○ A. Bastion host

○ B. Screened subnet

○ C. Screened host

○ D. Bastion subnet

Question 5

The main fan in your server died on Wednesday morning. It will be at least two days before it can be replaced. You decide to use another server instead but need to restore the data from the dead one. You have been doing differential backups and the last full backup was performed on Friday evening. The backup doesn't run on weekends. How many backup tapes will you need to restore the data?

- ○ A. Two
- ○ B. Four
- ○ C. One
- ○ D. Three

Question 6

You are planning to set up a network for remote users to use their own Internet connections to connect to shared folders on the network. Which technology would you implement?

- ○ A. DMZ
- ○ B. VPN
- ○ C. VLAN
- ○ D. NAT

Question 7

What type of algorithm is SHA-1?

- ○ A. Asymmetric encryption algorithm
- ○ B. Digital signature
- ○ C. Hashing algorithm
- ○ D. Certificate Authority

Question 8

A fire involving paper and wood products is likely to be considered what class of fire?

○ A. Class A

○ B. Class B

○ C. Class C

○ D. Class D

Question 9

Which of the following are *not* methods for minimizing a threat to a Web server? [Choose the two best answers.]

❑ A. Disable all non-Web services.

❑ B. Ensure telnet is running.

❑ C. Disable nonessential services.

❑ D. Enable logging.

Question 10

Which of the following are major security evaluation criteria efforts? [Choose the two best answers.]

❑ A. TCSEC

❑ B. CCSEC

❑ C. IPSec

❑ D. ITSEC

Question 11

Separation of duties is designed to guard against which of the following?

○ A. Social engineering

○ B. Viruses

○ C. Fraud

○ D. Nonrepudiation

Question 12

A system designed to lure an attacker away from a critical system is called a
_____.

- O A. Bastion host
- O B. Honeypot
- O C. Vulnerability system
- O D. Intrusion-detection system

Question 13

Your company is in the process of setting up a DMZ segment. You have to allow
Web traffic in the DMZ segment. Which TCP port do you have to open?

- O A. 80
- O B. 139
- O C. 25
- O D. 443

Question 14

Which of the following attacks is most likely to be successful, even if all devices
are properly secured and configured?

- O A. Trojan horse
- O B. Mantrap
- O C. Social engineering
- O D. All of the above

Question 15

When using CHAP, the challenge/response mechanism can happen when?

- O A. Only at the beginning of the connection
- O B. At the beginning and the end of the connection
- O C. Only at the end of the connection
- O D. At any time during the connection

Question 16

With Discretionary Access Control (DAC), how are access rights to resources determined?

○ A. Roles

○ B. Rules

○ C. Owner discretion

○ D. Security label

Question 17

Which of the following is a common name for an opening in a program that allows for additional, undocumented access to data?

○ A. Virus

○ B. Algorithm

○ C. Back door

○ D. Demilitarized zone

Question 18

Which is *not* a good choice for achieving security awareness among your users in your organization?

○ A. Periodic presentations

○ B. Monthly emails

○ C. Yearly seminars

○ D. Training during employee orientation

Question 19

Which of the following types of programs can be used to determine whether network resources are locked down correctly?

○ A. Password sniffers

○ B. Port scanners

○ C. Keystroke loggers

○ D. Cookies

Question 20

The enforcement of access control via tasks or groups for system users is achieved in which of the following?

- ○ A. IPSec
- ○ B. RBAC
- ○ C. IDS
- ○ D. DRP

Question 21

Which one of the following types of servers would be the target for an attack where a malicious individual attempts to change information by connecting to port 53?

- ○ A. FTP server
- ○ B. File server
- ○ C. Web server
- ○ D. DNS server

Question 22

What type of activity is not associated with computer forensics?

- ○ A. Collecting and analyzing data from disk drives
- ○ B. Collecting and analyzing data from memory
- ○ C. Collecting fingerprints from the computer case and input devices
- ○ D. Labeling and photographing the evidence

Question 23

You are checking your network to ensure that the servers have been hardened correctly. You plan on using a vulnerability-scanning program. Which of the following programs can you use? [Choose the two best answers.]

- ❑ A. John the Ripper
- ❑ B. SATAN
- ❑ C. L0phtCrack
- ❑ D. SAINT

Question 24

In encryption, when data is broken into several units of varying sizes (dependent on algorithm) and the encryption is applied to those chunks of data, what type of algorithm is that called?

- ○ A. Symmetric encryption algorithm
- ○ B. Elliptic curve
- ○ C. Block cipher
- ○ D. All of the above

Question 25

Your company decides it wants to implement a Virtual Private Network (VPN). Which of the following would you consider using because they are tunneling protocols? [Choose the two best answers.]

- ❑ A. MD5
- ❑ B. L2TP
- ❑ C. 3DES
- ❑ D. PPTP

Question 26

As the network administrator, you are implementing a policy for passwords. What is the best option for creating user passwords?

- ○ A. Uppercase and lowercase letters combined with numbers and symbols
- ○ B. A randomly generated password
- ○ C. A word that is familiar to the user with a number attached to the end
- ○ D. The user's last name spelled backwards

Question 27

Digital signatures are used to authenticate the sender. Which of the following is true of digital signatures? [Choose the two best answers.]

❑ A. They use the skipjack algorithm.

❑ B. They can be automatically timestamped.

❑ C. They allow the sender to repudiate that the message was sent.

❑ D. They cannot be imitated by someone else.

Question 28

Which of the following are parts of Kerberos authentication? [Choose the two best answers.]

❑ A. Authentication service

❑ B. Time-based induction

❑ C. Ticket-granting service

❑ D. TEMPEST

Question 29

A smartcard provides two-factor authentication. Which two of the following must be provided for proper authentication? [Choose the two best answers.]

❑ A. Something you have

❑ B. Something you know

❑ C. Something you are

❑ D. Something you do

Question 30

Which of the following describes an active attack?

○ A. Does not insert data into the stream but instead monitors information being sent

○ B. Records and replays previously sent valid messages

○ C. Inserts false packets into the data stream

○ D. Makes attempts to verify the identify of the source of information

Question 31

Which one of the following is considered a physical security component?

- ○ A. VPN tunnel
- ○ B. Mantrap
- ○ C. Bastion host
- ○ D. IPSec

Question 32

Which of the following statements about entrapment and enticement is true?

- ○ A. Enticement is ethical and legal. Entrapment is unethical and illegal.
- ○ B. Entrapment is ethical and legal. Enticement is unethical and illegal.
- ○ C. Neither enticement nor entrapment is ethical or legal. Companies can be prosecuted for using either one.
- ○ D. Both enticement and entrapment are ethical and legal. Companies cannot be prosecuted for using either one.

Question 33

Which of the following are methods of sending secure email messages? [Choose the two best answers.]

- ❑ A. POP3
- ❑ B. S/MIME
- ❑ C. PGP
- ❑ D. SMTP

Question 34

Which one of the following is a private IP address?

- ○ A. 11.1.2.1
- ○ B. 165.193.123.44
- ○ C. 176.18.36.4
- ○ D. 192.168.0.234

Question 35

Which of the following statements is true about SSL?

- ○ A. SSL provides security for both the connection and the data once it is received.
- ○ B. SSL only provides security for the connection, not the data once it is received.
- ○ C. SSL only provides security for the data once it is received, not the connection.
- ○ D. SSL does not provide security for either the connection or the data once it is received.

Question 36

Of the following, which is a characteristic of a hot site?

- ○ A. The facility is equipped with plumbing, flooring, and electricity only.
- ○ B. The facility resources are shared by mutual agreement.
- ○ C. The facility and equipment are already set up and ready to occupy.
- ○ D. The facility is equipped with some resources, but not computers.

Question 37

Which of the following algorithms in not an example of a symmetric encryption algorithm?

- ○ A. Rijndael
- ○ B. Diffie-Hellman
- ○ C. RC6
- ○ D. AES

Question 38

The RBAC model can use which of the following types of access? [Choose the three best answers.]

❑ A. Role based

❑ B. Task based

❑ C. Lattice based

❑ D. Discretionary based

Question 39

You are having problems with your DNS server. When the users try to open various Web sites, they receive an error saying that the site is not found. You go to one of the machines, open a DOS prompt, and type which command to find out what the problem is?

○ A. **netstat**

○ B. **tracert**

○ C. **ipconfig**

○ D. **nslookup**

Question 40

What is the security protocol that has been developed for 802.11?

○ A. Wired Equivalent Protocol

○ B. Wireless Encryption Protocol

○ C. Wired Equivalent Privacy

○ D. Wireless Protocol Encryption

Question 41

Which of the following is true about fiber-optic cable? [Choose the two best answers.]

❑ A. It is highly sensitive to electric and magnetic interference.

❑ B. It is insensitive to electric and magnetic interference.

❑ C. It is relatively inexpensive.

❑ D. It is expensive.

Question 42

CHAP uses a challenge/response mechanism. How many steps is this process?

- ○ A. Seven
- ○ B. Three
- ○ C. Four
- ○ D. Two

Question 43

What is the difference between HTTPS and S-HTTP?

- ○ A. S-HTTP protects each message sent, whereas HTTPS protects the communication channel.
- ○ B. S-HTTP does not support multiple encryption types, whereas HTTPS does.
- ○ C. HTTPS protects each message sent, whereas S-HTTP protects the communication channel.
- ○ D. There is no difference.

Question 44

What is the process of systematically dialing a range of phone numbers looking for unprotected dial-in modems?

- ○ A. Sniffing
- ○ B. War-driving
- ○ C. War-dialing
- ○ D. Social engineering

Question 45

Under MAC, the category of a resource can be changed by whom?

- ○ A. All managers
- ○ B. Administrators only
- ○ C. The owner/creator
- ○ D. All users

Question 46

You want to evaluate a user's ability to connect to a RAS server via telephony. Which of the following vulnerability assessment tests would you use?

○ A. Blind testing

○ B. Knowledgeable testing

○ C. Internet service testing

○ D. Dial-up service testing

○ E. Infrastructure testing

Question 47

Which protocol is used to enable remote access servers to communicate with a central server in order to authenticate and authorize access to resources?

○ A. Kerberos

○ B. IPSec

○ C. RADIUS

○ D. PPTP

Question 48

Which of the following statements are incorrect about Encapsulated Secure Payload (ESP) and Authentication Header (AH)? [Choose the two best answers.]

❑ A. AH can only verify data integrity.

❑ B. ESP can encrypt data and verify data integrity.

❑ C. AH can encrypt data and verify data integrity.

❑ D. ESP can only verify data integrity.

Question 49

Which of the following is a hardware or software solution used to protect a network from unauthorized access?

○ A. Intrusion-detection system

○ B. Digital certificate

○ C. Honeypot

○ D. Firewall

Question 50

Unauthorized access has been detected on the network. Someone had been logging in as one of the administrative assistants during off hours. Later, you find out she received an email from the network administrator asking her to supply her password so that he could make changes to her profile. What types of attacks have been executed? [Choose two correct answers.]

❑ A. Spoofing

❑ B. Man in the middle

❑ C. Replay

❑ D. Social engineering

Question 51

Which of the following is not true regarding log files?

○ A. They should be stored and protected on a machine that has been hardened.

○ B. Log information traveling on the network must be encrypted, if possible.

○ C. They should be stored in one location.

○ D. They must be modifiable, and there should be no record of the modification.

Question 52

Which PKI Trust model would be used by a CA with multiple subordinate CAs?

○ A. Cross-certified

○ B. Hierarchical

○ C. Bridge

○ D. Linked

Question 53

Which of the following are reasons why it is unsafe to allow signed code to run on your systems?

○ A. The fact that the code is signed only guarantees that the code belongs to a certain entity, not that it is absolutely harmless.

○ B. Malicious users are known to have attempted obtaining legitimate certificates to sign harmful code, with some succeeding.

○ C. Scripts may be used to employ signed code that comes preinstalled and signed with the operating system.

○ D. All of the above.

Question 54

What is the difference between a wet-pipe and a dry-pipe fire-suppression system?

○ A. A dry-pipe system uses air to suppress fire, whereas a wet-pipe system uses water.

○ B. A dry-pipe system uses dry chemicals, whereas a wet-pipe system uses wet chemicals.

○ C. A wet-pipe system has water in the pipe at all times, whereas in a dry-pipe system, water is used but is held back by a valve until a certain temperature is reached.

○ D. A wet-pipe system uses wet chemicals that deploy after the pipe loses air pressure, whereas a dry-pipe system uses dry chemicals that deploy before the pipe loses air pressure.

Question 55

Which of the following statements best describes a disaster recovery plan (DRP)?

○ A. A DRP reduces the impact of a hurricane on a facility.

○ B. A DRP is an immediate action plan used to bring a business back online immediately after a disaster has struck.

○ C. A DRP attempts to manage risks associated with theft of equipment.

○ D. A DRP is a plan that sets up actions for long-term recovery after a disaster has hit.

Question 56

You're the security administrator for a credit union. The users are complaining about the network being slow. It is not a particularly busy time of the day. You capture network packets and discover that there have been hundreds of ICMP packets being sent to the host. What type of attack is likely being executed against your network?

- ○ A. Spoofing
- ○ B. Man in the middle
- ○ C. Denial of service
- ○ D. Worm

Question 57

Which of the following PKI functions do SSL/TLS protocols currently support? [Choose the two best answers.]

- ❏ A. Authentication
- ❏ B. Certificate Revocation Lists
- ❏ C. Encryption
- ❏ D. Attribute certificates

Question 58

How many layers are there in the OSI model?

- ○ A. Four
- ○ B. Six
- ○ C. Nine
- ○ D. Seven

Question 59

Which of the following is true in regard to the principle of least privilege?

○ A. It ensures that all members of the user community are given the same privileges as long as they do not have administrator or root access to systems.

○ B. It requires that a user be given no more privilege than necessary to perform a job.

○ C. It is a control enforced through written security policies.

○ D. It assumes that job functions will be rotated frequently.

Question 60

You have found that someone has been running a program to crack passwords. This has been successful enough that files have been altered and you suspect that many of the users' passwords have been compromised. Which of the following techniques can be implemented to help protect against another brute-force password attack?

○ A. Increase the value of the password history to 8.

○ B. Have users present proper identification before being granted a password.

○ C. Lock the account after three unsuccessful password entry attempts.

○ D. Require password resets every 60 days.

Question 61

Which of the following best describes a service-level agreement?

○ A. A method by which a company can guarantee a level of service from another company.

○ B. A method of procuring services after a disaster has struck.

○ C. A method of protecting servers and computers from disasters.

○ D. A method of protecting a facility from disasters.

Question 62

You need to provide your users with the capability to log on once and retrieve any resource to which they have been granted access, regardless of where the resource is stored. Which configuration will you deploy?

- ○ A. Role-Based Access Control (RBAC)
- ○ B. Multifactor
- ○ C. Biometric
- ○ D. Single sign-on (SSO)

Question 63

You are a consultant for a company that wants to secure its Web services and provide a guarantee to its online customers that all credit card information is securely transferred. Which technology would you recommend?

- ○ A. S/MIME
- ○ B. VPN
- ○ C. SSL/TLS
- ○ D. SSH

Question 64

You are the primary investigator on a team that is investigating the theft of some important information from your network. You have collected and analyzed data and are preparing to present your information in court. What is the process called when presenting the path that the evidence took to the courtroom?

- ○ A. Evidenced path
- ○ B. Chain of custody
- ○ C. Forensics
- ○ D. Chain of evidence

Question 65

You are configuring a security policy for your company. Which of the following three components make up the security triad? [Choose the three best answers.]

❑ A. Encryption

❑ B. Confidentiality

❑ C. Integrity

❑ D. Authorization

❑ E. Availability

Question 66

Which of the following would you use if you wanted to check the validity of a digital certificate?

○ A. Certificate policy

○ B. Certificate Revocation List

○ C. Corporate security policy

○ D. Trust model

Question 67

Which of the following statements are true when discussing physical security? [Choose the three best answers.]

❑ A. Physical security attempts to control access to data from Internet users.

❑ B. Physical security attempts to control unwanted access to specified areas of a building.

❑ C. Physical security attempts to control the impact of natural disasters on facilities and equipment.

❑ D. Physical security attempts to control internal employee access into secure areas.

Question 68

SMTP relay is a common exploit used among hackers for what purpose?

- ○ A. DNS zone transfers
- ○ B. Spamming
- ○ C. Port scanning
- ○ D. Man-in-the-middle attacks

Question 69

CGI scripts can present vulnerabilities in which of the following ways? [Choose the two best answers.]

- ❑ A. They can be used to relay email.
- ❑ B. They can be tricked into executing commands.
- ❑ C. They may expose system information.
- ❑ D. They store the IP address of your computer.

Question 70

Your company has decided to deploy a hardware token system along with user-names and passwords. This technique of using more than one type of authentication is known as which of the following?

- ○ A. Parallel authentication
- ○ B. Factored authentication
- ○ C. Mutual authentication
- ○ D. Multifactor authentication

Question 71

Which of the following are included within a digital certificate? [Choose the three best answers.]

- ❑ A. User's private key
- ❑ B. Information about the user
- ❑ C. Digital signature of the issuing CA
- ❑ D. User's public key

Question 72

Which of the following is a correct definition of a Trojan horse?

○ A. It needs no user intervention to replicate.

○ B. It makes data appear to come from somewhere other than where it really originated.

○ C. It is open-source code and attacks only open source software.

○ D. It buries itself in the operating system software and infects other systems only after a user executes the application that it is buried in.

Question 73

You have implemented a proxy firewall technology that can distinguish between an FTP **get** command and an FTP **put** command. What type of firewall are you using?

○ A. Proxy gateway

○ B. Circuit-level gateway

○ C. Application-level gateway

○ D. SOCKS proxy

Question 74

When encrypting and decrypting data using an asymmetric encryption algorithm, you do which of the following?

○ A. Use only the public key to encrypt and only the private key to decrypt.

○ B. Use the public key to either encrypt or decrypt.

○ C. Use only the private key to encrypt and only the public key to decrypt.

○ D. Use only the private key to decrypt data encrypted with the public key.

Question 75

Which of the following is *not* a piece of information used by a cookie?

- ○ A. The operating system you are running
- ○ B. The type of browser you are using
- ○ C. Your network login and password
- ○ D. The name and IP address of your computer

Question 76

You are setting up a switched network and want to group users by department, which technology would you implement?

- ○ A. DMZ
- ○ B. VPN
- ○ C. VLAN
- ○ D. NAT

Question 77

What is the leading reason many incidents are never reported? [Choose the best answer.]

- ○ A. They do not break laws.
- ○ B. The reporting process is too time consuming.
- ○ C. The fear of losing business or shareholders.
- ○ D. They result in less than $1,000 in damage.

Question 78

Which of the following is true in regard to FTP? [Choose the two best answers.]

- ❏ A. Authentication credentials are sent in cleartext.
- ❏ B. Authentication credentials are encrypted.
- ❏ C. It is vulnerable to sniffing and eavesdropping.
- ❏ D. It is very secure and not vulnerable to either sniffing or eavesdropping.

Question 79

Which of the following best describes the relationship between centralized and decentralized security?

○ A. Centralized is more secure but less scalable, whereas decentralized security is less secure but more scalable.

○ B. Decentralized security is more scalable and more secure than centralized.

○ C. Centralized security is more scalable and less secure than decentralized.

○ D. Centralized and decentralized have about the same security, but centralized is more scalable.

Question 80

You have created a utility for purging old files. You have hidden code inside the utility that will install itself and cause the infected system to erase the hard drive's contents on April 1, 2004. Which of the following attacks has been used in your code?

○ A. Virus

○ B. Spoofing

○ C. Logic bomb

○ D. Trojan horse

Question 81

Which of the following components are not associated with risk? [Choose the two best answers.]

❑ A. Vulnerability

❑ B. Threat

❑ C. Value

❑ D. Probability

❑ E. Analysis

Question 82

What is an exposed device that is the foundation for firewall software to operate on called?

- ○ A. Bastion host
- ○ B. Screened subnet
- ○ C. Screened host
- ○ D. Bastion subnet

Question 83

A user using a known weakness in operating system code has made himself an administrator. This is an example of which of the following?

- ○ A. Privilege management
- ○ B. Trojan horse
- ○ C. Privilege escalation
- ○ D. Single sign-on

Question 84

Which of the following best describes a vulnerability?

- ○ A. A vulnerability is a weakness in the configuration of software or hardware that could allow a threat to damage the network.
- ○ B. A vulnerability is any agent that could do harm to your network or its components.
- ○ C. A vulnerability is the likelihood of a particular event happening given an asset and a threat.
- ○ D. A vulnerability measures the cost of a threat attacking your network.

Question 85

Your network is under attack. Traffic patterns indicate that an unauthorized service is relaying information to a source outside the network. What type of attack is being executed against you?

- ○ A. Spoofing
- ○ B. Man in the middle

○ C. Replay

○ D. Denial of service

Question 86

Which of the following best describes Secure FTP?

○ A. It allows for a secure connection via IPSec.

○ B. It allows for a secure connection via SSL.

○ C. It allows for a secure connection via HTTPS.

○ D. None of the above is true.

Question 87

Who is ultimately responsible for setting the tone of the role of security in an organization?

○ A. Staff

○ B. Management

○ C. Consultants

○ D. Everyone

Question 88

You are a consultant for a small company. You have just learned about a patch that is available for Windows servers. You download and install the patch and several of the servers stop functioning properly. What should your next step be to return the servers to a functional state? [Choose the best answer.]

○ A. Reload the patch and see if the problems stop.

○ B. Roll back the changes.

○ C. Call the manufacturer and see if there is a fix.

○ D. Document the changes and troubleshoot.

Question 89

Your company is in the process of setting up an IDS system. You want to scan for irregular header lengths and information in the TCP/IP packet. Which IDS methodology is suitable for this purpose?

- O A. Heuristic analysis
- O B. Anomaly analysis
- O C. Stateful inspection
- O D. Pattern matching

Question 90

Which protocol is installed to provide centralized management of computers through a remotely installed agent?

- O A. SMTP
- O B. SNMP
- O C. LDAP
- O D. L2TP

Question 91

What is a network device that works at the third layer of the OSI model and is responsible for forwarding packets between networks called?

- O A. Router
- O B. Hub
- O C. Switch
- O D. Modem

Question 92

When an attacker compromises systems with installed zombie software and initiates an attack against a victim from a widely distributed number of hosts, this is called what?

- O A. DoS
- O B. DDoS

○ C. Trojan horse

○ D. Masquerading

Question 93

Which of the following is not a tunneling protocol used in VPN connections?

○ A. PPTP

○ B. L2TP

○ C. CHAP

○ D. IPSec

Question 94

Which of the following statements best describes the behavior of a worm?

○ A. A worm is self-replicating and needs no user interaction.

○ B. A worm attacks only after triggered.

○ C. A worm only attacks system files.

○ D. A worm attempts to hide from antivirus software by garbling its code.

Question 95

What is the difference between TACACS and RADIUS?

○ A. There is no difference.

○ B. RADIUS is an actual Internet standard; TACACS is not.

○ C. TACACS is an actual Internet standard; RADIUS is not.

○ D. RADIUS is an encryption protocol; TACACS is an authentication protocol.

Question 96

What is Secure Electronic Transaction (SET)?

○ A. A system for ensuring the security of historical electronic transactions across the Internet.

○ B. An e-commerce technology that provides a safe way to do financial transactions over the Internet.

○ C. A system developed by Microsoft for ensuring the security of electronic messages across the Internet.

○ D. A program that combines the resources of multiple computers to secure the exchange of email.

Question 97

What Web-based protocol was developed to standardize the way wireless devices communicate?

○ A. Wireless Encryption Protocol (WEP)

○ B. Wireless Application Protocol (WAP)

○ C. Wired Equivalent Privacy (WEP)

○ D. Wireless Session Protocol (WSP)

Question 98

Which of the following is true of Pretty Good Privacy (PGP)? [Choose the two best answers.]

❑ A. It uses a web of trust.

❑ B. It uses a hierarchical structure.

❑ C. It uses public key encryption.

❑ D. It uses private key encryption.

Question 99

What type of algorithm does MD5 use?

○ A. Block cipher algorithm

○ B. Hashing algorithm

○ C. Asymmetric encryption algorithm

○ D. Cryptographic algorithm

Question 100

You are the consultant for a small manufacturing company that wants to implement a backup solution. Which method is most commonly used to protect data? [Choose the best answer.]

○ A. Site redundancy

○ B. Offsite, secure recovery

○ C. Onsite backup

○ D. High availability systems

Question 101

You are the network administrator for a small company that has recently been the victim of several attacks. Upon rebuild of the server, you want to uninstall all unnecessary services and protocols. This process is known as system
_____.

○ A. Nonrepudiation

○ B. Hardening

○ C. Auditing

○ D. Hashing

Question 102

Which of the following looks at the long-term actions taken by a company after a disaster has taken place?

○ A. Emergency response plan

○ B. Security plan

○ C. Disaster recovery plan

○ D. Business continuity plan

Question 103

User groups that are built around business units and then have privileges assigned to these groups instead of individual users is an example of which type of management?

○ A. Role-based privilege management

○ B. User-based privilege management

○ C. Group-based privilege management

○ D. Individual-based privilege management

Question 104

In which type of architecture is the user responsible for the creation of the private and public key?

○ A. Decentralized key management

○ B. Centralized key management

○ C. Revocation key management

○ D. Multilevel key management

Question 105

Which of the following statements best describes nonrepudiation?

○ A. A set of mathematical rules used in encryption

○ B. A means of proving that a transaction occurred

○ C. A method of hiding data in another message

○ D. A technology used for redundancy and performance improvement

Question 106

You are checking your network to ensure users are conforming to a new password security policy that requires them to use complex passwords. You plan on using a password-cracking program. Which of the following programs can you use?

❑ A. John the Ripper

❑ B. SATAN

❑ C. L0phtCrack

❑ D. SAINT

Question 107

Your company is in the process of setting up a management system on your network and you want to use SNMP. You have to allow this traffic through the router. Which UDP ports do you have to open?

❏ A. 161

❏ B. 139

❏ C. 138

❏ D. 162

Question 108

You are securing the network with IDS technologies. You want to be able to see malicious intent activity as well as provide some security and monitoring for users who are VPNing outside the network. Which IDS type is best suited for this job?

○ A. Host-based IDS

○ B. Network-based IDS

○ C. None of the above

○ D. A combination of A and B

Question 109

When a Certificate Authority revokes a certificate, how is notice of the revocation distributed?

○ A. A digital signature

○ B. A certificate policy

○ C. A Certificate Revocation List

○ D. A Certificate Practice Statement

Question 110

Which of the following are characteristics of Transport Layer Security (TLS)? [Choose the two best answers.]

❑ A. It is interoperable with SSL.

❑ B. It is based on Netscape's SSL3.

❑ C. It ensures privacy on the Internet.

❑ D. It has one layer.

Question 111

Wireless Application Protocol (WAP) has several layers. Which of the following is the security layer?

○ A. Wireless Security Layer (WSL)

○ B. Wireless Transport Layer (WTL)

○ C. Wireless Transport Layer Security (WTLS)

○ D. Wireless Security Layer Transport (WSLT)

Question 112

A private network that gives business partners and vendors access to company information is called a(n) _____.

○ A. Extranet

○ B. Intranet

○ C. Internet

○ D. ARPAnet

Question 113

Which of the following is the weakest link in a security policy?

○ A. Management

○ B. A misconfigured firewall

○ C. An unprotected Web server

○ D. Uneducated users

Question 114

If the code of a program does not check the length of variables, it can be subject to which type of attack?

○ A. Buffer overflow

○ B. Replay

○ C. Spoofing

○ D. Denial of service

Question 115

Access through a router may be granted or denied based on IP address. What is the name given to this method?

○ A. ACL

○ B. AP

○ C. ACLU

○ D. Answers A and B

Question 116

What are the major security concerns with using DHCP? [Choose the two best answers.]

❏ A. The network is vulnerable to man-in-the-middle attacks.

❏ B. Anyone hooking up to the network can automatically receive a network address.

❏ C. Clients might be redirected to an incorrect DNS address.

❏ D. There are no security concerns with using DHCP.

Question 117

What should you do upon finding out an employee is terminated?

○ A. Disable the user account and have the data kept for a specified period of time.

○ B. Maintain the user account and have the data kept for a specified period of time.

○ C. Disable the user account and delete the user's home directory.

○ D. Do nothing until the employee has cleaned out her desk and you get written notification.

Question 118

Which of the following is *not* a good security practice?

○ A. You should have a procedure in place to periodically test password strength.

○ B. Auditing should be enabled and logs should be monitored regularly.

○ C. Allow all programmers to have administrator access because they need a lot of rights.

○ D. You should ensure that there are no accounts with default passwords or that there aren't any without a password.

Question 119

Which of the following statements best describes the difference between authentication and identification?

○ A. Authentication is the same identification.

○ B. Authentication is a means to verify who you are, whereas identification is what you are authorized to perform.

○ C. Authentication is the byproduct of identification.

○ D. Authentication is what you are authorized to perform, whereas identification is a means to verify who you are.

Question 120

What is the IEEE standard for wireless LAN technology?

○ A. 802.5

○ B. 802.11

○ C. 802.2

○ D. 802.10

Question 121

Which of the following statements about Java and JavaScript is true?

○ A. Java applets can be used to execute arbitrary instructions on the server.

○ B. JavaScript code can continue running even after the applet is closed.

○ C. JavaScript can provide access to files of a known name and path.

○ D. Java applets can be used to send email as the user.

○ E. Java applets allow access to cache information.

Question 122

What is the proper way to dispose of confidential documents?

○ A. Rip them into small pieces and put them in the trash.

○ B. Shred them and put them in the trash.

○ C. Have them destroyed by an authorized destruction company.

○ D. Put them in the recycle bin.

Question 123

Ensuring that all data is sequenced, timestamped, and numbered is a characteristic of _____.

○ A. Data authentication

○ B. Data integrity

○ C. Data availability

○ D. Data confidentiality

Question 124

What is a potential concern to weaker encryption algorithms as time goes on? [Choose the best answer.]

○ A. Performance of the algorithm will worsen over time.

○ B. Keys generated by users will start to repeat on other users' systems.

○ C. Hackers using distributed computing may be able to finally crack an algorithm.

○ D. All of the above.

Question 125

You want to hide your internal network from the outside world. Which of the following servers can accomplish this?

○ A. NAT

○ B. DNS

○ C. DHCP

○ D. All of the above

Answer Key to Sample Test #1

1. A, C, D	**19.** B	**37.** B
2. B	**20.** B	**38.** A, B, C
3. C	**21.** D	**39.** B
4. B	**22.** C	**40.** C
5. A	**23.** B, D	**41.** B, D
6. B	**24.** C	**42.** C
7. C	**25.** B, D	**43.** A
8. A	**26.** A	**44.** C
9. B, D	**27.** B, D	**45.** B
10. A, D	**28.** A, C	**46.** D
11. C	**29.** A, B	**47.** C
12. B	**30.** C	**48.** A, B
13. A	**31.** B	**49.** D
14. C	**32.** A	**50.** A, D
15. D	**33.** B, C	**51.** D
16. C	**34.** D	**52.** B
17. C	**35.** B	**53.** D
18. B	**36.** C	**54.** C

55. B	**79.** A	**103.** C
56. C	**80.** C	**104.** A
57. A, C	**81.** C, E	**105.** B
58. D	**82.** A	**106.** A, C
59. B	**83.** C	**107.** A, D
60. C	**84.** A	**108.** D
61. A	**85.** B	**109.** C
62. D	**86.** B	**110.** B, C
63. C	**87.** B	**111.** C
64. B	**88.** B	**112.** A
65. B, C, E	**89.** C	**113.** D
66. B	**90.** B	**114.** A
67. B, C, D	**91.** A	**115.** A
68. B	**92.** B	**116.** B, C
69. B, C	**93.** C	**117.** A
70. D	**94.** A	**118.** C
71. B, C, D	**95.** B	**119.** D
72. D	**96.** A	**120.** B
73. C	**97.** C	**121.** C
74. D	**98.** A, C	**122.** C
75. C	**99.** B	**123.** B
76. C	**100.** C	**124.** C
77. C	**101.** B	**125.** A
78. A, C	**102.** D	

Question 1

Answers A, C, and D are correct. These answers all represent legitimate trust models. Another common model also exists, called *cross-certification*; however, it usually makes more sense to implement a bridge architecture over this type of model. Answer B is incorrect because it does not represent a valid trust model.

Question 2

Answer B is correct. NetBus, Back Orifice, and Sub7 have two essential parts: a server and client. These programs are known as *illicit servers*. Answer A is incorrect because a software virus is a small chunk of code designed to attach to other code. Answer C is incorrect because a worm is a form of malicious code. Answer D is incorrect because a Trojan horse appears to be useful software, but there's code hidden inside that will attack your system directly or allow the system to be infiltrated by the originator of the code once it is executed, making your machine a zombie.

Question 3

Answer C is correct. The email is likely a hoax, and although the policies may differ among organizations, given this scenario and the available choices, the best answer is to notify the system administrator. Answers A, B, and D are all therefore incorrect.

Question 4

Answer B is correct. A screened subnet is an isolated subnet between the Internet and the internal network. A bastion host is the first line of security that a company allows to be addressed directly from the Internet; therefore, answer A is incorrect. A bastion host on the private network communicating directly with a border router is a screened host; therefore, answer C incorrect. Answer D is a fictitious term and is therefore incorrect as well.

Question 5

Answer A is correct. You will need the full backup from Friday and the differential tape from Tuesday. Answer B is incorrect because four tapes are too many for any type of backup because Wednesday's backup has not been done yet. Answer C is incorrect because one tape would be enough only if full backups were done daily. Answer D is incorrect because three would be the number of tapes needed if the backup type was incremental.

Question 6

Answer B is correct. A VPN is used to provide secure remote access services to the company's employees and agents. Answer A is incorrect because a DMZ is a small network between the internal network and the Internet that provides a layer of security and privacy. Answer C is incorrect because the purpose of a VLAN is to unite network nodes logically into the same broadcast domain regardless of their physical attachment to the network. Answer D is incorrect because NAT acts as a liaison between an internal network and the Internet.

Question 7

Answer C is correct. SHA-1 is an update version of Secure Hash Algorithm (SHA), which is used with DSA. Answer A is incorrect because this is an algorithm that uses a public and private key pair and is not associated with the SHA-1. Answer B is incorrect because a digital signature is not an encryption algorithm. Answer D is incorrect because a Certificate Authority accepts or revokes certificates.

Question 8

Answer A is correct. Class A fires involve combustibles such as wood and paper. Answer B is incorrect because a class B fire involves flammables or combustible liquids. Answer C is incorrect because a class C fire involves energized electrical equipment and is usually suppressed with nonconducting agents. Answer D is incorrect because a class D fire involves combustible metals such as magnesium.

Question 9

Answers B and D are correct. Having Telnet enabled presents security issues and is not a primary method for minimizing threat. Logging is important for secure operations and is invaluable when recovering from a security incident. However, it is not a primary method for reducing threat. Answer A is incorrect because disabling all non-Web services may provide a secure solution for minimizing threats. Answer C is incorrect because each network service carries its own risks; therefore, it is important to disable all nonessential services.

Question 10

Answers A and D are correct. Trusted Computer System Evaluation Criteria (TCSEC) and Information Technology Security Evaluation Criteria (ITSEC) are major security criteria efforts. Answer B is incorrect because CCSEC is a nonexistent organization. IPSec is a set of protocols to enable encryption, authentication, and integrity; therefore, answer C incorrect.

Question 11

Answer C is correct. Separation of duties is considered valuable in deterring fraud, because fraud can occur if an opportunity exists for collaboration between various job-related capabilities. Separation of duty requires that for particular sets of transactions, no single individual be allowed to execute all transactions within the set. Answer A is incorrect because social engineering relies on the faults in human behavior. Answer B is incorrect because a virus is designed to attach itself to other code and replicate. Answer D is incorrect because nonrepudiation means that neither a sender nor a receiver can deny sending or receiving a message.

Question 12

Answer B is correct. Honeypots are decoy systems designed to lure potential attackers away from critical systems. A bastion host is the first line of security that a company allows to be addressed directly from the Internet; therefore, answer A is incorrect. Answer C is incorrect because it is a made-up term. Answer D is incorrect because an IDS is used for intrusion detection.

Question 13

Answer A is correct. Port 80 is used for HTTP traffic. Answer B is incorrect because UDP uses port 139 for network sharing. Answer C is incorrect because port 25 is used for SMTP outgoing mail. Answer D is incorrect because port 443 is used by HTTPS.

Question 14

Answer C is correct. In computer security systems, social engineering attacks are usually the most successful, especially when the security technology is properly implemented and configured. Usually, these attacks rely on the faults in human beings. Answer A is incorrect because a Trojan horse appears to be useful software but has code hidden inside that will attack your system directly or allow the system to be infiltrated by the originator of the code once it is executed. Answer B is incorrect because a mantrap is a physical barrier. Finally, because there is only one correct answer, answer D is incorrect.

Question 15

Answer D is correct. CHAP continues the challenge/response activity throughout the connection to be sure that the user holds the proper credentials to communicate with the authentication server. This makes answers A, B, and C incorrect.

Question 16

Answer C is correct. DAC enables the owner of the resources to specify who can access those resources. Answer A is incorrect because roles are used to group access rights by role name; the use of resources is restricted to those associated with an authorized role. Answer B is incorrect because rules are mandatory access control. Answer D is incorrect because security labels are also used in mandatory access control.

Question 17

Answer C is correct. A back door is an opening in a program, often left by a developer, that enables access through nontraditional means. Answer A is incorrect because a software virus is a small chunk of code designed to attach to other code. Answer B is incorrect because an algorithm comprises the steps to arrive at a result. Answer D is incorrect because a demilitarized zone is a zone within a network where publicly accessible servers are typically placed.

Question 18

Answer B is correct. The use of emails is passive; therefore, answer B is not the best choice. Security training during employee orientation, periodic presentations, and yearly seminars are the best choices because they are active methods of raising security awareness. Answers A, C, and D are the best choices and therefore the incorrect answers for this question.

Question 19

Answer B is correct. A port scanner is a program that searches for unsecured ports. The number of open ports can help determine whether the network is locked down enough to deter malicious activity. Answer A is incorrect because password sniffers monitor network traffic and record the packets sending passwords. Answer C is incorrect because a keystroke logger is able to capture passwords locally on the computer as they are typed and record them. Answer D is incorrect because cookies are small text files used to identify a Web user and enhance the browsing experience.

Question 20

Answer B is correct. Role-Based Access Control (RBAC) ensures the principle of least privilege by identifying the user's job function and ensuring a minimum set of privileges required to perform that job. IPSec is a set of protocols to enable encryption, authentication, and integrity; therefore, answer A is incorrect. Answer C is incorrect because an IDS is used for intrusion detection, and answer D is incorrect because a DRP is a plan used in the event of disaster.

Question 21

Answer D is correct. DNS is the UDP service that runs on port 53. Answer A is incorrect because FTP is a TCP service that runs on port 21 (or 20). Sharing runs on UDP port 139; therefore, answer B is incorrect. HTTP (Web server) is a TCP service that runs on port 80; therefore, answer C is incorrect.

Question 22

Answer C is correct. The dusting and collection of fingerprints is a law-enforcement forensics function. Collecting and analyzing data from disk drives, memory, and labeling and photographing evidence are all functions of computer forensics. Therefore, answers A, B, and D are incorrect.

Question 23

Answers B and D are correct. Both SATAN and SAINT are vulnerability testing tools. Answers A and C are incorrect because John the Ripper and L0phtCrack are both used to crack passwords.

Question 24

Answer C is correct. When data that is going to be encrypted is broken into chunks of data and then encrypted, the type of encryption is called a block cipher. Although many symmetric algorithms use a block cipher, answer A is incorrect because *block cipher* is a more precise and accurate term for the given question. Answer B is incorrect because elliptic curve is a type of asymmetric encryption algorithm. Answer D is an incorrect choice because only one answer is correct.

Question 25

Answers B and D are correct. L2TP and PPTP are both tunneling protocols used in Virtual Private Networks. Both MD5 and 3DES are cryptography algorithms; therefore, answers A and C are incorrect.

Question 26

Answer A is correct. A combination of both uppercase and lowercase letters along with numbers and symbols will make guessing the password difficult. It will also take longer to crack using brute force. Answer B is incorrect because randomly generated passwords are difficult if not impossible for users to remember. This causes them to be written down, thereby increasing the risk of other people finding them. Answers C and D are incorrect because both can easily be guessed or cracked.

Question 27

Answers B and D are correct. A digital signature is applied to a message, which keeps it from being modified or imitated. Digital signatures can also be automatically timestamped. Answer A is incorrect because digital signatures are based on an asymmetric scheme. Skipjack is a symmetric key algorithm designed by the U.S. National Security Agency (NSA). Answer C is incorrect because digital signatures allow for nonrepudiation. This means the sender cannot deny that the message was sent.

Question 28

Answers A and C are correct. The Key Distribution Center (KDC) used by Kerberos provides authentication services and ticket-distribution services. Time-based induction is a virtual machine used in IDS; therefore, answer B is incorrect. Answer D is incorrect because TEMPEST is the study and control of electrical signals.

Question 29

Answers A and B are correct. A smartcard provides for two-factor authentication. The user must enter something he knows (a user ID or PIN) to unlock the smartcard, which is something he has. A biometric technique based on distinct characteristics, such as a fingerprint scan, is considered something you are; therefore, answer C is incorrect. Answer D has nothing to do with authentication and is therefore incorrect.

Question 30

Answer C is correct. An active attack makes attempts to insert false packets into the data stream. A passive attack attempts to passively monitor data being sent between two parties and does not insert data into the data stream; therefore, answer A is incorrect. A reply attack records and replays previously sent valid messages; therefore, answer B is incorrect. Authentication is the process of verifying the identity of a source and is not a type of attack; therefore, answer D is incorrect.

Question 31

Answer B is correct. A mantrap is an area of physical security where people have to go through two doors so their credentials can be checked. A VPN tunnel, bastion host, and IPSec are all examples of data security, not physical security. Therefore, answers A, C, and D are incorrect.

Question 32

Answer A is correct. Enticement is ethical and legal. Entrapment is unethical and illegal. Answers B, C, and D are all incorrect because they do not properly describe enticement and entrapment.

Question 33

Answers B and C are correct. PGP (Pretty Good Privacy) uses encryption to secure email messages, as does S/MIME. Answers A and D are incorrect because these are both methods for sending unsecure email.

Question 34

Answer D is correct. The Internet Numbers Authority (IANA) has reserved three blocks of IP addresses for private networks. These include 10.0.0.0–10.255.255.255, 172.16.0.0–172.31.255.255, and 192.168.0.0–192.168.255.255. Additionally, the range 169.254.0.0–169.254.255.255 is reserved for Automatic Private IP Addressing. Therefore, answers A, B, and D are incorrect.

Question 35

Answer B is correct. SSL only provides security for the connection, not the data once it is received. The data is encrypted while it is being transmitted, but once received by the computer, it is no longer encrypted. Therefore, answers A, C, and D are incorrect.

Question 36

Answer C is correct. A hot site is a facility and equipment that are already set up and ready to occupy. Answer A is incorrect because a cold site requires the customer to provide and install all the equipment needed for operations. Answer B is incorrect because it describes a mutual agreement. Answer D is incorrect because it describes a warm site.

Question 37

Answer B is correct. Diffie-Hellman uses public and private keys, so it is considered an asymmetric encryption algorithm. Because Rijndael and AES are now one in the same, they both can be called symmetric encryption algorithms; therefore, answers A and D are incorrect. Answer C is incorrect because RC6 is symmetric as well.

Question 38

Answers A, B, and C are correct. The RBAC model can use role-based access, determined by the role the user has, task-based access, determined by the task assigned to the user, or lattice-based access, determined by the sensitivity level assigned to the role. Discretionary-based access is a characteristic of Discretionary Access Control (DAC); therefore, answer D is incorrect.

Question 39

Answer B is correct. `tracert` traces the route a packet takes and records the hops along the way. This is a good tool to use to find out where a packet is getting hung up. Answer A is incorrect because `netstat` displays all the ports on which the computer is listening. Answer C is incorrect because `ipconfig` is used to display the TCP/IP settings on a Windows machine. Answer D is also incorrect because `nslookup` is a command-line utility used to troubleshoot a Domain Name Server (DNS) database.

Question 40

Answer C is correct. Wired Equivalent Privacy (WEP) is part of the 802.11b standard and is designed to provide for the same level of security on a wired network. Answers A, B, and D are all incorrect.

Question 41

Answers B and D are correct. Fiber-optic cable is insensitive to electrical and magnetic interference but is expensive. Answers A and C are incorrect.

Question 42

Answer C is correct. CHAP is a four-step process. First, the user sends a logon request. Second, the server sends the user a challenge. Third, the challenge is returned to the server. Lastly, the server compares values and then determines whether to authorize the request. Answers A, B, and D are incorrect.

Question 43

Answer A is correct. S-HTTP protects each message sent, whereas HTTPS protects the communication channel. S-HTTP is used if an individual message needs to be encrypted. HTTPS is used if all communication needs to be encrypted. S-HTTP does support multiple encryption types. Therefore, answers B, C, and D are incorrect.

Question 44

Answer C is correct. War-dialing is the process of systematically dialing a range of phone numbers hoping to gain unauthorized access to a network via unprotected dial-in modems. Sniffing is the process of capturing packets traveling across the network; therefore, answer A is incorrect. Answer B is incorrect because war-driving involves using wireless technology to connect to unprotected networks from outside the building. Social engineering preys upon weaknesses in the human factor; therefore, answer D is incorrect.

Question 45

Answer B is correct. With mandatory controls, only administrators may change the category of a resource, and no one may grant a right of access that is explicitly forbidden in the access control. Therefore, answers A, C, and D are incorrect.

Question 46

Answer D is correct. Dial-up testing would involve attempting to penetrate a network's security through telephonic connectivity to a RAS server supporting modem dial-in. Answers A and B are incorrect because they involve a general audit, either with or without prior knowledge of the network, and do not target remote access servers specifically. Answer C is incorrect because an Internet services test would focus on Internet-accessible avenues of penetration rather than dial-up access. Answer E is incorrect because an infrastructure test involves the analysis of networking, protocols, and distributed resources and services, without focusing specifically on RAS services.

Question 47

Answer C is correct. RADIUS is a protocol for allowing authentication, authorization, and configuration information between an access server and a shared authentication server. Answer A is incorrect because Kerberos is a network authentication protocol that uses secret key cryptography. Answer B is incorrect because IPSec is used for the tunneling and transport of data. PPTP is an Internet tunneling protocol; therefore, answer D is incorrect.

Question 48

Answers A and B are correct. ESP can encrypt data as well as verify data integrity, but AH can only verify data integrity. Therefore, answers C and D are incorrect.

Question 49

Answer D is correct. A firewall is a hardware or software device used to prevent a network from unauthorized access. Many firewalls are also designed to prevent unauthorized traffic from leaving the network. Answer A is incorrect because intrusion-detection systems are designed to analyze data, identify attacks, and respond to the intrusion. Answer B is also incorrect because a digital certificate electronically identifies an individual. Answer C is incorrect because a honeypot is used as a decoy to lure malicious attacks.

Question 50

Answers A and D are correct. Spoofing involves modifying the source address of traffic or source of information. In this instance, the email was spoofed to make the user think it came from the administrator. By replying to the request, the user was tricked into supplying compromising information, which is a classic sign of social engineering. Answer B is incorrect because a man-in-the-middle attack is commonly used to gather information in transit between two hosts. In a replay, an attacker intercepts traffic between two endpoints and retransmits or replays it later; therefore, answer C is incorrect.

Question 51

Answer D is correct. Logs should be centralized for easy analysis and stored on a machine that has been hardened, logging information traveling on the network should be encrypted if possible, and log files must not be modifiable without a record of the modification. Therefore, answers A, B, and C are incorrect.

Question 52

Answer B is correct. A PKI structure with a single CA and multiple subordinate CAs would benefit the most from a hierarchical structure. This is because it allows the top CA to be the root CA and control trust throughout the PKI. Answer A is incorrect because a cross-certified model is where CAs have a trust relationship with each other; they trust certificates from other

CAs. Answer C is incorrect because a bridge is a central point for cross-certified model. Answer D is incorrect because linked is not a PKI trust model.

Question 53

Answer D is correct. All the statements are good reasons why it is unsafe to run signed code on your system.

Question 54

Answer C is correct. A wet-pipe system constantly has water in it. In dry-pipe systems, water is used but is held back by a valve until a certain temperature is reached. Therefore, answers A, B, and D are incorrect.

Question 55

Answer B is correct. A DRP is an immediate action plan to be implemented just following a disaster. Answer A is incorrect because it describes physical disasters. Answer C is incorrect because it describes loss prevention. Answer D is incorrect because it describes a business continuity plan.

Question 56

Answer C is correct. A DoS attack attempts to block service or reduce activity on a host by sending requests directly to the victim. Answer A is incorrect because spoofing involves modifying the source address of traffic or the source of information. Answer B is incorrect because a man-in-the middle attack is commonly used to gather information in transit between two hosts. Answer D is incorrect because a worm is a form of malicious code.

Question 57

Answers A and C are correct. SSL/TLS supports authentication and encryption. SSL/TLS does not support either Certificate Revocation Lists or attribute certificates; therefore, answers B and D are incorrect.

Question 58

Answer D is correct. The OSI reference model is based on seven layers for how data should be transmitted between any two points. The seven layers from bottom to top are Physical (1), Data Link (2), Network (3), Transport (4), Session (5), Presentation (6), and Application (7). Answers A, B, and C all provide the wrong number of layers and are therefore incorrect.

Question 59

Answer B is correct. Users should not be given privileges above those necessary to perform their job functions. The other choices do not adequately and accurately describe the principle of least privilege. Therefore, answers A, C, and D are incorrect.

Question 60

Answer C is correct. By an account being locked after a few consecutive attempts, the effectiveness of a brute-force attack is reduced. Increasing the value of the password history only prevents the user from using previously used passwords; therefore, answer A is incorrect. Having an employee show proper identification does nothing to reduce brute-force attacks; therefore, answer B is incorrect. The use of password resets is an adequate mechanism in case a password has been compromised; however, it does little to circumvent brute-force attacks; therefore, answer D is incorrect.

Question 61

Answer A is correct. A service-level agreement is a contract between two companies that guarantees service. Answers B, C, and D all describe plans that are not part of an SLA.

Question 62

Answer D is correct. The ability to log on once and gain access to all needed resources is referred to as *single sign-on*. Answer A is incorrect because it describes MAC. Answer B is incorrect because multifactor authentication uses two or more authentication techniques. Answer C is incorrect because biometrics have to do with authentication.

Question 63

Answer C is correct. SSL/TLS is used to secure Web communications and ensure that customer information is securely transferred. Answer A is incorrect because S/MIME is used to secure email communications. Answer B is incorrect because VPN is not used to secure public anonymous connections to Web servers but instead is used to provide secure remote access services to the company's agents. Answer D is incorrect because SSH is used to secure file transfers and terminal sessions.

Question 64

Answer B is correct. Verifying the path of evidence from the crime scene to the courtroom is called the *chain of custody*. Answers A, C, and D are incorrect.

Question 65

Answers B, C, and E are correct. Confidentiality, integrity, and availability make up the security triad. Answers A and D are incorrect because they are not associated with the security triad.

Question 66

Answer B is correct. The Certificate Revocation List (CRL) provides a detailed list of all the certificates that are no longer valid for a CA. Answers A and D are both incorrect because these terms relate to the polices and practices of certificates and the issuing authorities. Answer C is incorrect because a corporate security policy is a set of rules and procedures on how information is protected.

Question 67

Answers B, C, and D are correct. Natural disasters, unwanted access, and user restrictions are all physical security issues. Preventing Internet users from getting to data is data security, not physical security; therefore, answer A is incorrect.

Question 68

Answer B is correct. SMTP relay is a process whereby port 25 is used to forward email. If a hacker can exploit your system, he can send junk mail through your server. Answer A is incorrect because a DNS zone transfer is when a DNS server transfers its database information to another DNS server. DNS servers are used for name resolution, not mail. Answer C is incorrect because port scanning involves a utility being used to scan a machine for open ports that can be exploited. Answer D is incorrect because a man-in-the-middle attack is commonly used to gather information in transit between two hosts.

Question 69

Answers B and C are correct. CGI is a standard that allows a Web server to execute a separate program in order to output content. Because of this, CGI scripts can be tricked into executing commands and could also expose system information. Answer A is incorrect because SMTP is used for email relay. Answer D is incorrect because cookies store the IP address of your computer.

Question 70

Answer D is correct. Multifactor authentication uses two or more authentication techniques. Mutual authentication is a process that authenticates both sides of a connection; therefore, answer C is incorrect. Answers A and B are fictitious terms and are therefore incorrect as well.

Question 71

Answers B, C, and D are correct. Digital certificates include information about the user, the digital signature of the issuing CA, and the user's public key. A user's private key should never be distributed outside of the user's control; therefore, answer A is incorrect.

Question 72

Answer D is correct. A Trojan horse appears to be useful software but has code hidden inside that will attack your system directly or allow the system to be infiltrated by the originator of the code once it is executed. Answers A is incorrect because a Trojan horse is not self-executing. Answer B is incorrect because spoofing makes data appear to come from somewhere other than where it really originated, not a Trojan horse. Answer C is incorrect because viruses are based on exploits of Microsoft Visual Basic, not Trojan horses.

Question 73

Answer C is correct. An application-level gateway understands services and protocols. Answer A is incorrect because it is too generic to be a proper answer. Answer B is incorrect because a circuit-level gateway's decision is based on source and destination addresses. Answer D is incorrect because it is an example of a circuit-level gateway.

Question 74

Answer D is correct. When encrypting and decrypting data using an asymmetric encryption algorithm, you use only the private key to decrypt data encrypted with the public key. Answers A and B are both incorrect because in public key encryption, if one key is used to encrypt, you can use the other to decrypt the data. Answer C is incorrect because the public key cannot decrypt the same data it encrypted.

Question 75

Answer C is correct. Cookies are used in Web page viewing and do not use the network login or password. Cookies use the name and IP address of your machine, your browser type, your operating system, and the URLs of the last pages you visited. Therefore, answers A, B, and D are incorrect.

Question 76

Answer C is correct. The purpose of a VLAN is to unite network nodes logically into the same broadcast domain regardless of their physical attachment to the network. Answer A is incorrect because a DMZ is a small network between the internal network and the Internet that all provides a layer of security and privacy. Answer B is incorrect because a VPN is used to provide secure remote access services to the company's employees and agents. Answer D is incorrect because NAT acts as a liaison between an internal network and the Internet.

Question 77

Answer C is correct. Most companies do not report such attacks because they are afraid that customers will lose faith in their business or they will be accountable to the shareholders for failing to properly protect the company assets. Although the other answers may indicate why a specific incident was not reported, the most common reason is fear. Therefore, answers A, B, and D are incorrect.

Question 78

Answers A and C are correct. FTP is vulnerable because the authentication credentials are sent in cleartext, which makes it vulnerable to sniffing and eavesdropping. Answers B and D are incorrect because they do not accurately describe FTP.

Question 79

Answer A is correct. Centralized security requires that a single group of administrators manages privileges and access. This makes the model more secure but less scalable than decentralized security, which is made up of teams of administrators trained to implement security for their area. Therefore, answers B, C, and D are incorrect.

Question 80

Answer C is correct. A logic bomb is a virus or Trojan horse that is built to go off when a certain event occurs or when a period of time goes by. Answers A and D are incorrect because a specified time element is involved. Answer B is incorrect because spoofing involves modifying the source address of traffic or the source of information.

Question 81

Answers C and E are correct. Value is not a component of risk; however, value may affect your decision of whether to accept a risk. Also, analysis has nothing to do with risk. Risk can be defined as the probability of a threat exploiting a vulnerability. Therefore, answers A, B, and D are incorrect.

Question 82

Answer A is correct. A bastion host is the first line of security that a company allows to be addressed directly from the Internet. A screened subnet is an isolated subnet between the Internet and internal network; therefore, answer B is incorrect. A bastion host on the private network communicating directly with a border router is a screened host; therefore, answer C incorrect. Bastion subnet is a fictitious term; therefore, answer D is incorrect.

Question 83

Answer C is correct. The process of elevating privilege or access is referred to as privilege escalation. Answer A is incorrect because privilege management has to do with programming functions. A Trojan horse is a program used to perform hidden functions; therefore, answer B is incorrect. The ability to log on once and gain access to all needed resources is referred to as single sign-on; therefore, answer D is incorrect.

Question 84

Answer A is correct. A vulnerability is a weakness in hardware or software. Answer B is incorrect because it describes a threat. Answer C is incorrect because it describes a risk. Answer D is incorrect because it describes exposure factor.

Question 85

Answer B is correct. A man-in-the-middle attack is commonly used to gather information in transit between two hosts. Answer A is incorrect because spoofing involves modifying the source address of traffic or source of information. Answer C is incorrect because in a replay, an attacker intercepts traffic between two endpoints and retransmits or replays it later. Because the purpose of a DoS attack is to deny use of resources or services to legitimate users, answer D is incorrect.

Question 86

Answer B is correct. Secure FTP is a client software that allows for a secure connection via SSL. Therefore, answers A, C, and D are incorrect.

Question 87

Answer B is correct. It is management's responsibility to set the tone for what type of role security plays in the organization. Answers A, C, and D are incorrect because, although they all play a part in security, the ultimate responsibility lies with management.

Question 88

Answer B is correct. Rolling back changes should be the next step to recovering the servers and making them quickly available for users. Answers A, C, and D are incorrect. Even though they are all options, answer B is the best choice.

Question 89

Answer C is correct. Stateful inspection will look for strings in the data portion of the TCP/IP packet stream on a continuous basis. Answer A is incorrect because heuristics is all about detecting virus-like behavior, rather than looking for specific signatures. Answer B is incorrect because anomaly analysis is used to detect abnormal behavior patterns. Answer D is incorrect because pattern matching searches through thousands of patterns, including popular, obscure, and discontinued patterns.

Question 90

Answer B is correct. SNMP was developed specifically to manage devices. Answer A is incorrect because Simple Mail Transfer Protocol (SMTP) is a mail protocol used for outgoing mail service. Answer C is incorrect because Lightweight Directory Access Protocol (LDAP) is a directory services protocol. Answer D is incorrect because L2TP is used for packet encapsulation.

Question 91

Answer A is correct. A router is a networking device that works at layer 3 in the OSI model. Answer B is incorrect because a hub works at layer 1. Answer C is incorrect because a switch works at layer 2. Answer D is incorrect because a modem is a device used for dial-up connections.

Question 92

Answer B is correct. A distributed denial of service (DDoS) attack is similar to a denial of service (DoS) attack in that they both try to prevent legitimate access to services. However, a DDoS attack is a coordinated effort among many computer systems; therefore, answer A is incorrect. A Trojan horse is a program used to perform hidden functions; therefore, answer C is incorrect. Masquerading involves using someone else's identity to access resources; therefore, answer D is incorrect.

Question 93

Answer C is correct. CHAP is an authentication protocol that uses a challenge/response mechanism. Answers A, B, and D are all incorrect because they are the three main tunneling protocols used in VPN connections.

Question 94

Answer A is correct. A worm is similar to a virus and Trojan horse, except that it replicates by itself, without any user interaction; therefore, answer B is incorrect. A worm can propagate via email, TCP/IP, and disk drives; therefore, answer C is incorrect. Answer D is incorrect because it describes a self-garbling virus, not a worm.

Question 95

Answer B is correct. TACACS is a client/server protocol that provides the same functionality as RADIUS, except that RADIUS is an actual Internet standard; therefore, answers A and C are incorrect. Answer D is incorrect because both RADIUS and TACACS are authentication protocols.

Question 96

Answer A is correct. SET was developed by several technological companies, including credit card companies, to ensure the security of financial transactions. None of the other choices accurately completes the statement; therefore, answers B, C, and D are incorrect.

Question 97

Answer C is correct. The Wired Equivalent Privacy (WEP) was developed in response to the vulnerabilities present in wireless networks; its developers wanted to provide mechanisms to put wireless networks on par with their physically contained and more secure counterpart. Answer A is incorrect because Wireless Encryption Protocol is a bogus term. Answer B is incorrect because WAP is a standardized set of communication protocols used for wireless devices. Answer D is incorrect because WSP is part of WAP.

Question 98

Answers A and C are correct. PGP uses a web of trust rather than the hierarchical structure. It also uses public key encryption. Based on this, answers B and D are incorrect.

Question 99

Answer B is correct. Although the Message Digest series of algorithms is classified globally as a symmetric key encryption algorithm, the correct answer is hashing algorithm, which is the method that the algorithm uses to encrypt data. Answer A in incorrect because a block cipher divides the message into blocks of bits. Answer C is incorrect because MD5 is a symmetric key algorithm, not an asymmetric encryption algorithm (examples of this would be RC6, Twofish, and Rijndael). Answer D is incorrect because cryptographic algorithm is a bogus term.

Question 100

Answer C is correct. Onsite backup is the most common way for companies to protect their data. Although the other answers are viable solutions, for a small company, onsite backup is the best choice. Therefore, answers A, B, and D are incorrect.

Question 101

Answer B is correct. System hardening is a process by which all unnecessary services are removed to make the system more secure. Answer A is incorrect because nonrepudiation means that neither a sender nor a receiver can deny sending or receiving a message. Answer C is incorrect because auditing is a process whereby events are traced in log files. Answer D is incorrect because hashing is an algorithm method.

Question 102

Answer D is correct. A business continuity plan looks at the long-term actions taken by a company after a disaster has taken place. Answer A is incorrect because emergency response can be a part of disaster recovery. Answer B is incorrect because it deals with the security of a company as a whole, not disaster planning. Answer C is incorrect because a DRP is an immediate action plan to be implemented following a disaster.

Question 103

Answer C is correct. Group-based privilege management focuses on business units such as marketing to assign and control users. Answer A is incorrect because functions such as server maintenance are role based. Answer B is incorrect because users get to decide who has access to files used and the level of permissions that will be set. Answer D is incorrect because users are directly assigned privilege based on job function or business need.

Question 104

Answer A is correct. In a decentralized key-management scheme, the user will create both the private and public key and then submit the public key to the CA to allow it to apply its digital signature once it has authenticated the user. Answer B is incorrect because centralized key management allows the organization to have complete control over the creation, distribution, modification, and revocation of the electronic credentials that it issues. Answers C and D are incorrect because they are nonexistent terms.

Question 105

Answer B is correct. Nonrepudiation means that neither a sender nor a receiver can deny sending or receiving a message or data. Answer A is incorrect because it describes an algorithm. Answer C is incorrect because it describes steganography. Answer D is incorrect because it describes RAID.

Question 106

Answers A and C are correct. John the Ripper and L0phtCrack are both used to crack passwords. Answers B and D are incorrect because both SATAN and SAINT are vulnerability-testing tools.

Question 107

Answers A and D are correct. UDP ports 161 and 162 and used by SNMP. Answer B is incorrect because UDP uses port 139 for network sharing. Answer C is incorrect because port 138 is used to allow NetBIOS traffic for name resolution.

Question 108

Answer D is correct. A combination of both systems is likely to provide the best protection. Network-based IDS is the best option for monitoring malicious intent, but it will not see tunneled data traveling the VPN connections users establish outside.

Question 109

Answer C is correct. Certificate Revocation Lists are used to identify revoked certificates; however, they are being replaced by the Online Certificate Status Protocol (OSCP), which provides certificate status in real time. Answer A is incorrect because a digital signature is an electronic signature used for identity authentication. Answers B and D are both incorrect because these terms relate to the polices and practices of certificates and the issuing authorities.

Question 110

Answers B and C are correct. Transport Layer Security (TLS) is based on Netscape's SSL3 and ensures privacy on the Internet and that there is no tampering. Answer A is incorrect because TLS and SSL are not interoperable. Answer D is incorrect because TLS is composed of two layers: the TLS record protocol and the handshake protocol.

Question 111

Answer C is correct. Wireless Transport Layer Security (WTLS) is the security layer for WAP applications. Even though answer B is part of the WAP, it is not the security layer. Answers A and D are incorrect because the Wireless Security Layer and Wireless Security Layer Transport don't exist.

Question 112

Answer A is correct. An extranet is a connection to a private network accessed by outside business partners. Answer B is incorrect because an intranet is used by employees. Answer C is incorrect because an internet is a public network. Answer D is incorrect because ARPAnet is an early version of the Internet.

Question 113

Answer D is correct. Users who are uneducated about security policies are the weakest links. Answer A is incorrect because management is responsible for setting the security policies of a company. Answers B and C are incorrect because they are a result of poor security policies.

Question 114

Answer A is correct. Buffer overflows are a result of programming flaws that allow for too much data to be sent. When the program does not know what to do with all this date, it crashes, leaving the machine in a state of vulnerability. Answer B is incorrect because a reply attack records and replays previously sent valid messages. Answer C is incorrect because spoofing involves modifying the source address of traffic or the source of information. Answer D is incorrect because the purpose of a DoS attack is to deny the use of resources or services to legitimate users.

Question 115

Answer A is correct. An access control list (ACL) coordinates access to resources based on a list of allowed or denied items, such as users or network addresses. An access point (AP) is often used in relation to a wireless access point (WAP); therefore, answer B is incorrect. Answer C is incorrect because ACLU identifies a nonprofit organization that seeks to protect the basic civic liberties of Americans. Answer D is incorrect because only answer A is correct.

Question 116

Answers B and C are correct. Because DHCP dynamically assigns IP addresses, anyone hooking up to the network can be automatically configured for network access. Anyone can run her own DHCP server. Therefore, a rogue server can misdirect clients to the wrong DNS server. Answer A is incorrect because a man-in-the-middle attack is commonly used to gather information in transit between two hosts. This is a media concern, not a DHCP issue. Answer D is incorrect because there are security concerns with using DHCP.

Question 117

Answer A is correct. A record of user logins with time and date stamps must be kept. User accounts should be disabled and data kept for a specified period of time as soon as employment is terminated. Answers B, C, and D are incorrect because they are not actions you should take when you find out an employee has been terminated.

Question 118

Answer C is correct. In many organizations, accounts are created and then nobody ever touches those accounts again. This is a very poor security practice. Accounts should be monitored regularly; therefore, answer B is incorrect. You should look at unused accounts and should have a procedure in place to ensure that departing employees have their rights revoked prior to leaving the company. You should also have a procedure in place to verify password strength or to ensure that there are no accounts without passwords. Therefore, answers A and D are incorrect.

Question 119

Answer D is correct. Authentication is what you are authorized to perform, access, or do. The two processes are not the same; therefore, answer A is incorrect. Identification is a means to verify who you are; therefore, answers B and C are incorrect.

Question 120

Answer B is correct. 802.11 is the IEEE standard relating the family of specifications for wireless LAN technologies. 802.5 is the standard related to Token Ring LANs; therefore, answer A is incorrect. 802.2 is the standard for the Data Link layer in the OSI reference model; therefore, answer C is incorrect. 802.10 is the specification for network security; therefore, answer D is incorrect.

Question 121

Answer C is correct. An early exploit of JavaScript allowed access to files located on the client's system if the name and path were known. Answers A, D, and E are incorrect because JavaScript, not Java, can be used to execute arbitrary instructions on the server, send email as the user, and allow access to cache information. Answer B is incorrect because Java, not JavaScript, can continue running even after the applet has been closed.

Question 122

Answer C is correct. Confidential documents should be destroyed by an authorized destruction company. Shredding them or ripping them into small pieces and putting in the trash is not a safe way to dispose of them; therefore, answers A and B are incorrect. They should never be put in the recycle bin; therefore, answer D is incorrect.

Question 123

Answer B is correct. Data integrity ensures that data is sequenced, time-stamped, and numbered. Answer A is incorrect because data authentication ensures that the user is properly identified. Answer C is incorrect because data availability ensures that no disruption in the process occurs. Answer D is incorrect because data confidentiality ensures that the data is only available to authorized users.

Question 124

Answer C is correct. As computers get faster, so does the ability for hackers to use distributed computing as a method of breaking encryption algorithms. With computer performance, in some cases, increasing by 30 to 50 percent a year on average, this could become a concern for some older algorithms. Answer A is incorrect because weak keys exhibit regularities, and the weakness has nothing to do with performance. Answer B is incorrect because the weakness in keys comes from a block cipher regularity in the encryption of secret keys. The keys will not repeat themselves on other machines. Answer D is incorrect because there is only one correct answer.

Question 125

Answer A is correct. Network Address Translation (NAT) servers alter packets from internal hosts so they can be sent across the Internet. Answer B is incorrect because DNS resolves IP addresses to domain names. Answer C is incorrect because DHCP is used to configure clients with IP addresses.

Sample Test #2

In the computer-administered test, questions designated as having only one correct answer will have the radio button–style interface for option selection. Questions with more than one correct answer will have check boxes.

Note that there will always be at least one correct answer, so even if you are not sure, guessing is better than leaving a question blank.

Question 1

What is the name given to the process of collecting, processing, and storing evidence as well as analyzing computer systems after an attack has taken place?

- ○ A. Discovery
- ○ B. Due care
- ○ C. Due process
- ○ D. Forensics

Question 2

A _____ is an agent that could intentionally or unintentionally do harm to your computer systems and network.

- ○ A. Threat
- ○ B. Risk
- ○ C. Vulnerability
- ○ D. Both A and B

Question 3

Your company decides it wants to implement a Virtual Private Network (VPN). Which of the following would you *not* consider using because they are not tunneling protocols? [Choose the two best answers.]

- ❏ A. MD5
- ❏ B. L2TP
- ❏ C. 3DES
- ❏ D. PPTP

Question 4

Which of the following statements are correct about Encapsulated Secure Payload (ESP) and Authentication Header (AH)? [Choose the two best answers.]

- ❏ A. AH can only verify data integrity.
- ❏ B. ESP can encrypt data and verify data integrity.
- ❏ C. AH can encrypt data and verify data integrity.
- ❏ D. ESP can only verify data integrity.

Question 5

Of the following, which is a network device that works at the third layer of the OSI model and is responsible for forwarding packets between networks?

○ A. Hub

○ B. Switch

○ C. Router

○ D. Toaster

Question 6

Layer 2 Tunneling Protocol (L2TP) merges the best features of what other two tunneling protocols?

○ A. L2F and PPP

○ B. PPP and PPTP

○ C. L2F and IPSec

○ D. PPTP and L2F

Question 7

Which one of the following is an encryption system used to protect email?

○ A. L2TP

○ B. PPTP

○ C. S/MIME

○ D. MIME

Question 8

Which one of the following is issued by a CA and can be used as a sort of electronic identification card?

○ A. Digital certificate

○ B. Certificate Authority

○ C. Microsoft Passport

○ D. Password

Question 9

A password and a personal identification number (PIN) are examples of which of the following?

- ○ A. Something you have
- ○ B. Something you make
- ○ C. Something you know
- ○ D. Something you are

Question 10

Which of the following are types of access control mechanisms within computer systems? [Choose the two best answers.]

- ❏ A. LDAP
- ❏ B. MAC
- ❏ C. DAC
- ❏ D. TACACS

Question 11

Which one of the following best describes the type of attack that is designed to bring a network to a halt by flooding the systems with useless traffic?

- ○ A. DoS
- ○ B. Ping of death
- ○ C. Teardrop
- ○ D. Social engineering

Question 12

Which of the following describe a denial of service (Dos) attack? [Choose the three best answers.]

- ❏ A. Attempts to flood a network to prevent legitimate network traffic
- ❏ B. Attempts to prevent a particular individual from accessing a service

❑ C. Attempts to upload a back door within a system to allow later access

❑ D. Attempts to disrupt the connection between two machines to prevent access to a service

❑ E. All of the above

Question 13

Which of the following is a coordinated effort where multiple machines attack a single victim or host with the intent to prevent legitimate service?

○ A. DoS

○ B. Masquerading

○ C. DDoS

○ D. Trojan Horse

Question 14

Which of the following is a hardware or software system used to protect a network from unauthorized access?

○ A. Firepot

○ B. Windows XP

○ C. Honeypot

○ D. Firewall

Question 15

Which of the following describes a firewall technique that looks at each packet and accepts or rejects the packet based on defined rules?

○ A. Circuit-level gateway

○ B. Packet filtering

○ C. Application gateway

○ D. Proxy server

Question 16

Which one of the following best describes a worm or a virus?

- ○ A. A virus propagates itself and destroys data.
- ○ B. A worm attacks only after being triggered.
- ○ C. A worm attacks system files, and a virus only attacks email.
- ○ D. A worm is self-replicating, and a virus must be activated to replicate.

Question 17

Which of the following serves the purpose of trying to lure a malicious attacker into a system?

- ○ A. Honeypot
- ○ B. Pot of gold
- ○ C. Lucky charms
- ○ D. Bear trap

Question 18

What is the acronym WEP short for?

- ○ A. Wired Equivalent Privacy
- ○ B. Wireless Encryption Protocol
- ○ C. Wired Equivalency Privacy
- ○ D. Wireless Encryption Privacy

Question 19

Of the following characteristics, which one should be included in every password?

- ○ A. Uppercase letters
- ○ B. Lowercase letters
- ○ C. Numbers
- ○ D. Special characters
- ○ E. All of the above
- ○ F. Answers A and B only

Question 20

Which one of the following is the better password?

○ A. QwErTy

○ B. MacroEconomics32

○ C. ElizabethBallou

○ D. One4a11$

Question 21

Which one of the following is *not* considered a physical security component?

○ A. VPN tunnel

○ B. Mantrap

○ C. Fence

○ D. CCTV

Question 22

Which of the following is the study of measurable human characteristics? Examples include hand scanning, iris profiling, fingerprinting, and voice printing.

○ A. Geometrics

○ B. Biometrics

○ C. Photometrics

○ D. Telemetrics

Question 23

To filter incoming network traffic based on IP address, which one of the following should you implement?

○ A. Firewall

○ B. Intranet

○ C. DoS

○ D. Server

Question 24

What is the widely used standard for defining digital certificates?

- ○ A. X.25
- ○ B. X.400
- ○ C. X.200
- ○ D. X.509

Question 25

What is the name given to the system of digital certificates and Certificate Authorities used for public key cryptography over networks?

- ○ A. Protocol Key Instructions (PKI)
- ○ B. Public Key Extranet (PKE)
- ○ C. Protocol Key Infrastructure (PKI)
- ○ D. Public Key Infrastructure (PKI)

Question 26

Which of the following are not methods of sending secure email messages? [Choose the two best answers.]

- ❑ A. MIME
- ❑ B. S/MIME
- ❑ C. PGP
- ❑ D. S/PGP

Question 27

Public key encryption uses which of the following types of keys?

- ○ A. Public keys only
- ○ B. Private keys only
- ○ C. Public and private keys
- ○ D. A pair of public keys
- ○ E. A pair of private keys

Question 28

Which one of the following is *not* an example of a denial of service attack?

○ A. Fraggle

○ B. Smurf

○ C. Gargomel

○ D. Teardrop

○ E. Ping of death

○ F. Trinoo

Question 29

Which of the following are examples of suspicious activity? [Choose the two best answers.]

❑ A. A log report that indicates multiple login failures on a single account.

❑ B. Multiple connections that are in a half-open state.

❑ C. A user reporting that she is unable to print to the Finance printer.

❑ D. A user is prompted to change his password upon initial login.

Question 30

What does an administrator use to allow, restrict, or deny access to a network or local resource?

○ A. Access controls

○ B. Configuration properties

○ C. Control panel

○ D. PGP

Question 31

Which one of the following is designed to keep a system of checks and balances within a given security structure?

○ A. Principle of least privilege

○ B. Separation of duties

○ C. Access controls

○ D. Principal privileges

Question 32

Which one of the following is not considered one of the three tenets of information security?

○ A. Integrity

○ B. Confidentiality

○ C. Privacy

○ D. Availability

Question 33

What is the term given to an area within a network that sits between a public network and an internal, private network and typically contains devices accessible to the public network?

○ A. Web content zone

○ B. Safe-DMC

○ C. Safe area

○ D. Demilitarized zone

Question 34

What type of attack attempts to use every possible key until the correct key is found?

○ A. Brute-force attack

○ B. Denial of service attack

○ C. Passive attack

○ D. Private key cryptography

Question 35

Which one of the following is an example of a device a user possesses that stores information about the user's level of access?

○ A. Token

○ B. Ticket

○ C. Biometric

○ D. Password

Question 36

Your manager wants you to investigate a client/server system that allows your company's remote access servers to talk with a central server in order to authenticate dial-in users and authorize their access. What type of systems should you research?

○ A. Single sign-on

○ B. RAS servers

○ C. RADIUS

○ D. PPTP

Question 37

What is the name given to the process whereby a server authenticates a client and the client authenticates the server?

○ A. Reverse authentication

○ B. Mirrored authentication

○ C. Mutual authentication

○ D. Dual-factor authentication

Question 38

What is the most common form of authentication used on most systems currently?

○ A. Biometrics

○ B. Usernames and passwords

○ C. Tokens

○ D. Mutual authentication

Question 39

Wired Equivalent Privacy (WEP) is a security protocol for _____ and is defined in the _____ standard.

- ○ A. LANs, 802.11b
- ○ B. 802.11a, WLAN
- ○ C. WLANs, 802.11b
- ○ D. IEEE, X.509

Question 40

Which of the following are protocols for transmitting data securely over the Web? [Choose the two best answers.]

- ❑ A. SSL
- ❑ B. S-HTTP
- ❑ C. FTP
- ❑ D. TCP/IP

Question 41

What protocol was developed to perform encryption on data passing over networks in hopes that it would provide the same security inherent with wired networks?

- ○ A. Wireless Encryption Protocol (WEP)
- ○ B. Wireless Application Protocol (WAP)
- ○ C. Wireless Session Protocol (WSP)
- ○ D. Wired Equivalent Privacy (WEP)

Question 42

Risk is made up of which of the following components? [Choose the three best answers.]

- ❑ A. Vulnerability
- ❑ B. Threat

❑ C. Probability

❑ D. Value

Question 43

You are the security administrator for your company. The CIO wants to block the protocol that allows for the distribution, inquiry, retrieval, and posting of news articles. What port number should you block at the firewall?

○ A. 119

○ B. 80

○ C. 25

○ D. 110

Question 44

While performing regular security audits, you suspect your company is under attack and someone is attempting to use resources on your network. The IP addresses in the log files, however, belong to a trusted partner company. Assuming an attack, which of the following may be occurring?

○ A. Replay

○ B. Authorization

○ C. Social engineering

○ D. Spoofing

Question 45

What should be used to prevent specific types of traffic from certain IP addresses and subnets from entering into the secured segment of your network?

○ A. NAT

○ B. Static packet filter

○ C. VLAN

○ D. Intrusion-detection system

Question 46

Which of the following is a firewall architecture that monitors connections throughout the communication session and checks the validity of the IP packet stream?

- ○ A. Static packet filtering
- ○ B. Spoofing inspection
- ○ C. Stateful inspection
- ○ D. Nonstateful inspection

Question 47

Which of the following describes a passive attack?

- ○ A. Does not insert data into the stream but instead monitors information being sent
- ○ B. Records and replays previously sent valid messages
- ○ C. Inserts false packets into the data stream
- ○ D. Makes attempts to verify the identify of the source of information

Question 48

What is the name given to the government standard describing methods implemented to limit or block electromagnetic radiation from electronic equipment?

- ○ A. EMR
- ○ B. Electroleak
- ○ C. Wiretapping
- ○ D. TEMPEST

Question 49

What type of activities are associated with computer forensics? [Choose the two best answers.]

- ❑ A. Collecting and analyzing data from disk drives
- ❑ B. Collecting and analyzing data from memory
- ❑ C. Collecting fingerprints from the computer case and input devices
- ❑ D. All of the above

Question 50

What are the best choices for actively achieving security awareness among your users in your organization? [Choose the two best answers.]

❏ A. Training during employee orientation

❏ B. Monthly emails

❏ C. Security exhortations through posters

❏ D. Yearly seminars

Question 51

Which one of the following is a process where a user can enter a single user-name and password and have access across multiple resources, eliminating the need to authenticate when switching across resources?

○ A. Authentication

○ B. Single sign-on (SSO)

○ C. Lightweight Directory Access Protocol (LDAP)

○ D. None of the above

Question 52

What is an advantage of the NTFS file system over FAT16 and FAT32?

○ A. Support for network access

○ B. Support for file- and folder-level permissions

○ C. Support for multiple operating systems on a single system

○ D. Support for streaming video

Question 53

You are the network administrator for your organization, and you have noticed multiple unauthorized access attempts on one of your intranet Web servers. Which of the following should be used to control such unauthorized attempts?

○ A. Disable CGI scripting on the Web server.

○ B. Ensure antivirus software is enabled on all servers.

○ C. Implement controls at the firewall.

○ D. Place the Web server in the DMZ.

Question 54

What determines what a user can view and alter?

- ○ A. Confidentiality
- ○ B. Integrity
- ○ C. Authentication
- ○ D. Access control

Question 55

During a Secure Sockets Layer (SSL) handshake, what type of encryption is used to authenticate the server to the client?

- ○ A. Netscape
- ○ B. Keyless
- ○ C. Public key
- ○ D. Private key

Question 56

You suspect one of your servers may have succumbed to a SYN flood attack. Which one of the following tools might you consider using to help confirm your suspicions?

- ○ A. Netstat
- ○ B. Ping
- ○ C. Tracert
- ○ D. IPConfig

Question 57

Unsolicited and unwanted email is generally referred to as which of the following? [Choose the best answer.]

- ○ A. Exchange
- ○ B. Hoax
- ○ C. Spam
- ○ D. Biba

Question 58

Which port does the Simple Mail Transfer Protocol (SMTP) utilize?

- ○ A. 25
- ○ B. 80
- ○ C. 53
- ○ D. All of the above

Question 59

A service in the Windows network operating systems is referred to as a _____ in the Unix environment.

- ○ A. Uniservice
- ○ B. Daemon
- ○ C. Parser
- ○ D. Shell

Question 60

What is an opening left in a program that allows additional, undocumented access to data is known as?

- ○ A. Back door
- ○ B. Algorithm
- ○ C. Blowfish
- ○ D. Demilitarized zone

Question 61

An attacker trying to exploit a Web server will likely want to scan systems running Web services. What port will the attacker scan for?

- ○ A. 21
- ○ B. 25
- ○ C. 80
- ○ D. 110

Question 62

Covert channel communication can be used for which of the following?

- ○ A. Hardening a system
- ○ B. Protecting client/server communication
- ○ C. Strengthening a security policy
- ○ D. Violating a security policy

Question 63

Information that is combined and results in greater understanding is known as which of the following?

- ○ A. Data mining
- ○ B. Data aggregation
- ○ C. Data retrieval
- ○ D. Data composition

Question 64

Your company has several systems that contain sensitive data. This data is useless unless combined with data across the other systems. What is a method of ensuring against the aggregation of data?

- ○ A. Separation of duties
- ○ B. Classifying the data
- ○ C. Enforcing stronger passwords
- ○ D. Conducting background checks

Question 65

An FTP site contains a directory that appears empty because the files are hidden from view, yet files can still be uploaded and downloaded from the directory. This is an example of which of the following?

- ○ A. Blind FTP
- ○ B. SSH

○ C. Locked FTP

○ D. Anonymous FTP

Question 66

Which of the following standards ensures privacy between communicating applications and clients on the Web and has been designed to replace SSL?

○ A. Secure Sockets Layer

○ B. Point-to-Point Tunneling Protocol

○ C. Transport Layer Security

○ D. Internet Protocol Security

Question 67

Of the following, which one transmits logon credentials as cleartext?

○ A. CHAP

○ B. PAP

○ C. MS-CHAP v2

○ D. All of the above

Question 68

At what layer of the OSI model does the Point-to-Point Protocol (PPP) provide services?

○ A. Layer 1

○ B. Layer 2

○ C. Layer 3

○ D. Layer 4

Question 69

What is the correct order for the different layers of the Open Systems Interconnection (OSI) model?

○ A. Network, Transport, Physical, Session, Data Link, Application, Presentation

○ B. Presentation, Data Link, Application, Transport, Network, Session, Physical

○ C. Application, Data Link, Network, Transport, Session, Physical, Presentation

○ D. Physical, Data Link, Network, Transport, Session, Presentation, Application

Question 70

The Point-to-Point Protocol (PPP) is able to handle which of the following data communication methods?

○ A. Synchronous and asynchronous

○ B. Synchronous only

○ C. Asynchronous only

○ D. Synchronous, asynchronous, and half-synchronous

Question 71

With Role-Based Access Control (RBAC), how are access rights grouped?

○ A. Role name

○ B. Rules

○ C. Pole identification number

○ D. Rule identification name

Question 72

Within a router, access may be granted or denied based on IP address. What is the name given to this method?

○ A. ACLU

○ B. ACL

○ C. AP

○ D. Answers A and B

Question 73

Which of the following items is normally shared among multiple users?

○ A. Password

○ B. User home directory

○ C. Username

○ D. None of the above

Question 74

You are an accountant in finance and you receive an email warning you of a dev-astating virus that is going around. The email instructs you to be weary of any email containing a specific file and further instructs you to delete the specific file if found from your computer. Which of the following should you do? [Choose the best answer.]

○ A. Search for and delete the file from your computer.

○ B. Forward the email to your friends and coworkers.

○ C. Notify your system administrator of the email.

○ D. Delete the email and reboot your computer.

Question 75

What is the name given to the activity that consists of collecting information that will be later used for monitoring and review purposes?

○ A. Logging

○ B. Auditing

○ C. Inspecting

○ D. Vetting

Question 76

The principle of least privilege _____
_____
_____.

- ○ A. requires that a user be given no more privilege than necessary to perform a job
- ○ B. ensures that all members of the user community are given the same privileges so long that they do not have administrator or root access to systems
- ○ C. is a control enforced through written security policies
- ○ D. assumes that job functions will be rotated frequently

Question 77

The enforcement of separation of duties is a valuable deterrent to which one of the following?

- ○ A. Trojan horses
- ○ B. Viruses
- ○ C. Fraud
- ○ D. Corporate audits
- ○ E. Answers A and B

Question 78

A retinal scan is a check for which one of the following?

- ○ A. Something you have
- ○ B. Something you know
- ○ C. Something you are
- ○ D. Something you do

Question 79

Which of the following techniques will best help protect a system against a brute-force password attack?

- ○ A. Lock the account after three unsuccessful password entry attempts
- ○ B. Have users present proper identification before being granted a password
- ○ C. Increase the value of the password history control
- ○ D. Require password resets every 90 days

Question 80

Which of the following should be employed to help prevent against the mishandling of media?

- ○ A. Token
- ○ B. SSL
- ○ C. Labeling
- ○ D. Ticketing

Question 81

What provides the basis for the level of protection applied to information? [Choose the three best answers.]

- ❏ A. Data classification
- ❏ B. Value
- ❏ C. Risk of loss
- ❏ D. Size of the organization

Question 82

An intrusion-detection system (IDS) detects an attacker and seamlessly transfers the attacker to a special host. What is the name given to this host?

- ○ A. Honeypot
- ○ B. Padded cell
- ○ C. Remote access host
- ○ D. Byte host

Question 83

Which of the following are advantages of honeypot and padded-cell systems? [Choose the three best answers.]

❑ A. Attackers are diverted to systems that they cannot damage.

❑ B. Administrators are allotted time to decide how to respond to an attack.

❑ C. Attackers actions can more easily be monitored, and as a result steps can be taken to improve system security.

❑ D. Well-defined legal implications.

❑ E. They provide a structure that would require fewer security administrators.

Question 84

Which of the following is a formal set of statements that defines how systems or network resources can be utilized?

○ A. Policies

○ B. Standards

○ C. Guidelines

○ D. Procedures

Question 85

What is the IEEE standard for wireless LAN technology?

○ A. 802.2

○ B. 802.11

○ C. 802.1

○ D. 802.6

Question 86

Which of the following ranges represents the pool of well-known ports?

○ A. 0 through 255

○ B. 0 through 1023

○ C. 0 through 49151

○ D. 1024 through 49151

Question 87

Your company does not allow users to utilize the Internet for personal reasons during work hours. Where is this statement most likely documented?

○ A. Company standards

○ B. Company procedures

○ C. Company guidelines

○ D. Company policies

Question 88

How many keys does asymmetric encryption require?

○ A. 1

○ B. 2

○ C. 1024

○ D. 1025

Question 89

What file system is preferred for use on all systems running Microsoft Windows NT, Windows 2000, and Windows XP Professional operating systems?

○ A. CDFS

○ B. NFS

○ C. FAT

○ D. NTFS

Question 90

Which of the following ports are assigned to NetBIOS services? [Choose the three best answers.]

❏ A. 137

❏ B. 138

❏ C. 139

❏ D. 140

Question 91

What type of backup is normally done once a day and clears the archive bit once the files have been backed up?

- ○ A. Copy
- ○ B. Daily
- ○ C. Incremental
- ○ D. Differential

Question 92

What is the name by which the sender of data is provided with proof of delivery and that neither the sender nor receiver can deny either having sent or received the data?

- ○ A. Nonrepudiation
- ○ B. Repetition
- ○ C. Nonrepetition
- ○ D. Repudiation

Question 93

A disaster recovery plan (DRP) is an agreed-upon plan detailing how operations will be restored after a disaster. When is the DRP created?

- ○ A. After a disaster
- ○ B. During a disaster
- ○ C. Before a disaster
- ○ D. None of the above

Question 94

The process of making an operating system more secure by closing known vulnerabilities and addressing security issues is known as _____.

○ A. Handshaking

○ B. Hardening

○ C. Hotfixing

○ D. All of the above

Question 95

Netbus is an example of which of the following? [Choose the two best answers.]

❏ A. An IP testing tool

❏ B. An illicit server

❏ C. A network scanning tool

❏ D. A Trojan horse

Question 96

What is the name given to viruses that mutate and can appear differently, which makes them more difficult to detect?

○ A. Stealth

○ B. Cavity

○ C. Polymorphic

○ D. Multipartite

Question 97

What type of virus can most easily be created without knowledge of a complex programming knowledge and is found in electronic office documents?

○ A. Stealth

○ B. Macro

○ C. Polymorphic

○ D. Multipartite

Question 98

A hacker attempting to break into a server running Windows 2000 will most likely attempt to break into which account?

- ○ A. Supervisor
- ○ B. Root
- ○ C. Administrator
- ○ D. Group

Question 99

Which of the following is a Unix-based command interface and protocol for accessing a remote computer securely?

- ○ A. Secure Electronic Transaction (SET)
- ○ B. Secure Hash Algorithm (SHA)
- ○ C. Secure Socket Shell (SSH)
- ○ D. Telnet

Question 100

What port is used for a DNS zone transfer?

- ○ A. 53
- ○ B. 80
- ○ C. 137
- ○ D. 138

Question 101

A Web server must always runs on port 80.

- ○ A. True
- ○ B. False

Question 102

Packet activity is monitored on each individual computer for what type of intrusion-detection system?

- ○ A. Network-based IDS
- ○ B. LAN-based IDS
- ○ C. Host-based IDS
- ○ D. All of the above

Question 103

What occurs when a program tries to store more data in a temporary storage area than it was intended to hold?

- ○ A. Buffer overflow
- ○ B. Patch
- ○ C. SYN flood
- ○ D. SMTP relay

Question 104

Passwords can be intercepted as they move through networks via which of the following?

- ○ A. Keyboard sniffers
- ○ B. Password sniffers
- ○ C. Trojan horses
- ○ D. Cookies

Question 105

A fire involving computer equipment and other electronic appliances is likely to be considered what class of fire?

- ○ A. Class A
- ○ B. Class B
- ○ C. Class C
- ○ D. Class D

Question 106

Which of the following are items that a physical security plan should include? [Choose the three best answers.]

❏ A. Description of the physical assets being protected

❏ B. The threats you are protecting against and their likelihood

❏ C. Location of a hard disk's physical blocks

❏ D. Description of the physical areas where assets are located

Question 107

A Certificate Authority discovers it has issued a digital certificate to the wrong person. What needs to be completed?

○ A. Certificate Practice Statement (CPS)

○ B. Revocation

○ C. Private key compromise

○ D. Fraudulent Practices Statement (FPS)

Question 108

Which of the following is a primary method for minimizing the threat to a Web server?

○ A. Disable all non-Web services and enable Telnet for interactive logins.

○ B. Ensure finger and echo are running.

○ C. Disable nonessential services.

○ D. Enable logging.

Question 109

Which one of the following is the equivalent of a burglar alarm for computer networks?

○ A. DNS

○ B. NIDS

○ C. FTP

○ D. RFP

Question 110

The enforcement of minimum privileges for system users is achieved via which of the following?

- ○ A. IPSec
- ○ B. RBAC
- ○ C. IDS
- ○ D. DRP

Question 111

Which of the following is not a major security evaluation criteria effort?

- ○ A. TCSEC
- ○ B. Common Criteria
- ○ C. IPSec
- ○ D. ITSEC

Question 112

Which one of the following types of servers would be the target for an attack where a malicious individual attempts to change information during a zone transfer?

- ○ A. Database server
- ○ B. File and print server
- ○ C. Web server
- ○ D. DNS server

Question 113

What is the name given to an internal router when two routers are used together in a firewall configuration?

- ○ A. Choke
- ○ B. Hold
- ○ C. Dual inside
- ○ D. Choke hold

Question 114

What is the name given to the only host on an internal network that is visible to the Internet through the firewall?

○ A. Bastion host

○ B. Screened host

○ C. Answers A and B

○ D. None of the above

Question 115

Which of the following is a type of cable in which the signals cannot be detected by electronic eavesdropping equipment?

○ A. Fiber optic

○ B. Unshielded twisted pair (UTP)

○ C. Shielded twisted pair (STP)

○ D. Coaxial thicknet

Question 116

What is the space above a drop ceiling called?

○ A. Raised floor

○ B. Fire-retardant space

○ C. Plenum

○ D. Teflon

Question 117

A protocol named _____ is used to manage network devices, and it works by sending _____ to various parts of the network.

○ A. SNMP, MIBs

○ B. MIB, PDUs

○ C. SNMP, PDUs

○ D. PDU, MIBs

Question 118

Which one of the following is *not* a private IP address?

○ A. 10.1.2.1

○ B. 165.193.123.44

○ C. 172.18.36.4

○ D. 192.168.0.234

Question 119

Of the following, which is a characteristic of a cold site?

○ A. Setup time is required.

○ B. The company needs to bring its own equipment.

○ C. The facility and equipment are already set up and ready to occupy.

○ D. Answers A and B.

Question 120

Which of the following is used to trap and ground stray electrical signals?

○ A. TEMPEST

○ B. Faraday cage

○ C. EMR

○ D. None of the above

Question 121

Which one of the following best describes a service-level agreement (SLA)? [Choose the best answer.]

○ A. A method of procuring services after a disaster has struck

○ B. A contract between a service provider and the customer that specifies how the provider will ensure recovery in the event of a disaster

○ C. A contract between a service provider and the customer that specifies the measurable services the provider will furnish

○ D. A method of protecting a facility from disaster

Question 122

A situation in which a program or process attempts to store more data in a temporary data storage area than it was intended to hold is known as which of the following?

- ○ A. Buffer overflow
- ○ B. Denial of service
- ○ C. Distributed denial of service
- ○ D. Storage overrun

Question 123

Which of the following is used in many encryption algorithms and is the transformation of a string of characters into a shorter fixed-length value or key that represents the original string?

- ○ A. Cipher block chaining
- ○ B. Hashing
- ○ C. PKI
- ○ D. Ciphertext

Question 124

What is usually the first phase conducted before performing site penetration?

- ○ A. Information gathering
- ○ B. Cracking
- ○ C. Social engineering
- ○ D. Spoofing

Question 125

What type of server acts as an intermediary, intercepting all requests to a target server to see whether it can fulfill these requests itself?

- ○ A. Web server
- ○ B. Packet filter
- ○ C. Proxy server
- ○ D. Firewall

Answer Key to Sample Test #2

1. D	**17.** A	**33.** D
2. A	**18.** A	**34.** A
3. A, C	**19.** E	**35.** A
4. A, B	**20.** D	**36.** C
5. C	**21.** A	**37.** C
6. D	**22.** B	**38.** B
7. C	**23.** A	**39.** C
8. A	**24.** D	**40.** A, B
9. C	**25.** D	**41.** D
10. B, C	**26.** A, D	**42.** A, B, C
11. A	**27.** C	**43.** A
12. A, B, D	**28.** C	**44.** D
13. C	**29.** A, B	**45.** B
14. D	**30.** A	**46.** C
15. B	**31.** B	**47.** A
16. D	**32.** C	**48.** D

49. A, B

50. A, D

51. B

52. B

53. C

54. D

55. C

56. A

57. C

58. A

59. B

60. A

61. C

62. D

63. B

64. A

65. A

66. C

67. B

68. B

69. D

70. A

71. A

72. B

73. D

74. C

75. A

76. A

77. C

78. C

79. A

80. C

81. A, B, C

82. B

83. A, B, C

84. A

85. B

86. B

87. D

88. B

89. D

90. A, B, C

91. C

92. A

93. C

94. B

95. B, D

96. C

97. B

98. C

99. C

100. A

101. B

102. C

103. A

104. B

105. C

106. A, B, D

107. B

108. C

109. B

110. B

111. C

112. D

113. A

114. A

115. A

116. C

117. C

118. B

119. D

120. B

121. C

122. A

123. B

124. A

125. C

Question 1

Answer D is correct. Forensics is the practice of using tools to investigate and establish facts, usually for evidence within a court of law. According to the question, the attack has already taken place, and evidence is being retrieved; therefore, answer A is incorrect. Answer B and C are also both incorrect. Due care describes a process before an attack takes place, and due process describes the course taken during court proceedings designed to safeguard the legal rights of individuals.

Question 2

Answer A is correct. A threat is something that could intentionally (for example, a malicious hacker) or unintentionally (for example, a tornado) do harm to your computer systems and network. Answer B is incorrect because a risk describes the possibility of realizing a threat. Answer C is incorrect because a vulnerability describes the susceptibility to attack. Answer D is also incorrect because answer B is incorrect.

Question 3

Answers A and C are correct. Both MD5 and 3DES are cryptography algorithms, whereas answers B and D are both tunneling protocols used in Virtual Private Networks. Therefore, answers B and D are incorrect.

Question 4

Answers A and B are correct. Encapsulated Secure Payload can encrypt data as well as verify data integrity, but Authentication Header can only verify data integrity. Therefore, answers C and D are incorrect.

Question 5

Answer C is correct. A router is a networking device that works at layer 3 in the OSI model. Answer A is incorrect because a hub works at layer 1. A switch works at layer 2; therefore, answer B is incorrect. A toaster (a device typically used to crisp bread) is not a networking device (at least not yet); therefore, answer D is incorrect.

Question 6

Answer D is correct. Both PPTP and L2F are leveraged within L2TP. Answers A, B, and C are all incorrect because each answer contains a protocol that is not a tunneling protocol.

Question 7

Answer C is correct. S/MIME is the secure version of MIME and is used to protect email messages. Answers A and B are incorrect because L2TP and PPTP are tunneling protocols. Answer D is incorrect because MIME is used for plaintext, the unsecured version of S/MIME.

Question 8

Answer A is correct. Digital certificates are issued by Certificate Authorities (CAs) and serve as a virtual ID or passport, commonly used to conduct business over the Web. Answer B is incorrect because a Certificate Authority is the issuer of these certificates used to establish identification. Answer C is incorrect because this describes a Microsoft authentication service. A password is a secret word or phrase used to gain access; therefore, answer D is incorrect.

Question 9

Answer C is correct. A password and a PIN are usually private alphanumeric codes that are known by an individual. Something you have describes an item such as a swipe card or token; therefore, answer A is incorrect. Something you make is not associated with authentication; therefore, answer B is incorrect. Answer D is incorrect because something you are involves biometrics such as fingerprints and voiceprints.

Question 10

Answers B and C are correct. Mandatory Access Control (MAC) and Discretionary Access Control (DAC) are both common types of access control mechanisms used within computer systems. LDAP is a directory protocol; therefore, answer A is incorrect. TACACS is an authentication protocol; therefore, answer D is incorrect.

Question 11

Answer A is correct. A denial of service (DoS) attack is designed to bring down a network by flooding the system with an overabundance of useless traffic. Although answers B and C are both types of denial of service attacks, they are incorrect because DoS more accurately describes "the type of attack." Answer D is incorrect because social engineering describes the non-technical means of obtaining information.

Question 12

Answers A, B, and D are correct. These answers all describe attacks designed to prevent legitimate service. Answer C is incorrect because this is characteristic of a Trojan horse, and naturally answer E is also incorrect.

Question 13

Answer C is correct. A distributed denial of service (DDoS) attack is similar to a denial of service (DoS) attack in that they both try to prevent legitimate access to services. However, a DDoS attack is a coordinated effort among many computer systems; therefore, answer A is incorrect. Masquerading involves using someone else's identity to access resources; therefore, answer B is incorrect. A Trojan horse is a program used to perform hidden functions; therefore, answer D is incorrect.

Question 14

Answer D is correct. A firewall is a hardware or software device used to prevent a network from unauthorized access. Many firewalls are also designed to prevent unauthorized traffic from leaving the network. Answer A is incorrect because is not a legitimate term. Answer B is also incorrect because Windows XP is a Microsoft operating system. A honeypot is used as a decoy to lure malicious attacks; therefore, answer C is incorrect.

Question 15

Answer B is correct. A packet-filtering firewall inspects each packet and makes decisions based on user-defined rules. Although answers A, C, and D are all types of firewall techniques, each of these are incorrect. A circuit-level gateway applies security once a connection is established. An application gateway applies security to specific applications, and a proxy server hides the internal network by intercepting all traffic.

Question 16

Answer D is correct. Traditionally a worm replicates itself, and a virus must be activated in order to replicate. Answer A is incorrect because a virus must be activated to propagate. Answer B is incorrect because a worm can perform its functions without being triggered. Answer C is also an incorrect statement.

Question 17

Answer A is correct. A honeypot is used to serve as a decoy and lure a malicious attacker. Answers B, C, and D are all incorrect answers and do not reflect legitimate terms for testing purposes.

Question 18

Answer A is correct. Wired Equivalent Privacy (WEP) is part of the 802.11b standard, and it is designed to provide for the same level of security as on a wired network. You may find WEP spelled out incorrectly outside the exam, but answers B, C, and D are all incorrect.

Question 19

Answer E is correct. A good password will use uppercase and lowercase letters as well as numbers and special characters; therefore, answer F is incorrect.

Question 20

Answer D is correct. Answer D is a good password because it is eight characters long and uses mixed case, numbers, and a special character ($). Answer A is incorrect because it uses a familiar keyboard pattern. Although answer B might make a good password, it would be better if it incorporated numbers within the password (not at the beginning or end) and if it were not a word found in the dictionary; therefore, answer B is incorrect. Answer C is incorrect because a person's name shouldn't be used as a password.

Question 21

Answer A is correct. A VPN tunnel is an example of data security—not physical security. Mantrap, fence, and CCTV are all components of physical security; therefore, answers B, C, and D are incorrect.

Question 22

Answer B is correct. Biometrics is the study of biological characteristics. Geometrics describes geometric qualities or properties; therefore, answer A is incorrect. Answer C, photometrics, is incorrect because this is the study and measurement of the properties of light. Telemetrics is the study and measurement of the transmission of data over certain mediums; therefore, answer D is incorrect.

Question 23

Answer A is correct. A firewall is a hardware or software system designed to protect networks against threats, and it can be used to permit or deny traffic based on IP address. Answer B is incorrect because an intranet is a private network. Answer C is incorrect because DoS is a type of attack meant to disrupt service. Although a firewall may be called a firewall server, answer D is incorrect because it is not specific enough.

Question 24

Answer D is correct. X.509 is the defining standard on which digital certificates are based. Answer A is incorrect because X.25 is a standard for connecting packet-switched networks. X.400 is a standard for transmitting email; therefore, answer B is incorrect. X.200 deals with the top layer of the OSI model; therefore, answer C is incorrect.

Question 25

Answer D is correct. Public Key Infrastructure (PKI) describes the trust hierarchy system for implementing a secure public key cryptography system over TCP/IP networks. Answers A, B, and C are incorrect because these are bogus terms.

Question 26

Answers A and D are correct. MIME is a specification for formatting messages but does not support encryption, and S/PGP does not exist. However, Pretty Good Privacy (PGP) uses encryption to secure email messages, as does S/MIME. Therefore, answers B and C are incorrect because these are both methods for sending secure email.

Question 27

Answer C is correct. Public key encryption uses a public and private key pair. Answer A is incorrect because there are no encryption technologies that use only public keys. Answer B is incorrect because only a symmetric key cryptography system would use just a private key. Answer D is incorrect for the same reason as answer A, and answer E is incorrect for the same reason as answer B.

Question 28

Answer C is correct. A Gargomel attack, although cool sounding, does not actually exist. Fraggle, Smurf, Teardrop, ping of death, and Trinoo are names of specific denial of service attacks. Therefore, answers A, B, D, E, and F are incorrect.

Question 29

Answers A and B are correct. A log report that shows multiple login failures for a single account should raise suspicion because this might be an attempt by an unauthorized person to gain access. Multiple connections in a half-open state are likely waiting for a SYN-ACK and may be indicative of a SYN flood attack. Answers C and D are incorrect because these appear to be typical network problems or the results of controls that have been implemented by an administrator.

Question 30

Answer A is correct. Access controls allow an administrator to allow, restrict, or deny access to resources. Two common access control methods include Discretionary Access Control (DAC) and Mandatory Access Control (MAC). Answers B and C are both incorrect because neither of these relates to administrative controls for administering the security on resources. Answer D is incorrect because PGP is used for secure email.

Question 31

Answer B is correct. Separation of duties, as well as responsibilities, is used to ensure a system of checks and balances. Answer A is incorrect because the principle of least privilege is used to ensure that users are granted only the minimum level of access required to perform their job functions. Answer C is incorrect because access controls allow for the control of access to resources. Answer D is incorrect because this is an invalid term.

Question 32

Answer C is correct. The three tenets of information security are confidentiality, integrity, and availability. Privacy, although similar to confidentiality, is not considered one of the three. Therefore, answers A, B, and D are incorrect.

Question 33

Answer D is correct. A demilitarized zone (DMZ) sits between a public network, such as the Internet, and an organization's internal network. A Web content zone is a security term used in Microsoft's Web browser; therefore, answer A is incorrect. Both answers B and C are made-up terms; therefore, they are incorrect.

Question 34

Answer A is correct. A brute-force attack will attempt to use every key and relies on adequate processing power. Answer B is incorrect because a denial of service attack is an attempt to prevent legitimate service. Answer C is incorrect because this describes an attempt to intercept data without altering it. Answer D is incorrect because this is a crypto system that relies on secret keys.

Question 35

Answer A is correct. A token is a physical device used to gain access and is usually accompanied by something the user knows, such as a password. Answer B is incorrect because this term is typically used when describing software authentication systems. Biometrics is the study and measurement of biological characteristics; therefore, answer C is incorrect. Answer D is incorrect because a password is something a user knows in order to gain access.

Question 36

Answer C is correct. Remote Authentication Dial-In User Service (RADIUS) is a client/server system that facilitates the communication between remote access servers and a central server. The central server will authenticate the dial-in users and authorize their access. Answer A is incorrect because single sign-on provides the mechanism whereby a user only needs to authenticate to a system one time and is able to access multiple systems without the need to reauthenticate or maintain separate usernames and passwords. Answer B is incorrect because a Remote Access Server (RAS) is the system used to handle remote user access, and your manager wants a central server to communicate with these servers. Answer D is incorrect because PPTP is a tunneling protocol.

Question 37

Answer C is correct. Mutual authentication describes the process whereby a client and server both authenticate each other, rather than the server only authenticating the client. Answers A, B, and D are all invalid terms and are therefore incorrect.

Question 38

Answer B is correct. Most computer systems support the basic authentication method of using a username and password combination. Although biometrics is promising, its widespread use has still yet to be seen; therefore, answer A is incorrect. Tokens are gaining in popularity but are primarily used with usernames and passwords; therefore, answer C is incorrect. Answer D is also incorrect because it describes the process of clients and servers both authenticating to each other.

Question 39

Answer C is correct. Wired Equivalent Privacy (WEP) is a security protocol designed for wireless local area networks, and it is defined in the 802.11b standard. Answers A, B, and D are all incorrect. 802.11a is similar to 802.11b, but offers greater bandwidth capabilities at a shorter range. The IEEE (or

Institute of Electrical and Electronics Engineers) developed the 802.11 standards, and X.509 is the standard for defining digital certificates.

Question 40

Answers A and B are correct. Both Secure Sockets Layer (SSL) and Secure HTTP (S-HTTP) are protocols designed to transmit data securely across the Web. SSL uses public key encryption to encrypt the data, and S-HTTP creates a secure connection between the client and server. File Transfer Protocol (FTP) is a simple and unsecured protocol for the transfer of files across the Internet, and TCP/IP, which is inherently unsecured, is the language of the Internet. Therefore, answers C and D are incorrect.

Question 41

Answer D is correct. Wired Equivalent Privacy (WEP) was developed in response to the vulnerabilities present in wireless networks. Its developers wanted to provide mechanisms to put wireless networks on par with their physically contained and more secure counterpart. Answer A is incorrect because this is a bogus term. Answer B is incorrect because WAP is specification for a set of communication protocols to standardize Internet access for wireless devices. WSP is part of WAP; therefore, answer C is incorrect.

Question 42

Answers A, B, and C are correct. Risk can be defined as the probability of a threat exploiting a vulnerability. Answer D is incorrect. Value is not a component of risk; however, value may affect your decision of whether to accept a risk.

Question 43

Answer A is correct. The Network News Transfer Protocol (NNTP) provides access to newsgroups and uses TCP port 119. The Hypertext Transfer Protocol (Web) uses port 80; therefore, answer B is incorrect. Answers C and D are also incorrect because these ports are used to send and receive mail. Port 25 is for the Simple Mail Transfer Protocol (SMTP), and port 110 is for the Post Office Protocol (POP).

Question 44

Answer D is correct. The most likely answer is spoofing because this allows an attacker to misrepresent the source of the requests. Answer A is incorrect because this type of attack records and replays previously sent valid messages. Answer B is incorrect because this is not a type of attack but is instead the granting of access rights based on authentication. Answer C is incorrect because social engineering involves the nontechnical means of gaining information.

Question 45

Answer B is correct. On a firewall, static packet filtering provides a simple solution for the basic filtering of network traffic based on source, destination addresses, and protocol types. Answer A is incorrect because NAT is used to hide internal addresses. Answer C is incorrect because a VLAN is used to make computers on physically different network segments appear as if they are one physical segment. Answer D is incorrect because an intrusion-detection system is used to identify suspicious network activity.

Question 46

Answer C is correct. Stateful inspection (also called *dynamic packet filtering*) monitors the connection throughout the session and verifies the validity of IP packet streams. Answer A is incorrect because static packet filtering examines packets based on information in their headers. Answer B is incorrect because there is no such firewall architecture. As opposed to stateful inspection, nonstateful inspection does not maintain the state of the packets; therefore, answer D is incorrect.

Question 47

Answer A is correct. A passive attack attempts to passively monitor data being sent between two parties and does not insert data into the data stream. A reply attack records and replays previously sent valid messages; therefore, answer B is incorrect. An active attack makes attempts to insert false packets into the data stream; therefore, answer C is incorrect. Authentication is the process of verifying the identify of a source and is not a type of attack; therefore, answer D is incorrect.

Question 48

Answer D is correct. TEMPEST originated with the U.S. military and deals with the study of devices that emit electromagnetic radiation. Electromagnetic radiation (EMR) is emitted from devices; therefore, answer A is incorrect. Answer B is a bogus term and is therefore incorrect. Answer C is incorrect because wiretapping involves the secret monitoring of information being passed.

Question 49

Answers A and B are correct. Both collecting and analyzing data from disk drives' memory are functions of computer forensics; however, the dusting and collection of fingerprints is a law-enforcement forensics function; therefore, answer C is incorrect. Answer D is also incorrect because only answers A and B are correct.

Question 50

Answers A and D are correct. Security training during employee orientation as well as yearly seminars are the best choices because these are active methods of raising security awareness. On the other hand, using emails and posters are passive methods of raising security awareness. Therefore, answers B and C are incorrect.

Question 51

Answer B is correct. Single sign-on provides the mechanism whereby a user only needs to authenticate to a system one time and is able to access multiple systems without the need to reauthenticate or maintain separate usernames and passwords. Answer A is incorrect because authentication is simply the process of identification. Answer C is incorrect because LDAP is a protocol for directory access. Answer D is incorrect because answer B is correct.

Question 52

Answer B is correct. Unlike any of the FAT file systems, NTFS supports file- and folder-level permissions. FAT file systems provide complete access locally to the entire FAT partition. Network access can be achieved regardless of the file system used; therefore, answer A is incorrect. Support for multiple operating systems is not a feature of NTFS over FAT file systems; therefore, answer C is incorrect. Streaming video is not a function of the type of file system; therefore, answer D is incorrect.

Question 53

Answer C is correct. Although there might be better solutions, depending on the circumstances, implementing proper controls at the firewall is the best choice for this internal server. Although CGI scripts may present certain dangers, disabling them is not the best choice; therefore, answer A is incorrect. Antivirus software will protect your systems against viruses but will not control unauthorized access; therefore, answer B is incorrect. You would not want to place the server in the DMZ because it is a private Web server and is not meant for access by public users; therefore, answer D is incorrect.

Question 54

Answer D is correct. Access control defines what users can access as well as what they can specifically view and alter. Confidentiality ensures data remains private; therefore, answer A is incorrect. Integrity describes the reliability of the data in that it has not been altered; therefore, answer B is incorrect. Authentication verifies the identify of a user or system; therefore, answer C is incorrect.

Question 55

Answer C is correct. The SSL handshake uses public key cryptography to verify the identify of the server. Answer A is incorrect; however, Netscape did originally develop the SSL protocol. Encryption uses public keys, private keys, or a combination of both; therefore, answer B is incorrect. SSL uses public key encryption during the SSL handshake, and it does not use private key encryption; therefore, answer D is incorrect.

Question 56

Answer A is correct. By using the netstat command, you can check the number of open connections that have received a SYN but not an ACK, which may indicate connections left in a half-opened state. Ping, Tracert, and IPConfig are other useful utilities but will not show connection states like Netstat. Therefore, answers B, C, and D are incorrect.

Question 57

Answer C is correct. Spam or junk email is unsolicited and unwanted email usually sent in bulk. Although Exchange is a Microsoft Mail server, it is not the correct answer; therefore, answer A is incorrect. An email hoax may be considered spam; however, spam is the more accurate answer; therefore, answer B is incorrect. Answer D is incorrect because Biba is actually a security model used to define different levels of integrity.

Question 58

Answer A is correct. Port 25 is used for the Simple Mail Transfer Protocol (SMTP). The Hypertext Transfer Protocol (Web) uses port 80; therefore, answer B is incorrect. Answers C is incorrect because port 53 is used for DNS. Because only one of the listed ports is correct, answer D is also incorrect.

Question 59

Answer B is correct. The terms *service* and *daemon* are synonymous. They describe programs that run continuously and handle service requests to a computer system. Uniservice is a bogus term; therefore, answer A is incorrect. A parser is a program that is usually part of a compiler; therefore, answer C is incorrect. *Shell* is a commonly used Unix term given to the interactive interface; therefore, answer D is incorrect.

Question 60

Answer A is correct. A back door is an opening in a program, often left by a developer that enables access through nontraditional means. Answer B is incorrect because an algorithm is a series of steps to arrive at a result. Blowfish is a type of symmetric block cipher; therefore, answer C is incorrect. Answer D is incorrect because a demilitarized zone is a zone within a network where publicly accessible servers are typically placed.

Question 61

Answer C is correct. Port 80 is used for Web services, also known as Hypertext Transfer Protocol. Port 21 is used for the File Transfer Protocol (FTP); therefore, answer A is incorrect. Port 25 is used for the Simple Mail Transfer Protocol (SMTP); therefore, answer B is incorrect. Port 110 is used for the Post Office Protocol (POP); therefore, answer D is incorrect.

Question 62

Answer D is correct. Covert channel communication allows the transfer of information in a manner that violates the system's security policy. Answers A, B, and C are not legitimate uses of a covert channel; therefore, these answers are incorrect.

Question 63

Answer B is correct. Data aggregation is the process of combining separate pieces of data that, by themselves, may be of no use, but when combined with other bits of data they will provide greater understanding. The other choices are all invalid answers; therefore, answers A, C, and D are incorrect.

Question 64

Answer A is correct. Individuals granted widespread authorization to data have a much easier chance to perform data aggregation. Ensuring the separation of duties provides a countermeasure against such data collection. Classifying the data does not help against the risk that the information may be collected by authorized individuals; therefore, answer B is incorrect. Answers C and D are also incorrect because these are irrelevant to the process of piecing together separate pieces of data.

Question 65

Answer A is correct. Blind FTP is often used for files sensitive in nature. Files listed in the Blind FTP directory are hidden from view. Answer B is incorrect because Secure Shell (SSH) is a program that provides secure shell access. SSH is basically a secure version of Telnet. Answer C is incorrect as this choice serves as a distracter. Anonymous FTP allows access without proper identification. Although a Blind FTP implementation may also be anonymous, the question specifically relates to blind FTP.

Question 66

Answer C is correct. Although the two are not interoperable, TLS is based on SSL and provides security between Web applications and their clients. TLS was designed to be the successor to Secure Sockets Layer; therefore, answer A is incorrect. The Point-to-Point Tunneling Protocol is used to create secure tunnels, such as in a Virtual Private Network; therefore, answer B is incorrect. Internet Protocol Security (IPSec) is also used to create Virtual Private Networks; therefore, answer D is incorrect.

Question 67

Answer B is correct. The Password Authentication Protocol (PAP) is a basic form of authentication whereby the username and password are transmitted unencrypted. Both CHAP and MS-CHAP v2 support the secure transmission of usernames and passwords. Therefore, answers A, C, and D are all incorrect.

Question 68

Answer B is correct. PPP, a protocol for communicating between two points using a serial interface, provides service at the second layer of the OSI model—the Data Link layer. Layer 1 (Physical), layer 3 (Network), and layer

4 (Transport) are not the layers at which PPP provides its service. Therefore, answers A, C, and D are all incorrect.

Question 69

Answer D is correct. The OSI reference model is based on seven layers for how data should be transmitted between any two points. The seven layers from bottom to top are Physical, Data Link, Network, Transport, Session, Presentation, and Application. Answers A, B, and C are in the wrong order and are therefore incorrect.

Question 70

Answer A is correct. PPP is able to handle synchronous as well as asynchronous connections. Therefore, answers B, C, and D are all incorrect.

Question 71

Answer A is correct. Access rights are grouped by the role name, and the use of resources are restricted to those associated with the authorized role. Answers B, C, and D are all incorrect methods for describing how access rights are grouped within RBAC.

Question 72

Answer B is correct. An access control list (ACL) coordinates access to resources based on a list of allowed or denied items such as users or network addresses. Answer A is incorrect because ACLU identifies a nonprofit organization that seeks to protect the basic civic liberties of Americans. An access point (AP) is often used in relation to a wireless access point (WAP); therefore, answer C is incorrect. Answer D is also incorrect because only answer B is correct.

Question 73

Answer D is correct. Passwords, home directories, and usernames in most cases are unique to the individual users. Although the use of shared usernames and passwords is common in many instances, it is a practice that generally should not be used.

Question 74

Answer C is correct. The email is likely a hoax, and although the policies may differ among organizations, given this scenario and the available choices, the best answer is to notify the system administrator. Answers A, B, and D are therefore all incorrect.

Question 75

Answer A is correct. Logging is the process of collecting data to be used for monitoring and auditing purposes. Auditing is the process of verification that normally involves going through log files; therefore, answer B is incorrect. Typically, the log files are frequently inspected, and inspection is not the process of collecting the data; therefore, answer C is incorrect. Vetting is the process of thorough examination or evaluation; therefore, answer D is incorrect.

Question 76

Answer A is correct. Users should not be given privileges above those necessary to perform their job function. The other choices do not adequately and accurately describe the principle of least privilege. Therefore, answers B, C, and D are incorrect.

Question 77

Answer C is correct. The potential for fraudulent activity is greater when the opportunity exists for one who is able to execute all the transactions within a given set. The separation of duties is not a deterrent to Trojan horses, viruses, or corporate audits. Therefore, answers A, B, D, and E are all incorrect.

Question 78

Answer C is correct. A retinal scan is a biometric technique based on distinct characteristics within the human eye. This is considered something you are, in contrast to something you have, such as a token or smartcard. Something you know would be a password, for example. Therefore, answers A, B, and D are all incorrect.

Question 79

Answer A is correct. By locking an account after a few consecutive attempts, the likelihood of a brute-force attack is reduced. Having an employee show proper identification does nothing to reduce brute-force attacks; therefore, answer B is incorrect. Increasing the value of the password history only prevents the user from using previously used passwords; therefore, answer C is incorrect. Password resets is an adequate mechanism to use in case a password has been compromised; however, it does little to circumvent brute-force attacks; therefore, answer D is incorrect.

Question 80

Answer C is correct. Proper labeling concerning the sensitivity of information should be placed on media such as tapes and disks to prevent the mishandling of the information. A token is a hardware device; therefore, answer A is incorrect. SSL is a protocol for protecting documents on the Internet; therefore, answer B is incorrect. Answer D, ticketing, is also incorrect.

Question 81

Answers A, B, and C are correct. Protecting data against accidental or malicious events is based on the classification level of the data, the data's value, as well as the level of risk or compromise of the data. The size of the organization has no bearing on the level of protection to be provided; therefore, answer D is incorrect.

Question 82

Answer B is correct. Once an IDS detects an attacker, the attacker may then be transparently transferred to a padded-cell host, which is a simulated environment where harm cannot be done. In contrast, a honeypot exists with the purpose of attracting the attacker; therefore, answer A is incorrect. Both the terms in answers C and D are incorrect because these are not related to intrusion-detection systems.

Question 83

Answers A, B, and C are correct. All accept answers D and E are advantages of honeypots and padded-cell systems. Currently the legal implications of using such systems is not that well defined, and the use of these systems will typically require more administrative resources.

Question 84

Answer A is correct. A policy is the formal set of statements that defines how systems are to be used. Standards are definitions or formats that are approved and must be used; therefore, answer B is incorrect. Guidelines are similar to standards but serve as more of a suggestion; therefore, answer C is incorrect. Procedures typically provide step-by-step instructions to follow; therefore, answer D is incorrect.

Question 85

Answer B is correct. 802.11 is the IEEE standard relating to the family of specifications for wireless LAN technologies. 802.2 is the standard for the Data Link layer in the OSI reference model; therefore, answer A is incorrect. 802.1 is the standard related to network management; therefore, answer C is incorrect. 802.6 is the standard for metropolitan area networks (MANs); therefore, answer D is incorrect.

Question 86

Answer B is correct. The well-known ports are those from 0 through 1023. Registered ports are those from 1024 through 49151, and dynamic and/or private ports are those from 49152 through 65535. Therefore, answers A, C, and D are all incorrect.

Question 87

Answer D is correct. A policy is a formal set of statements that defines how systems are to be used. Standards are definitions or formats that are approved and must be used; therefore, answer A is incorrect. Procedures typically provide step-by-step instructions to follow; therefore, answer B is incorrect. Guidelines are similar to standards but serve as more of a suggestion; therefore, answer C is incorrect.

Question 88

Answer B is correct. Asymmetric encryption, also known as *public key encryption*, uses two keys. One key is the private key, and the other key is the public key. Symmetric encryption uses only one key; therefore, answer A is incorrect. Answers C and D are also incorrect.

Question 89

Answer D is correct. NTFS (NT File System) is the preferred system because it supports file and folder permissions, among many other benefits. CDFS (CD-ROM File System) is used to control the CD-ROM; therefore, answer A is incorrect. Network File System (NFS) is a protocol and a client/server application; therefore, answer B is incorrect. File Allocation Table (FAT) file systems are not recommended because they lack native file-level security support; therefore, answer C is incorrect.

Question 90

Answers A, B, and C are correct. The NetBIOS name service uses port 137. The NetBIOS datagram service uses port 138, and the NetBIOS session service uses port 139. Port 140 is used by a service called the EMFIS Data Service; therefore, answer D is incorrect.

Question 91

Answer C is correct. An incremental backup backs up daily files created or changed since the last normal or incremental backup and clears the archive bit. A copy backup backs up all selected files but doesn't clear the archive bit; therefore, answer A is incorrect. A daily backup copies all selected files that you have modified the day the backup is performed but does not clear the archive; therefore, answer B is incorrect. A differential backup is similar to an incremental backup; however, it does not clear the archive bit; therefore, answer D is incorrect.

Question 92

Answer A is correct. Nonrepudiation provides the means by which neither party can deny having either sent or received the data in question. Both answers B and C are incorrect because they are incorrect terms. Repudiation is defined as the act of repudiation or refusal; therefore, answer D is incorrect.

Question 93

Answer C is correct. A disaster recovery plan is an agreed-upon plan that details the restoration of operations in the event of a disaster, and it should already be in existence prior to a disaster striking. Therefore, answers A and B are incorrect.

Question 94

Answer B is correct. Hardening refers to the process of securing an operating system. Handshaking relates the agreement process before communication takes place; therefore, answer A is incorrect. A hotfix is simply a security patch that gets applied to an operating system; therefore, answer C is incorrect. Because hardening is the only correct answer, answer D is also incorrect.

Question 95

Answers B and D are correct. Netbus is an example of a well-known Trojan horse (also called an *illicit server*) that typically uses port 12345. Netbus is not an IP testing tool or network scanning tool. Therefore, answers A and C are incorrect.

Question 96

Answer C is correct. Polymorphic viruses are designed to change part of their code after they infect a file in an attempt to evade detection. A stealth virus tries to hide its existence by taking over portions of your system; therefore, answer A is incorrect. A cavity virus attempts to install itself within a program; therefore, answer B is incorrect. A multipartite virus uses multiple methods of infecting a system; therefore, answer D is incorrect.

Question 97

Answer B is correct. Macro viruses are easy to create, do not require knowledge of complex programming languages, and are known to infect office documents such as those created with Microsoft Word. Stealth, polymorphic, and multipartite viruses, unlike macro viruses, require programming and are associated with infecting the operating system. Therefore, answers A, C, and D are incorrect.

Question 98

Answer C is correct. On Windows 2000 systems, the account with the greatest privileges is referred to as Administrator; however, on Unix systems, this account is named *root*. Therefore, answers A, B, and D are all incorrect.

Question 99

Answer C is correct. SSH provides for the secure access of remote computers and uses RSA public key cryptography. SET is a system for ensuring the security of financial transactions on the Web; therefore, answer A is incorrect. Answer B is incorrect because SHA is a hashing algorithm used to create a condensed version of a message. Telnet is used to access a computer remotely; however, it is unsecured; therefore, answer D is incorrect.

Question 100

Answer A is correct. DNS uses port 53 for zone transfers. The Hypertext Transfer Protocol (Web) uses port 80; therefore, answer B is incorrect. The NetBIOS name service uses port 137, and the NetBIOS datagram service uses port 138. Therefore, answers C and D are incorrect.

Question 101

Answer B is correct. Although the assigned port for the Hypertext Transfer Protocol (Web) is port 80, it is not required. In most cases Web servers do run on port 80 because browsers use this port by default, and the port number does not need to be specified within the Uniform Resource Locator (URL).

Question 102

Answer C is correct. A host-based IDS monitors packet activity on each computer or host, whereas network-based IDS monitors and analyzes packets flowing through the network; therefore, answer A is incorrect. A LAN based IDS is synonymous with network-based IDS; therefore, answer B is incorrect. Answer D is also incorrect.

Question 103

Answer A is correct. A buffer overflow occurs when a program attempts to store more data than it was intended to hold in temporary storage areas, also known as *buffers*. Answer B is incorrect because a patch is a small program that typically provides a quick fix to another program. Answer C is incorrect because a SYN flood is an attempt to send TCP connection requests faster than the machine can process the requests. SMTP relay refers to a mail server that allows mail to be relayed from the system to other destinations; therefore, answer D is incorrect.

Question 104

Answer B is correct. Password sniffers monitor traffic and record the packets sending passwords. Answer A is incorrect because a keyboard sniffer is able to capture passwords locally on the computer as they are typed and recorded. A Trojan horse is a program that has a hidden function; therefore, answer C is incorrect. Answer D is incorrect because cookies are small text files used to identify a Web user and enhance the browsing experience.

Question 105

Answer C is correct. A class C fire involves energized electrical equipment and is usually suppressed with nonconducting agents. Class A fires involve combustibles such as wood and paper; therefore, answer A is incorrect. Answer B is incorrect because a class B fire involves flammables or combustible liquids. Answer D is incorrect because a class D fire involves combustible metals such as magnesium.

Question 106

Answers A, B, and D are correct. A physical security plan should be a written plan addressing your current physical security needs as well as future direction. Answer C is incorrect because all of the answers are correct and should be addressed in a physical security plan. A hard disk's physical blocks pertain to the file system.

Question 107

Answer B is correct. There are numerous reasons why a certificate may need to be revoked. Among these include a certificate being issued to the incorrect person. A CPS is a published document from the CA describing its policies and procedures for issuing and revoking certificates; therefore, answer A is incorrect. A private key compromise is actually another reason to perform revocation of a certificate; therefore, answer C is incorrect. Answer D is incorrect because this is a bogus term.

Question 108

Answer C is correct. Each network service carries its own risks; therefore, it is important to disable all nonessential services. Although disabling all non-Web services may provide a secure solution for minimizing threats, having Telnet enabled for interactive logins presents security issues and is not a primary method for minimizing threat; therefore, answer A is incorrect. Answer B is incorrect because neither of these services should be enabled on a Web server. Logging is important for secure operations and is invaluable when recovering from a security incident; however, it is not a primary method for reducing threat; therefore, answer D is incorrect.

Question 109

Answer B is correct. A network-based intrusion-detection system (NIDS) scans a computer network and can identify signs of a computer break-in. DNS describes the process of name translation used on the Internet; therefore, answer A is incorrect. Answer C is incorrect because FTP is a method for transferring files. Answer D is incorrect because an RFP is a written Internet standard.

Question 110

Answer B is correct. Role-Based Access Control (RBAC) ensures the principle of least privilege by identifying the user's job function and ensuring a minimum set of privileges required to perform that job. IPSec is a set of protocols to enable encryption, authentication, and integrity; therefore, answer A is incorrect. Answer C is incorrect because an IDS is used for intrusion detection, and answer D is incorrect because a DRP is a plan used in the event of disaster.

Question 111

Answer C is correct. Trusted Computer System Evaluation (TCSEC) and Information Technology Security Evaluation Criteria (ITSEC) are major security criteria efforts, and the Common Criteria is based on both TCSEC and ITSEC; therefore, answers A, B, and D are the three major security evaluation criteria efforts. IPSec, however, is a set of protocols to enable encryption, authentication, and integrity.

Question 112

Answer D is correct. Zone transfers are associated with DNS servers. If a malicious hacker were to obtain a DNS zone file, she could identify all the hosts present within the network. Zone transfers are not functions of a database, file and print, or Web server. Therefore, answers A, B, and C are incorrect.

Question 113

Answer A is correct. A choke or interior router is the internal router when used with another router in a firewall configuration. This router does most of the packet filtering for the firewall. Answers B, C, and D are all incorrect choices meant to distract you.

Question 114

Answer A is correct. A bastion host is the only host on an internal network visible to the Internet; therefore, it is exposed to attack. With a screened host, each host on the internal network is still exposed to the Internet. Therefore, answer B and C are incorrect. Answer D is also incorrect because there is a correct answer.

Question 115

Answer A is correct. Signals within fiber-optic cables are not electrical in nature. Therefore, they do not emit electromagnetic radiation to be detected. This makes fiber-optic cabling ideal for high-security networks. Both UTP and STP are susceptible to eavesdropping; however, STP is less susceptible than UTP. Therefore, answers B and C are incorrect. Answer D is incorrect because coaxial thicknet is also susceptible to eavesdropping, yet it is a better choice over UTP.

Question 116

Answer C is correct. The plenum is the space between the ceiling and the floor of a building's next level. It is commonly used to run network cables, which must be of plenum-grade. A raised floor, sometimes called a *plenum floor*, is open space below a floor; therefore, answer A is incorrect. Answer B is also incorrect. In fact, there the plenum is of concern during a fire because there is actually little if any barriers to contain fire and smoke. Answer D is incorrect because Teflon is a trademarked product of the DuPont corporation. Teflon is often used to coat wiring placed in the plenum of a building.

Question 117

Answer C is correct. Simple Network Management Protocol (SNMP) is a set of protocols used for managing networks. SNMP sends messages, called protocol data units (PDUs), across the network, and SNMP-enabled devices store data about themselves in Management Information Bases (MIBs). Therefore, answers A, B, and D are incorrect.

Question 118

Answer B is correct. The Internet Numbers Authority (IANA) has reserved three blocks of IP addresses for private networks: 10.0.0.0–10.255.255.255, 172.16.0.0–172.31.255.255, and 192.168.0.0–192.168.255.255. Additionally, the range 169.254.0.0–169.254.255.255 is reserved for Automatic Private IP Addressing. Therefore, answers A, C, and D are incorrect.

Question 119

Answer D is correct. A cold site is a disaster recovery service, similar to a hot site. A cold site, however, requires the customer to provide and install all the equipment needed for operations, whereas a hot site is all ready to go; therefore, answer C is incorrect. Naturally, a cold site is less expensive than a hot site.

Question 120

Answer B is correct. A Faraday cage is a solid or mesh metal box used to trap and ground stray electrical signals. The box completely surrounds the protected equipment and is well grounded to dissipate stray signals from traveling to or from the cage. TEMPEST is a government standard describing methods implemented to block or limit electromagnetic radiation (EMR) from electronic equipment. Therefore, answer A and C are incorrect. Answer D is also incorrect because there is a correct answer.

Question 121

Answer C is correct. An SLA is a written contract between a service provider and the customer, and it specifies the services the provider will furnish to the customer. Answers A, B, and D are all incorrect. However, answer B may describe a specific type of SLA, but it is not the best answer.

Question 122

Answer A is correct. A buffer overflow occurs when a program or process attempts to store more data in a buffer than the buffer was intended to hold. The overflow of data can flow over into other buffers, thus overwriting or deleting data. Denial of service is a type of attack in which too much traffic is sent to a host, preventing it from responding to legitimate traffic; therefore, answer B is incorrect. Distributed denial of service is similar but is initiated through multiple hosts; therefore, answer C is incorrect. Although answer D sounds correct, it is not.

Question 123

Answer B is correct. Hashing, which is used in many encryption algorithms, involves creating a smaller number achieved from a larger string of text. Cipher block chaining is an operation in which a sequence of bits is encrypted as a single unit; therefore, answer A is incorrect. PKI is composed of various components making up the infrastructure to provide public and private key cryptography over networks; therefore, answer C is incorrect. Answer D is incorrect because ciphertext is synonymous with encrypted text.

Question 124

Answer A is correct. Before attempting to break into a system, the hacker will first try to analyze and footprint as much information as possible. Cracking describes malicious attacks on network resources; therefore, answer B is incorrect. Answer C is incorrect because social engineering is the nontechnical means of intrusion that often relies on tricking people into divulging security information. Spoofing is the electronic means of pretending to be another; therefore, answer D is incorrect.

Question 125

Answer C is correct. A proxy server provides security and caching services by serving as the intermediary between the internal network and external resources. Answer A is incorrect because the Web server is usually the target server in question. Answer B is incorrect because a packet filter is a type of firewall in which each packet is examined and is either allowed or denied based on policy. A firewall is similar to a proxy server in the security it provides; however, a firewall does not seek to fulfill requests as does a proxy server, which will maintain previously accessed information in its cache; therefore, answer D is incorrect.

List of Resources

Chapter 1

➤ The CompTIA Security+ home page:
www.comptia.com/certification/security/default.asp

Chapter 2

➤ Allen, Julia H. *The CERT Guide to System and Network Security Practices*. Addison-Wesley. Upper Saddle River, NJ, 2001. ISBN 020173723X.

➤ Krause, Micki, and Harold F. Tipton. *Information Security Management Handbook, Fourth Edition*. Auerbach Publications. New York, NY, 1999. ISBN 0849398290.

➤ The SANS "The Twenty Most Critical Internet Security Vulnerabilities" list: www.sans.org/top20/

Chapter 3

➤ Chirillo, John. *Hack Attacks Denied: A Complete Guide to Network Lockdown for UNIX, Windows, and Linux, Second Edition*. John Wiley & Sons. Indianapolis, IN, 2002. ISBN 0471232831.

Refer to Chapter 1, "Common Ports and Services," and Chapter 4, "Safeguarding Against Penetration Attacks."

➤ Chirillo, John. *Hack Attacks Revealed: A Complete Reference for UNIX, Windows, and Linux with Custom Security Toolkit, Second Edition*. John Wiley & Sons. Indianapolis, IN, 2002. ISBN 0471232823.

Refer to Chapter 4, "Well-Known Ports and Their Services," and Chapter 5, "Discovery and Scanning Techniques."

➤ McClure, Stuart, Joel Scambray, and George Kurtz. *Hacking Exposed: Network Security Secrets and Solutions, Third Edition*. McGraw-Hill. New York, NY, 2001. ISBN 0072193816.

Refer to Chapter 12, "Denial of Service Attacks."

➤ Virus Bulletin Web site: www.virusbtn.com

➤ The Twenty Most Critical Internet Security Vulnerabilities list (SANS): www.sans.org/top20/

➤ The CERT Coordination Center (CERT/CC): www.cert.org

Chapter 4

➤ Allen, Julia H. *The CERT Guide to System and Network Security Practices*. Addison-Wesley. Upper Saddle River, NJ, 2001. ISBN 020173723X.

➤ SANS Information Security Reading Room: rr.sans.org/index.php

Chapter 5

➤ Allen, Julia H. *The CERT Guide to System and Network Security Practices*. Addison-Wesley, Upper Saddle River, NJ, 2001. ISBN 020173723X.

➤ The World Wide Web Security FAQ: www.w3.org/Security/Faq/

➤ SANS Information Security Reading Room: rr.sans.org/index.php

➤ IEEE Standards Association: standards.ieee.org/

Chapter 6

➤ Bragg, Roberta. *CISSP Training Guide*. Que. Indianapolis, IN, 2002. ISBN 078972801X.

Refer to Chapter 2, "Telecommunications and Network Security."

➤ Lammle, Todd. *CCNA Cisco Certified Network Associate Study Guide, Second Edition*. Sybex. Alameda, CA, 2000. ISBN 0782126472.

Refer to Chapter 6, "Virtual LANs (VLANs)."

➤ Maufer, Thomas A. *IP Fundamentals: What Everyone Needs to Know About Addressing & Routing*. Prentice Hall PTR. Upper Saddle River, NJ, 1999. ISBN 0139754830.

Refer to Chapter 12, "Introduction to Routing."

➤ Firewall Architectures: `www.invir.com/int-sec-firearc.html`

➤ Introduction to the Internet and Internet Security: `csrc.nist.gov/publications/nistpubs/800-10/node1.html`

➤ IP in IP Tunneling (RFC 1853): `www.faqs.org/rfcs/rfc1853.html`

➤ VLAN information: `net21.ucdavis.edu/newvlan.htm`

Chapter 7

➤ Shipley, Greg. *Maximum Security, Third Edition*. Sams Publishing. Indianapolis, IN, 2001. ISBN 0672318717.

➤ The World Wide Web Security FAQ: `www.w3.org/Security/Faq/`

➤ SANS Information Security Reading Room: `rr.sans.org/index.php`

➤ CERT Incident Reporting Guidelines:
`www.cert.org/tech_tips/incident_reporting.html`

Chapter 8

➤ Krutz, Ronald, and Russell Dean Vines. *The CISSP Prep Guide: Mastering the Ten Domains of Computer Security*. John Wiley & Sons. Indianapolis, IN, 2001. ISBN 0471413569.

➤ How Encryption Works reference Web site:
`www.howstuffworks.com/encryption.htm`

➤ RSA-Based Cryptographic Schemes Web site: `www.rsasecurity.com/rsalabs/rsa_algorithm/`

➤ W3C XML Encryption Working Group Web site:
`www.w3.org/Encryption/2001/`

➤ National Institute of Standards and Technology Web site: www.nist.gov

➤ Rijndael Web site: www.esat.kuleuven.ac.be/~rijmen/rijndael/

➤ Request for Comments (RFC) 2527, "Internet X.509 Public Key
Infrastructure Certificate Policy and Certification Practices
Framework," on the Internet Engineering Task Force (IETF) Web site:
www.ietf.org/rfc/rfc2527.txt

➤ Microsoft Kerberos deployment Web page:
www.microsoft.com/technet/treeview/default.asp?url=/TechNet/prodtechnol/
windows2000serv/deploy/kerberos.asp

➤ Security books, journals, bibliographies, and publications listing Web
site: www.cs.auckland.ac.nz/~pgut001/links/books.html

Chapter 9

➤ Housley, Russ and Tim Polk. *Planning for PKI*. John Wiley & Sons.
New York, NY, 2001. ISBN 0471397024.

➤ Krutz, Ronald, and Russell Dean Vines. *The CISSP Prep Guide:
Mastering the Ten Domains of Computer Security*. John Wiley & Sons.
Indianapolis, IN, 2001. ISBN 0471413569.

➤ PKI X.509 PKIX Charter Web page (which provides a description of the
working group and many related RFC and Internet-draft links):
www.ietf.org/html.charters/pkix-charter.html

➤ International Telecommunications Union Web site page with information on the data networks and open systems communications recommendations: www.itu.int/rec/recommendation.asp?type=products&lang=
e&parent=T-REC-X

➤ RSA Corporation "Public Key Cryptography Standards" Web page:
www.rsasecurity.com/rsalabs/pkcs/

➤ National Institute of Standards and Technology "Security Requirements
for Cryptographic modules" Web page: csrc.nist.gov/cryptval/
140-1/fr981023.htm

Chapter 10

➤ Chirillo, John. *Hack Attacks Denied*. John Wiley & Sons. New York, NY, 2001. ISBN 0471416258.

➤ Shipley, Greg. *Maximum Security, Third Edition*. Sams Publishing. Indianapolis, IN, 2001. ISBN 0672318717.

➤ SANS Information Security Reading Room: `rr.sans.org/index.php`

➤ CERT Incident Reporting Guidelines:
`www.cert.org/tech_tips/incident_reporting.html`

Chapter 11

➤ Chirillo, John. *Hack Attacks Denied*. John Wiley & Sons. New York, NY, 2001. ISBN 0471416258.

➤ Cole, Eric. *Hackers Beware*. Pearson Education. Indianapolis, IN, 2002. ISBN 0735710090.

➤ An Explanation of Computer Forensics, by Judd Robbins: `www.computerforensics.net/forensics.htm`

➤ CERT Incident Reporting Guidelines:
`www.cert.org/tech_tips/incident_reporting.html`

Other Resources

➤ `www.bluetooth.com/` is the official Bluetooth Web site.

➤ `www.bluetooth.org/` offers information about joining the Bluetooth SIG.

➤ `www.securityfocus.com/popups/forums/bugtraq/faq.shtml` provides information about the SecurityFocus BUGTRAQ mailing list FAQ.

➤ `www.informit.com/` includes IT-related articles, books, forums, and certification information (requires registration).

➤ `www.mcmcse.com/comptia/security/SY0101.shtml` is Microsoft's list of Security+ resources.

➤ www.certcities.com offers practice exams, exam review forums, and other information related to IT certification tests. The Security+ exam is discussed at certcities.com/editorial/exams/story.asp?EditorialsID=66.

➤ www.comptia.com/certification/security/default.asp is CompTIA's site for Security+ information.

List of Products
and Vendors

The following products, vendors, and technologies were mentioned in this book.

Chapter 2

➤ SecurID Tokens (user authenticators):

www.rsasecurity.com/products/securid/tokens.html

RSA Security
174 & 176 Middlesex Turnpike
Bedford, MA 01730
Phone: 877-RSA-4900 or 781-515-5000

Chapter 3

➤ T-sight (intrusion investigation and response tool): www.engarde.com/
software/t-sight/

En Garde Systems
4848 Tramway Ridge Dr. NE, Suite 122
Albuquerque, NM 87111
Phone: 505-346-1760

➤ HUNT (detects TCP/IP weaknesses):

lin.fsid.cvut.cz/~kra/index.html#HUNT

➤ VNC (Virtual Network Computing: remote desktop-display system): `www.uk.research.att.com/vnc/`

➤ Symantec PCAnywhere (remote-access system): `www.symantec.com/pcanywhere/`

➤ Terminal Services (Windows 2000 remote-viewing application): `www.microsoft.com/windows2000/technologies/terminal/default.asp`

➤ Symantec's Antivirus Web site: `www.symantec.com/avcenter/index.html`

➤ McAfee Security Antivirus Web site: `www.mcafee.com/anti-virus/default.asp`

➤ Sophos Antivirus Web site: `www.sophos.com/`

6 Kimball Lane, 4th Floor
Lynnfield, MA 01940
Phone: 781-973-0110

➤ Nessus (free remote security scanner): `www.nessus.org/`

➤ Symantec NetRecon (network vulnerability assessment tool): `enterprisesecurity.symantec.com/`

➤ Nmap (Network Mapper: open-source security auditing utility): `www.insecure.org/nmap/`

➤ SAINT (Security Administrator's Integrated Network Tool: network scanning engine): `www.wwdsi.com/products/saint_engine.html`

SAINT Corporation
4720 Montgomery Lane, Suite 800
Bethesda, MD 20814
Phone: 301-656-0521 or 800-596-2006

➤ TigerSuite (security hacking system): `www.tigertools.net/tt2k.htm`

Chapter 4

➤ MSN Messenger: `messenger.msn.com`

➤ ICQ: `icq.com`

➤ AOL Instant Messenger: `aim.com`

➤ Netscape: netscape.com

P.O. Box 7050
Mountain View, CA 94039-7050
Phone: 650-254-1900
Fax: 650-528-4124

Chapter 5

➤ Netscape: netscape.com

P.O. Box 7050
Mountain View, CA 94039-7050
Phone: 650-254-1900
Fax: 650-528-4124

➤ Sun Microsystems: www.sun.com

Sun Microsystems, Inc.
4150 Network Circle
Santa Clara, CA 95054
Phone: 800-555-9SUN (650-960-1300)

➤ Microsoft Outlook: www.microsoft.com/office/outlook/default.asp

➤ ToolTalk: docs.sun.com/db/doc/806-2910

➤ Linuxconf: www.solucorp.qc.ca/linuxconf

➤ DoubleClick: www.doubleclick.com/us

450 West 33rd Street
New York, NY 10001
Phone: 212-271-2542

➤ VeriSign: www.verisign.com

487 E. Middlefield Rd.
Mountain View, CA 94043
Phone: 866-447-8776 (4IR-VRSN)

➤ Thawte: www.thawte.com

P.O. Box
17648, Raleigh, NC 27619-7648
Phone: 919-831-8400
Fax: 650-237-8888

➤ CERT coordination center: www.cert.org/advisories/CA-2001-07.html

➤ SAINT, FTP Vulnerabilities: www.saintcorporation.com/demo/ saint_tutorials/FTP_vulnerabilities.html

SAINT Corporation
4720 Montgomery Lane, Suite 800
Bethesda, MD 20814
Phone: 301-656-0521 or 800-596-2006

➤ Linux: linux.com

➤ Snort: www.snort.org

➤ Sniffit: reptile.rug.ac.be/~coder/sniffit/sniffit.html

➤ Microsoft Network Monitor:
msdn.microsoft.com/library/default.asp?url=/library/
en-us/netmon/netmon/network_monitor.asp

➤ Internet Engineering Task Force (IETF): ietf.org

➤ World Wide Web Consortium (W3C): www.w3.org

Chapter 6

➤ Imation: www.imation.com

1 Imation Place
Oakdale, MN 55128
Phone: 651-704-4000
888-466-3456
Fax: 888-704-4200
Email: info@imation.com

➤ Sony AIT: www.storagebysony.com

Chapter 7

➤ Ethereal packet sniffer (free network protocol analyzer for Unix and Windows): www.ethereal.com

Chapter 8

➤ VeriSign: www.verisign.com

487 E. Middlefield Rd.
Mountain View, CA 94043
Phone: 866-447-8776 (4IR-VRSN)

➤ Entrust: www.entrust.com/

One Hanover Park
16633 Dallas Parkway, Suite 800
Addison, TX 75001
Phone: 972-713-5800

Chapter 9

➤ RSA Laboratories: www.rsasecurity.com/rsalabs

174 Middlesex Turnpike
Bedford, MA 01730
Phone: 877-RSA-4900
781-515-5000
Fax: 781-515-5010

➤ Cisco: www.cisco.com

Main Corporate HQ
Cisco Systems, Inc.
170 West Tasman Dr.
San Jose, CA 95134
Phone: 408-526-4000
800-553-6387

➤ VeriSign: www.verisign.com

487 E. Middlefield Rd.
Mountain View, CA 94043
Phone: 866-447-8776 (4IR-VRSN)

Chapter 10

➤ Department of Defense: www.defenselink.mil

What's on the CD-ROM

This appendix is a brief rundown of what you'll find on the CD-ROM that comes with this book. For a more detailed description of the *PrepLogic Practice Tests, Preview Edition* exam simulation software, see Appendix D, "Using *PrepLogic, Preview Edition* Software." In addition to the *PrepLogic Practice Tests, Preview Edition*, the CD-ROM includes the electronic version of the book in Portable Document Format (PDF), several utility and application programs, and a complete listing of test objectives and where they are covered in the book. Finally, a pointer list to online pointers and references are added to this CD. You will need a computer with Internet access and a relatively recent browser installed to use this feature.

PrepLogic Practice Tests, Preview Edition

PrepLogic is a leading provider of certification training tools. Trusted by certification students worldwide, we believe PrepLogic is the best practice exam software available. In addition to providing a means of evaluating your knowledge of the Exam Cram material, *PrepLogic Practice Tests, Preview Edition* features several innovations that help you to improve your mastery of the subject matter.

For example, the practice tests allow you to check your score by exam area or domain to determine which topics you need to study more. Another feature allows you to obtain immediate feedback on your responses in the form of explanations for the correct and incorrect answers.

PrepLogic Practice Tests, Preview Edition exhibits most of the full functionality of the *Premium Edition* but offers only a fraction of the total questions. To get the complete set of practice questions and exam functionality, visit PrepLogic.com and order the *Premium Edition* for this and other challenging exam titles.

Again, for a more detailed description of the *PrepLogic Practice Tests, Preview Edition* features, see Appendix D.

Exclusive Electronic Version of Text

The CD-ROM also contains the electronic version of this book in Portable Document Format (PDF). The electronic version comes complete with all figures as they appear in the book. You will find that the search capabilities of the reader comes in handy for study and review purposes.

Easy Access to Online Pointers and References

The Suggested Reading section at the end of each chapter in this Exam Cram contains numerous pointers to Web sites, newsgroups, mailing lists, and other online resources. To make this material as easy to use as possible, we include all this information in an HTML document entitled "Online Pointers" on the CD. Open this document in your favorite Web browser to find links you can follow through any Internet connection to access these resources directly.

Using the *PrepLogic Practice Tests, Preview Edition* Software

This Exam Cram includes a special version of PrepLogic Practice Tests—a revolutionary test engine designed to give you the best in certification exam preparation. PrepLogic offers sample and practice exams for many of today's most in-demand and challenging technical certifications. This special *Preview Edition* is included with this book as a tool to use in assessing your knowledge of the Exam Cram material, while also providing you with the experience of taking an electronic exam.

This appendix describes in detail what *PrepLogic Practice Tests, Preview Edition* is, how it works, and what it can do to help you prepare for the exam. Note that although the *Preview Edition* includes all the test simulation functions of the complete, retail version, it contains only a single practice test. The *Premium Edition*, available at PrepLogic.com, contains the complete set of challenging practice exams designed to optimize your learning experience.

Exam Simulation

One of the main functions of *PrepLogic Practice Tests, Preview Edition* is exam simulation. To prepare you to take the actual vendor certification exam, PrepLogic is designed to offer the most effective exam simulation available.

Question Quality

The questions provided in the *PrepLogic Practice Tests, Preview Edition* are written to the highest standards of technical accuracy. The questions tap the content of the Exam Cram chapters and help you to review and assess your knowledge before you take the actual exam.

Interface Design

The *PrepLogic Practice Tests, Preview Edition* exam simulation interface provides you with the experience of taking an electronic exam. This enables you to effectively prepare yourself for taking the actual exam by making the test experience a familiar one. Using this test simulation can help to eliminate the sense of surprise or anxiety you might experience in the testing center because you will already be acquainted with computerized testing.

Effective Learning Environment

The *PrepLogic Practice Tests, Preview Edition* interface provides a learning environment that not only tests you through the computer, but also teaches the material you need to know to pass the certification exam. Each question comes with a detailed explanation of the correct answer and often provides reasons the other options are incorrect. This information helps to reinforce the knowledge you already have and also provides practical information you can use on the job.

Software Requirements

PrepLogic Practice Tests requires a computer with the following:

➤ Microsoft Windows 98, Windows Me, Windows NT 4.0, Windows 2000, or Windows XP

➤ A 166MHz or faster processor is recommended

➤ A minimum of 32MB of RAM

➤ As with any Windows application, the more memory, the better your performance

➤ 10MB of hard drive space

Installing *PrepLogic Practice Tests, Preview Edition*

Install *PrepLogic Practice Tests, Preview Edition* by running the setup program on the *PrepLogic Practice Tests, Preview Edition* CD. Follow these instructions to install the software on your computer:

1. Insert the CD into your CD-ROM drive. The Autorun feature of Windows should launch the software. If you have Autorun disabled, click the Start button and select Run. Go to the root directory of the CD and select setup.exe. Click Open, and then click OK.

2. The Installation Wizard copies the *PrepLogic Practice Tests, Preview Edition* files to your hard drive; adds *PrepLogic Practice Tests, Preview Edition* to your Desktop and Program menu; and installs test engine components to the appropriate system folders.

Removing *PrepLogic Practice Tests, Preview Edition* from Your Computer

If you elect to remove the *PrepLogic Practice Tests,, Preview Edition* product from your computer, an uninstall process has been included to ensure that it is removed from your system safely and completely. Follow these instructions to remove PrepLogic Practice Tests, Preview Edition from your computer:

1. Select Start, Settings, Control Panel.

2. Double-click the Add/Remove Programs icon.

3. You are presented with a list of software currently installed on your computer. Select the appropriate *PrepLogic Practice Tests, Preview Edition* title you wish to remove. Click the Add/Remove button. The software is then removed from you computer.

Using *PrepLogic Practice Tests, Preview Edition*

PrepLogic is designed to be user friendly and intuitive. Because the software has a smooth learning curve, your time is maximized, as you will start practicing almost immediately. *PrepLogic Practice Tests, Preview Edition* has two major modes of study: Practice Test and Flash Review.

Using Practice Test mode, you can develop your test-taking abilities, as well as your knowledge through the use of the Show Answer option. While you are taking the test, you can reveal the answers along with a detailed explanation of why the given answers are right or wrong. This gives you the ability to better understand the material presented.

Flash Review is designed to reinforce exam topics rather than quiz you. In this mode, you will be shown a series of questions, but no answer choices. Instead, you will be given a button that reveals the correct answer to the question and a full explanation for that answer.

Starting a Practice Test Mode Session

Practice Test mode enables you to control the exam experience in ways that actual certification exams do not allow:

➤ *Enable Show Answer Button*—Activates the Show Answer button, allowing you to view the correct answer(s) and a full explanation for each question during the exam. When not enabled, you must wait until after your exam has been graded to view the correct answer(s) and explanation(s).

➤ *Enable Item Review Button*—Activates the Item Review button, allowing you to view your answer choices, marked questions, and facilitating navigation between questions.

➤ *Randomize Choices*—Randomize answer choices from one exam session to the next; makes memorizing question choices more difficult, therefore keeping questions fresh and challenging longer.

To begin studying in Practice Test mode, click the Practice Test radio button from the main exam customization screen. This will enable the options detailed above.

To your left, you are presented with the options of selecting the pre-configured Practice Test or creating your own Custom Test. The pre-configured test has a fixed time limit and number of questions. Custom Tests allow you to configure the time limit and the number of questions in your exam.

The *Preview Edition* included with this book includes a single pre-configured Practice Test. Get the compete set of challenging PrepLogic Practice Tests at PrepLogic.com and make certain you're ready for the big exam.

Click the Begin Exam button to begin your exam.

Starting a Flash Review Mode Session

Flash Review mode provides you with an easy way to reinforce topics covered in the practice questions. To begin studying in Flash Review mode, click the Flash Review radio button from the main exam customization screen. Select either the pre-configured Practice Test or create your own Custom Test.

Click the Best Exam button to begin your Flash Review of the exam questions.

Standard *PrepLogic Practice Tests, Preview Edition* Options

The following list describes the function of each of the buttons you see. Depending on the options, some of the buttons will be grayed out and inaccessible or missing completely. Buttons that are accessible are active. The buttons are as follows:

➤ *Exhibit*—This button is visible if an exhibit is provided to support the question. An exhibit is an image that provides supplemental information necessary to answer the question.

➤ *Item Review*—This button leaves the question window and opens the Item Review screen. From this screen you will see all questions, your answers, and your marked items. You will also see correct answers listed here when appropriate.

➤ *Show Answer*—This option displays the correct answer with an explanation of why it is correct. If you select this option, the current question is not scored.

➤ *Mark Item*—Check this box to tag a question you need to review further. You can view and navigate your Marked Items by clicking the Item Review button (if enabled). When grading your exam, you will be notified if you have marked items remaining.

➤ *Previous Item*—This option allows you to view the previous question.

➤ *Next Item*—This option allows you to view the next question.

➤ *Grade Exam*—When you have completed your exam, click this button to end your exam and view your detailed score report. If you have unanswered or marked items remaining you will be asked if you would like to continue taking your exam or view your exam report.

Time Remaining

If the test is timed, the time remaining is displayed on the upper right corner of the application screen. It counts down the minutes and seconds remaining to complete the test. If you run out of time, you will be asked if you want to continue taking the test or if you want to end your exam.

Your Examination Score Report

The Examination Score Report screen appears when the Practice Test mode ends—as the result of time expiration, completion of all questions, or your decision to terminate early.

This screen provides you with a graphical display of your test score with a breakdown of scores by topic domain. The graphical display at the top of the screen compares your overall score with the PrepLogic Exam Competency Score.

The PrepLogic Exam Competency Score reflects the level of subject competency required to pass this vendor's exam. While this score does not directly translate to a passing score, consistently matching or exceeding this score does suggest you possess the knowledge to pass the actual vendor exam.

Review Your Exam

From Your Score Report screen, you can review the exam that you just completed by clicking on the View Items button. Navigate through the items viewing the questions, your answers, the correct answers, and the explanations for those answers. You can return to your score report by clicking the View Items button.

Get More Exams

Each *PrepLogic Practice Tests, Preview Edition* that accompanies your Exam Cram contains a single PrepLogic Practice Test. Certification students worldwide trust PrepLogic Practice Tests to help them pass their IT certification exams the first time. Purchase the *Premium Edition* of PrepLogic Practice Tests and get the entire set of all new challenging Practice Tests for this exam. PrepLogic Practice Tests—Because You Want to Pass the First Time.

Contacting PrepLogic

If you would like to contact PrepLogic for any reason, including information about our extensive line of certification practice tests, we invite you to do so. Please contact us online at http://www.preplogic.com.

Customer Service

If you have a damaged product and need a replacement or refund, please call the following phone number:

800-858-7674

Product Suggestions and Comments

We value your input! Please email your suggestions and comments to the following address:

feedback@preplogic.com

License Agreement

YOU MUST AGREE TO THE TERMS AND CONDITIONS OUT-LINED IN THE END USER LICENSE AGREEMENT ("EULA") PRESENTED TO YOU DURING THE INSTALLATION PROCESS. IF YOU DO NOT AGREE TO THESE TERMS DO NOT INSTALL THE SOFTWARE.

Glossary

. . . .

accounting
The tracking of users' access to resources primarily for billing purposes.

active detection
Involves some action taken by the intrusion-detection system in response to a suspicious activity or an intrusion (in essence, it is reactive detection).

algorithm
A set of sequenced steps that are repeatable. In encryption, the algorithm is used to define how the encryption is applied to data.

asset
A company resource that has value.

asymmetric algorithms
A pair of key values—one public and the other private—used to encrypt and decrypt data. Only the holder of the private key can decrypt data encrypted with the public key, which means anyone

who obtains a copy of the public key can send data to the private key holder in confidence. Only data encrypted with the private key can be decrypted with the public key; this provides proof of identity, ensures nonrepudiation, and provides the basis for digital signatures.

attribute certificate
A digital certificate that binds data items to a user or system by using a name or public key certificate.

auditing
The tracking of users' access to resources primarily for security purposes.

authenticated header (AH)
A component of the IPSec protocol that provides integrity, authentication, and anti-replay capabilities.

authentication
The process of identifying users.

authorization

The process of identifying what a given user is allowed to do.

availability

Ensures any necessary data is available when it is requested.

back door

A method of gaining access to a system or resource that bypasses normal authentication or access control methods.

biometrics

Authentication based on some part of the human anatomy (retina, fingerprint, voice, and so on).

block cipher

Transforms a message from plaintext (unencrypted form) to ciphertext (encrypted form) one piece at a time, where the block size represents a standard chunk of data that is transformed in a single operation. Block ciphers also normally take prior encryption activity into account (called *block chaining* or *feedback modes*) to further strengthen the encryption they provide. (Adapted from www.counterpane.com/ crypto-gram-0001.html.)

business continuity plan

A plan that describes a long-term systems and services replacement and recovery strategy, designed for use when a complete loss of facilities occurs. A business continuity plan prepares for automatic failover of critical services to redundant offsite systems.

centralized key management

Involves a Certificate Authority generating both public and private key pairs for a user and then distributing them to the user.

certificate

Also known as a *digital certificate*, a certificate represents a unique way of establishing user identity and credentials to enable the conducting of business or other transactions online. Generally, digital certificates originate from a Certificate Authority (CA), which can be private (such as when a company or organization creates its own CAs) or public (such as when an individual, a company, or an organization obtains a digital certificate from a public CA such as those operated by GE or VeriSign). Typically, a digital certificate contains the holder's name, a serial number, expiration dates, a copy of the holder's public key (which can then be used to encrypt messages), and a digital certificate from the issuing authority to demonstrate its validity. Some digital certificates conform to the X.509 standard; numerous public registries of such certificates are maintained on the Internet and act as clearinghouses for such information.

Certificate Authority (CA)

A system that issues, distributes, and maintains currency information about digital certificates. Such authorities can be private (operated within a company or an organization for its own use) or public (operated on the Internet for general public access).

Certificate Enrollment Protocol (CEP)

A proprietary Cisco protocol that allows Cisco IOS–based routers to communicate with Certificate Authorities.

Certificate Management Protocol (CMP)

A protocol used for advanced PKI management functions. These functions include certificate issuance, exchange, invalidation, revocation, and key commission.

certificate policy

A statement that governs the usage of digital certificates.

Certificate Practice Statement (CPS)

A document that defines the practices and procedures a CA uses to manage the digital certificates it issues.

certificate revocation

The act of invalidating a digital certificate.

Certificate Revocation List (CRL)

A list generated by a CA that enumerates digital certificates that are no longer valid and the reasons they are no longer valid.

certificate suspension

The act of temporarily invalidating a certificate while its validity is being verified.

chain of custody

The documentation of all transfers of evidence from one person to another, showing the date, time, and reason for transfer, as well as the signatures of both parties involved in the transfer. Chain of custody also refers to the process of tracking evidence from a crime scene to the courtroom.

change management

A formal engineering discipline, change management describes the well-documented process for tracking and controlling changes to systems, as well as their design data and documentation, through agreed upon procedures and timelines. In security, this term indicates that a formal process to schedule, implement, track, and document changes to policies, configurations, systems, and software is employed in an organization.

Challenge Handshake Authentication Protocol (CHAP)

A widely used authentication method in which a hashed version of a user's password is transmitted during the authentication process (instead of sending the password itself). Using CHAP, a remote access server transmits a challenge string, to which the client responds with a message digest (MD5) hash based on the challenge string and the user's password. Upon receipt, the remote access server repeats the same calculation and compares that value to the value it was sent; if the two values match, the client credentials are deemed authentic. CHAP was created for use with dial-up networking and is commonly used with PPP-encapsulated

Windows remote access services. (Adapted from www.microsoft. com/technet/prodtechnol/ winxppro/proddocs/ auth_chap.asp.)

cipher

A method for encrypting text, the term *cipher* is also used to refer to an encrypted message (although the term *ciphertext* is preferred).

code escrow

The process of placing application source code in the care of some trusted third party. In the event of a disagreement, the dissolution of the development company, or a failure to perform on the part of the software programmers, the code can be released to the purchasing company.

code of ethics

A formal list of rules governing personal and professional behavior that is adopted by a group of individuals or organizations. Many security certifications, including Security+, require their holders to adhere to a code of ethics that's designed to foster ethical and legal behavior and discourage unethical or illegal behavior.

cold site

A remote site that has electricity, plumbing, and heating installed, ready for use when enacting disaster recovery or business continuity plans. At a cold site, all other equipment, systems, and configurations are supplied by the company

enacting the plan; therefore, basic facilities that are ready to receive necessary systems and equipment are the hallmarks of a cold site.

confidentiality

Involves a rigorous set of controls and classifications associated with sensitive information to ensure that such information is neither intentionally nor unintentionally disclosed.

cross-certification

When two or more CAs choose to trust each other and issue credentials on each other's behalf.

cryptographic module

Any combination of hardware, firmware, or software that implements cryptographic functions such as encryption, decryption, digital signatures, authentication techniques, and random number generation.

decentralized key management

Key management that occurs when a user generates a public and private key pair and then submits the public key to a Certificate Authority for validation and signature.

degaussing

A method of removing recorded magnetic fields from magnetic storage media by applying strong cyclic magnetic pulses, thereby erasing the content and making the media unreadable.

demilitarized zone (DMZ)

Also called the *free-trade zone* or *neutral zone*, a DMZ is an area in a network that allows limited and controlled access from the public Internet. A DMZ often hosts a corporation's Web and File Transfer Protocol (FTP) sites, email, external Domain Name Service (DNS) servers, and the like. The network segment for a DMZ usually sits between an internal corporate network and the public Internet, with firewalls on either side. Also, the border router (which defines the boundary between what a corporation or organization controls and the public Internet) normally sits between the DMZ and the public Internet, with a corporate or organizational firewall between the DMZ and internal network segments.

denial of service and distributed denial of service (DoS/DDoS)

A type of attack that denies legitimate users access to a server or services by consuming sufficient system resources or network bandwidth or by rendering a service unavailable. The difference between a DoS and a DDoS attack is in the point(s) of origination: A DoS attack typically originates from a single system, whereas a DDoS attack originates from multiple systems simultaneously (thereby causing even more extreme consumption of bandwidth and other resources).

dictionary attack

An attack in which software is used to compare hashed data, such as a password, to a word in a hashed dictionary. This is repeated until matches are found in the hash, with the goal being to match the password exactly to determine the original password that was used as the basis of the hash.

digital certificate

A formatted document that includes the user's public key as well as the digital signature of the Certificate Authority (CA) that has authenticated her. The digital certificate can also contain information about the user, the CA, and attributes that define what the user is allowed to do with systems she accesses using the digital certificate.

digital signature

A hash encrypted to a private key of the sender that proves user identity and authenticity of the message. Signatures do not encrypt the contents of an entire message. Also, in the context of certificates, a digital signature uses data to provide an electronic signature that authenticates the identity of the original sender of the message or data.

disaster recovery plan (DRP)

A plan outlining actions to be taken in case a business is hit with a natural or manmade disaster.

Discretionary Access Control (DAC)

A distributed security method that allows users to set permissions on a per-object basis. The NTFS permissions used in Windows NT, 2000, and XP/.NET use DAC.

distributed computing

A procedure in which multiple computers are networked and common sections of a larger task are distributed to the members of the group to process the larger task to complete that task more quickly.

dry-pipe fire suppression

A sprinkler system with pressurized air in the pipes. If a fire starts, there is a slight delay as the pipes fill with water. This system is used in areas where wet-pipe systems might freeze.

due care

Assurance that the necessary steps are followed to satisfy a specific requirement, which can be an internal or external requirement, as in an agency regulation.

electromagnetic emanation (EME)

A condition of electronic equipment in which electrons leak from cables and the equipment itself. These emanations can possibly be picked up and reconstructed.

Elliptic Curve Cryptography (ECC)

A method in which elliptic curve equations are used to calculate encryption keys for use in general-purpose encryption.

encryption algorithm

A mathematical formula or method used to scramble information before it is transmitted over unsecure media. Examples include RSA, DH, IDEA, Blowfish, MD5, and DSS/DSA.

environment

The physical conditions that affect and influence growth, development, and survival. Used in the security field to describe the surrounding conditions of an area to be protected.

escalation

The upward movement of privileges when using network resources or exercising rights (such as moving from read permissions to write).

evidence

Any hardware, software, or data that can be used to prove the identity and actions of an attacker.

Extensible Markup Language (XML)

Like HTML, this flexible markup language is based on standards from the World Wide Web Consortium at www.w3.org. Unlike HTML, XML can be used to generate standard or fully customized content-rich Web pages, documents, and applications. XML is used to provide widely accessible services and data to end users, exchange data among applications, and capture and represent data in a large variety of custom and standard formats. Numerous standard XML applications are security related, including the Security Assertion Markup Language (SAML), XML Signatures, XML Encryption, various XML key-handling applications, and the Extensible Access Control Markup Language (XACML). See `xml.coverpages.org` for more information on this topic and related standards.

extranet

A special internetwork architecture wherein a company's or organization's external partners and customers are granted access to some parts of its intranet and the services it provides in a secure, controlled fashion.

Faraday cage

A metal enclosure used to conduct stray EMEs (electromagnetic emissions) to ground, thereby eliminating signal leakage and the ability of external monitors or detectors to "read" network or computer activity. A Faraday cage can be very small or encompass an entire building, and it is generally used only when security concerns are extremely high (as in national defense, classified areas, or highly sensitive commercial environments).

Federal Information Processing Standard (FIPS)

A standard created by the United States government for the evaluation of cryptographic modules. It consists of four levels that escalate in their requirement for higher security levels.

firewall

A hardware device or software application designed to filter incoming or outgoing traffic based on predefined rules and patterns. Firewalls can filter traffic based on protocol uses, source or destination addresses, and port addresses, and they can even apply state-based rules to block unwanted activities or transactions. For an excellent source of information on this topic, see Matt Curtin and Marcus Ranum's Internet Firewalls FAQ at `www.interhack.net/pubs/fwfaq`.

forensics

As related to security, forensics is the process of analyzing and investigating a computer crime scene after an attack has occurred and of reconstructing the sequence of events and activities involved in such an attack.

guideline

Specific information on how standards should be implemented. A guideline is generally not mandatory, thus acting as a kind of flexible rule used to produce a desired behavior or action. A guideline allows freedom of choice on how to achieve the behavior.

hash value

The resultant output or data generated from an encryption hash when applied to a specific set of data. If computed and passed as part of an incoming message and then recomputed upon message receipt, such a hash value can be used to verify the received data when the two hash values match.

hashing

A methodology used to calculate a short, secret value from a data set of any size (usually for an entire message or for individual transmission units). This secret value is recalculated independently on the receiving end and compared to the submitted value to verify the sender's identity.

honeypot

A decoy system designed to attract hackers. A honeypot usually has all its logging and tracing enabled, and its security level is lowered on purpose. Likewise, such systems often include deliberate lures or bait, in hopes of attracting would-be attackers who think there are valuable items to be attained on these systems.

hot site

A site that is immediately available for occupation if an emergency arises. It typically has all the necessary hardware and software loaded and is available 24/7.

incident

Any violation, or threatened violation, of a security policy.

incident response

A clear action plan on what each response team member needs to do and when it has to be done in the event of an emergency or a security incident.

integrity

Involves a monitoring and management system that performs integrity checks and protects systems from unauthorized modifications to data, system, and application files. Normally, performing such checks requires access to a prior scan or original versions of the various files involved. When applied to messages or data in transit, integrity checks rely on calculating hash or digest values before and after transmission to ensure nothing changed between the time the data was sent and the time it was received.

Internet Key Exchange (IKE)

A method used in the IPSec protocol suite for public key exchange, security association parameter negotiation, identification, and authentication.

intranet

A portion of the Information Technology infrastructure that belongs to and is controlled by the company in question.

intrusion-detection system (IDS)

A sophisticated network-protection system designed to detect attacks in progress but not to prevent potential attacks from occurring (although many IDSs can trace attacks back to an apparent source; some can even automatically notify all hosts through which attack traffic passes that they are forwarding such traffic). IDSs can be used to monitor network communication patterns networkwide (in which case, they're called *network intrusion-detection systems*, or *NIDSs*) or on a per-host basis (in which case, they're called *host intrusion-detection systems*, or *HIDSs*). IDSs are equally good at detecting internal intrusions or attacks as they are external ones.

IP Security (IPSec)

Used for encryption of TCP/IP traffic, IP Security provides security extensions to the version of TCP/IP known as IPv4. IPSec defines mechanisms to negotiate encryption between pairs of hosts that want to communicate with one another at the Internet Protocol (IP) layer and can therefore handle all host-to-host traffic between pairs of machines. IPSec manages special relationships between pairs of machines, called *security associations*, and these govern which types of IPSec protocols are used, which types of keys are used, how they're exchanged, and how long such keys and security associations can last. For a good IPSec overview, visit www.networkmagazine.com/ article/DCM20000509S0082; for information about IPSec RFCs and standards, see www.ietf.org/html. charters/ipsec-charter.html.

Kerberos

A specific type of authentication developed at MIT, Kerberos takes its name from the three-headed beast that guards the gates of Hell in Greek mythology. Kerberos defines a set of authentication services, as defined in RFC 1510, and includes three protocols of particular importance: (1) the Authentication Service (AS) Exchange protocol, which enables a key distribution center (KDC) to grant clients a logon session key and the ticket-granting ticket (TGT) used to access other services Kerberos controls; (2) the Ticket-Granting Service (TGS) Exchange protocol, used to distribute service session keys and tickets for such services; and (3) the Client/Server (CS) Exchange protocol, which clients use to send a ticket to request a ticket for access to some specific service. For a good overview of Kerberos and a description of how Kerberos works with Windows, look up Knowledge Base Article Q217098 at www.microsoft.com/technet.

key escrow

Key escrow is a policy in which the Certificate Authority retains a copy of the private key it generates for the user for future use. This is most often used to allow an organization to access data that was encrypted by an employee using the private key.

key exchange

A technique in which a pair of keys is generated and then exchanged between two systems (typically a client and server) over a network connection to allow a secure connection to be established between them.

Layer 2 Tunneling Protocol (L2TP)

A technology used with VPN to establish a communication tunnel between communicating parties over unsecure media. L2TP permits a single logical connection to transport multiple protocols between a pair of hosts. L2TP is a member of the TCP/IP protocol suite and is defined in RFC 2661; a framework for creating Virtual Private Networks that uses L2TP appears in RFC 2764.

Lightweight Directory Access Protocol (LDAP)

A TCP/IP protocol that allows client systems to access directory services and related data. Examples of services that work with LDAP include the Windows 2000 Active Directory and Novell Directory Services (NDS), but LDAP works with any X.500-compliant directory service. In most cases, LDAP is used as part of management or other applications or in browsers to access directory services information. LDAP is defined in RFCs 1777 and 2559; numerous other RFCs address specific aspects of LDAP behavior or capabilities or define best practices for its use.

logic bomb

A piece of software designed to do damage at a predetermined point in time or in response to some type of condition (for example, "disk is 95 percent full") or event (for example, some particular account logs in or some value the system tracks exceeds a certain threshold).

M of N Control

The process of backing up private key material across multiple systems or devices.

man in the middle

An attack in which a hacker attempts to intercept data in a network stream and then inserts her own data into the communication with the goal of disrupting or taking over communications. The term itself is derived from the insertion of a third party—the proverbial "man in the middle"—between two parties engaged in communications.

Mandatory Access Control (MAC)

A centralized security method that doesn't allow users to change permissions on objects.

mantrap

A two-door configuration in a building or office that can lock unwanted individuals in a secured area, preventing them from entering other areas or even from exiting wherever it is they're being held.

message

The content and format a sender chooses to use to communicate with some receiver across a network, an intranet, an extranet, or the Internet.

message digest

The output of an encryption hash that's applied to some fixed-size chunk of data. A message digest provides a profound integrity check because even a change to one bit in the target data also changes the resulting digest value. This explains why digests are included so often in network transmissions.

mutual authentication

A situation in which a client provides authentication information to establish identity and related access permissions with a server and in which a server also provides authentication information to the client to ensure that illicit servers cannot masquerade as genuine servers.

Network Address Translation (NAT)

TCP/IP protocol technology that maps internal IP addresses to one or more external IP addresses through a NAT server of some type. NAT enables the conservation of public IP address space by mapping private IP addresses used in an internal LAN to one or more external public IP addresses to communicate with the external world. NAT also provides address-hiding services (thereby denying

outsiders access to "real" or private internal IP addresses), thus adding both security and simplicity to network addressing.

Online Certificate Status Protocol (OCSP)

A protocol defined by the IETF that is used to validate digital certificates issued by a CA.

passive detection

A method of intrusion detection that has an IDS present in the network in a silent fashion; it does not interfere with communications in progress.

pattern matching

A network-analysis method that uses a central box on the network. This approach compares each individual packet against a database of signatures (formats of packets known to be dangerous, offensive, or recognizable as parts of known attacks or vulnerability exploits). The inherent weakness in this method is that such patterns must be known (and definitions in place) before they can be used to recognize attacks or exploits. Therefore, similar to virus signature files, attack pattern files (also called *signatures*) must be present to be useful.

plenum

The space in a building between a false (drop) ceiling and the true ceiling or roof above. The plenum is typically used to run light fixtures and wiring, but it's also defined as a return air space in most building codes (which is why the coating on cables run through such space must be fire retardant and nontoxic when burned).

Point-to-Point Tunneling Protocol (PPTP)

A TCP/IP technology used to create Virtual Private Network (VPN) or remote access links between sites (usually from one server to another) or for remote access (usually from a remote client to a local communications server). PPTP is the work of a vendor group that includes Microsoft, 3Com, and Copper Mountain Networks. It is generally regarded as less secure than L2TP and is used less frequently for that reason. PPTP is described in RFC 2637.

policy

A broad statement of views and positions. A policy states high-level intent with respect to a specific area of security and is more properly called a *security policy*. Security policies typically address how passwords are to be constructed and used, how various classes of data should be classified, which access controls apply, and which job roles can be granted remote access to a network. The formulation of a security policy generally occurs after a risk analysis has been performed, represents an organization's formal attempts to describe how security works, and is applied in its IT systems and services.

Pretty Good Privacy (PGP)

A shareware encryption technology for communications that utilizes both public and private encryption technologies to speed up encryption without compromising security. Also available in commercial product form, PGP products offer personal and enterprise-level encryption services of many kinds; visit www.pgp.com for more information.

private key

A piece of data generated by an asymmetric algorithm that's used by the host to encrypt data. A matching public key can be used to decrypt data encrypted with the private key; this technique makes digital signatures and nonrepudiation possible. Likewise, anyone with access to the public key can encrypt data that only the private key holder can decrypt and read; this technique enables you to send information over public networks that only a designated recipient can read.

privilege management

The process of controlling users and their capabilities on a network.

probability

Used in risk assessment, probability measures the likelihood or chance that a threat will actually exploit some vulnerability.

procedure

A procedure specifies how policies will be put into practice in an environment (that is, it provides necessary how-to instructions).

Public Branch Exchange (PBX)

A telephone switch used on a company's or organization's premises to create a local telephone network. Using a PBX obviates the need to order numerous individual phone lines from a telephone company and permits PBX owners to offer advanced telephony features and functions to their users.

public key

A piece of data generated by an asymmetric algorithm distributed to the public for general use. Access to a public key provides tangible evidence of the identity of the corresponding private key holder because it can be used to decrypt information that only the private key holder can encrypt. Equally important, a public key can be used to encrypt information that only the private key holder can decrypt, thereby permitting messages to remain confidential and unreadable to any other user who does not possess a copy of the recipient's private key.

Public Key Infrastructure (PKI)

A paradigm that encompasses Certificate Authorities and X.509 certificates used with public encryption algorithms to distribute, manage, issue, and revoke public keys. Of course, such a system also includes mechanisms to manage corresponding private keys for individual key holders. Public Key Infrastructures typically also include registration authorities to issue and validate requests for digital certificates, a certificate-management system of some type, and a directory in which certificates are stored and can be accessed. Together, all these elements make up a PKI.

receiver

The party that receives a message from its sender.

Remote Authentication Dial-In User Services (RADIUS)

An Internet protocol, described in RFC 2138, used for remote access services. It conveys user authentication and configuration data between a centralized authentication server (also called a *RADIUS server*) and a remote access server (RADIUS client) to permit the remote access server to authenticate requests to use its network access ports. Users present the remote access server (RADIUS client) with credentials, which are in turn passed to the RADIUS server for authentication. If a user's access request is granted, the RADIUS server provides authorization and configuration information that the remote access server uses to establish a connection with that user; if a user's access request is denied, the connection with that user is terminated. In many ways, RADIUS offers a basic alternative to TACACS+, the Terminal Access Controller Access Control System described in RFC 1492.

replay

An attack that involves capturing valid traffic from a network and then retransmitting that traffic at a later time to gain unauthorized access to systems and resources.

risk

The potential that a threat might exploit some vulnerability.

role

A defined behavior for a user or group of users based on some specific activity or responsibilities (for example, a tape backup administrator is usually permitted to back up all files on one or more systems; that person might or might not be allowed to restore such files, depending on the local security policies in effect).

Role-Based Access Control (RBAC)

A security method that combines both MAC and DAC. RBAC uses profiles. Profiles are defined for specific roles within a company and then users are assigned to such roles. This facilitates administration in a large group of users because when you modify a role and assign it new permissions, those settings are automatically conveyed to all users assigned to that role.

rollback

A process used to undo changes or transactions when they do not complete, when they are suspected of being invalid or unwanted, or when they cause problems.

round

A selection of encrypted data that is split into two or more blocks of data. Each block of data is then run through an encryption algorithm that applies an encryption key to each block of data individually, rather than applying encryption to the entire selection of data in a single operation.

router

A device that connects multiple network segments and routes packets between them. Hardware routers run proprietary configurable software, and network operating systems often include routing functionality as well. Routers split broadcast domains.

Secure Hypertext Transfer Protocol (HTTPS or S-HTTP)

An Internet protocol that encrypts individual messages used for Web communications rather than establishing a secure channel, like in SSL/TLS. S-HTTP supports choices among multiple security policies, various key-management techniques, and encryption algorithms through a per-transaction negotiation mechanism.

Secure Multipurpose Internet Mail Extensions (S/MIME)

An Internet protocol governed by RFC 2633 and used to secure email communications through encryption and digital signatures for authentication. It generally works with PKI to validate digital signatures and related digital certificates.

Secure Shell (SSH)

A protocol designed to support secure remote login, along with secure access to other services across an unsecure network (for example, inherently unsecure services such as Telnet and FTP may be nevertheless used when those protocols are tunneled within a Secure Shell session). SSH includes a secure Transport layer protocol that provides server authentication, confidentiality (encryption), and integrity (message digest functions), along with a user-authentication protocol and a connection protocol that runs on top of the user-authentication protocol.

Secure Sockets Layer (SSL)

An Internet protocol originally created at Netscape Corporation that uses connection-oriented, end-to-end encryption to ensure that client/server communications are confidential (encrypted) and meet integrity constraints (message digests). SSL operates between the HTTP Application layer protocol and a reliable Transport layer protocol (usually TCP). Because SSL is independent of the Application layer, any application protocol can work with SSL transparently. SSL can also work with a secure Transport layer protocol, which is why the term *SSL/TLS* appears frequently. *See also* Transport Layer Security.

Security Association (SA)

A method in IPSec that accounts for individual security settings for IPSec data transmission.

security baseline

Defined in a company's or organization's security policy, a security baseline is a specific set of security-related modifications to and patches and settings for systems and services in use that underpins technical implementation of security.

sender

The party that originates a message.

sequence number

A counting mechanism in IPSec that increases incrementally each time a packet is transmitted in an IPSec communication path. It protects the receiver from replay attacks.

service-level agreement (SLA)

A contract between two companies or a company and individual that specifies, by contract, a level of service to be provided by one company to another. Supplying replacement equipment within 24 hours of loss of that equipment or related services is a simple example of an SLA.

shielded twisted pair (STP)

A form of twisted pair cabling that incorporates a metallic braid or foil shield in its construction, thereby making it more resistant to magnetic and radio interference (and also more expensive) than unshielded twisted pair cabling (UTP).

Simple Network Management Protocol (SNMP)

A UDP-based Application layer Internet protocol used for network management, SNMP is governed by RFCs 2570 and 2574. In converting management information between management consoles (managers) and managed nodes (agents), SNMP implements configuration and event databases on managed nodes that can be configured to respond to interesting events by notifying network managers.

single sign-on (SSO)

The concept or process of using a single logon authority to grant users access to resources on a network regardless of what operating system or application is used to make or handle a request for access. The concept behind the term is that users need to authenticate only once and can then access any resources available on a network.

smartcard

A credit card–sized device that contains an embedded chip. On this chip, varying and multiple types of data can be stored, such as a driver's license number, medical information, passwords or other authentication data, and even bank account data.

sniffer

A hardware device or software program used to capture and analyze network data in real time. Because such a device can typically read and interpret all unencrypted traffic on the cable segment to which it is attached, it can be a powerful tool in any competent hacker's arsenal.

social engineering

The process of using human behavior to attack a network or gain access to resources that would otherwise be inaccessible. Social engineering is a term that emphasizes the well-known fact that poorly or improperly trained individuals can be persuaded, tricked, or coerced into giving up passwords, phone numbers, or other data that can lead to unauthorized system access, even when strong technical security measures can otherwise prevent such access. User education and well-documented policies (for example, stating that no passwords should ever be given by telephone under any circumstances) are the only remedies that can foil attacks based on this technique.

spoofing

A technique for generating network traffic that contains a different (and usually quite specific) source address from that of the machine actually generating the traffic. Spoofing is used for many reasons in attacks: It foils easy identification of the true source; it permits attackers to take advantage of existing trust relationships; and it deflects responses to attacks against some (usually innocent) third party or parties.

standard

This term is used in many ways. In some contexts, it refers to best practices for specific platforms, implementations, OS versions, and so forth. Some standards are mandatory and ensure uniform application of a technology across an organization. In other contexts, a standard might simply describe a well-defined rule used to produce a desired behavior or action. In this case, a standard sets out specific actions for achieving a desired behavior or result.

switch

A hardware device that manages multiple, simultaneous pairs of connections between communicating systems. In some cases, a switch is used as a network concentrator that splits traditionally flat network segments into dedicated communication links (microsegmentation). Likewise, switches split collision domains, but switches can also provide greater aggregate bandwidth between pairs or groups of communicating devices because each switched link normally gets exclusive access to available bandwidth. Therefore, switches often improve overall performance as well as provide logical network segmentation and collision domain management capabilities.

symmetric encryption

An encryption technique in which a single encryption key is generated and used to encrypt data. This data is then passed across a network. After that data arrives at the recipient device, the same key used to encrypt that data is used to decrypt it. This technique requires a secure way to share keys because both the sender and receiver use the same key (also called a *shared secret* because that key should be unknown to third parties).

TACACS+

An enhanced version of Terminal Access Controller Access Control System. Whereas TACACS+ is TCP based, the original TACACS is a UDP-based authentication and access control Internet protocol governed by RFC 1492. In either implementation, TACACS recognizes three classes of devices: a network access server, an authentication server, and a remote terminal from which access requests originate. When a client requests access, a remote terminal passes an identifier and a password (or other authentication data that might originate from a smartcard, a security token-passing device, a biometric device, or even a multifactor authentication system) to the remote access server. In turn, the remote access server passes that information to an authentication server for validation. If the authentication server validates the credentials, the request is allowed to proceed; if it does not, the access request is denied.

TCP/IP hijacking

A process used to steal an ongoing TCP/IP session for the purposes of attacking a target computer. Essentially, hijacking works by spoofing network traffic so it appears to originate from a single computer, when in actuality, it originates elsewhere. Hijacking also depends on guessing or matching packet sequence numbers or other data so that the other party in the communication doesn't realize another computer has taken over an active communications session.

TEMPEST

A code word used by the United States government to describe a set of standards and specifications for reducing emanations from electronic equipment, thereby reducing vulnerability to eavesdropping. This term is sometimes (and incorrectly) expanded as an acronym for "test for electromagnetic propagation and evaluation for secure transmissions" or "telecommunications electronics material protected from emanating spurious transmissions," but this terminology is apocryphal or historical rather than real (visit www.acronymfinder.com for more information). Although this term has military origins, it is now used mostly in civilian circles; in military nomenclature, the replacement term is EMSEC (an abbreviation for *emissions security*). Whatever source one might seek for this term, it always refers to

limiting leakage of electronic signals from equipment to stop their unwanted monitoring.

threat

A danger to a computer network or system (for example, a hacker or virus represents a threat).

token

Also known as a *security token*, this is a hardware- or software-based system used for authentication wherein two or more sets of matched devices or software generate matching random passwords with a high degree of complexity. Thus, a token-based security device presents a complex password or security token that is difficult to guess within a short period of time. Then, it enhances that security by changing the token on a regularly scheduled basis to limit the size of any data set encrypted with a single password or token. Finally, because token-based security systems also require their users to supply an additional password or personal identification number, such systems also qualify as two-factor authentication systems.

Transport Layer Security (TLS, or sometimes TLSP)

An end-to-end encryption protocol originally specified in ISO Standard 10736 that provides security services as part of the Transport layer in a protocol stack. More commonly, however, TLS refers to an Internet protocol defined in RFC 2246 that is also called TLSP. Because this TLS is based on and similar to SSL version 3.0, it is really misnamed because it operates at the Application layer, not the Transport layer.

Trojan horse

Software that is hidden inside other software commonly used to infect systems with viruses, worms, or remote control software. Similar to the famous exploit that Odysseus perpetrated during the Trojan wars, a software Trojan horse represents itself as offering some type of capability or functionality when it also includes some means to destroy or take over systems on which it is installed.

unshielded twisted pair (UTP)

A type of cabling in which pairs of wires are twisted around one another to improve transmission and interference susceptibility characteristics. UTP is used extensively in wiring LANs.

virtual local area network (VLAN)

A software technology that allows for the grouping of network nodes connected to one or more network switches into a single logical network. By permitting logical aggregation of devices into virtual network segments, VLANs offer simplified user management and network resource access controls for switched networks.

Virtual Private Network (VPN)

A popular technology that supports reasonably secure, logical, private network links across some unsecure public network infrastructure, such as the Internet. VPNs reduce Public Switched Telephone Network (PSTN) costs by eliminating calls or requiring only local calls to be placed to an Internet service provider (ISP). VPNs are also more secure than traditional remote access because they can be encrypted. Finally, because VPNs support tunneling (the hiding of numerous types of protocols and sessions within a single host-to-host connection), they also support multiple connections that use the same wire.

virus

A piece of (usually) malicious code that's normally disguised as something legitimate or innocuous (for example, an email attachment that purports to be a picture or a document file) that causes unexpected or unwanted events to occur. The defining characteristic of a virus is that it spreads to other computers by design; although some viruses also damage the systems on which they reside, not all viruses inflict damage. Viruses can spread immediately upon reception or implement other unwanted actions, or they can lie dormant until a trigger in their code causes them to become active. Viruses usually belong to one of three classes: file infectors, which attach themselves to executable files of some type; system or boot sector infectors, which infect key system files or boot areas on hard disks or removable media; and macro viruses, which infect applications such as Microsoft Word to implement their actions. The hidden code a virus executes is called its *payload*.

vulnerability

A weakness in hardware or software that can be used to gain unauthorized or unwanted access to or information from a network or computer.

warm site

A backup site that has some of the equipment and infrastructure necessary for a business to begin operating at that location. Typically, companies or organizations bring their own computer systems and hardware to a warm site, but that site usually already includes a ready-to-use networking infrastructure and also might include reliable power, climate controls, lighting, and Internet access points.

wet-pipe fire suppression

A sprinkler system with pressurized water in its pipes. If a fire starts, the pipes release water immediately and offer the fastest and most effective means of water-based fire suppression.

Wired Equivalent Privacy (WEP)

A security protocol used in IEEE 802.11 wireless networking, WEP is designed to provide security equivalent to that found in regular wired networks. This is achieved by using basic symmetric encryption to protect data sent over wireless connections so that sniffing of wireless transmissions doesn't produce readable data and so that drive-by attackers cannot access a wireless LAN without additional effort and attacks.

Wireless Transport Layer Security (WTLS)

WTLS defines a security level for applications based on the Wireless Application Protocol (WAP). As its acronym indicates, WTLS is based on Transport layer security (TLS) but has been modified to work with the low-bandwidth, high latency, and limited processing capabilities found in many wireless networking implementations. WTLS also provides authentication, data integrity, and confidentiality mechanisms, all based on encryption methods using shared 56- or 128-bit symmetric keys.

worm

A special type of virus designed primarily to reproduce and replicate itself on as many computer systems as possible, a worm does not normally alter files but rather remains resident in a computer's memory. Worms typically rely on access to operating system capabilities that are invisible to users.

Often worms are detected by their side effects (unwanted consumption of system resources, diminished system performance, or reprioritization of normal system tasks) rather than by overt behavior. Antivirus software is a key ingredient in preventing infection from worms, as it is with other types of viruses.

X.500 directory

A standard that regulates global, distributed directory services databases, it's also known as a *white pages* directory (because lookup occurs by name, rather than by job role or other categorized information, as in a yellow pages type of system). For a detailed overview of X.500, search on that term at searchnetworking.techtarget.com.

X.509 digital certificate

A digital certificate that uniquely identifies a potential communications party or participant. Among other things, an X.509 digital certificate includes a party's name and public key, but it can also include organizational affiliation, service or access restrictions, and a host of other access- and security-related information.

XML Access Control Language (XACL)

An XML application that allows granular access controls within XML-generated Web pages, documents, or other XML-generated applications. XACL is designed to browse and update XML documents securely on a per-element basis. For more information on this topic, visit xml.coverpages.org and search on XACL.

Index

C

How can we make this index more useful? Email us at indexes@quepublishing.com

E

I

I Love You virus, 58

i-Mode standard, security vulnerabilities, 106-107

IDEA (International Data Encryption Algorithm), 77

identifying

  nonessential services, 44-47

  risks

    assessment guidelines, 259

    assets inventory, 258

    threat assessments, 259

    vulnerability-scanning tools, 259-260

IDSs (intrusion detection systems), 150

  attack signatures, 150

  bastion hosts, role of, 156

  behavior-based, 150

    common features, 151

    limitations, 152

  exam practice questions, 163-166

  honeynets, 156

  honeypots, 155

  host-based, 123, 154-155

  incident handling responses

    countermeasures, 156

    deflection, 156

    detection, 156

  Intrusion Countermeasure Equipment (ICE), 156

  knowledge-based

    known attack signatures, 150

    limitations, 151

  layered approach, 155

  network-based

    header signatures, 153

    port signatures, 153

    strengths, 154

    string signatures, 153

  versus intrusion-prevention systems, 124

IEEE 802.11x (wireless networks), 120

  Carrier Sense Multiple Access with Collision Avoidance (CSMA/CA), 105

  current specifications, 105

  remote access issues, 72-73

    clear-text data transmission, 73

    man-in-the-middle attacks, 73

    radio traffic detection, 73

    session hijacking, 73

    war chalking, 74

    war driving, 74

  wireless vulnerabilities, 105

IEEE 802.1Q standard, VLAN tagging, 139-140

IEEE Standards Association Web site, 114

IETF (Internet Engineering Task Force) Web site

  cryptographic resources, 195

  cryptography resources, 221

incident handling responses (IDSs), 244

  countermeasures, 156

  deflection, 156

  detection, 156

incremental backups (tapes), 131, 237

information leaks, CGI script vulnerability, 99

Information Security Management Handbook, 41

InformIT Web site, computer security resources, xxxii

infrastructure security

  exam practice questions, 143-147

  FAQS.org Web site, 148

  Invii.com Web site, 148

  NIST Web site, 148

  UC Davis Web site, 148

  vulnerability scanning, 260

instant messaging

  products, 82

  vulnerabilities

    file-sharing systems, 82

    packet-sniffing, 82

J - K

N

Q - R

X - Y - Z

What if Que

joined forces to deliver the best technology books in a common digital reference platform?

We have. Introducing
InformIT Online Books
powered by Safari.

■ Specific answers to specific questions.
InformIT Online Books' powerful search engine gives you relevance-ranked results in a matter of seconds.

■ Immediate results.
With InformIt Online Books, you can select the book you want and view the chapter or section you need immediately.

■ Cut, paste, and annotate.
Paste code to save time and eliminate typographical errors. Make notes on the material you find useful and choose whether or not to share them with your workgroup.

■ Customized for your enterprise.
Customize a library for you, your department, or your entire organization. You pay only for what you need.

As an InformIT partner, Que has shared the knowledge and hands-on advice of our authors with you online. Visit InformIT.com to see what you are missing.

Get your first 14 days FREE!
InformIT Online Books is offering its members a 10-book subscription risk free for 14 days.
Visit **http://www.informit.com/onlinebooks** for details.